INCIDENTS IN THE LIFE OF A SLAVE GIRL

broadview editions
series editor: Martin R. Boyne

INCIDENTS IN THE LIFE OF A SLAVE GIRL

WRITTEN BY HERSELF

Harriet Jacobs

edited by Koritha Mitchell

broadview editions

BROADVIEW PRESS – www.broadviewpress.com
Peterborough, Ontario, Canada

Founded in 1985, Broadview Press remains a wholly independent publishing house. Broadview's focus is on academic publishing; our titles are accessible to university and college students as well as scholars and general readers. With over 800 titles in print, Broadview has become a leading international publisher in the humanities, with world-wide distribution. Broadview is committed to environmentally responsible publishing and fair business practices.

© 2023 Koritha Mitchell

Library and Archives Canada Cataloguing in Publication

Title: Incidents in the life of a slave girl : written by herself / Harriet Jacobs ; edited by Koritha Mitchell.
Names: Jacobs, Harriet A. (Harriet Ann), 1813-1897, author. | Mitchell, Koritha, editor.
Description: Includes bibliographical references.
Identifiers: Canadiana (print) 2023022833X | Canadiana (ebook) 20230228399 | ISBN 9781554815029 (softcover) | ISBN 9781770488977 (PDF) | ISBN 9781460408292 (EPUB)
Subjects: LCSH: Jacobs, Harriet A. (Harriet Ann), 1813-1897. | LCSH: Enslaved women—United States—Biography. | LCSH: Enslaved persons—United States—Biography. | LCSH: Enslaved women—United States—Social conditions. | LCSH: Enslaved persons—United States—Social conditions. | LCSH: Slave narratives—United States. | LCGFT: Autobiographies. | LCGFT: Slave narratives.
Classification: LCC E444.J33 A3 2023 | DDC 306.3/62092—dc23

Advisory editor for this volume: Colleen Humbert

Broadview Press handles its own distribution in North America:
PO Box 1243, Peterborough, Ontario K9J 7H5, Canada
555 Riverwalk Parkway, Tonawanda, NY 14150, USA
Tel: (705) 743–8990; Fax: (705) 743–8353
email: customerservice@broadviewpress.com

For all territories outside of North America, distribution is handled by Eurospan Group.

Broadview Press acknowledges the financial support of the Government of Canada for our publishing activities. Canadä

Cover design and typesetting: George Kirkpatrick

PRINTED IN CANADA

Contents

Acknowledgements • 9
Introduction • 11
Harriet Jacobs: A Brief Chronology • 55
A Note on the Text • 63

Incidents in the Life of a Slave Girl. Written by Herself • 65

Appendix A: Historical Contexts • 261
  1. "Handed by the Blacks of New Haven City," Petition
     (1788) • 262
  2. From the *Fugitive Slave Act* (1850) • 262
  3. Notice warning Black people in Boston to be on guard
     after the passage of the *Fugitive Slave Act* (24 April
     1851) • 264
  4. United States Supreme Court Justice Roger Taney, The
     Dred Scott Decision (6 March 1857) • 265
  5. From the *First Confiscation Act* (1861) • 266
  6. From the *Second Confiscation Act* (1862) • 267
  7. The Emancipation Proclamation (1863) • 268
  8. From the *Freedmen's Bureau Act* (1865) • 271
  9. The Thirteenth Amendment (1865) • 273
  10. From the Fourteenth Amendment (1868) • 273
  11. From the Fifteenth Amendment (1870) • 274
  12. From United States Supreme Court Justice Billings Brown,
     Plessy v. Ferguson (1896) • 274

Appendix B: Additional Historical Connections • 277
  1. Laws of Virginia, Act XII (1662) • 277
  2. From Olive Gilbert, *The Narrative of Sojourner Truth*
     (1850) • 277
  3. Documents regarding Nat Turner's Insurrection • 280
    a. "Anonymus" to Governor John Floyd (28 August
       1831) • 281
    b. Proclamation by Governor John Floyd (17 September
       1831) • 281
  4. Advertisement, *American Beacon* (30 June 1835) • 282
  5. South Carolina *Negro Seamen Act* (1 December
     1822) • 283

Appendix C: The Composition, Publication, and Reception of
Incidents • 284
1. Harriet Jacobs's First Forays into Writing for
   Publication • 284
   a. From *New York Daily Tribune* (21 June 1853) • 284
   b. *New York Tribune* (25 July 1853) • 288
2. Correspondence from Harriet Jacobs to Amy Post • 289
   a. From Harriet Jacobs to Amy Post (after 28 December
      1852) • 289
   b. From Harriet Jacobs to Amy Post (14 February
      1853) • 291
   c. Harriet Jacobs to Amy Post (4 April 1853) • 292
   d. From Harriet Jacobs to Amy Post (c. May
      1853) • 293
   e. From Harriet Jacobs to Amy Post (9 October
      1853) • 294
   f. From Harriet Jacobs to Amy Post (March
      1854) • 295
3. Correspondence from Lydia Maria Child to Harriet
   Jacobs • 296
   a. Lydia Maria Child to Harriet Jacobs (13 August
      1860) • 296
   b. Lydia Maria Child to Harriet Jacobs (27 September
      1860) • 297
4. Original Title Page of Jacobs's Narrative • 298
5. Correspondence from John Greenleaf Whittier to Lydia
   Maria Child (1 April 1861) • 300
6. William C. Nell, "Linda, the Slave Girl," *Liberator*
   (24 January 1861) • 300
7. From Unsigned Book Review, *Weekly Anglo-African*
   (13 April 1861) • 302
8. From Unsigned Book Review, *Anti-Slavery Advocate*
   (1 May 1861) • 303

Appendix D: Life after *Incidents* • 305
1. From Linda [Harriet Jacobs], "Life among the
   Contrabands," *Liberator* (5 September 1862) • 305
2. From "Jacobs (Linda) School, Alexandria, Va.," *Freedmen's
   Record* (February 1865) • 308
3. "From Harriet Jacobs," *Freedman* (February
   1866) • 310
4. "From Louisa Jacobs," *Freedmen's Record* (March
   1866) • 311

5. Linda [Harriet] Jacobs, "Savannah Freedmen's Orphan Asylum," *Anti-Slavery Reporter* (2 March 1868) • 312
6. Letters by an Adult Louisa Jacobs (1880–84) • 314
   a. "Ah me!" (25 March 1880) • 314
   b. "Rest and quiet is what she needs" (7 September 1884) • 314
   c. "I was sure Mother would not refuse him" (21 December 1884) • 315
7. Remembrances upon Jacobs's Death • 317
   a. From the Eulogy by Reverend Francis Grimké • 317
   b. From the Obituary for Harriet Jacobs, *Woman's Journal* (May 1897) • 318

Appendix E: Enduring Legacy • 321
1. From Ellen Driscoll, "The Loophole of Retreat" (4 December 1991–8 February 1992) • 321
2. From Lydia Diamond, *Harriet Jacobs: A Play* (2011) • 322
3. Quotations from Lorna Ann Johnson, *Freedom Road* (2004) • 324

Appendix F: People and Places Relevant to *Incidents* • 326
1. Who Is Who in *Incidents* • 326
2. Image of Dr. Norcom • 327
3. Image of Mrs. Norcom • 328
4. Image of Louisa Jacobs • 329
5. Visual Rendering of Floor Plan of Grandmother's House and Hiding Place • 330
6. Visual Rendering of the Edenton Neighborhood in Which Jacobs Was Born and Hid • 332
7. Image of Amy Post • 333
8. Image of Harriet Beecher Stowe • 334
9. Image of Lydia Maria Child • 335

Works Cited and Select Bibliography • 337
Permissions Acknowledgements • 347

This volume is dedicated to my mother, Laverne Mitchell.

It is astonishing how much you made possible, Mama.
Absolutely astonishing.

Acknowledgements

As I submit the manuscript for this edition, I am reminded that its content is my responsibility. No one else is to blame for anything that someone might find blameworthy. Nevertheless, it could not have been completed without readers who answered my call. They helped me toward clarity so that I might have a chance of doing some measure of justice to Harriet Jacobs and her extraordinary life and work. These are the people I asked to read the Introduction with a ridiculously short turnaround time, and they obliged! Jessica Marie Johnson, Crystal Webster, Lori Harrison-Kahan, Ed Whitley, and Katherine Marino, I very much appreciate the care and rigor you brought.

I am also grateful to the anonymous reviewers of the original proposal, submitted so many years ago. I went back to those four reader reports every time I needed guidance, inspiration, or encouragement. Thank you for believing in my ability to deliver. Thank you for articulating your faith in me so explicitly.

I signed the contract for this edition before the pandemic, so it has taken longer to produce than expected. However, these years have created many opportunities for me to engage with people differently and appreciate our interactions even more. I therefore want to use this space to thank publicly some of the people who helped me survive and thrive during these challenging years. I won't even try to do it artfully. Many thanks to Margo Crawford, Sharon Holland, Patrick Anderson, Robert Reid-Pharr, Brittney Cooper, Treva Lindsey, Sandra Aya Enimil, Kyla Tompkins, Robin Bernstein, Brian Herrera, Denise Cruz, Martha S. Jones, Mark Anthony Neal, Harvey Young, Lisa Thompson, Soyica Diggs Colbert, Régine Jean-Charles, Salamishah Tillet, Guthrie Ramsey, Emily Field, Sarah Mesle, Alex Hardin, Emily Todd, Perin Gürel, Laura Barrio-Vilar, Kathleen Diffley, Ariel Nereson, Deborah Elizabeth Whaley, Anne Sullivan, Ryan Fong, Ivonne García, Brigitte Fielder, Nafissa Thompson-Spires, Honorée Fanonne Jeffers, Derrick Spires, Vincent Stephens, Pastor Leslie Callahan, Rev. Dr. Valerie Bridgeman, Katherine Marino, Leila Ben-Nasr, Martin Joseph Ponce, Richard Haberstroh, Amrita Dhar, Margaret Price, Nick White, Valencia Walker, Saeed Jones, Ashley Lucas, Joseph Flipper, Labib Rouhana, Teresa Ramírez, Steeve Buckridge, Rashawn Ray, Brendesha Tynes, Victor Ray,

Steven Thrasher, Hakeem Jefferson, Neil Lewis, Jr., Chanda Prescod-Weinstein, and Jedidah Isler.

I offer a special thank you to the fierce women of my Zora's House Memoir Circle. What would have become of me during these pandemic years without you? The same is true of Carie Brown, Deesha Philyaw, LaTida Smith, Peter Harmon, Brig Johnson, and, of course, the one and only Craig E. Jones.

Introduction

Can you get pregnant?

The answer to that question just might shape your life. It can dictate what you do or don't do, where you go, and at what time of day you venture out, whether addressing a frivolous want or a dire need. It can determine how much freedom you feel on a daily basis or how much fear you feel from moment to moment.

However, no matter your individual answer to the question above, pregnancy potential shapes the opinions we all have. We all know what we think people who can get pregnant should or should not do. Whether we consider something smart or stupid often depends on whether the person doing it can get pregnant. In other words, legislators are not the only ones who take strong stances regarding the behavior of people who can become pregnant, and the stakes are always high. Otherwise, abortion would not be a constant American controversy—either declared the ultimate gauge of someone's morality or identified as basic medical care for bodies that can be impregnated.

As high as the stakes are today, they were higher as the United States built its economic and political culture around treating people as chattels, as moveable pieces of property. When African Americans were legally considered chattels,[1] those who could become pregnant were treated as breeding animals that just happened to resemble human beings. To guarantee that procreation meant profit, American legislators—who were all white men— made the rape of Black women a "legitimate use of property" (Hartman, *Scenes* 80, 85, 86).

Slavery shaped life in what we now call the United States from 1619 to at least 1865—nearly 250 years, impacting at least twelve generations. For two and a half centuries, American law made the rape of enslaved Black women "legitimate use of property" because the women themselves were considered chattels

---

1   This is not to say that the evil of human bondage has ended, only this particular legalized form. For the evil's persistence to this day, consider what many activists call "human trafficking." Beyond US borders, examples include the treatment of African women by Arab elites, such as that recounted in Mende Nazer's *Slave: My True Story*. Also, African Americans were not the only people enslaved in what we now call the United States. See, for example, Tiya Miles, *All That She Carried*.

and because their exploitation could produce more people to be reduced to economic assets. Given that reality, we should ask, *What was it like to live in a society that saw your sexual violation as a necessary non-event?* To answer that question is to attend to a very particular American experience, that of an enslaved Black woman. But, make no mistake, that particular experience sheds light on the most defining features of American culture. As legal scholar Kimberlé Crenshaw explained by coining the term *intersectionality*,[1] systems that ensure the unequal distribution of resources routinely structure life along demographic lines. It is not enough to know, for example, that a person is considered white, but knowing that they are considered white and male will prove quite revealing. Because both racism and sexism have shaped the policies and practices of American culture, resources—not just food, clothing, and shelter but also citizenship rights—flow toward those who are white and male. Meanwhile, simply because society functions as designed, deprivation follows those who are Black and female.

When slavery was the law of the land, not every white man was an enslaver and not every African-descended woman was enslaved,[2] but every life was touched by the forces that made slavery possible because society doles out life chances according to identity. Even if focusing on two people in the same state, city, or household, one would find significant variations in their opportunities and hardships, according to their social status. And, for two and a half centuries, everyone's status was impacted by slavery's importance to the economy. After all, being considered a person, rather than a chattel, meant occupying a legal and social category whose meaning emerged from slavery's existence.[3] People who

---

1 The foundation for Crenshaw's term, concept, and theorization can be found in two essays: "Demarginalizing the Intersection of Race and Sex: A Black Feminist Critique of Antidiscrimination Doctrine, Feminist Theory and Antiracist Politics" (1989) and "Mapping the Margins: Intersectionality, Identity Politics, and Violence against Women of Color" (1991).

2 In fact, free African-descended people lived throughout the era of enslavement in every location where slavery reigned. For a thorough investigation of how women navigated this hostile terrain in early decades, see Johnson; Berry and Gross.

3 For the pervasiveness of slavery in society, see Hannah-Jones, who directly builds on the work of David Blight, Ira Berlin, Eric Foner, and others.

were not held in bondage as chattels had very different experiences, though. In the United States, free Black people lived in both the North and the South, but they were treated in ways that their white counterparts were not. At the same time, within any community of free Black people, many elements determined the kinds of interactions a person had, including whether they were seen as a man or woman, boy or girl.[1]

To examine American experience through the lens of profit-driven sexual exploitation would not explain African American life in its entirety, but enslaved people's lives specifically, and yet there was also variation in the lived realities of the enslaved. Generalizations are always risky, and no single person can represent an entire group. Therefore, even if trying to understand how sexual violence impacted enslaved populations, pregnancy potential is not the only factor to consider. People who could not be impregnated (to produce more chattels) were sexually abused, too. As historians increasingly document, being a man or boy, an elderly person, or a prepubescent child did not necessarily translate into escaping sexual violation.[2] Then, just like now, those convinced of their right to dominate other people often use sexual harassment and assault to intimidate and terrorize.

Still, especially given how much pregnancy potential structures American lives today, shouldn't we be curious about its role in earlier eras? I certainly am. So, again: *What was it like to live in a society that saw your sexual violation as a necessary non-event?* We can begin to answer that question because an exceptional woman named Harriet Ann Jacobs overcame extraordinary odds to make herself into a survivor, author, and advocate.

In 1861, Harriet Jacobs used the pseudonym Linda Brent and became the first formerly enslaved African American woman to publish a book-length account of her life. The narrative was originally titled *Linda; Or, Incidents in the Life of a Slave Girl, Written by Herself.*[3] Nearly two decades earlier, in 1845, Frederick

---

1 I speak in terms of being "considered" white or being "seen as" a man or woman to bring attention to how dominant assumptions, more than one's individual truth, shape experience. For help with thinking about how interpretations of people's gender and race can both align with and contradict what individuals know to be true about themselves, see, for example, Snorton.

2 See Berry and Harris.

3 Because Jacobs used a pseudonym and her editor handled the copyright paperwork on her behalf, the door was open for [*continued*]

Douglass (c. 1818–95) published his life story, which was "written by himself," and it became the foundation for why so many recognize his name today. Stripped of citizenship rights because he was born into slavery and not considered white, Douglass managed to become literate, escape bondage, and tell his story to strengthen support for the abolition of slavery. Once slavery was no longer legal, Douglass worked in solidarity with those targeted by other forms of oppression, and he did so for the rest of his life.

Douglass's experiences made him exceptional, but he was also exceptionally well positioned to demonstrate that his achievements were unusual only because the United States did so much to rob, brutalize, and impoverish African Americans. Of course, Douglass did not work alone in movements for human rights, including the struggle for women's suffrage. Black women were among the contemporaries who made significant contributions.[1]

If asked to name African American women of Douglass's time, most think of Sojourner Truth (1797–1883) and Harriet Tubman (c. 1820–1913). Like Douglass, these women changed the course of history, and while alive, they were appreciated orators for abolitionist and other progressive causes. However, unlike Douglass, they never penned their own life stories.[2] Given their prominence, there was significant biographical interest in both Truth and Tubman, so the fact that neither wrote autobiographies is worth

---

assumptions that Child wrote the book, but see Appendix C3b for the care with which Child attended to these issues. Also, see Foster for a discussion of the significance of the dropping of the name "Linda" from how the text is identified.

1   For example, see Jones.

2   Frederick Douglass escaped from slavery and became one of the most prominent African Americans of the nineteenth century. Sojourner Truth was born enslaved in New York as Isabella Baumfree. After freeing herself by running away, she became an outspoken abolitionist and advocate for women's voting rights. She never wrote her own story but used photography as a form of literacy and self-representation. See Painter; Gilbert. Harriet Tubman freed herself from bondage and returned several times to help others escape, becoming known during her lifetime as "Moses." She was also the first woman to serve as a spy for the United States Army and was constantly cheated out of a military pension. Her authorized biography appeared in 1869 (Bradford). Also see Dunbar, *She Came to Slay*.

noticing.[1] One explanation, of course, is that it was illegal for enslaved people to learn to read and write. Can you imagine an entire childhood and adolescence in which you were punished for showing a desire to learn? How could you "catch up" as an adult when you were finally free to do so?[2]

Still, the fact that Truth and Tubman were not only African American but also female undoubtedly played a part. Because slavery violently transformed people into property, living in a body that could be impregnated yielded particular experiences. The simple capacity to have children that were valuable as commodities—*not* as human beings—must have taken an extraordinary physical, emotional, and mental toll. Anticipating Crenshaw's intersectionality, Jacobs put it this way: "Slavery is terrible for men; but it is far more terrible for women. Superadded to the burden common to all, they have wrongs, and sufferings, and mortifications peculiarly their own" (pp. 141–42).

Surviving slavery in a child-bearing body was a feat, then. To write and publish about one's survival was nearly unheard of, but Harriet Jacobs did precisely that. Even more astonishing, it was only the beginning of her accomplishments.

When the United States wanted Black women to exist only as producers of people that could be treated as property, Harriet Jacobs became a survivor by maneuvering the sexual abuse she could not avoid. After escaping one type of injustice in the South, she maneuvered another version in the North and transformed herself into an author, believing her story could inspire passive Americans to actively oppose slavery. Once she had written her narrative, Jacobs encountered so many publishing obstacles that she ended up printing it herself. With copies of her life story in hand, she then became a traveling bookseller, determined to reach readers who might be inspired to help those still in bondage. And then, beginning in the first months of the Civil War, she used the platform she had earned as an author to advocate for others for the rest of her life.

---

1 This is not to suggest that their biographies are automatically less valuable. Indeed, as Joycelyn Moody's research demonstrates, especially when considering "dictated narratives," one finds that formerly enslaved Black women "purposefully did not pursue literacy despite a willingness to exploit the currency it gave them among reading Americans" ("Silenced" 222).

2 When she is a teacher, Jacobs's daughter Louisa offers a glimpse at a man determined to do precisely that. See Appendix D4.

Ultimately, Jacobs's achievement was exceptional beyond measure. We cannot truly understand its magnitude. But we must try because—like Douglass—she worked to expose how much violence it took to create a society in which so few African American women did what she did.

Harriet Jacobs: Survivor, Author, Advocate

Harriet Ann Jacobs was born in Edenton, North Carolina, in 1813[1] to enslaved parents. Because they managed to shield her, young Harriet did not become aware of her slave status until age six when her mother died. Though she began living in white households from that point, hardship became pronounced when she was nearly twelve and entered the home of James Norcom (1778–1850), whom she calls Dr. Flint in *Incidents*. Her struggle intensified when he began sexually harassing her as she approached her fifteenth year. From that point onward, she engaged in the battle to avoid being sexually conquered; she was determined to escape the spiritual and emotional devastation she believed would result. She also understood that Norcom disposed of his conquests by selling them and the children he impregnated them with, so her struggle was about protecting not only herself but also any children she might bear because her children would inherit her slave status.

The United States is structured—by law and by custom—to accommodate white men's desires, not Black women's and girls' dignity, so Jacobs's war of wills with Norcom impacted her entire life. As a teenager, she fell in love with a free Black man who wanted to purchase her freedom and marry her. Norcom not only refused to sell Jacobs; he also threatened to kill her sweetheart. Further, the fifty-year-old doctor planned to build a secluded cottage where Jacobs would be at a distance from his jealous wife and always sexually available as his concubine.[2] To foil these plans, the fifteen-year-old Jacobs encouraged the attentions of a nearly thirty-year-old white man who was sexually interested in her. The United States made her body available by default, so she at least wanted to influence how it would happen. She preferred Samuel

---

1 Though there has been discussion of different possible years of Jacobs's birth, historian Jean Fagan Yellin's research consistently confirms 1813.

2 A woman who lives with a man to whom she is not married, especially a woman regarded as socially subservient; a mistress.

Tredwell Sawyer (c. 1800–65), whom she names Mr. Sands in *Incidents*, because he was single, unlike her tormentor, and she did not hate him. Jacobs gave birth to a son, Joseph, in 1829 and a daughter, Louisa, in 1833, with Sawyer acknowledged as the father of both.[1]

The young mother had avoided being lodged in a secluded cabin, but Norcom did not lose interest—an interest that amounted to sexual terrorism.[2] Norcom consistently expressed his eagerness to make a "lady" of Jacobs, always urging her to accept the resources he promised and realize how fortunate she was to have his attention. The law made Jacobs's sexual consent meaningless, but Norcom nevertheless pursued it. As historian Emily Owens demonstrates, Norcom was like countless enslavers in that he did not simply want access to Jacobs's body; he wanted her to "willingly" give it. To know Jacobs's story is to glimpse "what it felt like to have not only her body, but also her desire, hunted" (Owens 74).

Norcom relentlessly pursued Jacobs, and when she continued to refuse his "kind offers," he sent her to his son's plantation, six miles from her children and the rest of her support system. Intent upon compounding her misery, he next planned to send her children to join her so that they could all be properly "broken in." At that point, Jacobs decided to run away to increase the likelihood

---

1 Gabrielle Foreman has emphasized that Jacobs was exerting control over who would be recognized as the father of her children because it is possible that Norcom had raped her and was the father of her first child (*Activist* 20–29). On another note, William Andrews draws attention to the fact that Sawyer's unreliability makes "Sands" an apt name for Jacobs to choose ("Class" 193).

2 Owens sees no ambiguity: "Jacobs makes clear that his begging and cajoling, his contracting and calculating was *terrifying* to her. It was not a site of confusion, affection, or love for her; rather, it was another version of slaveholding domination" (79). Also, "Jacobs is verbose, consistent, and, importantly, explicit about the sexualized terror that she lived under both during her time on Norcom's estate and, significantly, in the balance of the narrative, during her escape. Although Jacobs does not describe acts of physicalized sexual violence against her, she actively and clearly describes a climate of sexual terror through a narrative of pursuit" (76). As important, Owens notes how, when Flint considers a move to Louisiana, *Incidents* gestures toward it as a place where there are no limits on white men's ability to live out their concubine fantasies.

that Norcom would see the children as a burden and sell them to Sawyer, whom she believed would free them.

Trying to secure her children's freedom led to one of the battles in the war of wills that Jacobs won. It is also what she is most famous for: she hid for six years and eleven months in the crawl space above her grandmother's storage shed (see Appendix F5). Throughout this time, she was a block away from Norcom (see Appendix F6), but she wrote letters to keep him convinced that she had already escaped to the North. This battle was hard-won, to say the absolute least. Spending nearly seven years in a dark, cramped space took a tremendous toll on her body, and the spiritual, emotional, and mental suffering was no less extreme because she somehow managed to emerge from the ordeal with her sanity intact.[1]

Jacobs finally had a chance to go north in 1842, landing in Philadelphia, then making a life in New York. Before long, Jacobs became familiar with Northern racism, but she was also reunited with her daughter, Louisa, who had been sent north two years before she could escape the South herself. Her son later joined them, a real accomplishment for the oppressed mother.

Jacobs was constantly working for her children's freedom and education, so money dictated decisions. In 1845, the wife of her employer, Nathaniel Parker Willis (1806–67), died in childbirth, and the widower asked Jacobs to accompany him and his newly orphaned daughter, Imogen, to England, where they could spend time with his deceased wife's British family. As historian Jean Fagan Yellin explains, "Willis was offering more money than [Jacobs] was earning, and doubtless she was finding it extremely difficult to feed herself and her children on the wages she could make as a seamstress. It must have been hard for her—when she finally had both of her children under her roof—to decide to accept Willis's offer. But accept it she did" (*Life* 83). They remained abroad for ten months, and when Jacobs returned to the United States, she found that her teenaged son Joseph had left his apprenticeship (87). Jacobs's children were phenotypically white,[2] so Joseph's coworkers approached him with civility and decency until they learned he was "colored." Once they insisted upon treating him poorly, Joseph embarked on a whaling voyage, proving as adventurous as Jacobs's brother, John S., who spent time as a gold speculator and sailor.

---

1 Jacobs certainly faced mental health challenges, especially while in the crawl space. See Louis for a detailed discussion.

2 Having the observable characteristics associated with whiteness.

Trying to make enough money to secure her children's free-dom and education was always a struggle, and Jacobs undertook this struggle as a fugitive, constantly at risk of being returned to bondage. She often had to run and hide because Norcom contin-ued to pursue her in the North, and so did his family after he died in 1850. By the time Norcom's heirs arrived in New York to press their unjust claims, Willis had married an American, Cornelia Grinnell Willis (1825–1904). Jacobs was about to run again by joining her brother in California, but Mrs. Willis had begun nego-tiations to stop any further attempts at capturing Jacobs and her children.[1] Though the deal brought Jacobs some relief, to have money paid for her God-given liberty also made her feel like mer-chandise, and the debt it created was not easily discharged. Jacobs remained in Cornelia Willis's service for many years, helping to raise her children and run her household. Meanwhile, she des-perately wanted a home in which she could provide for her own beloved family, but Jacobs never had a "hearthstone of [her] own" (p. 257).

★ ★ ★

Incidents records the above in much more detail and with liter-ary flair and sophistication. Representing Jacobs's life story from childhood to adulthood and from enslavement to freedom, the remarkable events of the narrative nevertheless prove to be only the beginning. Jacobs wrote *Incidents* to "arouse the women of the North to a realizing sense of the condition of two millions of women at the South, still in bondage, suffering what I suffered, and most of them far worse" (p. 67).

However, Jacobs lived until 1897, and she used every decade after the completion of her autobiography for advocacy as well. Jacobs finished the manuscript[2] of her narrative in 1858 and trav-eled to London with it. Familiar with the abolitionist movement, she understood that a Black author's book project had a better chance with American printers if it had first been published in

---

1 Yellin offers further detail: "Cornelia Grinnell Willis had paid $150 cash down for Jacobs. She needed an equal amount to pay off [Daniel] Messmore [Mary Norcom's new husband], and all spring she tried to raise the money" including by writing fundraising letters to friends (*Life* 118).

2 The text of an author's work, handwritten or typed, that is meant to be submitted eventually to a publisher.

England.[1] Unfortunately, she returned to the United States without having secured a contract. Undeterred, she set about finding a Boston firm. These efforts led to her introduction to author Lydia Maria Child (1802–80), who offered to edit Jacobs's work. Using her experience and connections, Child also negotiated a contract on Jacobs's behalf with publishers Thayer and Eldridge. A publication date of December 1860 came and went, and the firm went bankrupt. Thayer and Eldridge had created the plates from which the book would be printed, though, so Jacobs bought those and then paid for the printing and binding of two thousand copies (Pottroff 231). *Incidents* was therefore "published for the author" in January 1861. Now a published author, Jacobs next became a traveling bookseller.

Ongoing conversations with activists William C. Nell (1816–74) and Amy Post (1802–89) had fueled Jacobs's writing because they convinced her that her story would bring people into the fight to end slavery; the task now was to reach as many readers as possible. Though she hadn't been able to secure a British publisher initially, once the book existed, *Incidents* "was popular enough for Jacobs to negotiate a British edition, titled *The Deeper Wrong*"; however, "unscrupulous printers produced pirated volumes," so someone other than Jacobs benefited financially (Foster and Yarborough vii). Refusing to let that personal injustice distract her, Jacobs spent the first months of 1862 traveling to sell books as she addressed audiences in Boston, New York City, Philadelphia, and Washington, DC. Following Jacobs's trail, literary historian Christy Pottroff finds that "she carried the weight of her story, book by book, to advance the abolitionist cause and to raise enough money to pay off the cost of the book's printing" (232).

Jacobs's book tour was in support of abolition, but after the Civil War started in April 1862, she saw the destitute populations it produced and decided to address their needs more directly. As cultural critic Kyla Schuller puts it, "Jacobs was well on her way to establishing herself as a major abolitionist speaker and writer, a career that would have enabled her greatest wish, a home of her own," but she shifted her priorities (71). Indeed, according to Pottroff, "Jacobs initially traveled to DC as part of her book tour,"

---

1   This was the case for abolitionist texts such as William Wells Brown's novel *Clotel; or, the President's Daughter* (1853) and William [and Ellen] Craft's autobiographical narrative *Running a Thousand Miles for Freedom* (1860).

but "finding people in urgent need, [she] stopped selling books and took direct action" (238–39).

By September 1862, Jacobs was in Washington, DC, where enslaved people congregated in hopes of attaining a freedom that was not at all guaranteed (see Appendices A5 and A6). They came for a better life but more often found starvation and disease. Jacobs alleviated their suffering; it was "solidarity work with her fellow self-emancipators" (Schuller 71). While offering direct services, Jacobs also published reports in newspapers, keeping other activists informed and ready to send resources. By January 1863, Jacobs began working with a very similar population of newly free African Americans in Alexandria, Virginia. With support from Philadelphia and New York Quakers, she taught, provided healthcare, and distributed clothing (Appendix D1). Her thirty-year-old daughter, Louisa, joined her in November 1863, and in partnership with Julia Wilbur (1815–95), a Quaker activist who became a true friend, she worked in Alexandria until July 1865.[1]

While in Alexandria, she had established the Jacobs Free School in 1864, another example of her commitment to community care and mutual aid. Jacobs wanted African Americans to provide for themselves and each other, so she and Louisa resisted the ever-present pressure to let white people determine every outcome. Louisa became head teacher, despite objections from residents who insisted they "could not claim the Building unless a white man controlled the school" (Yellin, *Life* 77–78). Pushing past intense opposition, Jacobs and her daughter also fundraised to pay off the building (178). As Schuller explains, "refusing to ask for cash from Northern [allies]," Jacobs and Louisa requested "surplus rummage sale items, which they then sold, an act closer to mutual aid than to charity" (72).

Every victory was hard won, but there was much to be proud of in Alexandria, and by November 1865, fifty-two-year-old Jacobs and her now thirty-two-year-old daughter took their school knowhow to Savannah, Georgia. As they provided education to the Black community there, the priorities that always shaped Jacobs's advocacy remained evident. She wanted Black people to control the institutions that served them, and she was committed to holistic care (see Appendix D3). Meanwhile, slavery may have ended

---

1 Jacobs's friendship with Wilbur was solidified as they worked to minimize the harm created by Rev. Albert Gladwin, who was put in charge of the contraband camp and treated everyone with condescension and cruelty (Yellin, *Life* 165–73).

on paper, but American brutality never let up. White Southerners abused African Americans physically and verbally to remind them of their "proper" place of subordination. They relentlessly drove home the message that Black people would never be their equals, would never enjoy the citizenship they claimed for themselves. Like her mother, Louisa wrote newspaper reports about the progress being made in the communities she served, and because African Americans were attacked for believing they were people, not animals or property, there was no shortage of stories of abuse (Appendix D4). Violence and hostility always hovered. Finally, Jacobs and her daughter fled Savannah after an acquaintance was killed in 1866 (Yellin, *Life* 200–01).

Jacobs could not escape the reality that white people always had more resources. Being considered white translated into never having been enslaved and thereby robbed of the fruit of one's labor. That is precisely what distinguished white Americans from Jacobs's own phenotypically white children. Determined to obtain a measure of life's necessities for those impoverished by the functions of society, Jacobs maximized her connections to white philanthropists. Always busy sharing resources, she visited her hometown of Edenton, North Carolina, in 1867, distributing clothes and seeds, donations she had gathered for the purpose of helping people help themselves.

In 1868, Jacobs traveled to London again to raise money for an orphanage in Savannah (Appendix D5). Though "she had withdrawn all of her savings to undertake this mission," the trip did not yield the desired results (Yellin, *Life* 212).[1] Black people's allies seemed to consider their work complete with the formal abolition of slavery, but Jacobs knew better. She had seen her fellow Americans' commitment to making Emancipation into what Saidiya Hartman labels a non-event, through "the resubordination of the emancipated" (*Scenes* 116). For instance, when the Union defeated the Confederacy, the government took possession of property that Confederates had held and redistributed it. Soon, although they had been promised land to work so that they could become self-sufficient, Jacobs saw how "the poor loyal freedmen are driven off the soil, that it may be given back to traitors" (Yellin, *Life* 198). Time and time again, African Americans were reminded

---

1 Even the money that was collected didn't ultimately yield a completed project, likely because of the violent opposition African Americans faced whenever they began making progress toward self-sufficiency. See Yellin, *Life* 194–95 for some detail.

of their country's belief that resources should always flow toward white people (see Appendices A7 and A8).

Wherever Jacobs went, she alleviated others' suffering, and she nurtured relationships with activists who supported such work, so when she had moved to Massachusetts after fleeing Savannah, her connections served her well. She spent a year clerking for the New England Women's Club, which had secured a building in Boston. As clerk, Jacobs kept track of the use of the club's bedrooms and recorded attendance at its lectures and social events. Around this time, Jacobs met Harriet Beecher Stowe (1811–96) when the latter visited Massachusetts. They had corresponded before, but this was their first in-person meeting. The famous author of *Uncle Tom's Cabin* (1852) gave Jacobs a signed copy.

By 1870, Jacobs was renting a house in Cambridge, Massachusetts, starting a practice that would mark the rest of her life: running boarding houses. In this way, she was a business owner. Her boarding house in Cambridge was well respected, bringing her into contact with Harvard faculty members and their friends. She also ran boarding houses in the nation's capital, where demand for temporary lodging was high because the political class had permanent homes elsewhere. Again, she interacted with many prominent people.

None of this allowed her to escape the nation's racism and sexism, though, so she could never gain ground financially (see Appendix D6). She was also often sick (Appendix D6), and the same was true of her daughter. Despite their own ailments and financial hardships, mutual aid and philanthropy were always priorities—indeed, a way of life.[1] Jacobs was known for offering holiday meals to destitute elderly people in Washington, DC, for example, and she carried food in 1885 to the widow of James Norcom, Jr., son of the man who had terrorized her (Yellin, *Life* 245–47).[2]

Jacobs had last received word of her son decades earlier from Melbourne, Australia,[3] so she no doubt cherished having her

---

1 In *Madam C.J. Walker's Gospel of Giving: Black Women's Philanthropy during Jim Crow*, historian Tyrone McKinley Freeman documents the extent to which Black women made philanthropy a way of life during the violent, economically oppressive Jim Crow era. That tradition was longstanding, and Jacobs represents an earlier manifestation of it.

2 James Norcom, Jr., was also the man on whose plantation Jacobs and her children were to have been "broken in" (pp. 149–57).

3 She last got word in 1866 from a source that asked Jacobs to send money because Joseph was too sick to hold a pen himself [*continued*]

adult daughter by her side. She and Louisa worked long hours to make money, but they also managed to stay connected to activist circles. In 1886, the eighteenth convention of the National Woman Suffrage Association took place in Washington, DC, and the mother-daughter duo attended (Yellin, *Harriet Jacobs Family Papers* 1.lxi).

Jacobs had long struggled with her health, but it was not until 1888 that she finally closed her boarding house at age seventy-five. Consider the grueling work: well into her seventies, she was cooking for, and hosting, a house full of people. Already suffering with various conditions, Jacobs was diagnosed with breast cancer in 1894. As she was recovering from surgery around the age of eighty-one, Louisa was now her full-time caregiver. Jacobs's former employer, Cornelia Willis, came to help and noticed that Louisa "felt embarrassed that her nursing responsibilities caring for her mother prevented her from earning money to support them" (Yellin, *Life* 258).

Jacobs was in her eighties, Louisa was in her sixties, and both had toiled their entire lives, but their circumstances were shaped less by their work ethic and more by the racism and sexism that kept resources flowing away from them and toward white women and men. After falling from her wheelchair and injuring her hip months before, Harriet Jacobs died at home in March 1897 in the nation's capital city.[1] In eulogizing her, Rev. Francis Grimké (1850–1937) said, "She was no reed shaken by the wind, vacillating, easily moved from a position. She did her own thinking" (Appendix D7a).

★ ★ ★

To appreciate the immensity of Jacobs's achievement in becoming a survivor, author, and advocate, we can begin by acknowledging how white supremacy shaped not only slavery but also efforts to end it, namely the abolitionist movement. African Americans, both free and enslaved, were often abolitionists with intellectual clarity about the injustice of slavery and with courage to risk life and limb in the struggle against it.[2] Nevertheless, the movement

---

to write a letter, but he wanted to come home to the United States. Jacobs managed to send money but never saw her son again. See Yellin, *Life* 224–25.

1 As cause of death, Yellin reports "interstitial nephritis and asthma" (*Harriet Jacobs Family Papers* 1.lxiii). The former is a kidney disorder.

2 See R. Kelley.

was dominated by whites because the United States made them free while enslaving and disfranchising Black people.

White anti-slavery activists courageously countered the idea undergirding American laws and customs, that African Americans should be stripped of every right white people enjoy,[1] but they were not exempt from believing the nation's lies about the inherent goodness and superiority of white folk. White abolitionists often saw themselves as morally superior to peers who refused to question slavery. In other words, they were righteous in comparison to other white people, their social equals. And if they were more advanced than their social counterparts, they certainly surpassed their social subordinates, the Black people they were righteous enough to help.[2]

Naturally, then, encounters with African Americans should always reinforce their image of themselves as saviors worthy of nothing but admiration and gratitude. Familiar with Frederick Douglass's undeniable impact, Jacobs understood that it was based on his lectures about having been born into slavery. As literature scholar Jacqueline Goldsby explains, "the typical procedure called for the slaves' narratives to be published *after* their oral presentation on the abolitionist lecture circuit" (17). Audiences open to opposing slavery required Black bodily presence coupled with leadership-approved stories of Black pain.[3] Sharing painful experiences provided occasion for white audiences to display sympathy—which affirmed their position above the Black victims they sympathized with and the white abusers who behaved in ways they presumably never would.

---

1 Without question, white abolitionists were courageous. As an example of the very real dangers they faced, Yoshiaki Furui reminds us, "In 1835 William Lloyd Garrison, editor of the antislavery paper the *Liberator*, was dragged by a rope through the Boston streets by a proslavery mob. In 1837 Elijah P. Lovejoy, another antislavery editor, was killed by a group of antiabolitionists" (46). On how consistently citizenship was based on the exclusion of African-descended people, see, for example, Jones; Spires.

2 Evidence for this logic is plentiful. See, for example, McBride.

3 As Frances Smith Foster puts it, "Jacobs had worked for a year in her brother's Rochester antislavery reading room. Since it was located over the offices of Frederick Douglass, she may have heard the history of the resistance that Douglass had encountered, especially from his most ardent abolitionist friends, when he decided to tell his story his way" (62).

To become an advocate for those still enslaved, Jacobs could not avoid the abolitionist movement's requirements for self-revelation that provided opportunities for white sympathy, but she seems to have been determined to work both with and around those demands. First, Jacobs did not follow the typical lecture-then-publish path.[1] Second, she offered her painful testimony according to her own priorities and aesthetic sensibilities—a powerful fusion of accuracy and bold creativity.[2]

Jacobs shared her experience in a way that highlights how inseparable fiction and nonfiction are. *Incidents* is a narrative of enslavement,[3] also known as a slave narrative, which means it is autobiographical—a life story written by the person whose life is represented. At the same time, it refuses to be understood simply as autobiography because Jacobs novelized her story, giving herself (and others) fictionalized names and using the strategies of popular genres, such as sentimental fiction, to hold readers' attention.

By investing in creativity no less than autobiographical accuracy, Jacobs gestured toward the fact that fiction is inescapable, and she highlighted not only the power of storytelling but also the uses and abuses of that power. Because she recognized how much creative effort it took for the nation to treat her as property, Jacobs understood that storytelling was rarely just fun and games. Especially in societies that insist certain groups are not people and therefore do not deserve rights, fictions have very real, nonfiction effects. In the hands of the powerful, that which is only make-believe can be used to mold nonfiction lives. For instance,

---

1 There may be many reasons why she did not follow the lecture-then-publish path. Sharing her story of sexual vulnerability in person might have been too painful for her and too scandalizing for audiences. For other possibilities, see Goldsby 18–19.

2 Changing names served many purposes, as countless scholars have argued, including putting some psychological distance between the story and herself while she composed, as Yellin suggests (*Life* 126). Still, I call attention to the effect of this choice because its impact is as important as any intention.

3 In the spirit of the community-sourced guide organized by Gabrielle Foreman, *Writing about Slavery? This Might Help*, I am bringing attention to the violence required to enslave one's fellow human beings. However, like Tiya Miles, I do not perform "linguistic acrobatics to avoid using the word 'slave' or 'owner'" (*All* 288). For some of the reasons why, see my discussion later in this Introduction about African Americans' use of the English language.

reality contradicted the stories Americans most often told, but that did not stop violent fictions from pressing in on every side. As historian Matthew Desmond explains, slavery required an intense mythology about Black people because "houses do not attempt to become non-property by running away. Cattle do not stage armed revolts. But humans treated as property were constantly doing both" (173). Everything about enslaved people screamed that they were human and should have rights, so American laws and popular culture generated more and more stories to make observable facts irrelevant. Accordingly, *Incidents* says of a person of color: "that intelligent, enterprising, noble-hearted man was a chattel! liable, by *the laws* of a country *that calls itself civilized*, to be sold with horses and pigs!" (p. 215, italics added).

Jacobs's autobiographical account also revolved around being a survivor of sexual abuse, and she survived to write that story because she recognized the fictions that made her vulnerable and decided to meet American inventiveness with her own. Jacobs had used her imagination to author a life of survival against the odds; she had "exhausted [her] ingenuity in avoiding the snares, and eluding the power of a hated tyrant" (p. 121). Now, she would author a narrative that adhered to her priorities, not those dictated by people who occupied elevated positions simply because they were considered white.[1]

Having identified the death-dealing creativity that put her at white people's mercy, Jacobs saw the value of life-affirming creativity. In the words of literary critic Rafia Zafar, she fashioned "the character of 'Linda Brent' to stand in for both her own self and those of the millions of her oppressed countrywomen" (3). Envisioning that which did not yet exist, Jacobs transformed herself into not only a survivor and trailblazing author but also an ardent advocate who operated in solidarity with countless others, including men targeted by sexual predators.[2]

By making herself into a survivor, author, and advocate, Jacobs confronted the dynamics most structuring American society and rejected the passivity they required of the sexually exploited female slave.[3] American culture cast Black people either as

---

1 For an example of Jacobs's awareness that whiteness confers unearned advantages, see Appendix C1b.

2 For instance, Jacobs made a point of sharing the story of someone she called Luke (pp. 247–48).

3 I use "female slave" here to emphasize the objectified position that Jacobs rejects. As Marianne Noble makes clear, the sexual [*continued*]

subhuman creatures whose destruction did not matter (except as a loss of property)[1] or as charity cases. When Black people can be understood in terms of charity, any white person who is not actively attacking them is presumed to be not simply decent but commendable. In Jacobs's time, white people who did not own slaves often fell into this category. They could see themselves as better than enslavers even if they did nothing to address the injustice that their charitable impulses suggested they acknowledged. Meanwhile, abolitionists were presumably even more admirable.

Because she took action based on creativity and never waited to be saved, Jacobs not only survived; she asserted power over her fate and refused the subordination preferred even by her allies. Literary historian Joycelyn Moody has found that by elevating certain kinds of people, "the abolitionist enterprise itself seems ironically to have silenced enslaved and ex-slave women" (Moody, "Silenced" 222). When she observed the movement, Jacobs apparently noticed its patterns. According to Sandra Gunning, in abolitionist discourse, a premium was placed on "the passivity rather than the resistance of the exploited" (146). Americans, even the most progressive ones, were prepared to receive Jacobs as a victim worthy of sympathy but not as "an authoritative commentator on slavery, *much less Northern morality*" (133, italics added). And there's no question that Jacobs understood what was expected. Gunning identifies Jacobs's keen awareness that she was "writing for a Northern audience not likely to grant her respect as a competent social commentator" (138). Nevertheless, Jacobs "shaped the evidence of her experience into a narrative that suggested not only *what* happened, but also *why*" (Owens 75). The refusal to

exploitation of enslaved women was supposed to prompt sympathy, but scenes of brutality also became masturbation material, according to Sigmund Freud. Jacobs herself also showed awareness of the countless consequences of seeing people as objects when detailing Mrs. Flint's night-time strategies for "discovering" that Linda is guilty of seducing her husband. As Hortense Spillers puts it, for Linda, becoming a teenager means being sexualized in ways that amount to "vulnerability to a gigantic sexualized repertoire that may be alternately expressed as male and/or female" (222). Both Dr. Flint and his wife project sexual fantasies onto the teenager in their purported care.

1 Throughout the time that the country of their birth insisted upon valuing them only in economic terms, enslaved people understood that calculus but also devised their own, what historian Daina Berry calls "soul value" (*Price*).

embody sympathy-inducing passivity characterizes Harriet Jacobs and Linda Brent, both the real-life historical figure and the narrating protagonist she created in *Incidents*. Asserting herself at every turn, Jacobs clearly recognized that "to depend on white feelings as a catalyst for change" only "reinscribes the world" (Yao 2) that sees a lower status as her "proper" place (Mitchell 5).

Both in life and in literature, because Jacobs/Brent resists being a charity case, her work exposes the unearned advantage white men and women enjoy—whether they are actively brutal enslavers or passively brutal in their inaction. Accordingly, *Incidents* exposes not only white villainy but also white mediocrity and incompetence. At one point, the text's main sexual predator, Dr. Flint, changes sleeping arrangements such that his four-year-old daughter remains with him, so fifteen-year-old Linda must, too. According to Gunning, "[h]ere one wonders if Flint expects the child to be present while he tries to rape her nurse" (143). When Mrs. Flint directs sexual suspicion and anger at Linda rather than her husband, she fails to protect not only a teenaged Linda but also her own daughter. Situations like this demonstrate that Jacobs had reason to view white Americans as anything but impressive. In fact, knowing that readers would likely join Mrs. Flint in judging Linda more harshly than they judge white men, Jacobs and her editor wrote carefully crafted prefaces to *Incidents*. These documents aim to help readers notice how downplaying the despicable behavior of "respectable" white men makes them complicit.[1] Whether she was impressed or not, however, Jacobs could not ignore reality: disfranchised groups needed help from white citizens.

The United States ensured that white people had a near monopoly on resources, so being an advocate involved working to recruit allies and accomplices. As Tiya Miles puts it, Jacobs was determined "to use her single voice as a lever to move women of privilege in defense of women in jeopardy" ("Introduction" viii). Even if she needed others' help, though, there would be nothing passive about how Jacobs operated.

In a culture that expected her to be an object of charity and geyser of gratitude, Jacobs was an ardent advocate, repeatedly achieving what seemed impossible and always with an eye toward empowering others. The composition of the text she used to

---

1   For excellent analysis of the folly of Northern readers trying to see their own domestic spaces as unrelated to what Jacobs describes, see Ernest; Rifkin.

advocate for herself and her community exemplifies her determination to take action against the odds, especially when she would not be the only beneficiary. First, it took years for Jacobs to even want to share her experience above a "whisper."[1] As Frances Smith Foster reports, "Harriet Jacobs was regularly asked to contribute her story to the antislavery effort, but she withstood those pleas for [many years] before she agreed to testify" (61). She did not want to speak her truth, let alone write and publish it, because it was painful to revisit what the United States allowed her to endure. In the words of Joycelyn Moody, "formerly enslaved women, such as Jacobs, who narrated their survival of sexual violence risked a psychic return to sites of trauma" ("Silenced" 226). Foster continues, "it was only after the Compromise of 1850 created the Fugitive Slave Law ... that Jacobs agreed to publicize some of her most personal experiences" (61). Jacobs devotes an entire chapter of *Incidents* to describing the terror prompted by the *Fugitive Slave Act*, so it surely contributed to her feeling that she "can nott be happy without trying to be useful" (Appendix C2b, p. 291). However, the early 1850s offered another prompt for making the effort to overcome her understandable hesitancy. Jacobs's grandmother, Molly Horniblow (c. 1771–1853), had made countless sacrifices on Jacobs's behalf, and she was a proud woman who was also uncompromising in sexual matters. Making public the ways that Jacobs's experience had not been "a life of a Heroine with no degradation associated with it" (Appendix C2a, p. 290) must have felt inappropriate while her grandmother might be affected. So, once the beloved matriarch died in 1853, Jacobs could take her story public without assuming she was bringing shame to the person to whom she owed so much.

Once determined to contribute to abolition by sharing her personal experience, Jacobs was willing to undertake the difficult work of writing, but the country's racism and sexism made doing so even more difficult; nevertheless, Jacobs overcame every obstacle. When she began drafting her narrative around 1853, she had been in the "free" North for a decade, but her circumstances reflected the nation's insistence upon making whiteness the prerequisite for opportunity. Black women, especially the formerly enslaved, were relegated to domestic service,[2] so Jacobs

---

1 Letter to Amy Post, 21 June 1857 (Yellin, *Harriet Jacobs Family Papers* 1.236–38).

2 The scholarship on constrained economic opportunity is extensive. As Tiya Miles summarizes, in every American city, "most African

had to carve out writing time while working a twenty-four-hours-a-day, seven-days-a-week job as a nanny and housekeeper. Her employer, Nathaniel Parker Willis, who founded the magazine now known as *Town and Country*, spent his days in the study, free from household concerns, including the care of his five children. Meanwhile, Jacobs "undertook her project in secret, and at night" (Yellin, *Life* 127). Transforming herself into an author also required overcoming odds because the literary marketplace worshipped white voices. She published the book on her own, at her own expense, after several tries[1]—the last of which fell through because the publisher had bankrupted itself by producing and promoting an extravagant third edition of Walt Whitman's 1855 poetry collection *Leaves of Grass* (Pottroff 220).

Once Jacobs managed to complete the book and publish it in 1861, she refused passivity again and undertook various forms of advocacy. Convinced that her personal history was a weapon in the fight to end slavery, she advocated for those still in bondage by traveling to sell copies of her book. Then, when the Civil War began in 1862, she addressed the crisis that emerged as large numbers of Black people used the chaos of war to escape from slavery. The Union declared them "contrabands,"[2] and Jacobs went to a contraband camp to lend a hand. While she directly cared for those suffering in the camp, she also advocated for them by writing newspaper accounts of the miserable conditions, soliciting donations and other support. Then, as the country transitioned out of war, Jacobs continued her advocacy by using her reputation as *Incidents* author, and her connections to activist circles, to publish reports in newspapers about how the experience of newly free people failed to match the government's promises to them.

Jacobs lived until 1897—nearly forty years after she published *Incidents*—and she spent those decades meeting other people's

---

American women were employed as domestic servants in private homes or institutions. Nearly 90 percent of Black women did some form of domestic labor in 1890; that number had decreased only to 84 percent by 1910" (*All* 238). Of course, opportunity was even more limited in earlier decades.

1 This is not surprising when one considers that every publisher required Jacobs to obtain written testimony from others about the value of her story and the quality of her character.

2 Declaring enslaved people "contraband" basically meant that the Union saw them as similar to any other resource that warring factions would use to defeat the opponent. Also see Appendix A5.

needs and trying to convince her fellow Americans to join her. Operating with an ethic of community care and mutual aid, Jacobs was an advocate who urged wide participation, but she never waited on others to act. She always worked to alleviate suffering herself, despite how meager the United States ensured her resources (including her health and vitality[1]) would always be.

Harriet Jacobs: Artist

Besides making herself into a survivor, author, and advocate, Jacobs was undeniably an artist. While telling the truth of her experience in an unjust society and working to make life better for herself and countless others, she contributed to the world through creativity and aesthetic innovation. Once again, *Incidents* is only the beginning of that contribution, but even this one aspect of Jacobs's legacy proves to be remarkably layered and dynamic.

To understand the ingenuity, experimentation, and sheer

---

1   There is much to be said about Jacobs's life when one uses the lens of (Dis)Ability Studies. Jacobs's personal correspondence reveals her struggles with various ailments, including "a severe attack of Rheumatism" (Yellin, *Harriet Jacobs Family Papers* 1.213), "trouble" with her "womb" (1.221), and "another attack of congestion of the lungs—but much slighter than the attack that I had a year ago" (1.235). However, it is not just her life experience that proves powerful for (Dis)Ability-informed analysis. Her literary text can be similarly examined, and Shari Goldberg's efforts in this regard have produced compelling results. "Once Linda's children are born, hardly a page goes by without a reference to her heart," Goldberg finds (5). *Incidents* can help advance work like that encouraged by researchers such as Michael Snediker, those who urge scholars to attend to the experience of "living in ongoing discomfort" (Goldberg 6). Indeed, "trauma theory would eventually catch up with what Jacobs already sensed" (10) because "her narrative is not one of enslavement's psychological damage, punctuated by physical illness: it shows how psychological damage is inextricable from physical illness" (9).

Questions of wellness productively arise in conversations around (Dis)Ability, so hearing Vivian Delchamps argue that Charlotte Forten Grimké used sewing and activism *as self-care* has stayed with me. Jacobs's sewing never seems to have been divorced from labor, if not drudgery, but activism surely helped her stave off despair, just as Delchamps finds it did for Grimké, who was a close friend of both Jacobs and Louisa.

originality of *Incidents*, begin with genre. To speak in terms of genre is to acknowledge the literary conventions (or patterns) that make texts recognizable. The reader's recognition of those conventions shapes the meaning they glean from the work as well as the emotional and intellectual connections they make when engaging it.

Incidents is an autobiography, not unlike forerunners such as *The Autobiography of Benjamin Franklin* (1793) and *The Narrative of the Life of Frederick Douglass* (1845). In autobiography, as opposed to biography, the person whose life is being represented is also the person telling the story. As Franklin (1706–90) narrates his life, the reader encounters a man who overcomes adversity to emerge as the admirable figure whom others can use as inspiration for their own self-development. Scholars see many similarities between the figure Franklin puts forth in his text and the one Douglass offers. However, any parallels between Franklin's and Douglass's life stories are both confirmed and complicated by the difference that being white (and therefore free) made for Franklin and being enslaved made for Douglass. At the most basic level, because enslavement was one of the adversities Douglass overcame, readers encounter his life story as a slave narrative more readily than as autobiography, the presumably more universal genre.

Of course, being free because one is considered white is not universal; it is as specific and socially constructed as enslavement, and the experience of Jacobs's phenotypically white children demonstrates that fact. Nevertheless, whiteness and universality are constantly equated, and readers typically accept the equation without noticing they have done so. Like Douglass, Jacobs had been enslaved, so her life story is recognizable as a slave narrative, a genre most readers equate with Douglass's contribution.[1]

Generic conventions reflect consistency and change over time. Once several texts exist, similarities and differences can be identified, and when male authors dominate a genre, masculinity

---

1 Slave narratives took many other forms. See William Andrews, *To Tell a Free Story*, and his essay on the postbellum slave narrative. However, it is also worth noting Eric Gardner's legitimate lament: despite the expansiveness of Black print culture, "for many scholars, slave narratives (and/or perhaps a novel or two that look like slave narratives) *are* nineteenth-century African American literature." Even worse, "this complex genre is embodied solely in a tiny number of texts—perhaps, in the worst cases, just two (albeit fascinating) texts, Douglass's *Narrative* and Jacobs's *Incidents*" (8).

shapes the unspoken agreement between creators and consumers of that literary form. With slave narratives, many have observed that the narrator emerges in the text as a singular figure whose experiences in enslavement emphasize his distinction from those around him. The narrator represents those distinctions as qualities that enabled him to conquer adversity and become the person who claimed freedom for himself and can now relate the story being told. *Incidents* revises those (masculine) conventions with a narrator uninterested in escaping solo (without her children) and by consistently representing the cooperation needed to secure safety and freedom. Jacobs's narrator regularly relies on her grandmother, her uncle, a family friend named Peter, boat captains,[1] and many others. She even enlists the help of white women who are themselves enslavers but agree to conceal her. As literary critic Valerie Smith argues, Jacobs's narrator Linda Brent does not tell a story of a triumphant individual so much as a "triumphant self-in-relation" (33).

Jacobs's text also differs from narratives of enslavement like Douglass's because it does not emphasize physical strength and mobility. Male narrators often highlight an instance of physically overpowering an abuser, and this experience leads to their determination to be free, so it drives their physical movement from the South to the North. In contrast, Jacobs's Linda never has a victorious physical confrontation, and her journey to freedom begins with nearly seven years cramped in an attic within walking distance of her abuser. As literature scholar Yoshiaki Furui puts it, *Incidents* distinguishes itself from most slave narratives with "Linda's sheer lack of physical movement" and because "physical strength does not really factor into her struggle to escape to the North" (59).[2] As important, Linda articulates a sophisticated

---

1 The helpful boat captains are usually white, but sailing and sailors are important throughout the narrative, partly because Black men enjoyed more freedom on water than on land. Curbing that freedom also became important to white Americans, as made clear in, for example, Wong; Jones. Also see Appendix B5.

2 Yellin explains the tremendous risk everyone was taking on: if Jacobs's whereabouts were discovered, "she would of course be sent back to Norcom. If Grandmother and [her uncle] were found guilty of concealing a fugitive slave, they would be fined and prosecuted by the state. If they were found guilty of assisting a runaway to escape from North Carolina, they would be subject to the mandatory death penalty" (*Life* 49).

understanding of geography. As critical geographer Katherine McKittrick explains, while making a life in her grandmother's attic, Linda's surroundings are "disabling, oppressive, dark, and cramped," but she finds them "more liberatory than moving about under the gaze of Dr. Flint" (41). Then, after she reaches the "free states," Linda constantly highlights how the racism of the North makes it similar to the South. Having experienced a kind of freedom in the South and a kind of bondage in the North, Linda rejects simplistic notions of what it means to move and what it means to move around the country.

Incidents also expands the boundaries for the slave narrative genre because it does not equate literacy and freedom in a straightforward way. For Douglass, acquiring literacy is an act of rebellion because his enslaver directly forbids it. Then literacy becomes the fuel for his quest for freedom (Smith 23). Learning to read convinces him that human bondage has no valid justification, and learning to write empowers him to manipulate language for his own benefit—enabling him to write passes saying he is allowed to travel, for example. For Jacobs's narrator, however, literacy is a gift bestowed by her first owner that later creates more avenues for her exploitation. As Goldsby puts it, "Dr. Flint's sexual transgressions and abuses against Linda are literally graphic because they assume linguistic forms" (26). At one point, Linda's brother delivers a note from Dr. Flint, and she shares with the reader, "The color mounted to my brother's face when he gave it to me; and he said, 'Don't you hate me, Linda, for bringing you these things?'" (p. 126). Flint has a "restless, craving, vicious nature" (p. 84), and Linda's literacy exposes her to it even when she is not in his physical presence.

Humans can use their ingenuity to destroy life or to preserve it, so anything can become a weapon or a shield, a poison or a cure, and *Incidents* reveals this to be true of both literacy and domesticity. A home can be a safe haven or a prison.[1] Furthermore, that which makes households safe for girls and women who are considered white is also what presses "the cup of sin, and shame, and misery" to the lips of those not considered white (p. 96).[2] This double-edged dynamic leads Linda to predict vastly

---

1 Jacobs's text can also be seen as engaging with gothic sensibilities and with the trope of the "madwoman in the attic."

2 Again, the purported safety and sacredness of white domesticity were built on the exploitation Jacobs details, as scholars such as Ernest and Rifkin elucidate.

different futures for two girls she sees playing together (p. 96). It also leads her to characterize the town jail as more of a home for her daughter than Mrs. Flint's household (pp. 164–65). Likewise, while Linda's literacy makes her vulnerable to additional forms of Flint's sexual abuse, it also empowers her to become a stage manager who literally directs Flint's movement by mailing letters that convince him she is already in the North.[1]

Besides complicating simplistic notions of domesticity and literacy, *Incidents* refuses a concluding move made by most narratives in the tradition: it does not end with the protagonist forgiving their former owner. Many narrators showcase their moral and intellectual evolution by forgiving the people who once enslaved them. Jacobs's own brother, who published *A True Tale of Slavery* in England in the very same month that *Incidents* appeared in the United States, made this expected rhetorical and literary move. Yellin urges readers to notice that *Incidents* does not (*Life* 247).

While contributing to the recognizable form of the narrative of enslavement, Jacobs also innovates by refusing to base the narrator's victories on having once believed the nation's favorite fictions. That is, many narrators represent their transformation into an admirable figure by admitting how thoroughly slavery had initially degraded them. The system's brutality succeeded in convincing them of their worthlessness until a turning point empowered them to reject the culture's dehumanizing lies. As Frances Smith Foster and Richard Yarborough powerfully assert, whereas Douglass takes pains to show "how a man was made a slave and … how a slave was made a man," Jacobs depicts "an enslaved woman who never doubted that she was entitled to life, liberty, and the pursuit of happiness" (x). Even as she admits to feeling shame as she looks back on her life, she critiques American culture, which legally placed her at the mercy of despicable men and hard-hearted women.

The aesthetic innovation of *Incidents* also becomes apparent when viewed in relationship to sentimental fiction, which was popular among middle-class white women, the group Jacobs most hoped to activate on behalf of those still in bondage. Aware of the conventions that readers found compelling, Jacobs put her own

---

1 My inspiration for thinking of Jacobs's deliberate use of letters in terms of stage management comes from Curseen's excellent essay. For how Jacobs's letters powerfully and deliberately intervene in print culture, see Furui; Fagan.

spin on them.[1] As a genre, sentimental fiction is capacious, or capable of holding much, but one way to understand its impact is to consider how it guided the development of the American *Bildungsroman*, or coming-of-age story. This is especially helpful given that Jacobs's narrative begins in childhood and traces her journey to adulthood.[2]

Especially when they crafted texts centering female characters, American writers of sentimental fiction reworked the seduction plot, exemplified by Samuel Richardson's British novel *Pamela; or, Virtue Rewarded* (1740). What made its American counterparts recognizable? "A persistent male of elevated social rank seeks to seduce a woman of a lower class" and "through her resistance and piety, she educates her would-be seducer into an awareness of his own depravity and his capacity for true, honorable love" (Smith 41). Of course, honorable love was possible for a man of elevated status only with a woman considered white. If she were phenotypically white but believed to have "one drop" of Black blood,[3] then she could be a sought-after concubine but not a prized, protected wife.

American laws and customs prevented happy romantic endings for real-life women who weren't considered white, and this reality was reflected in how rarely they had happy endings in literature. In fact, the "tragic mulatto" became a trope in creative works.[4]

---

1 For instance, Jacobs creates dialogue, and her narrator directly addresses the reader, as is the case in novels of the time. Also, she presents action within chapters to create suspense while offering a sense of completion of a certain arc. Likewise, she titles chapters in compelling ways. In short, Jacobs's writing reveals an avid reader.

2 As Nazera Wright reminds us, "Jacobs distinguishes between girlhood and womanhood, a rhetorical move that acknowledges the slave woman not as chattel but as human *and* female" (85).

3 In order to justify enslaving entire populations, including the children of white men who raped enslaved women, the United States functioned under a "one-drop rule" even before putting it into law. Being said to have one ancestor with African blood was enough to reduce a person to slavery and prevent them from being able to inherit property or anything of social value. Only after slavery was abolished, and non-white people had enjoyed a few decades of being able to eke out some kind of success, did these ideas become laws, thereby reinforcing the belief that only whiteness made one a citizen.

4 The term *mulatto* could be used to suggest the presence of any amount of African ancestry, even if only "one drop" of [*continued*]

The mixed-race woman who is abandoned by, and pines after, the man of elevated status recurred so much that Jacobs can be seen to innovate on that literary convention as well. As Yellin puts it, "in her hand, the pathetic seduced 'tragic mulatto' of white fiction is metamorphosed from a victim of white male deception and fickleness into an inexperienced girl making desperate choices in her struggle for autonomy" (*Incidents* xxxiv). As "tragic" indicates, such figures emerged in fiction as objects of sympathy, and their plight underscored the damage slavery did, making men callous and devastating women who otherwise might have contributed to society or at least been happy.[1]

In nineteenth-century US culture, the path to a life of joyous contribution was laid out in the ubiquitous guidance of "the cult of true womanhood." As historian Barbara Welter explains, a *true woman* embodied the ideals of (religious) piety, (sexual) purity, submissiveness, and domesticity. She was properly submissive to the man in her life—her father and/or husband—and her commitment to domesticity ensured that the household she inhabited was clean, provided a nurturing space for children, and was otherwise run efficiently (151).[2] In prioritizing submissiveness and domesticity, she was also so sexually pure and spiritually enlightened that she had a positive moral influence (indirectly, in

---

"Black blood," or it could specifically suggest that one parent was believed to be of African descent. Similar terms include *quadroon* and *octoroon*, indicating one-quarter "African blood" and one-eighth "African blood," respectively. All such terms are now considered derogatory, as people in these categories increasingly advocate for *mixed-race* or *multiracial*.

1 Examples of this figure in literature include characters in Child's short story "The Quadroons" (1842); Brown's *Clotel* (1853); and Stowe's Eliza in *Uncle Tom's Cabin* (1852). In *Relative Races*, Brigitte Fielder notes how rarely scholars examine Cassy, who is phenotypically very similar to the much-discussed Eliza and other characters in the tradition.

2 Mrs. Flint proves submissive and domestic in that she takes her anger out on Linda rather than her husband, and she lords over kitchen ingredients, like flour, to maximize output (p. 80). She clearly values being a good steward of the resources. She does so to the point of cruelty to the enslaved but for the benefit of her husband and their household, proving her worth as a woman even if she clearly isn't honored by his sexual predations. Readers do well to see this as part of her adherence to "true womanhood."

her thoroughly feminine way) on the men in her life. She helped her husband, especially, to be the upstanding citizen the nation needed, despite his inevitable exposure to the vices shaping the world outside the home.

The cult of true womanhood along with sentimentality built the social, political, and literary landscape that *Incidents* entered, and the fact that sentimental literature was so popular that it shaped coming-of-age stories provides useful context for readers today. After all, "sentimentality works as a set of rules for how to 'feel right'" (Samuels 5). Furthermore, sentimentality's cultural impact was both a reflection and a perpetuation of widespread faith in "the power of feeling to guide right conduct" (Williamson 3).

What it meant for Americans to believe that right action followed right feeling can be appreciated by considering Harriet Beecher Stowe's monumentally influential novel *Uncle Tom's Cabin*. Published in *The National Era* between June 1851 and April 1852, the forty-one weekly installments were so widely read (and inspired so many new subscriptions to the newspaper) that, before the serialization came to a close, Stowe landed a contract to publish the novel in two volumes. The motivation for Stowe's remarkable contribution is worth noting. In 1849, her son Charley (the youngest of seven) died, and two years later, still in grief, she wrote, "It was at his dying bed and at his grave that I learnt what a poor slave mother may feel when her child is torn away from her" (qtd. in Lowry).

In other words, Stowe's own "right" feeling of sympathy created a turning point in her life and her career. That feeling never faded, so she found the *Fugitive Slave Act* of 1850 absolutely infuriating. As literary critic Beverly Lowry puts it, Stowe was determined "to touch the hearts of readers and instill in their minds a new and more nearly accurate portrayal" of the horrors of slavery to disturb not just "Southerners and slaveholders but—even more to the point—[their] compromisers and virtual collaborators from the North." Without question, Stowe's ability to feel for the plight of enslaved women—especially through motherhood—shaped her text as well as the impact it had on countless Americans.[1]

Given Stowe's back story, it is even more telling that Jacobs's work disrupts the assumptions of sentimentality in two pointed ways. Linda resists being the object of someone else's sympathy,

---

1 Of course, it was an international hit, but I want to draw readers' attention to the cultural landscape of the United States.

and she doubts white women's capacity for identifying with her, even when they are mothers. After Linda is sent to a plantation to be humbled, a white friend visits. Trying to be comforting, the friend tells Linda that she "wished that I and all my grandmother's family were at rest in our graves, for not until then should she feel any peace about us" (p. 152). As Smith argues, "Jacobs is clearly fond of this woman, but as she tells the story, she admits that she resents Miss Fanny's attempts to sentimentalize her situation" by elevating death instead of considering "the more practical solution of freedom" (43). Even if feeling "right" ideally inspired action, it could affirm white people's preferred view of themselves without action. That's certainly how Linda interprets Miss Fanny's comment here—as being about a white woman seeing herself as righteous because she sympathizes so much that she wants relief. (So the relief is for her, not for African Americans.) Attentive readers will also notice that *Incidents* offers frequent testimony about how motherhood does nothing to make white women more empathetic, moral, or admirable.[1]

Jacobs also represented motherhood as the source of Black women's refusal to wait for white people to feel right or to act right, and her real-life experience with Stowe must have been part of the inspiration. Stowe became an example of the pitfalls of relying on white saviors when, in 1853, she treated Jacobs with condescension and disrespect (Yellin, *Life* 118–22). Jacobs had initially hoped to have Stowe write her biography, which would have put Jacobs even more firmly in the excellent company of Sojourner Truth and Harriet Tubman. Jacobs had her friend Amy Post write to Stowe with a sketch of her life. Before there was time to receive an answer, Jacobs saw newspaper announcements about Stowe preparing to visit abolitionists in England. Determined to contribute to the cause, Jacobs came up with the idea of having her daughter Louisa, who had just finished school, accompany Stowe. Jacobs would pay Louisa's expenses, of course, and the arrangement could be mutually beneficial, given each woman's commitment to the anti-slavery cause. Louisa could assist Stowe while gaining experience as an activist and speaker. After all, Jacobs believed her daughter to be "a very good representative of a Southern Slave" for British audiences to encounter (Appendix C2b). "And," in Yellin's words, "if Louisa were traveling with

---

1 In this way, Jacobs offers early testimony of the findings fleshed out by historians Thavolia Glymph in *Out of the House of Bondage* and Stephanie Jones-Rogers in *They Were Her Property.*

Stowe, she might be able to convince the famous author to write Jacobs's life story" (*Life* 120). Agreeing that it was a solid plan, Jacobs's employer, Cornelia Willis, wrote a letter to Stowe with the proposal. When Stowe answered, she offended Jacobs, broke her confidence, and revealed her inability to see African Americans as anything other than objects for sympathy and source material for her quite lucrative publications (see Appendices C2c and C2d).[1]

★ ★ ★

Jacobs's aesthetic contributions can also be observed in how *Incidents* engages visual culture. For instance, the text gestures toward portraiture and its role in shaping American understandings of how a person's outward appearance revealed inward truths. Americans increasingly treated portraits as "windows into the soul," but African Americans had many reasons to question what mainstream culture claimed was "apparent." Black people have long recognized that beauty does not exist simply to be detected.[2] Instead, culture shapes how and where one sees beauty because American society so relentlessly bombards everyone with dehumanizing, degrading images of those who are not white.

It is in this context that Jacobs recorded Linda's visit to an artist's studio in Philadelphia shortly after leaving the South. It is the first time Linda sees artistic renderings of Black children. The scene may appear to be an instance of "a Black American finding confirmation of her humanity in positive and nonracist visual representation of the Black self" (Blackwood 63). However, Linda says not that the images "are" beautiful but that they "seemed" beautiful to her (p. 221). Literary historian Sarah Blackwood therefore rightly emphasizes Jacobs's "assertion of an aesthetic value system outside of the 'visual authority' that undergirded white supremacy in artistic and cultural expression." Jacobs engaged portraiture in ways that show her alliance with many Black writers of the nineteenth century—writers "thinking hard about what, if anything, the appearance of a face indexes [or reveals]" (64).

---

1 For more on the significant amounts of money Stowe made, see (among others) Schuller.

2 This ability to question beauty remains vitally important because the investment in using beauty to bludgeon non-white people endures. For a powerful discussion of beauty's violent function, see Tressie McMillam Cottom's *Thick*.

Jacobs's interest in engaging portraiture was clearly tied to the country's visual logics, and those logics should remind readers of the inability to separate fiction and nonfiction. While highlighting the fictitious stories about African Americans that ensure unjust outcomes, Jacobs also called attention to how US culture limits vision so that African Americans are left out of the nation's family portraits. American visual culture made narrow "lines of inheritance" appear natural and right (Blackwood 65), thereby supporting the stories the law told about who should inherit property and who should become property to be inherited. As cultural critic Brigitte Fielder explains, legal kinship was "a function not of biology but of recognition," so it "excluded even biological kin from familial belonging and legitimacy" (127). "Tragic mulatto" motherhood was tragic precisely because this dynamic held when a white man impregnated an enslaved woman with children who looked as white as his "legitimate" heirs—but who would not appear in family portraits.

If a society says whiteness makes one beautiful, fully human, and entitled to rights, isn't it telling that it easily denies resources to white people said to have "one drop" of Black blood?

* * *

Jacobs's aesthetic commitment can also be gleaned in her engagement with vernacular culture[1] and the joy she apparently took from word choice and turns of phrase. For example, *Incidents* provides one of the earliest eyewitness accounts of Johnkannaus celebrations recorded by an African American (p. 180). Jacobs's way of capturing the critical humor of these Christmastime celebrations reveals them to be a distinctive contribution of kidnapped people. African and African-descended individuals who were enslaved did not simply have their labor stolen; every attempt was made to brutalize their culture out of them, too. By honoring the orality and physical activities of vernacular culture, Jacobs depicts Johnkannaus as evidence of a people who were surviving and were determined to have some African traditions survive with them. In short, she used her writing to honor cultural retentions whose enduring presence was evidenced by oral and embodied practices.[2]

---

1 With *vernacular culture*, I am referring to the language and practices specific to ordinary people in a specific place.

2 Black people's ability to forge rich culture in the midst of hostility is

Jacobs also honored vernacular culture by showcasing the virtuosity African Americans exhibit by making a language forced upon them speak truths otherwise denied. As I remind my students, I am a Black woman whose ancestors were enslaved in the United States. The only reason I speak English is that the British were colonizers, and their American counterparts were and are imperialists, spreading English around the globe by making it into currency: in countless countries, doing big business requires speaking English.[1] There are limits, then, to how much this language can be made to express my soul's truths or my ancestor's truths. As creative writer Toni Cade Bambara said, "English is a wonderful mercantile language. You can get a lot of trade done with English. But you would find it very difficult to validate the psychic and spiritual existence of your life" (Chandler 348).

African Americans have never let these very real limitations determine everything, though. They have always cultivated what I call "homemade citizenship," a deep sense of success and belonging in the midst of violence.[2] And one finds countless examples of this active cultivation by paying attention to their manipulation of the language deployed not only to strip them of citizenship but also to deny their humanity.

Considering "sass" is one way to appreciate the rigor and ingenuity of Black people's use of the English language. Literary historian Joanne Braxton characterizes sass as a decidedly feminine form of speech that talks back to oppression. When Linda is in conversation with Dr. Flint, Braxton explains, "sass preserves the slave girl's self-esteem and increases the psychological distance between herself and the master" (31). Linda speaks in ways that protect her own perspective and identify Flint's as false because accepting his view would mean believing that he is indeed making "kind offers." Ultimately, "Linda uses sass the way that Frederick Douglass used his fists and his feet, as a means of resistance" (32).[3]

---

beautifully represented in the National Museum of African American History and Culture (NMAAHC) in Washington, DC. Their permanent exhibition "Cultural Expression" on Level 4 highlights slang and gestures and is absolutely unforgettable. Excerpts available online at https://nmaahc.si.edu/explore/exhibitions/cultural-expressions.

1 See, for example, Hoang.

2 See Mitchell.

3 Aligned with these findings, DoVeanna Fulton argues, "Despite Jacobs's literacy, ... orality is central to the empowerment of Linda Brent and her children's freedom" (37).

Complementing these insights about language, literary historian Gabrielle Foreman calls attention to "vernacular reading" as a practice in African American culture through multiple generations. After all, "to 'get read' or 'be read' is to be dressed down, or told about yourself, as in 'girl, you just got read'" (3).[1] Examining nineteenth-century works, Foreman identifies how routinely "Black women's writing 'reads' multiple communities and ideologies: ostensible[2] allies, white abolitionists, and white women and families, for example" (3). Attentive audiences will notice Jacobs using *Incidents* to read those she encountered in real life and read its readers, too. One might say that *Incidents* reads American culture *for filth*.

My favorite examples of Jacobs using *Incidents* to read folk for filth include the following:

> the opening of Chapter XII: Fear of Insurrection: "Not far from this time Nat Turner's insurrection broke out; and the news threw our town into great commotion. Strange that they should be alarmed, when their slaves were so 'contented and happy'! But so it was." (p. 128)

> "My aunt was taken out of jail at the end of a month, because Mrs. Flint could not spare her any longer. She was tired of being her own housekeeper. It was quite too fatiguing to order her dinner and eat it too." (p. 164)

> "Hot weather brings out snakes and slaveholders, and I like one class of the venomous creatures as little as I do the other. What a comfort it is, to be free to say so!" (p. 231)

Another way to understand Jacobs's commitment to aesthetics is to acknowledge what it took for her to write while watching her employer, Nathaniel Parker Willis, craft texts under the luxurious conditions created by her never-ending labor. Willis's columns bragged about the beauty of Idlewild, the seventy-acre New York estate where Jacobs served his family. Like Willis, Jacobs "was

---

1 For one example of these practices reverberating through the generations, listen to any episode of *The Read*, a podcast hosted by Kid Fury and Crissle. During the last segment of each show, the hosts "read" someone or "pass the read" to a listener who wrote in with "a read" of their own.

2 Professed; outwardly appearing as such.

surrounded by a natural environment chosen to touch a writer's soul. Yet her days were destined not for the study, but for the nursery" (Yellin, *Life* 127). Caring for the family's five children was a twenty-four-hours-a-day, seven-days-a-week job, but it became even more demanding and hectic when Willis made grand gestures by inviting guests (Yellin, *Life* 130).

As Jacobs labored in the home of her white employers, duty constantly called (see Appendix C2), so her literary achievement is even more remarkable. Also, Foreman reminds readers that "Jacobs keeps her job by playing her own trickster—the faithful servant—and plays her role well enough to convince Willis's most thorough biographer that her 'attachment to the interests of the family during the whole period of her service was a beautiful instance of ... fidelity and affection.'" Meanwhile, it was during these years that Jacobs "composed her narrative and published articles in numerous journals without their knowledge or help" (35).

In other words, writing her earliest publications as well as *Incidents* required Jacobs to be a performance artist, too. American society made sure that only certain roles were available to her. Jacobs played her assigned part, but in ways that allowed her to exceed the script. As Schuller puts it, Willis "intended the gabled estate to be a writers' retreat for himself and his famous friends, including Edgar Allen Poe and Henry Wadsworth Longfellow. Yet the most significant text written at Idlewild was penned by the nanny, up in the servants' quarters, by the cover of night" (66).

To compose the beautifully rendered *Incidents* under these conditions required a fortitude few can imagine, but Jacobs was also a woman who somehow emerged from nearly seven years in a cramped attic with her sanity intact. Readers do well to consider that Jacobs's achievements did not simply evince strength, though.[1] Her accomplishments testify to an investment in beauty and aesthetic contribution.

---

1 The idea that Black women are naturally strong and can endure whatever the world dishes out is so commonly believed that the *Strong Black Woman* has long been a stereotype, even if it appears to be a positive one. It is so ingrained in Western cultures that many scholars and activists call attention to the dangers of accepting it. Trudier Harris and Melissa Harris-Perry have both done influential work in this vein, and The Nap Ministry aligns with it. Also see Treva Lindsey's *America Goddam* and her 2022 *Huffington Post* piece "The 'Strong Black Woman' Trope Is a Trap."

Throughout these years, Jacobs was an artist forced to put others' needs before her craft. For example, "instead of writing her book, her hands were busy sewing dolls for the Willis children" (Yellin, *Life* 129). Yet, despite these circumstances, Jacobs's personal correspondence revealed a woman clinging to her art and artistry. Yellin reports, "Her arms encircling the Willis children, Jacobs's head was swirling with literary imagery: 'the poor Book is in its Chrysalis state and though I can never make it a butterfly I am satisfied to have it creep meekly among some of the humbler bugs'" (*Life* 129; also see Appendix C2f). Jacobs clearly took joy in writing beautifully, given the vocabulary and syntax in her private correspondence (Yellin, *Incidents* xvii).

Viewing Jacobs as an artist helps readers understand why artists continue to build on her legacy. It must be an affinity for the creativity and dynamism of *Incidents* that draws those who work in so many different media—prize-winning fiction writer Colson Whitehead, playwright Lydia Diamond, visual artist Ellen Driscoll, and multimedia creator Roxana Walker-Canton, to name only a few.[1]

It is crucial that readers view Jacobs as an artist. Find instances of artistry beyond what I have described. Also, take time to notice the beauty of her language. The beauty is astonishing, given not only the ugly truths she told but also the violence inherent in the fact that being literate meant reading and writing English. Noticing her facility with the language that declared her property is one way to honor her and the many Black women brutalized by the normal workings of American society. Such women could not escape the nation's death-dealing tendencies—what Honorée Jeffers identifies as "soul assaults" (185)—but they somehow maintained, in Alice Walker's words, a deep "respect for all that illuminates and cherishes life" (408).[2] Their life-affirming artistic

---

1 Whitehead names *Incidents* as part of his inspiration for *The Underground Railroad*, his award-winning novel that was made into a television series directed by Barry Jenkins in 2021. Diamond's play and Driscoll's art appear excerpted in Appendices E1–E2. For a glimpse into Walker-Canton's *Incidents*-inspired work, visit https://vimeo.com/78098410.

2 I am citing here Walker's famous essay "In Search of Our Mothers' Gardens." To appreciate the weight of what Walker wants readers to grapple with, consider this: "How was the creativity of the black woman kept alive, year after year and century after century, when for most of the years black people have been in America, it was a

commitment in a brutal (and brutally ugly) society is evidence of "a continuation of radical vision that should have been impossible" (Miles, *All* 30). In a country devoted to dehumanizing violence, holding on to possibilities is no small feat. It deserves our recognition, at the very least.

How Studying Harriet Jacobs Illuminates American Culture[1]

Storytelling is a human activity the world over, and stories can be powerful whether they cling to reality or contradict it. With the stories we tell, humans make sense of the world and make meaning of our lives. In this very human endeavor, fiction and nonfiction are inseparable; even when conveying basic truths, we compose with our imaginations. However, storytelling plays a particular role in societies that insist certain groups are not people and therefore do not deserve rights. In these contexts, the powerful (who also have violence at their disposal) use storytelling to mold environments to match their worldview.

Deeming humans to be subhuman requires forcing fictions onto nonfiction lives, and the Founding Fathers built American culture on precisely that practice. Telling stories about how the inhabitants of North America did not use the land as God intended became the justification for attacking Indigenous peoples while declaring that stealing land was not stealing when the people doing it were considered white. Likewise, stories about how shallow a Black person's feelings are equipped white folk to separate children from parents as if they were puppies, and there was somehow nothing barbaric or evil about those white Americans.[2]

---

punishable crime for a black person to read and write? And the freedom to paint, to sculpt, to expand the mind with action did not exist. Consider, if you can bear to imagine it, what might have been the result if singing, too, had been forbidden by law" (403).

1 Though I do not use "America" to refer to the United States because the country is far from the only part of the Americas that matters, I use "American" as an adjective to describe US national culture.

2 Sharon Holland's research highlights how assumptions about people's right to dominate animals destroys harmony and can fuel barbarity toward puppies, too, but especially given the need to declare #BlackLivesMatter, I am often struck by how much more gentleness white Americans feel toward pets than toward African Americans. On violence against the people who first occupied the land, see Dunbar-Ortiz.

Harriet Jacobs highlighted how those in power made sure that fictions became a very real, nonfiction force, so her example remains relevant today. Studying Jacobs illuminates fundamental truths about American culture because her signature text demands recognition of a simultaneity that impacts everyone's experience in the United States. Namely, because *Incidents* invests equally in accuracy and creativity, it underscores the interplay of fiction and nonfiction that continues to structure the environment.

Because the nation makes being a cisgender[1] straight white man the basis for citizenship, it constantly fabricates justifications for doing so. When legislators declared voting to be a right for citizens, denying white women the franchise seemed like common sense. Why? Stories (that, from birth, no one could avoid) circulated constantly to convince everyone that white women were delicate, irrational, and in need of guidance. Likewise, stories about the God-given superiority and benevolence of white men set the stage for insisting that human beings are entitled to self-defense even as white men brutalized Black and Brown people and made their defense of themselves illegal.[2] To this very day, "while self-defense laws are interpreted generously when applied to white men who feel threatened by men of color, they are applied very narrowly to women and gender nonconforming people" (Kaba 50). Whether self-defense is at issue or not, "Black skin is a repellant to empathy" (32). Meanwhile, whenever white men have done something truly horrific, stories cast them as justified and therefore innocent of wrongdoing. This dynamic is clearest today when one considers serial killers. As scholar David Leonard has shown, serial killers in the United States are overwhelmingly white men, so popular culture and the legal system produce empathetic stories about them in order to "manufacture innocence" for them.[3]

---

1 As a prefix, *cis-* means on the same side (as opposed to *trans-*, meaning on the opposite side). Therefore, "cisgender" refers to gender expression that is on the same side as the gender assumed on the basis of how one's sex was assigned at birth.

2 Voting wasn't always a citizenship right, but when it became one, women were generally excluded. Scholarship on that as well as the denial of self-defense is plentiful, but see, for example, Hyde on the former and Anderson on the latter.

3 In addition to Leonard's powerful essay, for examples of how white violence is justified and rendered somehow natural and right, consider Wild West stories about "Cowboys" and "Indians." See Deloria; Olou.

Even as white men fail to measure up to what the country says it respects—morality, decency, a basic work ethic—American culture bombards everyone with stories about how they are the best and brightest to be found!

For anyone capable of recognizing dominant cultural fictions and the human truths those fictions suppress, *Incidents* provides countless opportunities for noticing that white men of high social status are not admirable; they are simply licensed. Because of how Jacobs told her story in 1861 as a survivor of sexual abuse, she laid a foundation for #MeToo. Jacobs paved a path that many have been compelled to walk when they expose "the national scandal of their private shame" (Berlant 99). When survivors of sexual harassment and assault come forward, they inevitably highlight how national culture produces their vulnerability because it is so invested in the social status and potential of white men and boys that it ignores evidence to the contrary and treats their simply being white men and boys as proof of their harmlessness.[1] Jacobs exposed the respectable facade that unjustly empowers men, including the "superior person" who acknowledged fathering her children but showed little regard for their fates as he built his political career (pp. 120, 197–98). "If the secret memoirs of many members of Congress should be published," she wrote, "curious details would be unfolded" (p. 202).[2] Corroborating Jacobs, Southern scholar Imani Perry puts it this way: "there is nothing new about ugliness in a dressed-up place" (46) so "gentlemen were not gentlemen at all" (17).

---

1 The priority placed on white men and boys took center stage in 2018 as Dr. Christine Blasey Ford testified about having been sexually assaulted by Supreme Court nominee Brett Kavanaugh and as the pain and trauma of Emily Doe took a back seat to the presumed student-athlete potential of Brock Turner, whom witnesses saw rape her by a dumpster in 2015. In these cases and many others, American culture's tendency toward "himpathy" shines through. Philosopher Kate Manne defines "himpathy" as "the disproportionate or inappropriate sympathy extended to a male perpetrator over his similarly or less privileged female targets or victims, in cases of sexual assault, harassment, and other misogynistic behavior" (37).

2 Of course, this aligns with the open secret of Thomas Jefferson's "relationship" with Sally Hemings, which began when she was fourteen and he was forty-four. See Gordon-Reed, *Thomas*; Winters. I call it an "open secret" because it was widely known and discussed but never kept Jefferson from ascending politically. See DuCille.

In other words, Jacobs understood fictions to be the source of white men's authority, and just as important, she recognized the fictitious stories told to deny Black people everything that white men and white women claim for themselves. In this way, she left a blueprint for #BlackLivesMatter and #SayHerName, movements that expose the lies dominant culture tells about Black people to excuse brutality toward them. Ultimately, efforts like #MeToo and #BlackLivesMatter build on Jacobs's legacy because her work encourages recognition of the dominant fictions that circulate relentlessly as well as the realities they aim to overshadow.[1]

Human ingenuity—including our storytelling—can be used to destroy lives or to save them. Because she understood that fact, Harriet Jacobs chose deliberately and took concrete action accordingly. To do the same, we must begin by facing what is clear from the evidence of the past and present: decency is not an American inheritance; it requires deliberate effort.

This Volume and Its Resources

Incidents in the Life of a Slave Girl is now read all over the world, taught in a variety of educational settings, and studied by scholars in countless disciplines. As Yellin put it in 2005, "translated and published in German, Portuguese, French, and Japanese, it is in print in a score of editions in English and is read in high schools and colleges around the country" (*Life* 262). The compelling narrative reaches beyond classrooms, though. It finds its way into book clubs and community spaces as well as spaces of therapy and healing.[2] And the narrative's circulation is only increasing. A Spanish translation was published in 2005 and a Chinese

---

1 #MeToo was actually initiated by Tarana Burke to advocate for Black women and girls who were survivors of sexual abuse. Black women's activism on these issues is extensive. They have consistently explained (advancing awareness of intersectionality) why the humanity of women, girls, and LGBT people of color can be disregarded when perpetrators are also of color. Famous cases involve Clarence Thomas, Bill Cosby, and R. Kelly, but activists are clear about how painfully common these dynamics are. See (among many others) community efforts undertaken by Burke, Mariame Kaba, Dream Hampton, and Salamishah and Scheherazade Tillet, including *A Long Walk Home*.

2 For example, the short film *Freedom Road* shows how reading *Incidents* provides opportunities for incarcerated women to find their voices (Appendix E3). Likewise, Foster and Yarborough suggest that the

translation in 2015.[1] In short, *Incidents* is largely understood to be a crucial contribution to many fields of study and to the knowledge of ordinary people who want to be informed citizens of the world.

Incidents occupies this status today because renowned historian Jean Fagan Yellin followed the archival trail with remarkable persistence. Though Jacobs was well known as the author of *Incidents* during her lifetime, historians later began asserting that it was fiction[2] and written by its editor, Lydia Maria Child. In 1981, Yellin authenticated the text with archival research by documenting the people, places, and events that shaped Jacobs's life and her book. In 1987, Yellin published a scholarly edition of *Incidents*, foregrounding the proof that Jacobs's narrative is true, that she is its author, and that Child served as editor.

Incidents is only one part of Jacobs's legacy, though, and that fact is becoming more broadly recognized as well. Historical markers memorialize Jacobs in Philadelphia; at the site of her house in Cambridge, Massachusetts; and along US Highway 17 in her North Carolina hometown of Edenton. Likewise, as Foster and Yarborough report, the county in which Jacobs was born, Chowan County, offers tours highlighting the experiences she and her family had there, and the HarrietJacobs.org website represents cooperation among several entities, including the National Park Service (xviii–xix). These developments reflect a deep appreciation for Jacobs's legacy beyond *Incidents*—an appreciation fostered in part by Yellin because she oversaw the compilation of *The Harriet Jacobs Family Papers*. This two-volume set of letters, property deeds, contracts, and other documents sheds unparalleled light on Jacobs's life not only before but also during and after the years chronicled in her narrative.

---

work helps those seeking to understand "their own traumas and those of predecessors who survived them" (viii).

1 The Chinese translation was published by Shanghai Jiao Tong University Press, and scholar Carme Manuel i Cuenca of the University of Valencia did the Spanish translation.

2 The copyright was taken out in Child's name, so the assumption that she was the author and not simply acting on the pseudonymous author's behalf isn't outlandish. However, see the care with which Child operated on this issue in Appendix C3b. Even when the Library of Congress listed Child as author, activist Black librarians refused to comply. The Library of Congress finally identified the work with Jacobs in 1987 (Schuller 267).

Though there are many English-language editions of *Incidents*, I offer this one in order to give readers the context needed to appreciate what has long been understood by those whose efforts have resulted in historical markers and other tributes. Namely, *Incidents* was a monumental achievement, yet it is only one part of what Jacobs accomplished in her lifelong determination to make the world better. For instance, this edition offers a brief Chronology. It highlights events in this extraordinary woman's life and gestures toward interactions Jacobs had with leading figures of her day, including Frederick Douglass, William Lloyd Garrison (1805–79), William C. Nell, Amy Post, Harriet Beecher Stowe, Lydia Maria Child, and Susan B. Anthony (1820–1906), whom she and her grown daughter Louisa met with several times (Maillard 10). Next, the edition reproduces the narrative itself but with extensive footnotes, clarifying anything that might be unfamiliar.

After having engaged Jacobs's signature text, readers can delve into the six appendices, which provide opportunities to consider the issues raised by studying Jacobs's autobiography and her life beyond it. The various documents also give readers ample opportunity to make connections of their own. For instance, Appendix A places at readers' fingertips material that reflects the values shaping American culture. The *Fugitive Slave Act*, ratified in 1850, reminds readers that slavery could not have survived without cooperation from the North, and the *Dred Scott* decision of 1857 demonstrates that enslaving people was not the only way to disregard African Americans' rights and basic humanity. Likewise, when actually encountering the Emancipation Proclamation or the act establishing the Freedmen's Bureau, one sees how they place a priority on white people's elevated status (without reference to their merit) at every turn. The priorities evident in these documents help illuminate what was only more forcefully stated in the *Plessy v. Ferguson* Supreme Court decision, namely that African Americans "had no rights which the white man was bound to respect."

Appendix B illuminates other dynamics informing Jacobs's narrative and its incisive cultural critiques, including how the United States empowered white people to disregard familial bonds of every sort, based purely on what was convenient for those in power. In Appendix C, readers find material confirming that Jacobs authored her own story as well as reviews that suggest not only how the text contributed to the abolitionist movement but also, again, how widely known her authorship was. Appendix D gives a sense of the wide-ranging advocacy work Jacobs undertook in the decades after she published *Incidents*. Appendix E offers a glimpse into how artists today continue to be inspired by Jacobs's autobiography, and Appendix F puts at readers' fingertips the real-life people and places relevant to the story *Incidents* tells.

Harriet Jacobs: A Brief Chronology

1813	Born enslaved in Edenton, North Carolina
1815	John S. Jacobs, Harriet's brother, is born
1819	Harriet's mother dies; Harriet is six years old
1825	Harriet and her younger brother, John S. Jacobs, move into the Norcom household
1826	Harriet's father dies; Harriet is about twelve
1828	Harriet's grandmother is sold and freed from Norcom's direct control
1829	Harriet prevented from marrying her first love Son, Joseph, is born, with Samuel Tredwell Sawyer acknowledged as the father
1831	William Lloyd Garrison founds the abolitionist newspaper *The Liberator* in Boston; he publishes it every week for thirty-five years, despite violence and threats of violence August: Nat Turner's rebellion in Southampton, Virginia
1833	Daughter, Louisa, is born, with Samuel Tredwell Sawyer acknowledged as the father
1835	Harriet is sent to Norcom's son's plantation, six miles from her grandmother and support system; she later runs away
1837	Sawyer is elected to Congress
1838	Sawyer marries; later that year, John S. runs away from Sawyer
1840	Louisa is sent to Washington, DC, to be with Sawyer and his family
1842	Harriet escapes to the North, initially landing in Philadelphia
1843	Flees New York, where she works for Mary Stace Willis, goes to Boston, and sends for her daughter Louisa
1845	Travels to England with widower Nathaniel Parker Willis as caretaker for his daughter Imogen; they remain abroad for 10 months *The Narrative of the Life of Frederick Douglass* is published
1846	Back in the US, Jacobs is harassed by Mary Matilda

	Norcom and her new husband, Daniel Messmore
1849	Moves to Rochester to be with her brother, who is trying to create an anti-slavery reading room; interacts with abolitionists such as Frederick Douglass and William C. Nell and stays in the home of Isaac and Amy Post
	February: John S. and Frederick Douglass embark on a two-week speaking tour together
1850	Returns to New York and works for Cornelia Willis, the second wife of Nathaniel Parker Willis
	As-told-to biography *The Narrative of the Life of Sojourner Truth* is published
1852	Norcom's heirs arrive in New York to capture Jacobs, she hides in Massachusetts, and without Jacobs's knowledge, Cornelia Willis enlists the help of the New York Colonization Society to pay a down payment of $150 to stop the constant anxiety; Willis then spends months raising the remaining $150
	The serialization of *Uncle Tom's Cabin* by Harriet Beecher Stowe ends and it appears as a two-volume bound book set; it continues to garner widespread attention in the United States and abroad
	Jacobs makes attempts to interest Harriet Beecher Stowe in writing life story, to no avail
1853	Stowe responds to letters from Amy Post and Jacobs's employer Cornelia Willis, offending Jacobs and revealing her children's origin to her employer
	Jacobs publishes "Letter from a Fugitive Slave" in June and "Cruelty to Slaves" in July in the *New York Tribune*, which prove to be seeds for *Incidents*
	In the fall, her grandmother dies
1854	June: William C. Nell visits Jacobs at Idlewild, the New York estate of her employer Nathaniel Parker Willis; they discuss her interactions with Stowe, and Nell encourages Jacobs to complete and publish her book; the evening he leaves, she falls ill and is in bed for three weeks
	One of many periods of illness severe enough to force Jacobs to get away from her New York nanny/housekeeping job
1856	After having helped Jacobs at the Willis country home at Idlewild, Louisa moves to Brooklyn to be governess in Fanny Fern's household (she is

	Nathaniel Parker Willis's sister and the siblings do not get along)
1857/58	Jacobs finishes book manuscript, travels to Boston to obtain letters of endorsement and introduction to present to abolitionists in England, and travels to England in hopes of securing a publishing contract
1859	Places her book manuscript with Boston publishers Phillips & Sampson, who agree to publish it if she can secure a preface from Harriet Beecher Stowe or Nathaniel Parker Willis; Willis had recently published "Negro Happiness in Virginia," so Jacobs continues avoiding exposing herself to him; she approaches Stowe again and is again rejected; meanwhile, Phillips & Sampson go out of business
	John Brown's raid on Harpers Ferry
1860	Places her book manuscript with Boston publishers Thayer & Eldridge
	They want a preface from Lydia Maria Child; Nell introduces Jacobs to Child, who offers to edit the manuscript and begins acting on Jacobs's behalf, ultimately securing a publishing contract; shortly thereafter, Thayer & Eldridge go bankrupt, but they had produced the stereotype plates for Jacobs's book
1861	January: Having purchased the plates, Jacobs pays for the printing and binding of her book, publishing *Incidents* using the pseudonym Linda Brent
	February: Travels with her book to sell copies, determined to make a difference in the movement for abolition
	12 April: Civil War begins with the Confederacy's attack on federal property at Fort Sumter
	Publication of *Incidents* places Jacobs in the circle of William Lloyd Garrison
	1 August: Jacobs among the Boston crowd at the annual commemoration of West Indian Independence, where speakers included William Lloyd Garrison and Wendell Phillips; the next day, Lydia Maria Child stops in at the offices of *The Liberator* where she sees Jacobs, who is carrying a testimonial from her employer, Cornelia Willis, about the truth of her narrative
1862	*Incidents* appears in England under the title *The Deeper Wrong* because Jacobs mailed the stereotype

plates to her British ally Frederick Chesson

April: After votes in the Congress and the Senate, Abraham Lincoln signs the bill emancipating the capital city's enslaved population; the Union Army also begins accepting Black troops

Jacobs goes to Washington, DC, to help contrabands

June: Takes three days to attend the tenth annual meeting of Progressive Friends (Quakers) in Longwood, Pennsylvania, where William Lloyd Garrison is among the speakers; Jacobs tells him about her relief work, and he encourages her to write about it

September: Publishes "Life among the Contrabands" in *The Liberator*, about her work in several locations

1863   Sends money to Australia for Joseph, on whose behalf someone purportedly communicates to say he is too ill to write; she never hears from him again

Jacobs shares podium with William Wells Brown in Alexandria, Virginia

May: Travels to Boston with eight orphaned girls, seeking homes for them away from the harsh conditions of the contraband camps

1864   Establishes the Jacobs Free School in Alexandria, Virginia

1865   9 April: Confederate surrender ends the Civil War

15 April: Abraham Lincoln is assassinated, and Southerner Andrew Johnson ascends to the presidency

Thirteenth Amendment ends slavery on paper

Order for the formerly enslaved to receive forty acres of land is reversed

1866   January: Jacobs and her daughter Louisa move to Savannah to educate and otherwise facilitate mutual aid for Black residents; military rule had ended shortly before their arrival, leaving African Americans even more vulnerable to racist violence

Jacobs and Louisa leave Savannah, fearing for their lives and for the community's fate

Frances E.W. Harper delivers "We Are All Bound Up Together" speech at the Eleventh National Woman's Rights Convention, at which it was

	reconstituted as the American Equal Rights Association; Harper shares the platform with Frederick Douglass, Susan B. Anthony, and Elizabeth Cady Stanton
1867	January: Nathaniel Parker Willis dies and Jacobs is there to support his family
	February: Louisa, now in her mid-thirties, arrives in New York to lecture on behalf of the American Equal Rights Association, thereby continuing the work of Frances E.W. Harper as well as her uncle John S. and working alongside Charles Lenox Remond; Elizabeth Cady Stanton had made their arrangements
	May: Jacobs visits Edenton, North Carolina, where she was born, though the family no longer owns her grandmother's house
	Howard University is founded
1868	Jacobs and Louisa are in England, hoping to raise money to help Savannah communities; they do not see John S., Jacobs's seafaring brother
	President Johnson is impeached
	Fourteenth Amendment establishes the idea that citizenship should be automatic for those born in the United States
c. 1869	Jacobs retreats to Massachusetts as the US government turns its back on Black people in the South
	Scenes in the Life of Harriet Tubman is published
1870	Rents in Cambridge, Massachusetts, and runs a boarding house there
1871	Meets Stowe face to face in Cambridge; Stowe inscribes a copy of *Uncle Tom's Cabin* to Jacobs that remains in the family for a century
c. 1872	Jacobs's half-brother Elijah is in nearby New Bedford, Massachusetts; by 1873, John S. and his family are also in Cambridge, but John S. dies suddenly, so Jacobs enjoys having so much family around for mere months before tragedy strikes
1873	William Lloyd Garrison attends the memorial services for John S., honoring his contributions to anti-slavery efforts
	Jacobs establishes a larger boarding house in Cambridge

1877	Closes the Cambridge boarding house
	March: Congratulates Frederick Douglass on his appointment as US marshal
	At age sixty-four, Jacobs moves to Washington, DC; she and Louisa are close to Charlotte Forten Grimké, although they do not at all share her high social class
	Jacobs hopes to open a school, but she and Louisa must abandon the idea, instead operating another boarding house
	Compromise of 1877 installs Rutherford B. Hayes as president and federal troops leave the South, effectively ending Reconstruction efforts to ensure that African Americans' citizenship rights would be recognized
1879	Establishes a boarding house in Washington, DC, for elite whites; it stays in operation until 1881
1885	Learns that the widow and children of James Norcom, Jr. (son of "Dr. Flint") are in Washington, DC, and in need; Jacobs takes food to the family
	Establishes a boarding house serving elite African Americans
1886	Jacobs and Louisa attend Eighteenth Convention of National Woman Suffrage Association in Washington, DC
	Publication of *Harriet Tubman, the Moses of Her People*
1888	Jacobs, now seventy-five, continues to be ill; finally closes boarding house
1889	Goes to Edenton to rest
1892	Frances E.W. Harper publishes the novel *Iola Leroy*, with the title character's mother being named Harriet—paying homage to Jacobs, according to Yellin
1894	Already suffering with various conditions, Jacobs is diagnosed with breast cancer and undergoes surgery
	Recovers despite advanced age (approximately eighty-one), and her unbroken ties with Mrs. Willis show again, as Willis arrives to help her and Louisa
1897	Dies in Washington, DC, and is buried in Mount Auburn Cemetery next to her brother in Cambridge, Massachusetts

c. 1899	Now in her sixties, Louisa becomes assistant matron and then matron of the National Home for the Relief of Destitute Colored Women and Children, an establishment that Elizabeth Keckley, former dressmaker for Abraham Lincoln's wife and author of *Behind the Scenes*, had helped make successful when it was founded in 1863 but Keckley entered as a patron in 1903
1904	Now in her seventies, Louisa resigns from the National Home and accepts a position as matron of Howard University's Miner Hall
1908	Louisa resigns from Howard University position, departing with assurance that her contributions have been appreciated; she is seventy-five before she stops working
1917	Louisa dies and is buried in Mount Auburn alongside her mother and uncle

A Note on the Text

This edition is based on the first edition of *Incidents in the Life of a Slave Girl*, published for the author. It was transcribed and made digitally accessible as part of The New York Public Library's project The Digital Schomburg. Obvious errors of spelling or punctuation, of which there were very few, have been silently corrected.

INCIDENTS

IN THE

LIFE OF A SLAVE GIRL.

WRITTEN BY HERSELF.

"Northerners know nothing at all about Slavery. They think it is perpetual bondage only. They have no conception of the depth of degradation involved in that word, SLAVERY; if they had, they would never cease their efforts until so horrible a system was overthrown."

A Woman of North Carolina.

"Rise up, ye women that are at ease! Hear my voice, ye careless daughters! Give ear unto my speech."

Isaiah xxxii.9.

EDITED BY L MARIA CHILD.
BOSTON:
PUBLISHED FOR THE AUTHOR.
1861.

PREFACE
BY THE AUTHOR.

Reader, be assured this narrative is no fiction. I am aware that some of my adventures may seem incredible; but they are, nevertheless, strictly true. I have not exaggerated the wrongs inflicted by Slavery; on the contrary, my descriptions fall far short of the facts. I have concealed the names of places, and given persons fictitious names. I had no motive for secrecy on my own account, but I deemed it kind and considerate towards others to pursue this course.

I wish I were more competent to the task I have undertaken. But I trust my readers will excuse deficiencies in consideration of circumstances. I was born and reared in Slavery; and I remained in a Slave State twenty-seven years. Since I have been at the North, it has been necessary for me to work diligently for my own support, and the education of my children. This has not left me much leisure to make up for the loss of early opportunities to improve myself; and it has compelled me to write these pages at irregular intervals, whenever I could snatch an hour from household duties.

When I first arrived in Philadelphia, Bishop Paine[1] advised me to publish a sketch of my life, but I told him I was altogether incompetent to such an undertaking. Though I have improved my mind somewhat since that time, I still remain of the same opinion; but I trust my motives will excuse what might otherwise seem presumptuous. I have not written my experiences in order to attract attention to myself; on the contrary, it would have been more pleasant to me to have been silent about my own history. Neither do I care to excite sympathy for my own sufferings. But I do earnestly desire to arouse the women of the North to a realizing sense of the condition of two millions of women at the South, still in bondage, suffering what I suffered, and most of them far worse. I want to add my testimony to that of abler pens to convince the people of the Free States what Slavery really is. Only

---

1 Reverend Daniel Payne (1811–93) was part of the Philadelphia community of the African Methodist Episcopal Church and one of the people Jacobs met upon arriving in the city after nearly seven years of hiding in the South. He immediately urged her to write her remarkable story.

by experience can any one realize how deep, and dark, and foul is that pit of abominations. May the blessing of God rest on this imperfect effort in behalf of my persecuted people!

Linda Brent.

INTRODUCTION
BY THE EDITOR.

The author of the following autobiography is personally known to me, and her conversation and manners inspire me with confidence. During the last seventeen years, she has lived the greater part of the time with a distinguished family in New York,[1] and has so deported herself as to be highly esteemed by them. This fact is sufficient, without further credentials of her character. I believe those who know her will not be disposed to doubt her veracity, though some incidents in her story are more romantic than fiction.[2]

At her request, I have revised her manuscript;[3] but such changes as I have made have been mainly for purposes of condensation and orderly arrangement. I have not added any thing to the incidents, or changed the import of her very pertinent remarks. With trifling exceptions, both the ideas and the language are her own. I pruned excrescences[4] a little, but otherwise I had no reason for changing her lively and dramatic way of telling her own story. The names of both persons and places are known to me; but for good reasons I suppress them.

It will naturally excite surprise that a woman reared in Slavery should be able to write so well. But circumstances will explain this. In the first place, nature endowed her with quick perceptions. Secondly, the mistress, with whom she lived till she was twelve years old, was a kind, considerate friend, who taught her to read and spell. Thirdly, she was placed in favorable circumstances after

---

1 This is a reference to Nathaniel Parker Willis and his family. Willis founded the magazine now known as *Town and Country*, and though his family would have been viewed as anti-slavery allies, Jacobs experienced the head of household as "too proslavery" (Appendix C2a) for her to do anything but hide her writing in support of abolition.

2 Child suggests that the autobiographical narrative readers are about to encounter will remind them of creative works that exemplify the literary movement known as Romanticism. Even if those literary features stand out for the reader, Child explains, this story is *not* fictional.

3 The text of an author's work, handwritten or typed, that is meant to be submitted eventually to a publisher.

4 Outgrowths that can create an odd appearance even though they are probably harmless.

she came to the North; having frequent intercourse with intelligent persons, who felt a friendly interest in her welfare, and were disposed to give her opportunities for self-improvement.

I am well aware that many will accuse me of indecorum for presenting these pages to the public; for the experiences of this intelligent and much-injured woman belong to a class which some call delicate subjects, and others indelicate. This peculiar phase of Slavery has generally been kept veiled; but the public ought to be made acquainted with its monstrous features, and I willingly take the responsibility of presenting them with the veil withdrawn. I do this for the sake of my sisters in bondage, who are suffering wrongs so foul, that our ears are too delicate to listen to them. I do it with the hope of arousing conscientious and reflecting women at the North to a sense of their duty in the exertion of moral influence on the question of Slavery, on all possible occasions. I do it with the hope that every man who reads this narrative will swear solemnly before God that, so far as he has power to prevent it, no fugitive from Slavery shall ever be sent back to suffer in that loathsome den of corruption and cruelty.

L. Maria Child.

INCIDENTS
IN THE
LIFE OF A SLAVE GIRL,
SEVEN YEARS CONCEALED.

CONTENTS.

I. Childhood ... 73
II. The New Master and Mistress ... 76
III. The Slaves' New Year's Day ... 82
IV. The Slave Who Dared to Feel Like a Man ... 84
V. The Trials of Girlhood ... 94
VI. The Jealous Mistress ... 97
VII. The Lover ... 103
VIII. What Slaves Are Taught to Think of the North ... 109
IX. Sketches of Neighboring Slaveholders ... 111
X. A Perilous Passage in the Slave Girl's Life ... 119
XI. The New Tie to Life ... 123
XII. Fear of Insurrection ... 128
XIII. The Church and Slavery ... 133
XIV. Another Link to Life ... 140
XV. Continued Persecutions ... 143
XVI. Scenes at the Plantation ... 149
XVII. The Flight ... 158
XVIII. Months of Peril ... 160
XIX. The Children Sold ... 167
XX. New Perils ... 172
XXI. The Loophole of Retreat ... 176
XXII. Christmas Festivities ... 179
XXIII. Still in Prison ... 182
XXIV. The Candidate for Congress ... 185
XXV. Competition in Cunning ... 188
XXVI. Important Era in My Brother's Life ... 193
XXVII. New Destination for the Children ... 197
XXVIII. Aunt Nancy ... 203
XXIX. Preparations for Escape ... 207
XXX. Northward Bound ... 215
XXXI. Incidents in Philadelphia ... 218
XXXII. The Meeting of Mother and Daughter ... 222
XXXIII. A Home Found ... 225
XXXIV. The Old Enemy Again ... 228
XXXV. Prejudice against Color ... 231

XXXVI. The Hair-Breadth Escape ... 233
XXXVII. A Visit to England ... 238
XXXVIII. Renewed Invitations to Go South ... 241
XXXIX. The Confession ... 243
XL. The Fugitive Slave Law ... 245
XLI. Free at Last ... 250
Appendix ... 258

INCIDENTS IN THE LIFE OF A SLAVE GIRL, SEVEN YEARS CONCEALED.

CHAPTER I.
CHILDHOOD.

I was born a slave; but I never knew it till six years of happy childhood had passed away. My father was a carpenter, and considered so intelligent and skillful in his trade, that, when buildings out of the common line were to be erected, he was sent for from long distances, to be head workman. On condition of paying his mistress two hundred dollars a year, and supporting himself, he was allowed to work at his trade, and manage his own affairs. His strongest wish was to purchase his children; but, though he several times offered his hard earnings for that purpose, he never succeeded. In complexion my parents were a light shade of brownish yellow, and were termed mulattoes.[1] They lived together in a comfortable home; and, though we were all slaves, I was so fondly shielded that I never dreamed I was a piece of merchandise, trusted to them for safe keeping, and liable to be demanded of them at any moment. I had one brother, William, who was two years younger than myself—a bright, affectionate child. I had also a great treasure in my maternal grandmother, who was a remarkable woman in many respects. She was the daughter of a planter in South Carolina, who, at his death, left her mother and his three children free, with money to go to St. Augustine, where they had relatives. It was during the Revolutionary War;[2] and they were captured on their passage, carried back, and sold to different purchasers. Such was the story my grandmother used to tell me; but I do not remember all the particulars. She was a little girl when she was captured and sold to the keeper of a large hotel. I have often heard her tell how hard she fared during childhood.

---

1 *Mulatto* could be used to suggest the presence of any amount of African ancestry, even if only "one drop," or it could specifically suggest that one parent was believed to be of African descent. Similar terms include *quadroon* and *octoroon*, indicating one-quarter "African blood" and one-eighth "African blood," respectively. All such terms are now considered derogatory, as people in these categories increasingly advocate for *mixed-race* or *multiracial*.

2 The war between Great Britain and its colonies that would become the United States (1775–83).

But as she grew older she evinced so much intelligence, and was so faithful, that her master and mistress could not help seeing it was for their interest to take care of such a valuable piece of property. She became an indispensable personage in the household, officiating in all capacities, from cook and wet nurse[1] to seamstress. She was much praised for her cooking; and her nice crackers became so famous in the neighborhood that many people were desirous of obtaining them. In consequence of numerous requests of this kind, she asked permission of her mistress to bake crackers at night, after all the household work was done; and she obtained leave to do it, provided she would clothe herself and her children from the profits. Upon these terms, after working hard all day for her mistress, she began her midnight bakings, assisted by her two oldest children. The business proved profitable; and each year she laid by a little, which was saved for a fund to purchase her children. Her master died, and the property was divided among his heirs. The widow had her dower[2] in the hotel, which she continued to keep open. My grandmother remained in her service as a slave; but her children were divided among her master's children. As she had five, Benjamin, the youngest one, was sold, in order that each heir might have an equal portion of dollars and cents. There was so little difference in our ages that he seemed more like my brother than my uncle. He was a bright, handsome lad, nearly white; for he inherited the complexion my grandmother had derived from Anglo-Saxon ancestors. Though only ten years old, seven hundred and twenty dollars were paid for him. His sale was a terrible blow to my grandmother; but she was naturally hopeful, and she went to work with renewed energy, trusting in time to be able to purchase some of her children. She had laid up three hundred dollars, which her mistress one day begged as a loan, promising to pay her soon. The reader probably knows that no promise or writing given to a slave is legally binding; for, according to Southern laws, a slave, being property, can hold no property. When my grandmother lent her hard earnings to her mistress, she trusted solely to her honor. The honor of a slaveholder to a slave!

---

1 A servant who breastfeeds another woman's baby. Historian Stephanie Jones-Rogers provides details on the high demand for this kind of labor and the disregard for Black women that drove this robust market.

2 The portion of a deceased husband's real property allowed to his widow for her lifetime.

To this good grandmother I was indebted for many comforts. My brother Willie and I often received portions of the crackers, cakes, and preserves she made to sell; and after we ceased to be children we were indebted to her for many more important services.

Such were the unusually fortunate circumstances of my early childhood. When I was six years old, my mother died; and then, for the first time, I learned, by the talk around me, that I was a slave. My mother's mistress was the daughter of my grand-mother's mistress. She was the foster sister of my mother; they were both nourished at my grandmother's breast. In fact, my mother had been weaned at three months old, that the babe of the mistress might obtain sufficient food. They played together as children; and, when they became women, my mother was a most faithful servant to her whiter foster sister. On her death-bed her mistress promised that her children should never suffer for any thing; and during her lifetime she kept her word. They all spoke kindly of my dead mother, who had been a slave merely in name, but in nature was noble and womanly. I grieved for her, and my young mind was troubled with the thought who would now take care of me and my little brother. I was told that my home was now to be with her mistress; and I found it a happy one. No toilsome or disagreeable duties were imposed upon me. My mistress was so kind to me that I was always glad to do her bidding, and proud to labor for her as much as my young years would permit. I would sit by her side for hours, sewing diligently, with a heart as free from care as that of any free-born white child. When she thought I was tired, she would send me out to run and jump; and away I bounded, to gather berries or flowers to decorate her room. Those were happy days—too happy to last. The slave child had no thought for the morrow; but there came that blight,[1] which too surely waits on every human being born to be a chattel.[2]

When I was nearly twelve years old, my kind mistress sickened and died. As I saw the cheek grow paler, and the eye more glassy, how earnestly I prayed in my heart that she might live! I loved her; for she had been almost like a mother to me. My prayers were not answered. She died, and they buried her in the little churchyard, where, day after day, my tears fell upon her grave.

I was sent to spend a week with my grandmother. I was now old enough to begin to think of the future; and again and again

---

1 Any cause of ruin, impairment, or destruction.
2 Moveable piece of personal property.

I asked myself what they would do with me. I felt sure I should never find another mistress so kind as the one who was gone. She had promised my dying mother that her children should never suffer for any thing; and when I remembered that, and recalled her many proofs of attachment to me, I could not help having some hopes that she had left me free. My friends were almost certain it would be so. They thought she would be sure to do it, on account of my mother's love and faithful service. But, alas! we all know that the memory of a faithful slave does not avail much to save her children from the auction block.

After a brief period of suspense, the will of my mistress was read, and we learned that she had bequeathed me to her sister's daughter, a child of five years old. So vanished our hopes. My mistress had taught me the precepts of God's Word: "Thou shalt love thy neighbor as thyself." "Whatsoever ye would that men should do unto you, do ye even so unto them." But I was her slave, and I suppose she did not recognize me as her neighbor. I would give much to blot out from my memory that one great wrong. As a child, I loved my mistress; and, looking back on the happy days I spent with her, I try to think with less bitterness of this act of injustice. While I was with her, she taught me to read and spell; and for this privilege, which so rarely falls to the lot of a slave, I bless her memory.

She possessed but few slaves; and at her death those were all distributed among her relatives. Five of them were my grandmother's children, and had shared the same milk that nourished her mother's children. Notwithstanding my grandmother's long and faithful service to her owners, not one of her children escaped the auction block. These God-breathing machines are no more, in the sight of their masters, than the cotton they plant, or the horses they tend.

CHAPTER II.
THE NEW MASTER AND MISTRESS.

Dr. Flint, a physician in the neighborhood, had married the sister of my mistress, and I was now the property of their little daughter. It was not without murmuring that I prepared for my new home; and what added to my unhappiness, was the fact that my brother William was purchased by the same family. My father, by his nature, as well as by the habit of transacting business as a skillful mechanic, had more of the feelings of a freeman than is common among slaves. My brother was a spirited boy; and being brought up under such influences, he early detested the name of master and mistress. One day, when his father and his mistress both happened to call him at the same time, he hesitated between the two; being perplexed to know which had the strongest claim upon his obedience. He finally concluded to go to his mistress. When my father reproved him for it, he said, "You both called me, and I didn't know which I ought to go to first."

"You are my child," replied our father, "and when I call you, you should come immediately, if you have to pass through fire and water."

Poor Willie! He was now to learn his first lesson of obedience to a master. Grandmother tried to cheer us with hopeful words, and they found an echo in the credulous[1] hearts of youth.

When we entered our new home we encountered cold looks, cold words, and cold treatment. We were glad when the night came. On my narrow bed I moaned and wept, I felt so desolate and alone.

I had been there nearly a year, when a dear little friend of mine was buried. I heard her mother sob, as the clods fell on the coffin of her only child, and I turned away from the grave, feeling thankful that I still had something left to love. I met my grandmother, who said, "Come with me, Linda;" and from her tone I knew that something sad had happened. She led me apart from the people, and then said, "My child, your father is dead." Dead! How could I believe it? He had died so suddenly I had not even heard that he was sick. I went home with my grandmother. My heart rebelled against God, who had taken from me mother, father, mistress, and friend. The good grandmother tried to comfort me. "Who knows the ways of God?" said she. "Perhaps they have been kindly taken from the evil days to come." Years afterwards I often thought of this. She promised to be a mother to her grandchildren, so far as she might be permitted to do so; and strengthened by her love, I returned to my master's. I thought I should be allowed to go to my father's house the next morning; but I was ordered to go for flowers, that my mistress's house might be decorated for an evening party. I spent the day gathering flowers and weaving them into festoons,[2] while the dead body of my father was lying within a

---

1 Willing to believe or trust too readily, especially without proper or adequate evidence.

2 Strings or chains of flowers, foliage, ribbon, etc., suspended in a curve between two points.

mile of me. What cared my owners for that? he was merely a piece of property. Moreover, they thought he had spoiled his children, by teaching them to feel that they were human beings.

This was blasphemous doctrine for a slave to teach; presumptuous in him, and dangerous to the masters.

The next day I followed his remains to a humble grave beside that of my dear mother. There were those who knew my father's worth, and respected his memory.

My home now seemed more dreary than ever. The laugh of the little slave-children sounded harsh and cruel. It was selfish to feel so about the joy of others. My brother moved about with a very grave face. I tried to comfort him, by saying, "Take courage, Willie; brighter days will come by and by."

"You don't know any thing about it, Linda," he replied. "We shall have to stay here all our days; we shall never be free."

I argued that we were growing older and stronger, and that perhaps we might, before long, be allowed to hire our own time, and then we could earn money to buy our freedom. William declared this was much easier to say than to do; moreover, he did not intend to buy his freedom. We held daily controversies upon this subject.

Little attention was paid to the slaves' meals in Dr. Flint's house. If they could catch a bit of food while it was going, well and good. I gave myself no trouble on that score, for on my various errands I passed my grandmother's house, where there was always something to spare for me. I was frequently threatened with punishment if I stopped there; and my grandmother, to avoid detaining me, often stood at the gate with something for my breakfast or dinner. I was indebted to her for all my comforts, spiritual or temporal.

It was her labor that supplied my scanty wardrobe. I have a vivid recollection of the linsey-woolsey dress given me every winter by Mrs. Flint. How I hated it! It was one of the badges of slavery.

While my grandmother was thus helping to support me from her hard earnings, the three hundred dollars she had lent her mistress were never repaid. When her mistress died, her son-in-law, Dr. Flint, was appointed executor. When grandmother applied to him for payment, he said the estate was insolvent, and the law prohibited payment. It did not, however, prohibit him from retaining the silver candelabra,[1] which had been purchased with

---

1 Ornamental branched holders for more than one candle (plural of *candelabrum*).

that money. I presume they will be handed down in the family, from generation to generation.

My grandmother's mistress had always promised her that, at her death, she should be free; and it was said that in her will she made good the promise. But when the estate was settled, Dr. Flint told the faithful old servant that, under existing circumstances, it was necessary she should be sold.

On the appointed day, the customary advertisement was posted up, proclaiming that there would be a "public sale of negroes, horses, &c." Dr. Flint called to tell my grandmother that he was unwilling to wound her feelings by putting her up at auction, and that he would prefer to dispose of her at private sale. My grandmother saw through his hypocrisy; she understood very well that he was ashamed of the job. She was a very spirited woman, and if he was base enough to sell her, when her mistress intended she should be free, she was determined the public should know it. She had for a long time supplied many families with crackers and preserves; consequently, "Aunt Marthy," as she was called, was generally known, and every body who knew her respected her intelligence and good character. Her long and faithful service in the family was also well known, and the intention of her mistress to leave her free. When the day of sale came, she took her place among the chattels, and at the first call she sprang upon the auction-block. Many voices called out, "Shame! Shame! Who is going to sell you, aunt Marthy? Don't stand there! That is no place for you." Without saying a word, she quietly awaited her fate. No one bid for her. At last, a feeble voice said, "Fifty dollars." It came from a maiden lady, seventy years old, the sister of my grandmother's deceased mistress. She had lived forty years under the same roof with my grandmother; she knew how faithfully she had served her owners, and how cruelly she had been defrauded of her rights; and she resolved to protect her. The auctioneer waited for a higher bid; but her wishes were respected; no one bid above her. She could neither read nor write; and when the bill of sale was made out, she signed it with a cross. But what consequence was that, when she had a big heart overflowing with human kindness? She gave the old servant her freedom.[1]

---

1 Historian Jean Fagan Yellin's archival research reveals that the money paid actually came from the enslaved person (Jacobs's grandmother), not the white friend (*Life* 21–22). It may be worth considering why writers of color paint white people as generous heroes based on their having done so little.

At that time, my grandmother was just fifty years old. Laborious years had passed since then; and now my brother and I were slaves to the man who had defrauded her of her money, and tried to defraud her of her freedom. One of my mother's sisters, called Aunt Nancy, was also a slave in his family. She was a kind, good aunt to me; and supplied the place of both housekeeper and waiting maid to her mistress. She was, in fact, at the beginning and end of every thing.

Mrs. Flint, like many southern women, was totally deficient in energy. She had not strength to superintend her household affairs; but her nerves were so strong, that she could sit in her easy chair and see a woman whipped, till the blood trickled from every stroke of the lash. She was a member of the church; but partaking of the Lord's supper did not seem to put her in a Christian frame of mind. If dinner was not served at the exact time on that particular Sunday, she would station herself in the kitchen, and wait till it was dished, and then spit in all the kettles and pans that had been used for cooking. She did this to prevent the cook and her children from eking out their meagre fare with the remains of the gravy and other scrapings. The slaves could get nothing to eat except what she chose to give them. Provisions were weighed out by the pound and ounce, three times a day. I can assure you she gave them no chance to eat wheat bread from her flour barrel. She knew how many biscuits a quart of flour would make, and exactly what size they ought to be.

Dr. Flint was an epicure. The cook never sent a dinner to his table without fear and trembling; for if there happened to be a dish not to his liking, he would either order her to be whipped, or compel her to eat every mouthful of it in his presence. The poor, hungry creature might not have objected to eating it; but she did object to having her master cram it down her throat till she choked.

They had a pet dog, that was a nuisance in the house.

The cook was ordered to make some Indian mush[1] for him. He refused to eat, and when his head was held over it, the froth flowed from his mouth into the basin. He died a few minutes after. When Dr. Flint came in, he said the mush had not been well cooked, and that was the reason the animal would not eat it. He sent for the cook, and compelled her to eat it. He thought that the woman's stomach was stronger than the dog's; but her sufferings afterwards

---

1 Likely a dish based on cornmeal, which white colonists called "Indian meal."

proved that he was mistaken. This poor woman endured many cruelties from her master and mistress; sometimes she was locked up, away from her nursing baby, for a whole day and night.

When I had been in the family a few weeks, one of the plantation slaves was brought to town, by order of his master. It was near night when he arrived, and Dr. Flint ordered him to be taken to the work house, and tied up to the joist, so that his feet would just escape the ground. In that situation he was to wait till the doctor had taken his tea. I shall never forget that night. Never before, in my life, had I heard hundreds of blows fall, in succession, on a human being. His piteous groans, and his "O, pray don't, massa," rang in my ear for months afterwards. There were many conjectures as to the cause of this terrible punishment. Some said master accused him of stealing corn; others said the slave had quarrelled with his wife, in presence of the overseer, and had accused his master of being the father of her child. They were both black, and the child was very fair.

I went into the work house next morning, and saw the cowhide still wet with blood, and the boards all covered with gore. The poor man lived, and continued to quarrel with his wife. A few months afterwards Dr. Flint handed them both over to a slave-trader. The guilty man put their value into his pocket, and had the satisfaction of knowing that they were out of sight and hearing. When the mother was delivered into the trader's hands, she said, "You promised to treat me well." To which he replied, "You have let your tongue run too far; damn you!" She had forgotten that it was a crime for a slave to tell who was the father of her child.

From others than the master persecution also comes in such cases. I once saw a young slave girl dying soon after the birth of a child nearly white. In her agony she cried out, "O Lord, come and take me!" Her mistress stood by, and mocked at her like an incarnate fiend. "You suffer, do you?" she exclaimed. "I am glad of it. You deserve it all, and more too."

The girl's mother said, "The baby is dead, thank God; and I hope my poor child will soon be in heaven, too."

"Heaven!" retorted the mistress. "There is no such place for the like of her and her bastard."

The poor mother turned away, sobbing. Her dying daughter called her, feebly, and as she bent over her, I heard her say, "Don't grieve so, mother; God knows all about it; and HE will have mercy upon me."

Her sufferings, afterwards, became so intense, that her mistress felt unable to stay; but when she left the room, the scornful smile was still on her lips. Seven children called her mother. The poor black woman had but the one child, whose eyes she saw closing in death, while she thanked God for taking her away from the greater bitterness of life.

CHAPTER III.
THE SLAVES' NEW YEAR'S DAY.

Dr. Flint owned a fine residence in town, several farms, and about fifty slaves, besides hiring a number by the year.

Hiring-day at the south takes place on the 1st of January. On the 2d, the slaves are expected to go to their new masters. On a farm, they work until the corn and cotton are laid. They then have two holidays. Some masters give them a good dinner under the trees. This over, they work until Christmas eve. If no heavy charges are meantime brought against them, they are given four or five holidays, whichever the master or overseer may think proper. Then comes New Year's eve; and they gather together their little alls, or more properly speaking, their little nothings, and wait anxiously for the dawning of day. At the appointed hour the grounds are thronged with men, women, and children, waiting, like criminals, to hear their doom pronounced. The slave is sure to know who is the most humane, or cruel, master within forty miles of him.

It is easy to find out, on that day, who clothes and feeds his slaves well; for he is surrounded by a crowd, begging, "Please, massa, hire me this year. I will work very hard, massa."

If a slave is unwilling to go with his new master, he is whipped, or locked up in jail, until he consents to go, and promises not to run away during the year.

Should he chance to change his mind, thinking it justifiable to violate an extorted promise, woe unto him if he is caught! The whip is used till the blood flows at his feet; and his stiffened limbs are put in chains, to be dragged in the field for days and days!

If he lives until the next year, perhaps the same man will hire him again, without even giving him an opportunity of going to the hiring-ground. After those for hire are disposed of, those for sale are called up.

O, you happy free women, contrast your New Year's day with that of the poor bond-woman! With you it is a pleasant season, and the light of the day is blessed. Friendly wishes meet you every where, and gifts are showered upon you. Even hearts that have been estranged from you soften at this season, and lips that have been silent echo back, "I wish you a happy New Year." Children bring their little offerings, and raise their rosy lips for a caress. They are your own, and no hand but that of death can take them from you.

But to the slave mother New Year's day comes laden with peculiar sorrows. She sits on her cold cabin floor, watching the children who may all be torn from her the next morning; and often does she wish that she and they might die before the day dawns. She may be an ignorant creature, degraded by the system that has brutalized her from childhood; but she has a mother's instincts, and is capable of feeling a mother's agonies.

On one of these sale days, I saw a mother lead seven children to the auction-block. She knew that some of them would be taken from her; but they took all. The children were sold to a slave-trader, and their mother was bought by a man in her own town. Before night her children were all far away. She begged the trader to tell her where he intended to take them; this he refused to do. How could he, when he knew he would sell them, one by one, wherever he could command the highest price? I met that mother in the street, and her wild, haggard face lives to-day in my mind. She wrung her hands in anguish, and exclaimed, "Gone! All gone! Why don't God kill me?" I had no words wherewith to comfort her. Instances of this kind are of daily, yea, of hourly occurrence.

Slaveholders have a method, peculiar to their institution, of getting rid of old slaves, whose lives have been worn out in their service. I knew an old woman, who for seventy years faithfully served her master. She had become almost helpless, from hard labor and disease. Her owners moved to Alabama, and the old black woman was left to be sold to any body who would give twenty dollars for her.

CHAPTER IV.
THE SLAVE WHO DARED TO FEEL
LIKE A MAN.

Two years had passed since I entered Dr. Flint's family, and those years had brought much of the knowledge that comes from experience, though they had afforded little opportunity for any other kinds of knowledge. My grandmother had, as much as possible, been a mother to her orphan grandchildren. By perseverance and unwearied industry, she was now mistress of a snug little home, surrounded with the necessaries of life. She would have been happy could her children have shared them with her. There remained but three children and two grandchildren, all slaves. Most earnestly did she strive to make us feel that it was the will of God: that He had seen fit to place us under such circumstances; and though it seemed hard, we ought to pray for contentment.

It was a beautiful faith, coming from a mother who could not call her children her own. But I, and Benjamin, her youngest boy, condemned it. We reasoned that it was much more the will of God that we should be situated as she was. We longed for a home like hers. There we always found sweet balsam[1] for our troubles. She was so loving, so sympathizing! She always met us with a smile, and listened with patience to all our sorrows. She spoke so hopefully, that unconsciously the clouds gave place to sunshine. There was a grand big oven there, too, that baked bread and nice things for the town, and we knew there was always a choice bit in store for us.

But, alas! even the charms of the old oven failed to reconcile us to our hard lot. Benjamin was now a tall, handsome lad, strongly and gracefully made, and with a spirit too bold and daring for a slave. My brother William, now twelve years old, had the same aversion to the word master that he had when he was an urchin[2] of seven years. I was his confidant. He came to me with all his troubles. I remember one instance in particular. It was on a lovely spring morning, and when I marked the sunlight dancing here and there, its beauty seemed to mock my sadness. For my master, whose restless, craving, vicious nature roved about day and night, seeking whom to devour, had just left me, with stinging,

---

1 Any of various fragrant outputs from certain trees, such as balm-of-Gilead.

2 Any small boy or youngster.

scorching words; words that scathed ear and brain like fire. O, how I despised him! I thought how glad I should be, if some day when he walked the earth, it would open and swallow him up, and disencumber[1] the world of a plague.

When he told me that I was made for his use, made to obey his command in every thing; that I was nothing but a slave, whose will must and should surrender to his, never before had my puny arm felt half so strong.

So deeply was I absorbed in painful reflections afterwards, that I neither saw nor heard the entrance of any one, till the voice of William sounded close beside me. "Linda," said he, "what makes you look so sad? I love you. O, Linda, isn't this a bad world? Every body seems so cross and unhappy. I wish I had died when poor father did."

I told him that every body was not cross, or unhappy; that those who had pleasant homes, and kind friends, and who were not afraid to love them, were happy. But we, who were slave-children, without father or mother, could not expect to be happy. We must be good; perhaps that would bring us contentment.

"Yes," he said, "I try to be good; but what's the use? They are all the time troubling me." Then he proceeded to relate his afternoon's difficulty with young master Nicholas. It seemed that the brother of master Nicholas had pleased himself with making up stories about William. Master Nicholas said he should be flogged, and he would do it. Whereupon he went to work; but William fought bravely, and the young master, finding he was getting the better of him, undertook to tie his hands behind him. He failed in that likewise. By dint[2] of kicking and fisting, William came out of the skirmish none the worse for a few scratches.

He continued to discourse on his young master's meanness; how he whipped the little boys, but was a perfect coward when a tussle ensued between him and white boys of his own size. On such occasions he always took to his legs. William had other charges to make against him. One was his rubbing up pennies with quicksilver, and passing them off for quarters of a dollar on an old man who kept a fruit stall. William was often sent to buy fruit, and he earnestly inquired of me what he ought to do under such circumstances. I told him it was certainly wrong to deceive the old man, and that it was his duty to tell him of the impositions practised by his young master. I assured him the old man would

---

1 To free from a burden.
2 Force or power.

not be slow to comprehend the whole, and there the matter would end. William thought it might with the old man, but not with him. He said he did not mind the smart of the whip, but he did not like the idea of being whipped.

While I advised him to be good and forgiving I was not unconscious of the beam in my own eye. It was the very knowledge of my own shortcomings that urged me to retain, if possible, some sparks of my brother's God-given nature. I had not lived fourteen years in slavery for nothing. I had felt, seen, and heard enough, to read the characters, and question the motives, of those around me. The war of my life had begun; and though one of God's most powerless creatures, I resolved never to be conquered. Alas, for me!

If there was one pure, sunny spot for me, I believed it to be in Benjamin's heart, and in another's, whom I loved with all the ardor of a girl's first love. My owner knew of it, and sought in every way to render me miserable. He did not resort to corporal punishment, but to all the petty, tyrannical ways that human ingenuity could devise.

I remember the first time I was punished. It was in the month of February. My grandmother had taken my old shoes, and replaced them with a new pair. I needed them; for several inches of snow had fallen, and it still continued to fall. When I walked through Mrs. Flint's room, their creaking grated harshly on her refined nerves. She called me to her, and asked what I had about me that made such a horrid noise. I told her it was my new shoes. "Take them off," said she; "and if you put them on again, I'll throw them into the fire."

I took them off, and my stockings also. She then sent me a long distance, on an errand. As I went through the snow, my bare feet tingled. That night I was very hoarse; and I went to bed thinking the next day would find me sick, perhaps dead. What was my grief on waking to find myself quite well!

I had imagined if I died, or was laid up for some time, that my mistress would feel a twinge of remorse that she had so hated "the little imp," as she styled me. It was my ignorance of that mistress that gave rise to such extravagant imaginings.

Dr. Flint occasionally had high prices offered for me; but he always said, "She don't belong to me. She is my daughter's property, and I have no right to sell her." Good, honest man! My young mistress was still a child, and I could look for no protection from her. I loved her, and she returned my affection. I once heard her father allude to her attachment to me; and his wife promptly replied that it proceeded from fear. This put unpleasant doubts into my mind. Did the child feign what she did not feel? or was her mother jealous of the mite[1] of love she bestowed on me? I concluded it must be the latter. I said to myself, "Surely, little children are true."

One afternoon I sat at my sewing, feeling unusual depression of spirits. My mistress had been accusing me of an offence, of which I assured her I was perfectly innocent; but I saw, by the contemptuous curl of her lip, that she believed I was telling a lie.

I wondered for what wise purpose God was leading me through such thorny paths, and whether still darker days were in store for me. As I sat musing thus, the door opened softly, and William came in. "Well, brother," said I, "what is the matter this time?"

"O Linda, Ben and his master have had a dreadful time!" said he.

My first thought was that Benjamin was killed. "Don't be frightened, Linda," said William; "I will tell you all about it."

It appeared that Benjamin's master had sent for him, and he did not immediately obey the summons. When he did, his master was angry, and began to whip him. He resisted. Master and slave fought, and finally the master was thrown. Benjamin had cause to tremble; for he had thrown to the ground his master—one of the richest men in town. I anxiously awaited the result.

That night I stole to my grandmother's house, and Benjamin also stole thither from his master's. My grandmother had gone to spend a day or two with an old friend living in the country.

"I have come," said Benjamin, "to tell you good by. I am going away."

I inquired where.

"To the north," he replied.

I looked at him to see whether he was in earnest. I saw it all in his firm, set mouth. I implored him not to go, but he paid no heed to my words. He said he was no longer a boy, and every day made his yoke[2] more galling.[3] He had raised his hand against his master, and was to be publicly whipped for the offence. I reminded him of the poverty and hardships he must encounter among strangers. I told him he might be caught and brought back; and that was terrible to think of.

---

1 Something small, perhaps nearly microscopic.

2 A device placed around the heads of animals of burden to control their movement.

3 Extremely irritating, to the point of being offensive.

He grew vexed,[1] and asked if poverty and hardships with freedom, were not preferable to our treatment in slavery. "Linda," he continued, "we are dogs here; foot-balls, cattle, every thing that's mean.[2] No, I will not stay. Let them bring me back. We don't die but once."

He was right; but it was hard to give him up. "Go," said I, "and break your mother's heart."

I repented of my words ere[3] they were out.

"Linda," said he, speaking as I had not heard him speak that evening, "how could you say that? Poor mother! be kind to her, Linda; and you, too, cousin Fanny."

Cousin Fanny was a friend who had lived some years with us.

Farewells were exchanged, and the bright, kind boy, endeared to us by so many acts of love, vanished from our sight.

It is not necessary to state how he made his escape. Suffice it to say, he was on his way to New York when a violent storm overtook the vessel. The captain said he must put into the nearest port. This alarmed Benjamin, who was aware that he would be advertised in every port near his own town. His embarrassment was noticed by the captain. To port they went. There the advertisement met the captain's eye. Benjamin so exactly answered its description, that the captain laid hold on him, and bound him in chains. The storm passed, and they proceeded to New York. Before reaching that port Benjamin managed to get off his chains and throw them overboard. He escaped from the vessel, but was pursued, captured, and carried back to his master.

When my grandmother returned home and found her youngest child had fled, great was her sorrow; but, with characteristic piety, she said, "God's will be done." Each morning, she inquired if any news had been heard from her boy. Yes, news was heard. The master was rejoicing over a letter, announcing the capture of his human chattel.

That day seems but as yesterday, so well do I remember it. I saw him led through the streets in chains, to jail. His face was ghastly pale, yet full of determination. He had begged one of the sailors to go to his mother's house and ask her not to meet him. He said the sight of her distress would take from him all self-control. She yearned to see him, and she went; but she

---

1 Irritated; annoyed.
2 Inferior in grade, quality, or character; low in status, rank, or dignity; of little importance or consequence.
3 Before.

screened herself in the crowd, that it might be as her child had said.

We were not allowed to visit him; but we had known the jailer for years, and he was a kind-hearted man. At midnight he opened the jail door for my grandmother and myself to enter, in disguise. When we entered the cell not a sound broke the stillness. "Benjamin, Benjamin!" whispered my grandmother. No answer. "Benjamin!" she again faltered. There was a jingle of chains. The moon had just risen, and cast an uncertain light through the bars of the window. We knelt down and took Benjamin's cold hands in ours. We did not speak. Sobs were heard, and Benjamin's lips were unsealed; for his mother was weeping on his neck. How vividly does memory bring back that sad night! Mother and son talked together. He asked her pardon for the suffering he had caused her. She said she had nothing to forgive; she could not blame his desire for freedom. He told her that when he was captured, he broke away, and was about casting himself into the river, when thoughts of her came over him, and he desisted. She asked if he did not also think of God. I fancied I saw his face grow fierce in the moonlight. He answered, "No, I did not think of him. When a man is hunted like a wild beast he forgets there is a God, a heaven. He forgets every thing in his struggle to get beyond the reach of the bloodhounds."

"Don't talk so, Benjamin," said she. "Put your trust in God. Be humble, my child, and your master will forgive you."

"Forgive me for what, mother? For not letting him treat me like a dog? No! I will never humble myself to him. I have worked for him for nothing all my life, and I am repaid with stripes and imprisonment. Here I will stay till I die, or till he sells me."

The poor mother shuddered at his words. I think he felt it; for when he next spoke, his voice was calmer. "Don't fret about me, mother. I ain't worth it," said he. "I wish I had some of your goodness. You bear every thing patiently, just as though you thought it was all right. I wish I could."

She told him she had not always been so; once, she was like him; but when sore troubles came upon her, and she had no arm to lean upon, she learned to call on God, and he lightened her burdens. She besought him to do likewise.

We overstaid our time, and were obliged to hurry from the jail.

Benjamin had been imprisoned three weeks, when my grandmother went to intercede for him with his master. He was immovable. He said Benjamin should serve as an example to the rest of his slaves; he should be kept in jail till he was subdued, or be sold if he got but one dollar for him. However, he afterwards relented in some degree. The chains were taken off, and we were allowed to visit him.

As his food was of the coarsest kind, we carried him as often as possible a warm supper, accompanied with some little luxury for the jailer.

Three months elapsed, and there was no prospect of release or of a purchaser. One day he was heard to sing and laugh. This piece of indecorum was told to his master, and the overseer was ordered to re-chain him. He was now confined in an apartment with other prisoners, who were covered with filthy rags. Benjamin was chained near them, and was soon covered with vermin.[1] He worked at his chains till he succeeded in getting out of them. He passed them through the bars of the window, with a request that they should be taken to his master, and he should be informed that he was covered with vermin.

This audacity was punished with heavier chains, and prohibition of our visits.

My grandmother continued to send him fresh changes of clothes. The old ones were burned up. The last night we saw him in jail his mother still begged him to send for his master, and beg his pardon. Neither persuasion nor argument could turn him from his purpose. He calmly answered, "I am waiting his time."

Those chains were mournful to hear.

Another three months passed, and Benjamin left his prison walls. We that loved him waited to bid him a long and last farewell. A slave trader had bought him. You remember, I told you what price he brought when ten years of age. Now he was more than twenty years old, and sold for three hundred dollars. The master had been blind to his own interest. Long confinement had made his face too pale, his form too thin; moreover, the trader had heard something of his character, and it did not strike him as suitable for a slave. He said he would give any price if the handsome lad was a girl. We thanked God that he was not.

Could you have seen that mother clinging to her child, when they fastened the irons upon his wrists; could you have heard her heart-rending groans, and seen her bloodshot eyes wander wildly from face to face, vainly pleading for mercy; could you have

---

1 Objectionable or disgusting animals collectively, especially those of small size that are difficult to control, such as flies, lice, bedbugs, cockroaches, mice, and rats.

witnessed that scene as I saw it, you would exclaim, Slavery is damnable!

Benjamin, her youngest, her pet, was forever gone! She could not realize it. She had had an interview with the trader for the purpose of ascertaining if Benjamin could be purchased. She was told it was impossible, as he had given bonds not to sell him till he was out of the state. He promised that he would not sell him till he reached New Orleans.

With a strong arm and unvaried trust, my grandmother began her work of love. Benjamin must be free. If she succeeded, she knew they would still be separated; but the sacrifice was not too great. Day and night she labored. The trader's price would treble[1] that he gave; but she was not discouraged.

She employed a lawyer to write to a gentleman, whom she knew, in New Orleans. She begged him to interest himself for Benjamin, and he willingly favored her request. When he saw Benjamin, and stated his business, he thanked him; but said he preferred to wait a while before making the trader an offer. He knew he had tried to obtain a high price for him, and had invariably failed. This encouraged him to make another effort for freedom. So one morning, long before day, Benjamin was missing. He was riding over the blue billows, bound for Baltimore.

For once his white face did him a kindly service. They had no suspicion that it belonged to a slave; otherwise, the law would have been followed out to the letter, and the thing rendered back to slavery. The brightest skies are often overshadowed by the darkest clouds. Benjamin was taken sick, and compelled to remain in Baltimore three weeks. His strength was slow in returning; and his desire to continue his journey seemed to retard his recovery. How could he get strength without air and exercise? He resolved to venture on a short walk. A by-street was selected, where he thought himself secure of not being met by any one that knew him; but a voice called out, "Halloo, Ben, my boy! what are you doing here?"

His first impulse was to run; but his legs trembled so that he could not stir. He turned to confront his antagonist, and behold, there stood his old master's next door neighbor! He thought it was all over with him now; but it proved otherwise. That man was a miracle. He possessed a goodly number of slaves, and yet was not quite deaf to that mystic clock, whose ticking is rarely heard in the slaveholder's breast.

---

1 To make or become three times as much or as many; triple.

"Ben, you are sick," said he. "Why, you look like a ghost. I guess I gave you something of a start. Never mind, Ben, I am not going to touch you. You had a pretty tough time of it, and you may go on your way rejoicing for all me. But I would advise you to get out of this place plaguy[1] quick, for there are several gentlemen here from our town." He described the nearest and safest route to New York, and added, "I shall be glad to tell your mother I have seen you. Good by, Ben."

Benjamin turned away, filled with gratitude, and surprised that the town he hated contained such a gem—a gem worthy of a purer setting.

This gentleman was a Northerner by birth, and had married a southern lady. On his return, he told my grandmother that he had seen her son, and of the service he had rendered him.

Benjamin reached New York safely, and concluded to stop there until he had gained strength enough to proceed further. It happened that my grandmother's only remaining son had sailed for the same city on business for his mistress. Through God's providence, the brothers met. You may be sure it was a happy meeting. "O Phil," exclaimed Benjamin, "I am here at last." Then he told him how near he came to dying, almost in sight of free land, and how he prayed that he might live to get one breath of free air. He said life was worth something now, and it would be hard to die. In the old jail he had not valued it; once, he was tempted to destroy it; but something, he did not know what, had prevented him; perhaps it was fear. He had heard those who profess to be religious declare there was no heaven for self-murderers; and as his life had been pretty hot here, he did not desire a continuation of the same in another world. "If I die now," he exclaimed, "thank God, I shall die a freeman!"

He begged my uncle Phillip not to return south; but stay and work with him, till they earned enough to buy those at home. His brother told him it would kill their mother if he deserted her in her trouble. She had pledged her house, and with difficulty had raised money to buy him. Would he be bought?

"No, never!" he replied. "Do you suppose, Phil, when I have got so far out of their clutches, I will give them one red cent? No! And do you suppose I would turn mother out of her home in her old age? That I would let her pay all those hard-earned dollars for me, and never to see me? For you know she will stay south as long as her other children are slaves. What a good mother! Tell her to

1 Excessively.

buy you, Phil. You have been a comfort to her, and I have been a trouble. And Linda, poor Linda; what'll become of her? Phil, you don't know what a life they lead her. She has told me something about it, and I wish old Flint was dead, or a better man. When I was in jail, he asked her if she didn't want him to ask my master to forgive me, and take me home again. She told him, No; that I didn't want to go back. He got mad, and said we were all alike. I never despised my own master half as much as I do that man. There is many a worse slaveholder than my master; but for all that I would not be his slave."

While Benjamin was sick, he had parted with nearly all his clothes to pay necessary expenses. But he did not part with a little pin I fastened in his bosom when we parted. It was the most valuable thing I owned, and I thought none more worthy to wear it. He had it still.

His brother furnished him with clothes, and gave him what money he had.

They parted with moistened eyes; and as Benjamin turned away, he said, "Phil, I part with all my kindred." And so it proved. We never heard from him again.

Uncle Phillip came home; and the first words he uttered when he entered the house were, "Mother, Ben is free! I have seen him in New York." She stood looking at him with a bewildered air. "Mother, don't you believe it?" he said, laying his hand softly upon her shoulder. She raised her hands, and exclaimed, "God be praised! Let us thank him." She dropped on her knees, and poured forth her heart in prayer. Then Phillip must sit down and repeat to her every word Benjamin had said. He told her all; only he forbore to mention how sick and pale her darling looked. Why should he distress her when she could do him no good?

The brave old woman still toiled on, hoping to rescue some of her other children. After a while she succeeded in buying Phillip. She paid eight hundred dollars, and came home with the precious document that secured his freedom. The happy mother and son sat together by the old hearthstone that night, telling how proud they were of each other, and how they would prove to the world that they could take care of themselves, as they had long taken care of others. We all concluded by saying, "He that is Willing to be a slave, let him be a slave."

CHAPTER V.
THE TRIALS OF GIRLHOOD.

During the first years of my service in Dr. Flint's family, I was accustomed to share some indulgences with the children of my mistress. Though this seemed to me no more than right, I was grateful for it, and tried to merit the kindness by the faithful discharge of my duties. But I now entered on my fifteenth year—a sad epoch in the life of a slave girl. My master began to whisper foul words in my ear. Young as I was, I could not remain ignorant of their import. I tried to treat them with indifference or contempt. The master's age, my extreme youth, and the fear that his conduct would be reported to my grandmother, made him bear this treatment for many months. He was a crafty man, and resorted to many means to accomplish his purposes. Sometimes he had stormy, terrific ways, that made his victims tremble; sometimes he assumed a gentleness that he thought must surely subdue. Of the two, I preferred his stormy moods, although they left me trembling. He tried his utmost to corrupt the pure principles my grandmother had instilled. He peopled my young mind with unclean images, such as only a vile monster could think of. I turned from him with disgust and hatred. But he was my master. I was compelled to live under the same roof with him—where I saw a man forty years my senior daily violating the most sacred commandments of nature. He told me I was his property; that I must be subject to his will in all things. My soul revolted against the mean tyranny.[1] But where could I turn for protection? No matter whether the slave girl be as black as ebony or as fair as her mistress. In either case, there is no shadow of law to protect her from insult, from violence, or even from death; all these are inflicted by fiends who bear the shape of men. The mistress, who ought to protect the helpless victim, has no other feelings towards her but those of jealously and rage. The degradation, the wrongs, the vices, that grow out of slavery, are more than I can describe. They are greater than you would willingly believe. Surely, if you credited one half the truths that are told you concerning the helpless millions suffering in this cruel bondage, you at the north would not help to tighten the yoke. You surely would refuse to do for the master, on your own soil, the mean and cruel work which trained bloodhounds and the lowest class of whites do for him at the south.

---

1 Unrestrained exercise of power.

Every where the years bring to all enough of sin and sorrow; but in slavery the very dawn of life is darkened by these shadows. Even the little child, who is accustomed to wait on her mistress and her children, will learn, before she is twelve years old, why it is that her mistress hates such and such a one among the slaves. Perhaps the child's own mother is among those hated ones. She listens to violent outbreaks of jealous passion, and cannot help understanding what is the cause. She will become prematurely knowing in evil things. Soon she will learn to tremble when she hears her master's footfall. She will be compelled to realize that she is no longer a child. If God has bestowed beauty upon her, it will prove her greatest curse. That which commands admiration in the white woman only hastens the degradation of the female slave. I know that some are too much brutalized by slavery to feel the humiliation of their position; but many slaves feel it most acutely, and shrink from the memory of it. I cannot tell how much I suffered in the presence of these wrongs, nor how I am still pained by the retrospect. My master met me at every turn, reminding me that I belonged to him, and swearing by heaven and earth that he would compel me to submit to him. If I went out for a breath of fresh air, after a day of unwearied toil, his footsteps dogged me. If I knelt by my mother's grave, his dark shadow fell on me even there. The light heart which nature had given me became heavy with sad forebodings. The other slaves in my master's house noticed the change. Many of them pitied me; but none dared to ask the cause. They had no need to inquire. They knew too well the guilty practices under that roof; and they were aware that to speak of them was an offence that never went unpunished.

I longed for some one to confide in. I would have given the world to have laid my head on my grandmother's faithful bosom, and told her all my troubles. But Dr. Flint swore he would kill me, if I was not as silent as the grave. Then, although my grandmother was all in all to me, I feared her as well as loved her. I had been accustomed to look up to her with a respect bordering upon awe. I was very young, and felt shamefaced about telling her such impure things, especially as I knew her to be very strict on such subjects. Moreover, she was a woman of a high spirit. She was usually very quiet in her demeanor; but if her indignation was once roused, it was not very easily quelled. I had been told that she once chased a white gentleman with a loaded pistol, because he insulted one of her daughters. I dreaded the consequences of a violent outbreak; and both pride and fear kept me silent. But though I did not confide in my grandmother, and even evaded her vigilant watchfulness and inquiry, her presence in the neighborhood was some protection to me. Though she had been a slave, Dr. Flint was afraid of her. He dreaded her scorching rebukes. Moreover, she was known and patronized by many people; and he did not wish to have his villainy made public. It was lucky for me that I did not live on a distant plantation, but in a town not so large that the inhabitants were ignorant of each other's affairs. Bad as are the laws and customs in a slaveholding community, the doctor, as a professional man, deemed it prudent to keep up some outward show of decency.

O, what days and nights of fear and sorrow that man caused me! Reader, it is not to awaken sympathy for myself that I am telling you truthfully what I suffered in slavery. I do it to kindle a flame of compassion in your hearts for my sisters who are still in bondage, suffering as I once suffered.

I once saw two beautiful children playing together. One was a fair white child; the other was her slave, and also her sister. When I saw them embracing each other, and heard their joyous laughter, I turned sadly away from the lovely sight. I foresaw the inevitable blight that would fall on the little slave's heart. I knew how soon her laughter would be changed to sighs. The fair child grew up to be a still fairer woman. From childhood to womanhood her pathway was blooming with flowers, and overarched by a sunny sky. Scarcely one day of her life had been clouded when the sun rose on her happy bridal morning.

How had those years dealt with her slave sister, the little playmate of her childhood? She, also, was very beautiful; but the flowers and sunshine of love were not for her. She drank the cup of sin, and shame, and misery, whereof her persecuted race are compelled to drink.

In view of these things, why are ye silent, ye free men and women of the north? Why do your tongues falter in maintenance of the right? Would that I had more ability! But my heart is so full, and my pen is so weak! There are noble men and women who plead for us, striving to help those who cannot help themselves. God bless them! God give them strength and courage to go on! God bless those, every where, who are laboring to advance the cause of humanity!

CHAPTER VI.
THE JEALOUS MISTRESS.

I would ten thousand times rather that my children should be the half-starved paupers of Ireland than to be the most pampered among the slaves of America. I would rather drudge out my life on a cotton plantation, till the grave opened to give me rest, than to live with an unprincipled master and a jealous mistress. The felon's home in a penitentiary is preferable. He may repent, and turn from the error of his ways, and so find peace; but it is not so with a favorite slave. She is not allowed to have any pride of character. It is deemed a crime in her to wish to be virtuous.

Mrs. Flint possessed the key to her husband's character before I was born. She might have used this knowledge to counsel and to screen the young and the innocent among her slaves; but for them she had no sympathy. They were the objects of her constant suspicion and malevolence. She watched her husband with unceasing vigilance; but he was well practised in means to evade it. What he could not find opportunity to say in words he manifested in signs. He invented more than were ever thought of in a deaf and dumb asylum.[1] I let them pass, as if I did not understand what he meant; and many were the curses and threats bestowed on me for my stupidity. One day he caught me teaching myself to write. He frowned, as if he was not well pleased; but I suppose he came to the conclusion that such an accomplishment might help to advance his favorite scheme. Before long, notes were often slipped into my hand. I would return them, saying, "I can't read them, sir." "Can't you?" he replied; "then I must read them to you." He always finished the reading by asking, "Do you understand?" Sometimes he would complain of the heat of the tea room, and order his supper to be placed on a small table in the piazza. He would seat himself there with a well-satisfied smile, and tell me to stand by and brush away the flies. He would eat very slowly, pausing between the mouthfuls. These intervals were employed in describing the happiness I was so foolishly throwing away, and in threatening me with the penalty that finally awaited my stubborn disobedience. He boasted much of the forbearance he had exercised towards me, and reminded me that there was a limit to his patience. When I succeeded in avoiding opportunities for him to talk to me at home, I was ordered to come to his office,

---

1 An institution for the maintenance and care of persons requiring specialized assistance.

to do some errand. When there, I was obliged to stand and listen to such language as he saw fit to address to me. Sometimes I so openly expressed my contempt for him that he would become violently enraged, and I wondered why he did not strike me. Circumstanced as he was, he probably thought it was better policy to be forbearing. But the state of things grew worse and worse daily. In desperation I told him that I must and would apply to my grandmother for protection. He threatened me with death, and worse than death, if I made any complaint to her. Strange to say, I did not despair. I was naturally of a buoyant[1] disposition, and always I had a hope of somehow getting out of his clutches. Like many a poor, simple slave before me, I trusted that some threads of joy would yet be woven into my dark destiny.

I had entered my sixteenth year, and every day it became more apparent that my presence was intolerable to Mrs. Flint. Angry words frequently passed between her and her husband. He had never punished me himself, and he would not allow any body else to punish me. In that respect, she was never satisfied; but, in her angry moods, no terms were too vile for her to bestow upon me. Yet I, whom she detested so bitterly, had far more pity for her than he had, whose duty it was to make her life happy. I never wronged her, or wished to wrong her; and one word of kindness from her would have brought me to her feet.

After repeated quarrels between the doctor and his wife, he announced his intention to take his youngest daughter, then four years old, to sleep in his apartment. It was necessary that a servant should sleep in the same room, to be on hand if the child stirred. I was selected for that office, and informed for what purpose that arrangement had been made. By managing to keep within sight of people, as much as possible, during the day time, I had hitherto succeeded in eluding my master, though a razor was often held to my throat to force me to change this line of policy. At night I slept by the side of my great aunt, where I felt safe. He was too prudent to come into her room. She was an old woman, and had been in the family many years. Moreover, as a married man, and a professional man, he deemed it necessary to save appearances in some degree. But he resolved to remove the obstacle in the way of his scheme; and he thought he had planned it so that he should evade suspicion. He was well aware how much I prized my refuge by the side of my old aunt, and he determined to dispossess me of it. The first night the doctor had the little child in his room alone. The

---

1 Not easily depressed; cheerful.

next morning, I was ordered to take my station as nurse the following night. A kind Providence interposed in my favor. During the day Mrs. Flint heard of this new arrangement, and a storm followed. I rejoiced to hear it rage.

After a while my mistress sent for me to come to her room. Her first question was, "Did you know you were to sleep in the doctor's room?"

"Yes, ma'am."

"Who told you?"

"My master."

"Will you answer truly all the questions I ask?"

"Yes, ma'am."

"Tell me, then, as you hope to be forgiven, are you innocent of what I have accused you?"

"I am."

She handed me a Bible, and said, "Lay your hand on your heart, kiss this holy book, and swear before God that you tell me the truth."

I took the oath she required, and I did it with a clear conscience.

"You have taken God's holy word to testify your innocence," said she. "If you have deceived me, beware! Now take this stool, sit down, look me directly in the face, and tell me all that has passed between your master and you."

I did as she ordered. As I went on with my account her color changed frequently, she wept, and sometimes groaned. She spoke in tones so sad, that I was touched by her grief. The tears came to my eyes; but I was soon convinced that her emotions arose from anger and wounded pride. She felt that her marriage vows were desecrated, her dignity insulted; but she had no compassion for the poor victim of her husband's perfidy.[1] She pitied herself as a martyr;[2] but she was incapable of feeling for the condition of shame and misery in which her unfortunate, helpless slave was placed.

Yet perhaps she had some touch of feeling for me; for when the conference was ended, she spoke kindly, and promised to protect me. I should have been much comforted by this assurance if I could have had confidence in it; but my experiences in slavery had filled me with distrust. She was not a very refined woman, and had not much control over her passions. I was an object of her jealousy, and, consequently, of her hatred; and I knew I could not expect kindness or confidence from her under the circumstances

---

1 Deliberate breach of faith or trust; faithlessness.
2 A person who undergoes severe or constant suffering.

in which I was placed. I could not blame her. Slaveholders' wives feel as other women would under similar circumstances. The fire of her temper kindled from small sparks, and now the flame became so intense that the doctor was obliged to give up his intended arrangement.

I knew I had ignited the torch, and I expected to suffer for it after wards; but I felt too thankful to my mistress for the timely aid she rendered me to care much about that. She now took me to sleep in a room adjoining her own. There I was an object of her especial care, though not of her especial comfort, for she spent many a sleepless night to watch over me. Sometimes I woke up, and found her bending over me. At other times she whispered in my ear, as though it was her husband who was speaking to me, and listened to hear what I would answer. If she startled me, on such occasions, she would glide stealthily away; and the next morning she would tell me I had been talking in my sleep, and ask who I was talking to. At last, I began to be fearful for my life. It had been often threatened; and you can imagine, better than I can describe, what an unpleasant sensation it must produce to wake up in the dead of night and find a jealous woman bending over you. Terrible as this experience was, I had fears that it would give place to one more terrible.

My mistress grew weary of her vigils; they did not prove satisfactory. She changed her tactics. She now tried the trick of accusing my master of crime, in my presence, and gave my name as the author of the accusation. To my utter astonishment, he replied, "I don't believe it; but if she did acknowledge it, you tortured her into exposing me." Tortured into exposing him! Truly, Satan had no difficulty in distinguishing the color of his soul! I understood his object in making this false representation. It was to show me that I gained nothing by seeking the protection of my mistress; that the power was still all in his own hands. I pitied Mrs. Flint. She was a second wife, many years the junior of her husband; and the hoary-headed miscreant was enough to try the patience of a wiser and better woman. She was completely foiled, and knew not how to proceed. She would gladly have had me flogged for my supposed false oath; but, as I have already stated, the doctor never allowed any one to whip me. The old sinner was politic.[1] The application of the lash might have led to remarks that would have exposed him in the eyes of his children and grandchildren. How often did I rejoice that I lived in a town where all the inhabitants

1 Tactful; diplomatic.

knew each other! If I had been on a remote plantation, or lost among the multitude of a crowded city, I should not be a living woman at this day.

The secrets of slavery are concealed like those of the Inquisition.[1] My master was, to my knowledge, the father of eleven slaves. But did the mothers dare to tell who was the father of their children? Did the other slaves dare to allude to it, except in whispers among themselves? No, indeed! They knew too well the terrible consequences.

My grandmother could not avoid seeing things which excited her suspicions. She was uneasy about me, and tried various ways to buy me; but the never-changing answer was always repeated: "Linda does not belong to me. She is my daughter's property, and I have no legal right to sell her." The conscientious man! He was too scrupulous to sell me; but he had no scruples whatever about committing a much greater wrong against the helpless young girl placed under his guardianship, as his daughter's property. Sometimes my persecutor would ask me whether I would like to be sold. I told him I would rather be sold to any body than to lead such a life as I did. On such occasions he would assume the air of a very injured individual, and reproach me for my ingratitude. "Did I not take you into the house, and make you the companion of my own children?" he would say. "Have I ever treated you like a negro? I have never allowed you to be punished, not even to please your mistress. And this is the recompense I get, you ungrateful girl!" I answered that he had reasons of his own for screening me from punishment, and that the course he pursued made my mistress hate me and persecute me. If I wept, he would say, "Poor child! Don't cry! don't cry! I will make peace for you with your mistress. Only let me arrange matters in my own way. Poor, foolish girl! you don't know what is for your own good. I would cherish you. I would make a lady of you. Now go, and think of all I have promised you."

I did think of it.

Reader, I draw no imaginary pictures of southern homes. I am telling you the plain truth. Yet when victims make their escape

---

1 An official investigation, especially one of a political or religious nature, distinctive for its lack of regard for individual rights, the prejudice of the examiners, and the cruelty of its punishments. Because Jacobs capitalizes here, she is likely referring to The Tribunal of the Holy Office of the Inquisition, established in Spain in 1478 and finally disbanded in 1834, commonly known as the Spanish Inquisition.

from this wild beast of Slavery, northerners consent to act the part of bloodhounds, and hunt the poor fugitive back into his den, "full of dead men's bones, and all uncleanness."[1] Nay, more, they are not only willing, but proud, to give their daughters in marriage to slaveholders. The poor girls have romantic notions of a sunny clime, and of the flowering vines that all the year round shade a happy home. To what disappointments are they destined! The young wife soon learns that the husband in whose hands she has placed her happiness pays no regard to his marriage vows. Children of every shade of complexion play with her own fair babies, and too well she knows that they are born unto him of his own household. Jealousy and hatred enter the flowery home, and it is ravaged of its loveliness.

Southern women often marry a man knowing that he is the father of many little slaves. They do not trouble themselves about it. They regard such children as property, as marketable as the pigs on the plantation; and it is seldom that they do not make them aware of this by passing them into the slavetrader's hands as soon as possible, and thus getting them out of their sight. I am glad to say there are some honorable exceptions.

I have myself known two southern wives who exhorted their husbands to free those slaves towards whom they stood in a "parental relation;" and their request was granted. These husbands blushed before the superior nobleness of their wives' natures. Though they had only counselled them to do that which it was their duty to do, it commanded their respect, and rendered their conduct more exemplary. Concealment was at an end, and confidence took the place of distrust.

Though this bad institution deadens the moral sense, even in white women, to a fearful extent, it is not altogether extinct. I have heard southern ladies say of Mr. Such a one, "He not only thinks it no disgrace to be the father of those little niggers, but he is not ashamed to call himself their master. I declare, such things ought not to be tolerated in any decent society!"

---

1 From biblical scripture, Matthew 23.27: Woe unto you, scribes and Pharisees, hypocrites! for ye are like unto whited sepulchres, which indeed appear beautiful outward, but are within full of dead men's bones, and of all uncleanness.

CHAPTER VII.
THE LOVER.

Why does the slave ever love? Why allow the tendrils of the heart to twine around objects which may at any moment be wrenched away by the hand of violence? When separations come by the hand of death, the pious soul can bow in resignation, and say, "Not my will, but thine be done, O Lord!" But when the ruthless hand of man strikes the blow, regardless of the misery he causes, it is hard to be submissive. I did not reason thus when I was a young girl. Youth will be youth. I loved, and I indulged the hope that the dark clouds around me would turn out a bright lining. I forgot that in the land of my birth the shadows are too dense for light to penetrate. A land

"Where laughter is not mirth; nor thought the mind;
Nor words a language; nor e'en men mankind.
Where cries reply to curses, shrieks to blows,
And each is tortured in his separate hell."[1]

There was in the neighborhood a young colored carpenter; a free born man. We had been well acquainted in childhood, and frequently met together afterwards. We became mutually attached, and he proposed to marry me. I loved him with all the ardor of a young girl's first love. But when I reflected that I was a slave, and that the laws gave no sanction to the marriage of such, my heart sank within me. My lover wanted to buy me; but I knew that Dr. Flint was too wilful and arbitrary a man to consent to that arrangement. From him, I was sure of experiencing all sorts of opposition, and I had nothing to hope from my mistress. She would have been delighted to have got rid of me, but not in that way. It would have relieved her mind of a burden if she could have seen me sold to some distant state, but if I was married near home I should be just as much in her husband's power as I had previously been,—for the husband of a slave has no power to protect her. Moreover, my mistress, like many others, seemed to think that slaves had no right to any family ties of their own; that they were created merely to wait upon the family of the mistress. I once heard her abuse a young slave girl, who told her that a colored man wanted to make her his wife. "I will have you peeled

---

1 From "The Lament of Tasso" (1817) by English poet Lord Byron (1788–1824).

and pickled, my lady," said she, "if I ever hear you mention that subject again. Do you suppose that I will have you tending my children with the children of that nigger?" The girl to whom she said this had a mulatto child, of course not acknowledged by its father. The poor black man who loved her would have been proud to acknowledge his helpless offspring.

Many and anxious were the thoughts I revolved in my mind. I was at a loss what to do. Above all things, I was desirous to spare my lover the insults that had cut so deeply into my own soul. I talked with my grandmother about it, and partly told her my fears. I did not dare to tell her the worst. She had long suspected all was not right, and if I confirmed her suspicions I knew a storm would rise that would prove the overthrow of all my hopes.

This love-dream had been my support through many trials; and I could not bear to run the risk of having it suddenly dissipated.[1] There was a lady in the neighborhood, a particular friend of Dr. Flint's, who often visited the house. I had a great respect for her, and she had always manifested a friendly interest in me. Grandmother thought she would have great influence with the doctor. I went to this lady, and told her my story. I told her I was aware that my lover's being a free-born man would prove a great objection; but he wanted to buy me; and if Dr. Flint would consent to that arrangement, I felt sure he would be willing to pay any reasonable price. She knew that Mrs. Flint disliked me; therefore, I ventured to suggest that perhaps my mistress would approve of my being sold, as that would rid her of me. The lady listened with kindly sympathy, and promised to do her utmost to promote my wishes. She had an interview with the doctor, and I believe she pleaded my cause earnestly; but it was all to no purpose.

How I dreaded my master now! Every minute I expected to be summoned to his presence; but the day passed, and I heard nothing from him. The next morning, a message was brought to me: "Master wants you in his study." I found the door ajar, and I stood a moment gazing at the hateful man who claimed a right to rule me, body and soul. I entered, and tried to appear calm. I did not want him to know how my heart was bleeding. He looked fixedly at me, with an expression which seemed to say, "I have half a mind to kill you on the spot." At last he broke the silence, and that was a relief to both of us.

"So you want to be married, do you?" said he, "and to a free nigger."

---

1 Dispersed; dispelled.

"Yes, sir."

"Well, I'll soon convince you whether I am your master, or the nigger fellow you honor so highly. If you must have a husband, you may take up with one of my slaves."

What a situation I should be in, as the wife of one of his slaves, even if my heart had been interested!

I replied, "Don't you suppose, sir, that a slave can have some preference about marrying? Do you suppose that all men are alike to her?"

"Do you love this nigger?" said he, abruptly.

"Yes, sir."

"How dare you tell me so!" he exclaimed, in great wrath. After a slight pause, he added, "I supposed you thought more of yourself; that you felt above the insults of such puppies."

I replied, "If he is a puppy I am a puppy, for we are both of the negro race. It is right and honorable for us to love each other. The man you call a puppy never insulted me, sir; and he would not love me if he did not believe me to be a virtuous woman."

He sprang upon me like a tiger, and gave me a stunning blow. It was the first time he had ever struck me; and fear did not enable me to control my anger. When I had recovered a little from the effects, I exclaimed, "You have struck me for answering you honestly. How I despise you!"

There was silence for some minutes. Perhaps he was deciding what should be my punishment; or, perhaps, he wanted to give me time to reflect on what I had said, and to whom I had said it. Finally, he asked, "Do you know what you have said?"

"Yes, sir; but your treatment drove me to it."

"Do you know that I have a right to do as I like with you,—that I can kill you, if I please?"

"You have tried to kill me, and I wish you had; but you have no right to do as you like with me."

"Silence!" he exclaimed, in a thundering voice.

"By heavens, girl, you forget yourself too far! Are you mad? If you are, I will soon bring you to your senses. Do you think any other master would bear what I have borne from you this morning? Many masters would have killed you on the spot. How would you like to be sent to jail for your insolence?"

"I know I have been disrespectful, sir," I replied; "but you drove me to it; I couldn't help it. As for the jail, there would be more peace for me there than there is here."

"You deserve to go there," said he, "and to be under such treatment, that you would forget the meaning of the word peace. It would do you good. It would take some of your high notions out of you. But I am not ready to send you there yet, notwithstanding your ingratitude for all my kindness and forbearance. You have been the plague of my life. I have wanted to make you happy, and I have been repaid with the basest ingratitude; but though you have proved yourself incapable of appreciating my kindness, I will be lenient towards you, Linda. I will give you one more chance to redeem your character. If you behave yourself and do as I require, I will forgive you and treat you as I always have done; but if you disobey me, I will punish you as I would the meanest slave on my plantation. Never let me hear that fellow's name mentioned again. If I ever know of your speaking to him, I will cowhide you both; and if I catch him lurking about my premises, I will shoot him as soon as I would a dog. Do you hear what I say? I'll teach you a lesson about marriage and free niggers! Now go, and let this be the last time I have occasion to speak to you on this subject."

Reader, did you ever hate? I hope not. I never did but once; and I trust I never shall again. Somebody has called it "the atmosphere of hell;"[1] and I believe it is so.

For a fortnight[2] the doctor did not speak to me. He thought to mortify[3] me; to make me feel that I had disgraced myself by receiving the honorable addresses of a respectable colored man, in preference to the base proposals of a white man. But though his lips disdained to address me, his eyes were very loquacious.[4] No animal ever watched its prey more narrowly than he watched me. He knew that I could write, though he had failed to make me read his letters; and he was now troubled lest I should exchange letters with another man. After a while he became weary of silence; and I was sorry for it. One morning, as he passed through the hall, to leave the house, he contrived to thrust a note into my hand. I thought I had better read it, and spare myself the vexation of having him read it to me. It expressed regret for the blow he had given me, and reminded me that I myself was wholly to blame for it. He hoped I had become convinced of the injury I was doing myself by incurring his displeasure. He wrote that he had made up his mind to go to Louisiana; that he should take several slaves

---

1 Likely a reference to *Proverbial Philosophy* (1839) by British author Martin Farquhar Tupper (1810–89): "Hatred is the atmosphere of hell."

2 Fourteen nights and days; two weeks.

3 To subjugate by abstinence; to humiliate or shame.

4 Wordy; characterized by excessive talk.

with him, and intended I should be one of the number. My mistress would remain where she was; therefore I should have nothing to fear from that quarter. If I merited kindness from him, he assured me that it would be lavishly bestowed. He begged me to think over the matter, and answer the following day.

The next morning I was called to carry a pair of scissors to his room. I laid them on the table, with the letter beside them. He thought it was my answer, and did not call me back. I went as usual to attend my young mistress to and from school. He met me in the street, and ordered me to stop at his office on my way back. When I entered, he showed me his letter, and asked me why I had not answered it. I replied, "I am your daughter's property, and it is in your power to send me, or take me, wherever you please." He said he was very glad to find me so willing to go, and that we should start early in the autumn. He had a large practice in the town, and I rather thought he had made up the story merely to frighten me. However that might be, I was determined that I would never go to Louisiana with him.

Summer passed away, and early in the autumn Dr. Flint's eldest son was sent to Louisiana to examine the country, with a view to emigrating.[1] That news did not disturb me. I knew very well that I should not be sent with him. That I had not been taken to the plantation before this time, was owing to the fact that his son was there. He was jealous of his son; and jealousy of the overseer had kept him from punishing me by sending me into the fields to work. Is it strange that I was not proud of these protectors? As for the overseer, he was a man for whom I had less respect than I had for a bloodhound.

Young Mr. Flint did not bring back a favorable report of Louisiana, and I heard no more of that scheme. Soon after this, my lover met me at the corner of the street, and I stopped to speak to him. Looking up, I saw my master watching us from his window. I hurried home, trembling with fear. I was sent for, immediately, to go to his room. He met me with a blow. "When is mistress to be married?" said he, in a sneering tone. A shower of oaths and imprecations[2] followed. How thankful I was that my lover was a free man! that my tyrant had no power to flog him for speaking to me in the street!

Again and again I revolved in my mind how all this would end. There was no hope that the doctor would consent to sell me on

---

1 Leaving one region and settling in another.
2 Curses.

any terms. He had an iron will, and was determined to keep me, and to conquer me. My lover was an intelligent and religious man. Even if he could have obtained permission to marry me while I was a slave, the marriage would give him no power to protect me from my master. It would have made him miserable to witness the insults I should have been subjected to. And then, if we had children, I knew they must "follow the condition of the mother."[1] What a terrible blight that would be on the heart of a free, intelligent father! For his sake, I felt that I ought not to link his fate with my own unhappy destiny. He was going to Savannah to see about a little property left him by an uncle; and hard as it was to bring my feelings to it, I earnestly entreated him not to come back. I advised him to go to the Free States, where his tongue would not be tied, and where his intelligence would be of more avail to him. He left me, still hoping the day would come when I could be bought. With me the lamp of hope had gone out. The dream of my girlhood was over. I felt lonely and desolate.

Still I was not stripped of all. I still had my good grandmother, and my affectionate brother. When he put his arms round my neck, and looked into my eyes, as if to read there the troubles I dared not tell, I felt that I still had something to love. But even that pleasant emotion was chilled by the reflection that he might be torn from me at any moment, by some sudden freak of my master. If he had known how we loved each other, I think he would have exulted in separating us. We often planned together how we could get to the north. But, as William remarked, such things are easier said than done. My movements were very closely watched, and we had no means of getting any money to defray our expenses. As for grandmother, she was strongly opposed to her children's undertaking any such project. She had not forgotten poor Benjamin's sufferings, and she was afraid that if another child tried to escape, he would have a similar or a worse fate. To me, nothing seemed more dreadful than my present life. I said to myself, "William must be free. He shall go to the north, and I will follow him." Many a slave sister has formed the same plans.

---

1 Latin: *Partus sequitur ventrem*, meaning "That which is born follows the womb." See Appendix B1.

CHAPTER VIII.
WHAT SLAVES ARE TAUGHT TO THINK OF THE NORTH.

Slaveholders pride themselves upon being honorable men; but if you were to hear the enormous lies they tell their slaves, you would have small respect for their veracity.[1] I have spoken plain English. Pardon me. I cannot use a milder term. When they visit the north, and return home, they tell their slaves of the runaways they have seen, and describe them to be in the most deplorable condition. A slaveholder once told me that he had seen a runaway friend of mine in New York, and that she besought him to take her back to her master, for she was literally dying of starvation; that many days she had only one cold potato to eat, and at other times could get nothing at all. He said he refused to take her, because he knew her master would not thank him for bringing such a miserable wretch to his house. He ended by saying to me, "This is the punishment she brought on herself for running away from a kind master."

This whole story was false. I afterwards staid with that friend in New York, and found her in comfortable circumstances. She had never thought of such a thing as wishing to go back to slavery. Many of the slaves believe such stories, and think it is not worth while to exchange slavery for such a hard kind of freedom. It is difficult to persuade such that freedom could make them useful men, and enable them to protect their wives and children. If those heathens in our Christian land had as much teaching as some Hindoos, they would think otherwise. They would know that liberty is more valuable than life. They would begin to understand their own capabilities, and exert themselves to become men and women.

But while the Free States sustain a law which hurls fugitives back into slavery, how can the slaves resolve to become men? There are some who strive to protect wives and daughters from the insults of their masters; but those who have such sentiments have had advantages above the general mass of slaves. They have been partially civilized and Christianized by favorable circumstances. Some are bold enough to utter such sentiments to their masters. O, that there were more of them!

Some poor creatures have been so brutalized by the lash that they will sneak out of the way to give their masters free access to

---

1 Truthfulness.

their wives and daughters. Do you think this proves the black man to belong to an inferior order of beings? What would you be, if you had been born and brought up a slave, with generations of slaves for ancestors? I admit that the black man is inferior. But what is it that makes him so? It is the ignorance in which white men compel him to live; it is the torturing whip that lashes manhood out of him; it is the fierce bloodhounds of the South, and the scarcely less cruel human bloodhounds of the north, who enforce the Fugitive Slave Law. They do the work.

Southern gentlemen indulge in the most contemptuous expressions about the Yankees, while they, on their part, consent to do the vilest work for them, such as the ferocious bloodhounds and the despised negro-hunters are employed to do at home. When southerners go to the north, they are proud to do them honor; but the northern man is not welcome south of Mason and Dixon's line, unless he suppresses every thought and feeling at variance with their "peculiar institution."[1] Nor is it enough to be silent. The masters are not pleased, unless they obtain a greater degree of subservience than that; and they are generally accommodated. Do they respect the northerner for this? I trow[2] not. Even the slaves despise "a northern man with southern principles;" and that is the class they generally see. When northerners go to the south to reside, they prove very apt scholars. They soon imbibe the sentiments and disposition of their neighbors, and generally go beyond their teachers. Of the two, they are proverbially the hardest masters.

They seem to satisfy their consciences with the doctrine that God created the Africans to be slaves. What a libel upon the heavenly Father, who "made of one blood all nations of men!"[3] And then who are Africans? Who can measure the amount of Anglo-Saxon blood coursing in the veins of American slaves?

I have spoken of the pains slaveholders take to give their slaves

---

1 A phrase used to refer to enslavement in subtle, euphemistic terms (i.e., in terms that substitute mild, indirect, or vague language for more direct or blunt expression). Some used the euphemism to highlight its irony, but it began with John C. Calhoun's tendency to defend the "peculiar labor" that was the hallmark of the South. Calhoun (1782–1850) was a staunch advocate of slavery who also served as US secretary of war and as vice president.

2 Believe, think, or suppose.

3 From biblical scripture, Acts 17.25: God hath made of one blood all nations of men.

a bad opinion of the north; but, notwithstanding this, intelligent slaves are aware that they have many friends in the Free States. Even the most ignorant have some confused notions about it. They knew that I could read; and I was often asked if I had seen any thing in the newspapers about white folks over in the big north, who were trying to get their freedom for them. Some believe that the abolitionists have already made them free, and that it is established by law, but that their masters prevent the law from going into effect.[1] One woman begged me to get a newspaper and read it over. She said her husband told her that the black people had sent word to the queen of 'Merica that they were all slaves; that she didn't believe it, and went to Washington city to see the president about it. They quarrelled; she drew her sword upon him, and swore that he should help her to make them all free.

That poor, ignorant woman thought that America was governed by a Queen, to whom the President was subordinate. I wish the President was subordinate to Queen Justice.

CHAPTER IX.
SKETCHES OF NEIGHBORING SLAVEHOLDERS.

There was a planter in the country, not far from us, whom I will call Mr. Litch. He was an ill-bred, uneducated man, but very wealthy. He had six hundred slaves, many of whom he did not know by sight. His extensive plantation was managed by well-paid overseers. There was a jail and a whipping post on his grounds; and whatever cruelties were perpetrated there, they passed without comment. He was so effectually screened by his great wealth that he was called to no account for his crimes, not even for murder.

---

1 This belief was not outlandish, as illustrated by Juneteenth, which the United States made a federal holiday in 2021. On 19 June 1865, enslaved people in Texas first heard a reading of the Emancipation Proclamation that had gone into effect on 1 January 1863 (see Appendix A7). More than two years after they were no longer legally in bondage, they learned of their declared freedom. This delay was by design, given that many enslavers had flocked to Texas and Oklahoma for the express purpose of avoiding potential demands that they emancipate those whose labor they stole. See, for example, Gordon-Reed, *On Juneteenth.*

Various were the punishments resorted to. A favorite one was to tie a rope round a man's body, and suspend him from the ground. A fire was kindled over him, from which was suspended a piece of fat pork. As this cooked, the scalding drops of fat continually fell on the bare flesh. On his own plantation, he required very strict obedience to the eighth commandment.[1] But depredations on the neighbors were allowable, provided the culprit managed to evade detection or suspicion. If a neighbor brought a charge of theft against any of his slaves, he was browbeaten by the master, who assured him that his slaves had enough of every thing at home, and had no inducement to steal. No sooner was the neighbor's back turned, than the accused was sought out, and whipped for his lack of discretion. If a slave stole from him even a pound of meat or a peck of corn, if detection followed, he was put in chains and imprisoned, and so kept till his form was attenuated by hunger and suffering.

A freshet[2] once bore his wine cellar and meat house miles away from the plantation. Some slaves followed, and secured bits of meat and bottles of wine. Two were detected; a ham and some liquor being found in their huts. They were summoned by their master. No words were used, but a club felled them to the ground. A rough box was their coffin, and their interment was a dog's burial. Nothing was said.

Murder was so common on his plantation that he feared to be alone after nightfall. He might have believed in ghosts.

His brother, if not equal in wealth, was at least equal in cruelty. His bloodhounds were well trained. Their pen was spacious, and a terror to the slaves. They were let loose on a runaway, and, if they tracked him, they literally tore the flesh from his bones. When this slaveholder died, his shrieks and groans were so frightful that they appalled his own friends. His last words were, "I am going to hell; bury my money with me."

After death his eyes remained open. To press the lids down, silver dollars were laid on them. These were buried with him. From this circumstance, a rumor went abroad that his coffin was filled with money. Three times his grave was opened, and his coffin taken out. The last time, his body was found on the ground, and a flock of buzzards were pecking at it. He was again interred,

---

1 A reference to biblical scripture. Exodus 20 offers what Christians commonly call The Ten Commandments, the eighth of which is "Thou shalt not steal."
2 Flooding or a sudden rise in the level of a stream.

and a sentinel[1] set over his grave. The perpetrators were never discovered.

Cruelty is contagious in uncivilized communities. Mr. Conant, a neighbor of Mr. Litch, returned from town one evening in a partial state of intoxication. His body servant gave him some offence. He was divested of his clothes, except his shirt, whipped, and tied to a large tree in front of the house. It was a stormy night in winter. The wind blew bitterly cold, and the boughs of the old tree crackled under falling sleet. A member of the family, fearing he would freeze to death, begged that he might be taken down; but the master would not relent. He remained there three hours; and, when he was cut down, he was more dead than alive. Another slave, who stole a pig from this master, to appease his hunger, was terribly flogged. In desperation, he tried to run away. But at the end of two miles, he was so faint with loss of blood, he thought he was dying. He had a wife, and he longed to see her once more. Too sick to walk, he crept back that long distance on his hands and knees. When he reached his master's, it was night. He had not strength to rise and open the gate. He moaned, and tried to call for help. I had a friend living in the same family. At last his cry reached her. She went out and found the prostrate man at the gate. She ran back to the house for assistance, and two men returned with her. They carried him in, and laid him on the floor. The back of his shirt was one clot of blood. By means of lard, my friend loosened it from the raw flesh. She bandaged him, gave him cool drink, and left him to rest. The master said he deserved a hundred more lashes. When his own labor was stolen from him, he had stolen food to appease his hunger. This was his crime.

Another neighbor was a Mrs. Wade. At no hour of the day was there cessation of the lash on her premises. Her labors began with the dawn, and did not cease till long after nightfall. The barn was her particular place of torture. There she lashed the slaves with the might of a man. An old slave of hers once said to me, "It is hell in missis's house. 'Pears I can never get out. Day and night I prays to die."

The mistress died before the old woman, and, when dying, entreated her husband not to permit any one of her slaves to look on her after death. A slave who had nursed her children, and had still a child in her care, watched her chance, and stole with it in her arms to the room where lay her dead mistress. She gazed a while on her, then raised her hand and dealt two blows on her

---

1 A person or thing that watches or stands as if watching.

face, saying, as she did so, "The devil is got you now!" She forgot that the child was looking on. She had just begun to talk; and she said to her father, "I did see ma, and mammy did strike ma, so," striking her own face with her little hand. The master was startled. He could not imagine how the nurse could obtain access to the room where the corpse lay; for he kept the door locked. He questioned her. She confessed that what the child had said was true, and told how she had procured the key. She was sold to Georgia.

In my childhood I knew a valuable slave, named Charity, and loved her, as all children did. Her young mistress married, and took her to Louisiana. Her little boy, James, was sold to a good sort of master. He became involved in debt, and James was sold again to a wealthy slaveholder, noted for his cruelty. With this man he grew up to manhood, receiving the treatment of a dog. After a severe whipping, to save himself from further infliction of the lash, with which he was threatened, he took to the woods. He was in a most miserable condition—cut by the cowskin, half naked, half starved, and without the means of procuring a crust of bread.

Some weeks after his escape, he was captured, tied, and carried back to his master's plantation. This man considered punishment in his jail, on bread and water, after receiving hundreds of lashes, too mild for the poor slave's offence. Therefore he decided, after the overseer should have whipped him to his satisfaction, to have him placed between the screws of the cotton gin, to stay as long as he had been in the woods. This wretched creature was cut with the whip from his head to his feet, then washed with strong brine,[1] to prevent the flesh from mortifying, and make it heal sooner than it otherwise would. He was then put into the cotton gin, which was screwed down, only allowing him room to turn on his side when he could not lie on his back. Every morning a slave was sent with a piece of bread and bowl of water, which were placed within reach of the poor fellow. The slave was charged, under penalty of severe punishment, not to speak to him.

Four days passed, and the slave continued to carry the bread and water. On the second morning, he found the bread gone, but the water untouched.

When he had been in the press four days and five nights, the slave informed his master that the water had not been used for four mornings, and that a horrible stench came from the gin house. The overseer was sent to examine into it. When the press was unscrewed, the dead body was found partly eaten by rats and

---

1 Water saturated with salt.

vermin. Perhaps the rats that devoured his bread had gnawed him before life was extinct. Poor Charity! Grandmother and I often asked each other how her affectionate heart would bear the news, if she should ever hear of the murder of her son. We had known her husband, and knew that James was like him in manliness and intelligence. These were the qualities that made it so hard for him to be a plantation slave. They put him into a rough box, and buried him with less feeling than would have been manifested for an old house dog. Nobody asked any questions. He was a slave; and the feeling was that the master had a right to do what he pleased with his own property. And what did he care for the value of a slave? He had hundreds of them. When they had finished their daily toil, they must hurry to eat their little morsels, and be ready to extinguish their pine knots[1] before nine o'clock, when the overseer went his patrol rounds. He entered every cabin, to see that men and their wives had gone to bed together, lest the men, from over-fatigue, should fall asleep in the chimney corner, and remain there till the morning horn called them to their daily task. Women are considered of no value, unless they continually increase their owner's stock. They are put on a par with animals. This same master shot a woman through the head, who had run away and been brought back to him. No one called him to account for it. If a slave resisted being whipped, the bloodhounds were unpacked, and set upon him, to tear his flesh from his bones. The master who did these things was highly educated, and styled a perfect gentleman. He also boasted the name and standing of a Christian, though Satan never had a truer follower.

I could tell of more slaveholders as cruel as those I have described. They are not exceptions to the general rule. I do not say there are no humane slaveholders. Such characters do exist, notwithstanding the hardening influences around them. But they are "like angels' visits—few and far between."

I knew a young lady who was one of these rare specimens. She was an orphan, and inherited as slaves a woman and her six children. Their father was a free man. They had a comfortable home of their own, parents and children living together. The mother and eldest daughter served their mistress during the day, and at night returned to their dwelling, which was on the premises. The young lady was very pious, and there was some reality in her religion. She taught her slaves to lead pure lives, and wished them to enjoy the fruit of their own industry. Her religion was not a garb put on

---

1 A joint of pine wood used for fuel.

for Sunday, and laid aside till Sunday returned again. The eldest daughter of the slave mother was promised in marriage to a free man; and the day before the wedding this good mistress emancipated her, in order that her marriage might have the sanction of law.

Report said that this young lady cherished an unrequited affection for a man who had resolved to marry for wealth. In the course of time a rich uncle of hers died. He left six thousand dollars to his two sons by a colored woman, and the remainder of his property to this orphan niece. The metal soon attracted the magnet. The lady and her weighty purse became his. She offered to manumit[1] her slaves—telling them that her marriage might make unexpected changes in their destiny, and she wished to insure their happiness. They refused to take their freedom, saying that she had always been their best friend, and they could not be so happy any where as with her. I was not surprised. I had often seen them in their comfortable home, and thought that the whole town did not contain a happier family. They had never felt slavery; and, when it was too late, they were convinced of its reality.

When the new master claimed this family as his property, the father became furious, and went to his mistress for protection. "I can do nothing for you now, Harry," said she. "I no longer have the power I had a week ago. I have succeeded in obtaining the freedom of your wife; but I cannot obtain it for your children." The unhappy father swore that nobody should take his children from him. He concealed them in the woods for some days; but they were discovered and taken. The father was put in jail, and the two oldest boys sold to Georgia. One little girl, too young to be of service to her master, was left with the wretched mother. The other three were carried to their master's plantation. The eldest soon became a mother; and, when the slaveholder's wife looked at the babe, she wept bitterly. She knew that her own husband had violated the purity she had so carefully inculcated.[2] She had a second child by her master, and then he sold her and his offspring to his brother. She bore two children to the brother, and was sold again. The next sister went crazy. The life she was compelled to lead drove her mad. The third one became the mother of five daughters. Before the birth of the fourth the pious mistress died. To the last, she rendered every kindness to the slaves that her unfortunate circumstances permitted. She passed away

1 To release from bondage.
2 Implanted by consistent, earnest teaching.

peacefully, glad to close her eyes on a life which had been made so wretched by the man she loved.

This man squandered the fortune he had received, and sought to retrieve his affairs by a second marriage; but, having retired after a night of drunken debauch, he was found dead in the morning. He was called a good master; for he fed and clothed his slaves better than most masters, and the lash was not heard on his plantation so frequently as on many others. Had it not been for slavery, he would have been a better man, and his wife a happier woman.

No pen can give an adequate description of the all pervading corruption produced by slavery. The slave girl is reared in an atmosphere of licentiousness[1] and fear. The lash and the foul talk of her master and his sons are her teachers. When she is fourteen or fifteen, her owner, or his sons, or the overseer, or perhaps all of them, begin to bribe her with presents. If these fail to accomplish their purpose, she is whipped or starved into submission to their will. She may have had religious principles inculcated by some pious mother or grandmother, or some good mistress; she may have a lover, whose good opinion and peace of mind are dear to her heart; or the profligate[2] men who have power over her may be exceedingly odious[3] to her. But resistance is hopeless.

> "The poor worm
> Shall prove her contest vain. Life's little day
> Shall pass, and she is gone!"[4]

The slaveholder's sons are, of course, vitiated,[5] even while boys, by the unclean influences every where around them. Nor do the master's daughters always escape. Severe retributions[6] sometimes come upon him for the wrongs he does to the daughters of the slaves. The white daughters early hear their parents quarrelling about some female slave. Their curiosity is excited, and they soon learn the cause. They are attended by the young slave girls whom their father has corrupted; and they hear such talk as should never

---

1 Extreme lack of sexual restraint.
2 Shamelessly immoral.
3 Causing hatred; deserving hatred.
4 *Elfrida, A Dramatic Poem* (1752) by English poet William Mason (1724–97).
5 Debased.
6 Repayments according to merits, especially for evil.

meet youthful ears, or any other ears. They know that the women slaves are subject to their father's authority in all things; and in some cases they exercise the same authority over the men slaves.[1] I have myself seen the master of such a household whose head was bowed down in shame; for it was known in the neighborhood that his daughter had selected one of the meanest slaves on his plantation to be the father of her first grandchild. She did not make her advances to her equals, nor even to her father's more intelligent servants. She selected the most brutalized, over whom her authority could be exercised with less fear of exposure. Her father, half frantic with rage, sought to revenge himself on the offending black man; but his daughter, foreseeing the storm that would arise, had given him free papers, and sent him out of the state.

In such cases the infant is smothered, or sent where it is never seen by any who know its history. But if the white parent is the father, instead of the mother, the offspring are unblushingly reared for the market. If they are girls, I have indicated plainly enough what will be their inevitable destiny.

You may believe what I say; for I write only that whereof I know. I was twenty-one years in that cage of obscene birds. I can testify, from my own experience and observation, that slavery is a curse to the whites as well as to the blacks. It makes the white fathers cruel and sensual; the sons violent and licentious; it contaminates the daughters, and makes the wives wretched.[2] And as for the colored race, it needs an abler pen than mine to describe the extremity of their sufferings, the depth of their degradation.

Yet few slaveholders seem to be aware of the widespread moral ruin occasioned by this wicked system. Their talk is of blighted cotton crops—not of the blight on their children's souls.

If you want to be fully convinced of the abominations of slavery, go on a southern plantation, and call yourself a negro trader. Then there will be no concealment; and you will see and hear things that will seem to you impossible among human beings with immortal souls.

---

1 For more on this issue, see Berry and Harris, *Sexuality and Slavery*, especially the essay by Thomas A. Foster (pp. 124–44).

2 Miserable; pitiable.

CHAPTER X.
A PERILOUS PASSAGE IN THE SLAVE GIRL'S LIFE.

After my lover went away, Dr. Flint contrived a new plan. He seemed to have an idea that my fear of my mistress was his greatest obstacle. In the blandest tones, he told me that he was going to build a small house for me, in a secluded place, four miles away from the town. I shuddered; but I was constrained to listen, while he talked of his intention to give me a home of my own, and to make a lady of me. Hitherto, I had escaped my dreaded fate, by being in the midst of people. My grandmother had already had high words with my master about me. She had told him pretty plainly what she thought of his character, and there was considerable gossip in the neighborhood about our affairs, to which the open-mouthed jealousy of Mrs. Flint contributed not a little. When my master said he was going to build a house for me, and that he could do it with little trouble and expense, I was in hopes something would happen to frustrate his scheme; but I soon heard that the house was actually begun. I vowed before my Maker that I would never enter it. I had rather toil on the plantation from dawn till dark; I had rather live and die in jail, than drag on, from day to day, through such a living death. I was determined that the master, whom I so hated and loathed, who had blighted the prospects of my youth, and made my life a desert, should not, after my long struggle with him, succeed at last in trampling his victim under his feet. I would do any thing, every thing, for the sake of defeating him. What could I do? I thought and thought, till I became desperate, and made a plunge into the abyss.

And now, reader, I come to a period in my unhappy life, which I would gladly forget if I could. The remembrance fills me with sorrow and shame. It pains me to tell you of it; but I have promised to tell you the truth, and I will do it honestly, let it cost me what it may. I will not try to screen myself behind the plea of compulsion from a master; for it was not so. Neither can I plead ignorance or thoughtlessness. For years, my master had done his utmost to pollute my mind with foul images, and to destroy the pure principles inculcated by my grandmother, and the good mistress of my childhood. The influences of slavery had had the same effect on me that they had on other young girls; they had made me prematurely knowing, concerning the evil ways of the world. I knew what I did, and I did it with deliberate calculation.

But, O, ye happy women, whose purity has been sheltered from childhood, who have been free to choose the objects of your affection, whose homes are protected by law, do not judge the poor desolate slave girl too severely! If slavery had been abolished, I, also, could have married the man of my choice; I could have had a home shielded by the laws; and I should have been spared the painful task of confessing what I am now about to relate; but all my prospects had been blighted by slavery. I wanted to keep myself pure; and, under the most adverse circumstances, I tried hard to preserve my self-respect; but I was struggling alone in the powerful grasp of the demon Slavery; and the monster proved too strong for me. I felt as if I was forsaken by God and man; as if all my efforts must be frustrated; and I became reckless in my despair.

I have told you that Dr. Flint's persecutions and his wife's jealousy had given rise to some gossip in the neighborhood. Among others, it chanced that a white unmarried gentleman had obtained some knowledge of the circumstances in which I was placed. He knew my grandmother, and often spoke to me in the street. He became interested for me, and asked questions about my master, which I answered in part. He expressed a great deal of sympathy, and a wish to aid me. He constantly sought opportunities to see me, and wrote to me frequently. I was a poor slave girl, only fifteen years old.

So much attention from a superior person was, of course, flattering; for human nature is the same in all. I also felt grateful for his sympathy, and encouraged by his kind words. It seemed to me a great thing to have such a friend. By degrees, a more tender feeling crept into my heart. He was an educated and eloquent gentleman; too eloquent, alas, for the poor slave girl who trusted in him. Of course I saw whither all this was tending. I knew the impassable gulf between us; but to be an object of interest to a man who is not married, and who is not her master, is agreeable to the pride and feelings of a slave, if her miserable situation has left her any pride or sentiment. It seems less degrading to give one's self, than to submit to compulsion. There is something akin to freedom in having a lover who has no control over you, except that which he gains by kindness and attachment. A master may treat you as rudely as he pleases, and you dare not speak; moreover, the wrong does not seem so great with an unmarried man, as with one who has a wife to be made unhappy. There may be sophistry[1] in all this; but the condition of a slave confuses all principles of morality, and, in fact, renders the practice of them impossible.

---

1 A superficially plausible, but generally faulty method of reasoning.

When I found that my master had actually begun to build the lonely cottage, other feelings mixed with those I have described. Revenge, and calculations of interest, were added to flattered vanity and sincere gratitude for kindness. I knew nothing would enrage Dr. Flint so much as to know that I favored another; and it was something to triumph over my tyrant even in that small way. I thought he would revenge himself by selling me, and I was sure my friend, Mr. Sands, would buy me. He was a man of more generosity and feeling than my master, and I thought my freedom could be easily obtained from him. The crisis of my fate now came so near that I was desperate. I shuddered to think of being the mother of children that should be owned by my old tyrant. I knew that as soon as a new fancy took him, his victims were sold far off to get rid of them; especially if they had children. I had seen several women sold, with his babies at the breast. He never allowed his offspring by slaves to remain long in sight of himself and his wife. Of a man who was not my master I could ask to have my children well supported; and in this case, I felt confident I should obtain the boon.[1] I also felt quite sure that they would be made free. With all these thoughts revolving in my mind, and seeing no other way of escaping the doom I so much dreaded, I made a headlong plunge. Pity me, and pardon me, O virtuous reader! You never knew what it is to be a slave; to be entirely unprotected by law or custom; to have the laws reduce you to the condition of a chattel, entirely subject to the will of another. You never exhausted your ingenuity in avoiding the snares, and eluding the power of a hated tyrant; you never shuddered at the sound of his footsteps, and trembled within hearing of his voice. I know I did wrong. No one can feel it more sensibly than I do. The painful and humiliating memory will haunt me to my dying day. Still, in looking back, calmly, on the events of my life, I feel that the slave woman ought not to be judged by the same standard as others.

The months passed on. I had many unhappy hours. I secretly mourned over the sorrow I was bringing on my grandmother, who had so tried to shield me from harm. I knew that I was the greatest comfort of her old age, and that it was a source of pride to her that I had not degraded myself, like most of the slaves. I wanted to confess to her that I was no longer worthy of her love; but I could not utter the dreaded words.

As for Dr. Flint, I had a feeling of satisfaction and triumph in the thought of telling him. From time to time he told me of his

---

1 Blessing; benefit.

intended arrangements, and I was silent. At last, he came and told me the cottage was completed, and ordered me to go to it. I told him I would never enter it. He said, "I have heard enough of such talk as that. You shall go, if you are carried by force; and you shall remain there."

I replied, "I will never go there. In a few months I shall be a mother."

He stood and looked at me in dumb amazement, and left the house without a word. I thought I should be happy in my triumph over him. But now that the truth was out, and my relatives would hear of it, I felt wretched. Humble as were their circumstances, they had pride in my good character. Now, how could I look them in the face? My self-respect was gone! I had resolved that I would be virtuous, though I was a slave. I had said, "Let the storm beat! I will brave it till I die." And now, how humiliated I felt!

I went to my grandmother. My lips moved to make confession, but the words stuck in my throat. I sat down in the shade of a tree at her door and began to sew. I think she saw something unusual was the matter with me. The mother of slaves is very watchful. She knows there is no security for her children. After they have entered their teens she lives in daily expectation of trouble. This leads to many questions. If the girl is of a sensitive nature, timidity keeps her from answering truthfully, and this well-meant course has a tendency to drive her from maternal counsels. Presently, in came my mistress, like a mad woman, and accused me concerning her husband. My grandmother, whose suspicions had been previously awakened, believed what she said. She exclaimed, "O Linda! has it come to this? I had rather see you dead than to see you as you now are. You are a disgrace to your dead mother." She tore from my fingers my mother's wedding ring and her silver thimble. "Go away!" she exclaimed, "and never come to my house, again." Her reproaches fell so hot and heavy, that they left me no chance to answer. Bitter tears, such as the eyes never shed but once, were my only answer. I rose from my seat, but fell back again, sobbing. She did not speak to me; but the tears were running down her furrowed cheeks, and they scorched me like fire. She had always been so kind to me! So kind! How I longed to throw myself at her feet, and tell her all the truth! But she had ordered me to go, and never to come there again. After a few minutes, I mustered strength, and started to obey her. With what feelings did I now close that little gate, which I used to open with such an eager hand in my childhood! It closed upon me with a sound I never heard before.

Where could I go? I was afraid to return to my master's. I walked on recklessly, not caring where I went, or what would become of me. When I had gone four or five miles, fatigue compelled me to stop. I sat down on the stump of an old tree. The stars were shining through the boughs[1] above me. How they mocked me, with their bright, calm light! The hours passed by, and as I sat there alone a chilliness and deadly sickness came over me. I sank on the ground. My mind was full of horrid thoughts. I prayed to die; but the prayer was not answered. At last, with great effort I roused myself, and walked some distance further, to the house of a woman who had been a friend of my mother. When I told her why I was there, she spoke soothingly to me; but I could not be comforted. I thought I could bear my shame if I could only be reconciled to my grandmother. I longed to open my heart to her. I thought if she could know the real state of the case, and all I had been bearing for years, she would perhaps judge me less harshly. My friend advised me to send for her. I did so; but days of agonizing suspense passed before she came. Had she utterly forsaken me? No. She came at last. I knelt before her, and told her the things that had poisoned my life; how long I had been persecuted; that I saw no way of escape; and in an hour of extremity I had become desperate. She listened in silence. I told her I would bear any thing and do any thing, if in time I had hopes of obtaining her forgiveness. I begged of her to pity me, for my dead mother's sake. And she did pity me. She did not say, "I forgive you;" but she looked at me lovingly, with her eyes full of tears. She laid her old hand gently on my head, and murmured, "Poor child! Poor child!"

CHAPTER XI.
THE NEW TIE TO LIFE.

I returned to my good grandmother's house. She had an interview with Mr. Sands. When she asked him why he could not have left her one ewe lamb,[2]—whether there were not plenty of slaves who did not care about character,—he made no answer; but he spoke kind and encouraging words. He promised to care for my child, and to buy me, be the conditions what they might.

I had not seen Dr. Flint for five days. I had never seen him

---

1 Large or main branches of trees.
2 A young female sheep.

since I made the avowal to him. He talked of the disgrace I had brought on myself; how I had sinned against my master, and mortified my old grandmother. He intimated that if I had accepted his proposals, he, as a physician, could have saved me from exposure. He even condescended to pity me. Could he have offered wormwood more bitter? He, whose persecutions had been the cause of my sin!

"Linda," said he, "though you have been criminal towards me, I feel for you, and I can pardon you if you obey my wishes. Tell me whether the fellow you wanted to marry is the father of your child. If you deceive me, you shall feel the fires of hell."

I did not feel as proud as I had done. My strongest weapon with him was gone. I was lowered in my own estimation, and had resolved to bear his abuse in silence. But when he spoke contemptuously of the lover who had always treated me honorably; when I remembered that but for him I might have been a virtuous, free, and happy wife, I lost my patience. "I have sinned against God and myself," I replied; "but not against you."

He clinched his teeth, and muttered, "Curse you!" He came towards me, with ill-suppressed rage, and exclaimed, "You obstinate girl! I could grind your bones to powder! You have thrown yourself away on some worthless rascal. You are weak-minded, and have been easily persuaded by those who don't care a straw for you. The future will settle accounts between us. You are blinded now; but hereafter you will be convinced that your master was your best friend. My lenity[1] towards you is a proof of it. I might have punished you in many ways. I might have had you whipped till you fell dead under the lash. But I wanted you to live; I would have bettered your condition. Others cannot do it. You are my slave. Your mistress, disgusted by your conduct, forbids you to return to the house; therefore I leave you here for the present; but I shall see you often. I will call tomorrow."

He came with frowning brows, that showed a dissatisfied state of mind. After asking about my health, he inquired whether my board was paid, and who visited me. He then went on to say that he had neglected his duty; that as a physician there were certain things that he ought to have explained to me. Then followed talk such as would have made the most shameless blush. He ordered me to stand up before him. I obeyed. "I command you," said he, "to tell me whether the father of your child is white or black." I hesitated. "Answer me this instant!" he exclaimed. I did answer.

---

1 The quality of being mild or gentle.

He sprang upon me like a wolf, and grabbed my arm as if he would have broken it. "Do you love him?" said he, in a hissing tone.

"I am thankful that I do not despise him," I replied.

He raised his hand to strike me; but it fell again. I don't know what arrested the blow. He sat down, with lips tightly compressed. At last he spoke. "I came here," said he, "to make you a friendly proposition; but your ingratitude chafes me beyond endurance. You turn aside all my good intentions towards you. I don't know what it is that keeps me from killing you." Again he rose, as if he had a mind to strike me.

But he resumed. "On one condition I will forgive your insolence and crime. You must henceforth have no communication of any kind with the father of your child. You must not ask any thing from him, or receive any thing from him. I will take care of you and your child. You had better promise this at once, and not wait till you are deserted by him. This is the last act of mercy I shall show towards you."

I said something about being unwilling to have my child supported by a man who had cursed it and me also. He rejoined, that a woman who had sunk to my level had no right to expect any thing else. He asked, for the last time, would I accept his kindness? I answered that I would not.

"Very well," said he; "then take the consequences of your wayward course. Never look to me for help. You are my slave, and shall always be my slave. I will never sell you, that you may depend upon."

Hope died away in my heart as he closed the door after him. I had calculated that in his rage he would sell me to a slave-trader; and I knew the father of my child was on the watch to buy me.

About this time my uncle Phillip was expected to return from a voyage. The day before his departure I had officiated as bridesmaid to a young friend. My heart was then ill at ease, but my smiling countenance did not betray it. Only a year had passed; but what fearful changes it had wrought! My heart had grown gray in misery. Lives that flash in sunshine, and lives that are born in tears, receive their hue from circumstances. None of us know what a year may bring forth.

I felt no joy when they told me my uncle had come. He wanted to see me, though he knew what had happened. I shrank from him at first; but at last consented that he should come to my room. He received me as he always had done. O, how my heart smote[1]

---

1 Dealt a blow; delivered a pang.

me when I felt his tears on my burning cheeks! The words of my grandmother came to my mind,—"Perhaps your mother and father are taken from the evil days to come." My disappointed heart could now praise God that it was so. But why, thought I, did my relatives ever cherish hopes for me? What was there to save me from the usual fate of slave girls? Many more beautiful and more intelligent than I had experienced a similar fate, or a far worse one. How could they hope that I should escape?

My uncle's stay was short, and I was not sorry for it. I was too ill in mind and body to enjoy my friends as I had done. For some weeks I was unable to leave my bed. I could not have any doctor but my master, and I would not have him sent for. At last, alarmed by my increasing illness, they sent for him. I was very weak and nervous; and as soon as he entered the room, I began to scream. They told him my state was very critical. He had no wish to hasten me out of the world, and he withdrew.

When my babe was born, they said it was premature. It weighed only four pounds; but God let it live. I heard the doctor say I could not survive till morning. I had often prayed for death; but now I did not want to die, unless my child could die too. Many weeks passed before I was able to leave my bed. I was a mere wreck of my former self. For a year there was scarcely a day when I was free from chills and fever. My babe also was sickly. His little limbs were often racked with pain. Dr. Flint continued his visits, to look after my health; and he did not fail to remind me that my child was an addition to his stock of slaves.

I felt too feeble to dispute with him, and listened to his remarks in silence. His visits were less frequent; but his busy spirit could not remain quiet. He employed my brother in his office, and he was made the medium of frequent notes and messages to me. William was a bright lad, and of much use to the doctor. He had learned to put up medicines, to leech, cup, and bleed. He had taught himself to read and spell. I was proud of my brother; and the old doctor suspected as much. One day, when I had not seen him for several weeks, I heard his steps approaching the door. I dreaded the encounter, and hid myself. He inquired for me, of course; but I was nowhere to be found. He went to his office, and dispatched William with a note. The color mounted to my brother's face when he gave it to me; and he said, "Don't you hate me, Linda, for bringing you these things?" I told him I could not blame him; he was a slave, and obliged to obey his master's will. The note ordered me to come to his office. I went. He demanded to know where I was when he called. I told him I was at home. He flew into a passion, and said he knew better. Then he launched out upon his usual themes,—my crimes against him, and my ingratitude for his forbearance. The laws were laid down to me anew, and I was dismissed. I felt humiliated that my brother should stand by, and listen to such language as would be addressed only to a slave. Poor boy! He was powerless to defend me; but I saw the tears, which he vainly strove to keep back. This manifestation of feeling irritated the doctor. William could do nothing to please him. One morning he did not arrive at the office so early as usual; and that circumstance afforded his master an opportunity to vent his spleen.[1] He was put in jail. The next day my brother sent a trader to the doctor, with a request to be sold. His master was greatly incensed at what he called his insolence.[2] He said he had put him there to reflect upon his bad conduct, and he certainly was not giving any evidence of repentance. For two days he harassed himself to find somebody to do his office work; but every thing went wrong without William. He was released, and ordered to take his old stand, with many threats, if he was not careful about his future behavior.

As the months passed on, my boy improved in health. When he was a year old, they called him beautiful. The little vine was taking deep root in my existence, though its clinging fondness excited a mixture of love and pain. When I was most sorely oppressed I found a solace in his smiles. I loved to watch his infant slumbers; but always there was a dark cloud over my enjoyment. I could never forget that he was a slave. Sometimes I wished that he might die in infancy. God tried me. My darling became very ill. The bright eyes grew dull, and the little feet and hands were so icy cold that I thought death had already touched them. I had prayed for his death, but never so earnestly as I now prayed for his life; and my prayer was heard. Alas, what mockery it is for a slave mother to try to pray back her dying child to life! Death is better than slavery. It was a sad thought that I had no name to give my child. His father caressed him and treated him kindly, whenever he had a chance to see him. He was not unwilling that he should bear his name; but he had no legal claim to it; and if I had bestowed it upon him, my master would have regarded it as a new crime, a new piece of insolence, and would, perhaps, revenge it on the boy. O, the serpent of Slavery has many and poisonous fangs!

---

1 Ill humor, irritated temper, or spite.
2 Rude behavior or speech.

CHAPTER XII.
FEAR OF INSURRECTION.

Not far from this time Nat Turner's insurrection[1] broke out; and the news threw our town into great commotion. Strange that they should be alarmed, when their slaves were so "contented and happy"! But so it was.

It was always the custom to have a muster[2] every year. On that occasion every white man shouldered his musket.[3] The citizens and the so-called country gentlemen wore military uniforms. The poor whites took their places in the ranks in every-day dress, some without shoes, some without hats. This grand occasion had already passed; and when the slaves were told there was to be another muster, they were surprised and rejoiced. Poor creatures! They thought it was going to be a holiday. I was informed of the true state of affairs, and imparted it to the few I could trust. Most gladly would I have proclaimed it to every slave; but I dared not. All could not be relied on. Mighty is the power of the torturing lash.

By sunrise, people were pouring in from every quarter within twenty miles of the town. I knew the houses were to be searched; and I expected it would be done by country bullies and the poor whites. I knew nothing annoyed them so much as to see colored people living in comfort and respectability; so I made arrangements for them with especial care. I arranged every thing in my grandmother's house as neatly as possible. I put white quilts on the beds, and decorated some of the rooms with flowers. When

---

1 Nat Turner (1800–31) was an enslaved man and a devout Christian who believed that God inspired him to lead one of the nation's bloodiest and most effective slave rebellions. For two days in August 1831, he and his allies killed dozens of slaveholding whites as they systematically attacked plantations in Southampton County, Virginia. Many African Americans, whether they had joined with Turner or not, were summarily executed, but Turner remained at large for more than two months. Upon his capture in October 1831, he was hanged publicly, and a white lawyer released what he claimed to be a definitive account of the entire ordeal, *The Confessions of Nat Turner*. See Appendix B3. For how Turner stayed at large for so long, see Holden.

2 An assembling of troops or persons for formal inspection or other purposes.

3 A heavy, large-caliber gun, introduced in the 1500s: the predecessor of the modern rifle.

all was arranged, I sat down at the window to watch. Far as my eye could reach, it rested on a motley crowd of soldiers. Drums and fifes were discoursing martial music. The men were divided into companies of sixteen, each headed by a captain. Orders were given, and the wild scouts rushed in every direction, wherever a colored face was to be found.

It was a grand opportunity for the low whites, who had no negroes of their own to scourge. They exulted in such a chance to exercise a little brief authority, and show their subserviency to the slaveholders; not reflecting that the power which trampled on the colored people also kept themselves in poverty, ignorance, and moral degradation. Those who never witnessed such scenes can hardly believe what I know was inflicted at this time on innocent men, women, and children, against whom there was not the slightest ground for suspicion. Colored people and slaves who lived in remote parts of the town suffered in an especial manner. In some cases the searchers scattered powder and shot among their clothes, and then sent other parties to find them, and bring them forward as proof that they were plotting insurrection. Every where men, women, and children were whipped till the blood stood in puddles at their feet. Some received five hundred lashes; others were tied hands and feet, and tortured with a bucking paddle, which blisters the skin terribly. The dwellings of the colored people, unless they happened to be protected by some influential white person, who was nigh at hand, were robbed of clothing and every thing else the marauders thought worth carrying away. All day long these unfeeling wretches went round, like a troop of demons, terrifying and tormenting the helpless. At night, they formed themselves into patrol bands, and went wherever they chose among the colored people, acting out their brutal will. Many women hid themselves in woods and swamps, to keep out of their way. If any of the husbands or fathers told of these outrages, they were tied up to the public whipping post, and cruelly scourged for telling lies about white men. The consternation[1] was universal. No two people that had the slightest tinge of color in their faces dared to be seen talking together.

I entertained no positive fears about our household, because we were in the midst of white families who would protect us. We were ready to receive the soldiers whenever they came. It was not long before we heard the tramp of feet and the sound of voices. The door was rudely pushed open; and in they tumbled, like a

---

1 A sudden, alarming dread resulting in utter confusion.

pack of hungry wolves. They snatched at every thing within their reach. Every box, trunk, closet, and corner underwent a thorough examination. A box in one of the drawers containing some silver change was eagerly pounced upon. When I stepped forward to take it from them, one of the soldiers turned and said angrily, "What d'ye foller us fur? D'ye s'pose white folks is come to steal?"

I replied, "You have come to search; but you have searched that box, and I will take it, if you please."

At that moment I saw a white gentleman who was friendly to us; and I called to him, and asked him to have the goodness to come in and stay till the search was over. He readily complied. His entrance into the house brought in the captain of the company, whose business it was to guard the outside of the house, and see that none of the inmates left it. This officer was Mr. Litch, the wealthy slaveholder whom I mentioned, in the account of neighboring planters, as being notorious for his cruelty. He felt above soiling his hands with the search. He merely gave orders; and, if a bit of writing was discovered, it was carried to him by his ignorant followers, who were unable to read.

My grandmother had a large trunk of bedding and table cloths. When that was opened, there was a great shout of surprise; and one exclaimed, "Where'd the damned niggers git all dis sheet an' table clarf?"

My grandmother, emboldened by the presence of our white protector, said, "You may be sure we didn't pilfer 'em from your houses."

"Look here, mammy," said a grim-looking fellow without any coat, "you seem to feel mighty gran' 'cause you got all them 'ere fixens. White folks oughter have 'em all."

His remarks were interrupted by a chorus of voices shouting, "We's got 'em! We's got 'em! Dis 'ere yaller gal's got letters!"

There was a general rush for the supposed letter, which, upon examination, proved to be some verses written to me by a friend. In packing away my things, I had overlooked them. When their captain informed them of their contents, they seemed much disappointed. He inquired of me who wrote them.

I told him it was one of my friends. "Can you read them?" he asked. When I told him I could, he swore, and raved, and tore the paper into bits. "Bring me all your letters!" said he, in a commanding tone. I told him I had none. "Don't be afraid," he continued, in an insinuating way. "Bring them all to me. Nobody shall do you any harm." Seeing I did not move to obey him, his pleasant tone changed to oaths and threats. "Who writes to you? half free niggers?" inquired he. I replied, "O, no; most of my letters are from white people. Some request me to burn them after they are read, and some I destroy without reading."

An exclamation of surprise from some of the company put a stop to our conversation. Some silver spoons which ornamented an old-fashioned buffet had just been discovered. My grandmother was in the habit of preserving fruit for many ladies in the town, and of preparing suppers for parties; consequently she had many jars of preserves. The closet that contained these was next invaded, and the contents tasted. One of them, who was helping himself freely, tapped his neighbor on the shoulder, and said, "Wal done! Don't wonder de niggers want to kill all de white folks, when dey live on 'sarves" [meaning preserves].[1] I stretched out my hand to take the jar, saying, "You were not sent here to search for sweetmeats."

"And what were we sent for?" said the captain, bristling up to me. I evaded the question.

The search of the house was completed, and nothing found to condemn us. They next proceeded to the garden, and knocked about every bush and vine, with no better success. The captain called his men together, and, after a short consultation, the order to march was given. As they passed out of the gate, the captain turned back, and pronounced a malediction on the house. He said it ought to be burned to the ground, and each of its inmates receive thirty nine lashes. We came out of this affair very fortunately; not losing any thing except some wearing apparel.

Towards evening the turbulence increased. The soldiers, stimulated by drink, committed still greater cruelties. Shrieks and shouts continually rent the air. Not daring to go to the door, I

---

1 Jacobs's brackets. Jacobs "translates" the uneducated man's speech to call attention to how ignorant elite white Southerners keep the poor white people in their midst. If poor white citizens were less invested in denigrating Black people, they might work to make conditions better for more of the population. Jacobs's understanding of the class dynamics used to reinforce racism was not uncommon among African Americans. To this day, some US citizens love to insist that Black people obsess about race and don't understand class, but that has never been the case. Indeed, African Americans' class analysis gave birth to public education in the South. As historian Heather Andrea Williams has shown, elite white Southerners educated their children privately, so poor and middle-class white people didn't have access to education until African Americans created public options.

peeped under the window curtain. I saw a mob dragging along a number of colored people, each white man, with his musket upraised, threatening instant death if they did not stop their shrieks. Among the prisoners was a respectable old colored minister. They had found a few parcels of shot in his house, which his wife had for years used to balance her scales. For this they were going to shoot him on Court House Green. What a spectacle was that for a civilized country! A rabble, staggering under intoxication, assuming to be the administrators of justice!

The better class of the community exerted their influence to save the innocent, persecuted people; and in several instances they succeeded, by keeping them shut up in jail till the excitement abated. At last the white citizens found that their own property was not safe from the lawless rabble they had summoned to protect them. They rallied the drunken swarm, drove them back into the country, and set a guard over the town.

The next day, the town patrols were commissioned to search colored people that lived out of the city; and the most shocking outrages were committed with perfect impunity.[1] Every day for a fortnight, if I looked out, I saw horsemen with some poor panting negro tied to their saddles, and compelled by the lash to keep up with their speed, till they arrived at the jail yard. Those who had been whipped too unmercifully to walk were washed with brine, tossed into a cart, and carried to jail. One black man, who had not fortitude to endure scourging, promised to give information about the conspiracy. But it turned out that he knew nothing at all. He had not even heard the name of Nat Turner. The poor fellow had, however, made up a story, which augmented his own sufferings and those of the colored people.

The day patrol continued for some weeks, and at sundown a night guard was substituted. Nothing at all was proved against the colored people, bond or free. The wrath of the slaveholders was somewhat appeased by the capture of Nat Turner. The imprisoned were released. The slaves were sent to their masters, and the free were permitted to return to their ravaged homes. Visiting was strictly forbidden on the plantations. The slaves begged the privilege of again meeting at their little church in the woods, with their burying ground around it. It was built by the colored people, and they had no higher happiness than to meet there and sing hymns together, and pour out their hearts in spontaneous prayer. Their request was denied, and the church was demolished. They

---

1 Exemption from punishment.

were permitted to attend the white churches, a certain portion of the galleries being appropriated to their use. There, when every body else had partaken of the communion, and the benediction had been pronounced, the minister said, "Come down, now, my colored friends." They obeyed the summons, and partook of the bread and wine, in commemoration of the meek and lowly Jesus, who said, "God is your Father, and all ye are brethren."

CHAPTER XIII.
THE CHURCH AND SLAVERY.

After the alarm caused by Nat Turner's insurrection had subsided, the slaveholders came to the conclusion that it would be well to give the slaves enough of religious instruction to keep them from murdering their masters. The Episcopal clergyman offered to hold a separate service on Sundays for their benefit. His colored members were very few, and also very respectable—a fact which I presume had some weight with him. The difficulty was to decide on a suitable place for them to worship. The Methodist and Baptist churches admitted them in the afternoon; but their carpets and cushions were not so costly as those at the Episcopal church. It was at last decided that they should meet at the house of a free colored man, who was a member.

I was invited to attend, because I could read. Sunday evening came, and, trusting to the cover of night, I ventured out. I rarely ventured out by daylight, for I always went with fear, expecting at every turn to encounter Dr. Flint, who was sure to turn me back, or order me to his office to inquire where I got my bonnet, or some other article of dress. When the Rev. Mr. Pike came, there were some twenty persons present. The reverend gentleman knelt in prayer, then seated himself, and requested all present, who could read, to open their books, while he gave out the portions he wished them to repeat or respond to.

His text was, "Servants, be obedient to them that are your masters according to the flesh, with fear and trembling, in singleness of your heart, as unto Christ."

Pious Mr. Pike brushed up his hair till it stood upright, and, in deep, solemn tones, began: "Hearken, ye servants! Give strict heed unto my words. You are rebellious sinners. Your hearts are filled with all manner of evil. 'Tis the devil who tempts you. God is angry with you, and will surely punish you, if you don't forsake your wicked ways. You that live in town are eye-servants behind your master's back. Instead of serving your masters faithfully, which is pleasing in the sight of your heavenly Master, you are idle, and shirk your work. God sees you. You tell lies. God hears you. Instead of being engaged in worshipping him, you are hidden away somewhere, feasting on your master's substance; tossing coffee-grounds with some wicked fortuneteller, or cutting cards with another old hag. Your masters may not find you out, but God sees you, and will punish you. O, the depravity of your hearts! When your master's work is done, are you quietly together, thinking of the goodness of God to such sinful creatures? No; you are quarrelling, and tying up little bags of roots to bury under the door-steps to poison each other with. God sees you. You men steal away to every grog shop[1] to sell your master's corn, that you may buy rum to drink. God sees you. You sneak into the back streets, or among the bushes, to pitch coppers.[2] Although your masters may not find you out, God sees you; and he will punish you. You must forsake your sinful ways, and be faithful servants. Obey your old master and your young master—your old mistress and your young mistress. If you disobey your earthly master, you offend your heavenly Master. You must obey God's commandments. When you go from here, don't stop at the corners of the streets to talk, but go directly home, and let your master and mistress see that you have come."

The benediction was pronounced. We went home, highly amused at brother Pike's gospel teaching, and we determined to hear him again. I went the next Sabbath evening, and heard pretty much a repetition of the last discourse. At the close of the meeting, Mr. Pike informed us that he found it very inconvenient to meet at the friend's house, and he should be glad to see us, every Sunday evening, at his own kitchen.

I went home with the feeling that I had heard the Reverend Mr. Pike for the last time. Some of his members repaired to his house, and found that the kitchen sported two tallow candles;[3] the first time, I am sure, since its present occupant owned it, for the servants never had any thing but pine knots. It was so long before the reverend gentleman descended from his comfortable parlor that the slaves left, and went to enjoy a Methodist shout. They never seem so happy as when shouting and singing at religious meetings. Many of them are sincere, and nearer to the gate of heaven than sanctimonious Mr. Pike, and other long faced

---

1 Barroom or saloon, especially a cheap one.
2 To gamble.
3 Candles made from an animal's fatty tissue.

Christians, who see wounded Samaritans,[1] and pass by on the other side.

The slaves generally compose their own songs and hymns; and they do not trouble their heads much about the measure. They often sing the following verses:

> "Old Satan is one busy ole man;
> He rolls dem blocks all in my way;
> But Jesus is my bosom friend;
> He rolls dem blocks away.

> "If I had died when I was young,
> Den how my stam'ring tongue would have sung;
> But I am ole, and now I stand
> A narrow chance for to tread dat heavenly land."

I well remember one occasion when I attended a Methodist class meeting. I went with a burdened spirit, and happened to sit next a poor, bereaved mother, whose heart was still heavier than mine. The class leader was the town constable—a man who bought and sold slaves, who whipped his brethren and sisters of the church at the public whipping post, in jail or out of jail. He was ready to perform that Christian office any where for fifty cents. This white-faced, black-hearted brother came near us, and said to the stricken woman, "Sister, can't you tell us how the Lord deals with your soul? Do you love him as you did formerly?"

She rose to her feet, and said, in piteous tones, "My Lord and Master, help me! My load is more than I can bear. God has hid himself from me, and I am left in darkness and misery." Then, striking her breast, she continued, "I can't tell you what is in here! They've got all my children. Last week they took the last one. God only knows where they've sold her. They let me have her sixteen years, and then—O! O! Pray for her brothers and sisters! I've got nothing to live for now. God make my time short!"

She sat down, quivering in every limb. I saw that constable class leader become crimson in the face with suppressed laughter,

---

1 Referring to biblical scripture, Luke 10.25–37, when Jesus offers what has come to be known as the parable of the Good Samaritan. Jacobs is playing on the story, though, because the Samaritan isn't wounded himself; he helps the wounded. It is therefore worth considering the dynamism of Jacobs's critique of the white Christians whom she has observed.

while he held up his handkerchief, that those who were weeping for the poor woman's calamity might not see his merriment. Then, with assumed gravity, he said to the bereaved mother, "Sister, pray to the Lord that every dispensation[1] of his divine will may be sanctified to the good of your poor needy soul!"

The congregation struck up a hymn, and sung as though they were as free as the birds that warbled[2] round us,—

> "Ole Satan thought he had a mighty aim;
> He missed my soul, and caught my sins.
> Cry Amen, cry Amen, cry Amen to God!

> "He took my sins upon his back;
> Went muttering and grumbling down to hell.
> Cry Amen, cry Amen, cry Amen to God!

> "Ole Satan's church is here below.
> Up to God's free church I hope to go.
> Cry Amen, cry Amen, cry Amen to God!"

Precious are such moments to the poor slaves. If you were to hear them at such times, you might think they were happy. But can that hour of singing and shouting sustain them through the dreary week, toiling without wages, under constant dread of the lash?

The Episcopal clergyman, who, ever since my earliest recollection, had been a sort of god among the slaveholders, concluded, as his family was large, that he must go where money was more abundant. A very different clergyman took his place. The change was very agreeable to the colored people, who said, "God has sent us a good man this time." They loved him, and their children followed him for a smile or a kind word. Even the slaveholders felt his influence. He brought to the rectory[3] five slaves. His wife taught them to read and write, and to be useful to her and themselves. As soon as he was settled, he turned his attention to the needy slaves around him. He urged upon his parishioners the duty of having a meeting expressly for them every Sunday, with a sermon adapted to their comprehension. After much argument and importunity,[4] it was finally agreed that they might occupy the gallery of the

---

1 Something given out.
2 Sang with melodic embellishments.
3 The clergyman's house.
4 Persistence in requests or demands.

church on Sunday evenings. Many colored people, hitherto unaccustomed to attend church, now gladly went to hear the gospel preached. The sermons were simple, and they understood them. Moreover, it was the first time they had ever been addressed as human beings. It was not long before his white parishioners began to be dissatisfied. He was accused of preaching better sermons to the negroes than he did to them. He honestly confessed that he bestowed more pains upon those sermons than upon any others; for the slaves were reared in such ignorance that it was a difficult task to adapt himself to their comprehension. Dissensions arose in the parish. Some wanted he should preach to them in the evening, and to the slaves in the afternoon. In the midst of these disputings his wife died, after a very short illness. Her slaves gathered round her dying bed in great sorrow. She said, "I have tried to do you good and promote your happiness; and if I have failed, it has not been for want of interest in your welfare. Do not weep for me; but prepare for the new duties that lie before you. I leave you all free. May we meet in a better world." Her liberated slaves were sent away, with funds to establish them comfortably. The colored people will long bless the memory of that truly Christian woman. Soon after her death her husband preached his farewell sermon, and many tears were shed at his departure.

Several years after, he passed through our town and preached to his former congregation. In his afternoon sermon he addressed the colored people. "My friends," said he, "it affords me great happiness to have an opportunity of speaking to you again. For two years I have been striving to do something for the colored people of my own parish; but nothing is yet accomplished. I have not even preached a sermon to them. Try to live according to the word of God, my friends. Your skin is darker than mine; but God judges men by their hearts, not by the color of their skins." This was strange doctrine from a southern pulpit. It was very offensive to slaveholders. They said he and his wife had made fools of their slaves, and that he preached like a fool to the negroes.

I knew an old black man, whose piety and child-like trust in God were beautiful to witness. At fifty-three years old he joined the Baptist church. He had a most earnest desire to learn to read. He thought he should know how to serve God better if he could only read the Bible. He came to me, and begged me to teach him. He said he could not pay me, for he had no money; but he would bring me nice fruit when the season for it came. I asked him if he didn't know it was contrary to law; and that slaves were whipped and imprisoned for teaching each other to read. This brought the tears into his eyes. "Don't be troubled, uncle Fred," said I. "I have no thoughts of refusing to teach you. I only told you of the law, that you might know the danger, and be on your guard." He thought he could plan to come three times a week without its being suspected. I selected a quiet nook, where no intruder was likely to penetrate, and there I taught him his A, B, C. Considering his age, his progress was astonishing. As soon as he could spell in two syllables he wanted to spell out words in the Bible. The happy smile that illuminated his face put joy into my heart. After spelling out a few words, he paused, and said, "Honey, it 'pears when I can read dis good book I shall be nearer to God. White man is got all de sense. He can larn easy. It ain't easy for ole black man like me. I only wants to read dis book, dat I may know how to live; den I hab no fear 'bout dying."

I tried to encourage him by speaking of the rapid progress he had made. "Hab patience, child," he replied. "I learns slow."

I had no need of patience. His gratitude, and the happiness I imparted, were more than a recompense for all my trouble.

At the end of six months he had read through the New Testament, and could find any text in it. One day, when he had recited unusually well, I said,

"Uncle Fred, how do you manage to get your lessons so well?"

"Lord bress you, chile," he replied. "You nebber gibs me a lesson dat I don't pray to God to help me to understan' what I spells and what I reads. And he does help me, chile. Bress his holy name!"

There are thousands, who, like good uncle Fred, are thirsting for the water of life; but the law forbids it, and the churches withhold it. They send the Bible to heathen abroad, and neglect the heathen at home. I am glad that missionaries go out to the dark corners of the earth; but I ask them not to overlook the dark corners at home. Talk to American slaveholders as you talk to savages in Africa. Tell them it is wrong to traffic in men. Tell them it is sinful to sell their own children, and atrocious to violate their own daughters. Tell them that all men are brethren, and that man has no right to shut out the light of knowledge from his brother. Tell them they are answerable to God for sealing up the Fountain of Life from souls that are thirsting for it.

There are men who would gladly undertake such missionary work as this; but, alas! their number is small. They are hated by the south, and would be driven from its soil, or dragged to prison to die, as others have been before them. The field is ripe for the harvest, and awaits the reapers. Perhaps the great grandchildren of uncle Fred may have freely imparted to them the divine treasures, which he sought by stealth, at the risk of the prison and the scourge.

Are doctors of divinity blind, or are they hypocrites?

I suppose some are the one, and some the other; but I think if they felt the interest in the poor and the lowly, that they ought to feel, they would not be so easily blinded. A clergyman who goes to the south, for the first time, has usually some feeling, however vague, that slavery is wrong. The slaveholder suspects this, and plays his game accordingly. He makes himself as agreeable as possible; talks on theology, and other kindred topics. The reverend gentleman is asked to invoke a blessing on a table loaded with luxuries. After dinner he walks round the premises, and sees the beautiful groves and flowering vines, and the comfortable huts of favored household slaves. The southerner invites him to talk with these slaves. He asks them if they want to be free, and they say, "O, no, massa." This is sufficient to satisfy him. He comes home to publish a "South-Side View of Slavery,"[1] and to complain of the exaggerations of abolitionists. He assures people that he has been to the south, and seen slavery for himself; that it is a beautiful "patriarchal institution;" that the slaves don't want their freedom; that they have hallelujah meetings, and other religious privileges.

What does he know of the half-starved wretches toiling from dawn till dark on the plantations? of mothers shrieking for their children, torn from their arms by slave traders? of young girls dragged down into moral filth? of pools of blood around the whipping post? of hounds trained to tear human flesh? of men screwed into cotton gins to die? The slaveholder showed him none of these things, and the slaves dared not tell of them if he had asked them.

There is a great difference between Christianity and religion at the south. If a man goes to the communion table, and pays money into the treasury of the church, no matter if it be the price of blood, he is called religious. If a pastor has offspring by a woman not his wife, the church dismiss him, if she is a white woman; but if she is colored, it does not hinder his continuing to be their good shepherd.

When I was told that Dr. Flint had joined the Episcopal church, I was much surprised. I supposed that religion had a purifying effect on the character of men; but the worst persecutions I endured from him were after he was a communicant.[2] The

---

1 Published in 1854 by Boston minister Nehemiah Adams (1806–78). He is also referenced in Appendix C5.

2 A person entitled to partake in church rituals; a member of the church.

conversation of the doctor, the day after he had been confirmed, certainly gave me no indication that he had "renounced the devil and all his works."[1] In answer to some of his usual talk, I reminded him that he had just joined the church. "Yes, Linda," said he. "It was proper for me to do so. I am getting in years, and my position in society requires it, and it puts an end to all the damned slang. You would do well to join the church, too, Linda."

"There are sinners enough in it already," rejoined I. "If I could be allowed to live like a Christian, I should be glad."

"You can do what I require; and if you are faithful to me, you will be as virtuous as my wife," he replied.

I answered that the Bible didn't say so.

His voice became hoarse with rage. "How dare you preach to me about your infernal Bible!" he exclaimed. "What right have you, who are my negro, to talk to me about what you would like, and what you wouldn't like? I am your master, and you shall obey me."

No wonder the slaves sing,—

"Ole Satan's church is here below;
Up to God's free church I hope to go."

CHAPTER XIV.
ANOTHER LINK TO LIFE.

I had not returned to my master's house since the birth of my child. The old man raved to have me thus removed from his immediate power; but his wife vowed, by all that was good and great, she would kill me if I came back; and he did not doubt her word. Sometimes he would stay away for a season. Then he would come and renew the old threadbare discourse about his forbearance and my ingratitude. He labored, most unnecessarily, to convince me that I had lowered myself. The venomous old reprobate had no need of descanting[2] on that theme. I felt humiliated enough. My unconscious babe was the ever-present witness of my shame. I listened with silent contempt when he talked about my having forfeited his good opinion; but I shed bitter tears that I was no longer worthy of being respected by the good and pure. Alas!

---

1 The renunciation of the devil and all his works is required of one who wishes baptism in the Christian church.

2 Commenting at length.

slavery still held me in its poisonous grasp. There was no chance for me to be respectable. There was no prospect of being able to lead a better life.

Sometimes, when my master found that I still refused to accept what he called his kind offers, he would threaten to sell my child. "Perhaps that will humble you," said he.

Humble me! Was I not already in the dust? But his threat lacerated my heart. I knew the law gave him power to fulfil it; for slaveholders have been cunning enough to enact that "the child shall follow the condition of the mother,"[1] not of the father; thus taking care that licentiousness shall not interfere with avarice. This reflection made me clasp my innocent babe all the more firmly to my heart. Horrid visions passed through my mind when I thought of his liability to fall into the slave trader's hands. I wept over him, and said, "O my child! perhaps they will leave you in some cold cabin to die, and then throw you into a hole, as if you were a dog."

When Dr. Flint learned that I was again to be a mother, he was exasperated beyond measure. He rushed from the house, and returned with a pair of shears. I had a fine head of hair; and he often railed about my pride of arranging it nicely. He cut every hair close to my head, storming and swearing all the time. I replied to some of his abuse, and he struck me. Some months before, he had pitched me down stairs in a fit of passion; and the injury I received was so serious that I was unable to turn myself in bed for many days. He then said, "Linda, I swear by God I will never raise my hand against you again;" but I knew that he would forget his promise.

After he discovered my situation, he was like a restless spirit from the pit. He came every day; and I was subjected to such insults as no pen can describe. I would not describe them if I could; they were too low, too revolting. I tried to keep them from my grandmother's knowledge as much as I could. I knew she had enough to sadden her life, without having my troubles to bear. When she saw the doctor treat me with violence, and heard him utter oaths terrible enough to palsy a man's tongue, she could not always hold her peace. It was natural and motherlike that she should try to defend me; but it only made matters worse.

When they told me my new-born babe was a girl, my heart was heavier than it had ever been before. Slavery is terrible for men;

---

1 One of countless ways in which Jacobs demonstrates her understanding of how US law articulates and enforces the preferred fictions of powerful people. See Appendix B1.

but it is far more terrible for women. Superadded to the burden common to all, they have wrongs, and sufferings, and mortifications peculiarly their own.

Dr. Flint had sworn that he would make me suffer, to my last day, for this new crime against him, as he called it; and as long as he had me in his power he kept his word. On the fourth day after the birth of my babe, he entered my room suddenly, and commanded me to rise and bring my baby to him. The nurse who took care of me had gone out of the room to prepare some nourishment, and I was alone. There was no alternative. I rose, took up my babe, and crossed the room to where he sat. "Now stand there," said he, "till I tell you to go back!" My child bore a strong resemblance to her father, and to the deceased Mrs. Sands, her grandmother. He noticed this; and while I stood before him, trembling with weakness, he heaped upon me and my little one every vile epithet he could think of. Even the grandmother in her grave did not escape his curses. In the midst of his vituperations[1] I fainted at his feet. This recalled him to his senses. He took the baby from my arms, laid it on the bed, dashed cold water in my face, took me up, and shook me violently, to restore my consciousness before any one entered the room. Just then my grandmother came in, and he hurried out of the house. I suffered in consequence of this treatment; but I begged my friends to let me die, rather than send for the doctor. There was nothing I dreaded so much as his presence. My life was spared; and I was glad for the sake of my little ones. Had it not been for these ties to life, I should have been glad to be released by death, though I had lived only nineteen years.

Always it gave me a pang that my children had no lawful claim to a name. Their father offered his; but, if I had wished to accept the offer, I dared not while my master lived. Moreover, I knew it would not be accepted at their baptism. A Christian name they were at least entitled to; and we resolved to call my boy for our dear good Benjamin, who had gone far away from us.

My grandmother belonged to the church; and she was very desirous of having the children christened. I knew Dr. Flint would forbid it, and I did not venture to attempt it. But chance favored me. He was called to visit a patient out of town, and was obliged to be absent during Sunday. "Now is the time," said my grandmother; "we will take the children to church, and have them christened."

---

1 Violent denunciations and condemnations.

When I entered the church, recollections of my mother came over me, and I felt subdued in spirit. There she had presented me for baptism, without any reason to feel ashamed. She had been married, and had such legal rights as slavery allows to a slave. The vows had at least been sacred to her, and she had never violated them.[1] I was glad she was not alive, to know under what different circumstances her grandchildren were presented for baptism. Why had my lot been so different from my mother's? Her master had died when she was a child; and she remained with her mistress till she married. She was never in the power of any master; and thus she escaped one class of the evils that generally fall upon slaves.

When my baby was about to be christened, the former mistress of my father stepped up to me, and proposed to give it her Christian name. To this I added the surname of my father, who had himself no legal right to it; for my grandfather on the paternal side was a white gentleman. What tangled skeins are the genealogies of slavery! I loved my father; but it mortified me to be obliged to bestow his name on my children.

When we left the church, my father's old mistress invited me to go home with her. She clasped a gold chain round my baby's neck. I thanked her for this kindness; but I did not like the emblem. I wanted no chain to be fastened on my daughter, not even if its links were of gold. How earnestly I prayed that she might never feel the weight of slavery's chain, whose iron entereth into the soul!

CHAPTER XV.
CONTINUED PERSECUTIONS.

My children grew finely; and Dr. Flint would often say to me, with an exulting smile, "These brats will bring me a handsome sum of money one of these days."

I thought to myself that, God being my helper, they should never pass into his hands. It seemed to me I would rather see them killed than have them given up to his power. The money for the freedom of myself and my children could be obtained; but I derived no advantage from that circumstance. Dr. Flint loved money, but he

---

1 Jacobs consistently calls attention to how the nation's disregard did not stop African Americans from operating based on their own beliefs and emotional ties. For more, see Hunter. On how oppressed groups can preserve values and standards that differ from what dominant culture tries to impose, see Berry; Mitchell.

loved power more. After much discussion, my friends resolved on making another trial. There was a slaveholder about to leave for Texas, and he was commissioned to buy me. He was to begin with nine hundred dollars, and go up to twelve. My master refused his offers. "Sir," said he, "she don't belong to me. She is my daughter's property, and I have no right to sell her. I mistrust that you come from her paramour.[1] If so, you may tell him that he cannot buy her for any money; neither can he buy her children."

The doctor came to see me the next day, and my heart beat quicker as he entered. I never had seen the old man tread with so majestic a step. He seated himself and looked at me with withering scorn. My children had learned to be afraid of him. The little one would shut her eyes and hide her face on my shoulder whenever she saw him; and Benny, who was now nearly five years old, often inquired, "What makes that bad man come here so many times? Does he want to hurt us?" I would clasp the dear boy in my arms, trusting that he would be free before he was old enough to solve the problem. And now, as the doctor sat there so grim and silent, the child left his play and came and nestled up by me. At last my tormentor spoke. "So you are left in disgust, are you?" said he. "It is no more than I expected. You remember I told you years ago that you would be treated so. So he is tired of you? Ha! ha! ha! The virtuous madam don't like to hear about it, does she? Ha! ha! ha!" There was a sting in his calling me virtuous madam. I no longer had the power of answering him as I had formerly done. He continued: "So it seems you are trying to get up another intrigue.[2] Your new paramour came to me, and offered to buy you; but you may be assured you will not succeed. You are mine; and you shall be mine for life. There lives no human being that can take you out of slavery. I would have done it; but you rejected my kind offer."

I told him I did not wish to get up any intrigue; that I had never seen the man who offered to buy me.

"Do you tell me I lie?" exclaimed he, dragging me from my chair. "Will you say again that you never saw that man?"

I answered, "I do say so."

He clinched my arm with a volley of oaths. Ben began to scream, and I told him to go to his grandmother.

"Don't you stir a step, you little wretch!"[3] said he. The child

---

1 Unlawful or unauthorized lover.
2 The use of deceitful strategies.
3 A person of despicable character. (Notice that a doctor in his fifties is basically cursing a child. The levels of abuse are unending.)

drew nearer to me, and put his arms round me, as if he wanted to protect me. This was too much for my enraged master. He caught him up and hurled him across the room. I thought he was dead, and rushed towards him to take him up.

"Not yet!" exclaimed the doctor. "Let him lie there till he comes to."

"Let me go! Let me go!" I screamed, "or I will raise the whole house." I struggled and got away; but he clinched me again. Somebody opened the door, and he released me. I picked up my insensible child, and when I turned my tormentor was gone. Anxiously I bent over the little form, so pale and still; and when the brown eyes at last opened, I don't know whether I was very happy.

All the doctor's former persecutions were renewed. He came morning, noon, and night. No jealous lover ever watched a rival more closely than he watched me and the unknown slaveholder, with whom he accused me of wishing to get up an intrigue. When my grandmother was out of the way he searched every room to find him.

In one of his visits, he happened to find a young girl, whom he had sold to a trader a few days previous. His statement was, that he sold her because she had been too familiar with the over-seer. She had had a bitter life with him, and was glad to be sold. She had no mother, and no near ties. She had been torn from all her family years before. A few friends had entered into bonds for her safety, if the trader would allow her to spend with them the time that intervened between her sale and the gathering up of his human stock. Such a favor was rarely granted. It saved the trader the expense of board and jail fees, and though the amount was small, it was a weighty consideration in a slave-trader's mind.

Dr. Flint always had an aversion to meeting slaves after he had sold them. He ordered Rose out of the house; but he was no longer her master, and she took no notice of him. For once the crushed Rose was the conqueror. His gray eyes flashed angrily upon her; but that was the extent of his power. "How came this girl here?" he exclaimed. "What right had you to allow it, when you knew I had sold her?"

I answered, "This is my grandmother's house, and Rose came to see her. I have no right to turn any body out of doors, that comes here for honest purposes."

He gave me the blow that would have fallen upon Rose if she had still been his slave. My grandmother's attention had been attracted by loud voices, and she entered in time to see a second blow dealt. She was not a woman to let such an outrage, in her own house, go unrebuked. The doctor undertook to explain that I had been insolent. Her indignant feelings rose higher and higher, and finally boiled over in words. "Get out of my house!" she exclaimed. "Go home, and take care of your wife and children, and you will have enough to do, without watching my family."

He threw the birth of my children in her face, and accused her of sanctioning the life I was leading. She told him I was living with her by compulsion of his wife; that he needn't accuse her, for he was the one to blame; he was the one who had caused all the trouble. She grew more and more excited as she went on. "I tell you what, Dr. Flint," said she, "you ain't got many more years to live, and you'd better be saying your prayers. It will take 'em all, and more too, to wash the dirt off your soul."

"Do you know whom you are talking to?" he exclaimed.

She replied, "Yes, I know very well who I am talking to."

He left the house in a great rage. I looked at my grandmother. Our eyes met. Their angry expression had passed away, but she looked sorrowful and weary—weary of incessant strife. I wondered that it did not lessen her love for me; but if it did she never showed it. She was always kind, always ready to sympathize with my troubles. There might have been peace and contentment in that humble home if it had not been for the demon Slavery.

The winter passed undisturbed by the doctor. The beautiful spring came; and when Nature resumes her loveliness, the human soul is apt to revive also. My drooping hopes came to life again with the flowers. I was dreaming of freedom again; more for my children's sake than my own. I planned and I planned. Obstacles hit against plans. There seemed no way of overcoming them; and yet I hoped.

Back came the wily[1] doctor. I was not at home when he called. A friend had invited me to a small party, and to gratify her I went. To my great consternation, a messenger came in haste to say that Dr. Flint was at my grandmother's, and insisted on seeing me. They did not tell him where I was, or he would have come and raised a disturbance in my friend's house. They sent me a dark wrapper; I threw it on and hurried home. My speed did not save me; the doctor had gone away in anger. I dreaded the morning, but I could not delay it; it came, warm and bright. At an early hour the doctor came and asked me where I had been last night. I told him. He did not believe me, and sent to my friend's house to

1 Cunning; crafty.

ascertain the facts. He came in the afternoon to assure me he was satisfied that I had spoken the truth. He seemed to be in a facetious[1] mood, and I expected some jeers were coming. "I suppose you need some recreation," said he, "but I am surprised at your being there, among those negroes. It was not the place for you. Are you allowed to visit such people?"

I understood this covert fling at the white gentleman who was my friend; but I merely replied, "I went to visit my friends, and any company they keep is good enough for me."

He went on to say, "I have seen very little of you of late, but my interest in you is unchanged. When I said I would have no more mercy on you I was rash. I recall my words. Linda, you desire freedom for yourself and your children, and you can obtain it only through me. If you agree to what I am about to propose, you and they shall be free. There must be no communication of any kind between you and their father. I will procure a cottage, where you and the children can live together. Your labor shall be light, such as sewing for my family. Think what is offered you, Linda—a home and freedom! Let the past be forgotten. If I have been harsh with you at times, your willfulness drove me to it. You know I exact obedience from my own children, and I consider you as yet a child."

He paused for an answer, but I remained silent.

"Why don't you speak?" said he. "What more do you wait for?"

"Nothing, sir."

"Then you accept my offer?"

"No, sir."

His anger was ready to break loose; but he succeeded in curbing it, and replied, "You have answered without thought. But I must let you know there are two sides to my proposition; if you reject the bright side, you will be obliged to take the dark one. You must either accept my offer, or you and your children shall be sent to your young master's plantation, there to remain till your young mistress is married; and your children shall fare like the rest of the negro children. I give you a week to consider of it."

He was shrewd; but I knew he was not to be trusted. I told him I was ready to give my answer now.

"I will not receive it now," he replied. "You act too much from impulse. Remember that you and your children can be free a week from to-day if you choose."

On what a monstrous chance hung the destiny of my children! I knew that my master's offer was a snare, and that if I entered it

---

1 Humorous, especially in an inappropriate way.

escape would be impossible. As for his promise, I knew him so well that I was sure if he gave me free papers, they would be so managed as to have no legal value. The alternative was inevitable. I resolved to go to the plantation. But then I thought how completely I should be in his power, and the prospect was appalling. Even if I should kneel before him, and implore him to spare me, for the sake of my children, I knew he would spurn[1] me with his foot, and my weakness would be his triumph.

Before the week expired, I heard that young Mr. Flint was about to be married to a lady of his own stamp. I foresaw the position I should occupy in his establishment. I had once been sent to the plantation for punishment, and fear of the son had induced the father to recall me very soon. My mind was made up; I was resolved that I would foil my master and save my children, or I would perish in the attempt. I kept my plans to myself; I knew that friends would try to dissuade me from them, and I would not wound their feelings by rejecting their advice.

On the decisive day the doctor came, and said he hoped I had made a wise choice.

"I am ready to go to the plantation, sir," I replied.

"Have you thought how important your decision is to your children?" said he.

I told him I had.

"Very well. Go to the plantation, and my curse go with you," he replied. "Your boy shall be put to work, and he shall soon be sold; and your girl shall be raised for the purpose of selling well. Go your own ways!" He left the room with curses, not to be repeated.

As I stood rooted to the spot, my grandmother came and said, "Linda, child, what did you tell him?"

I answered that I was going to the plantation.

"Must you go?" said she. "Can't something be done to stop it?"

I told her it was useless to try; but she begged me not to give up. She said she would go to the doctor, and remind him how long and how faithfully she had served in the family, and how she had taken her own baby from her breast to nourish his wife. She would tell him I had been out of the family so long they would not miss me; that she would pay them for my time, and the money would procure a woman who had more strength for the situation than I had. I begged her not to go; but she persisted in saying, "He will listen to me, Linda." She went, and was treated as I expected. He coolly listened to what she said, but denied her request. He

---

1 Reject with the implication that one is not even worthy of notice.

told her that what he did was for my good, that my feelings were entirely above my situation, and that on the plantation I would receive treatment that was suitable to my behavior.

My grandmother was much cast down. I had my secret hopes; but I must fight my battle alone. I had a woman's pride, and a mother's love for my children; and I resolved that out of the darkness of this hour a brighter dawn should rise for them. My master had power and law on his side; I had a determined will. There is might in each.

CHAPTER XVI.
SCENES AT THE PLANTATION.

Early the next morning I left my grandmother's with my youngest child. My boy was ill, and I left him behind. I had many sad thoughts as the old wagon jolted on. Hitherto, I had suffered alone; now, my little one was to be treated as a slave. As we drew near the great house, I thought of the time when I was formerly sent there out of revenge. I wondered for what purpose I was now sent. I could not tell. I resolved to obey orders so far as duty required; but within myself, I determined to make my stay as short as possible. Mr. Flint was waiting to receive us, and told me to follow him up stairs to receive orders for the day. My little Ellen was left below in the kitchen. It was a change for her, who had always been so carefully tended. My young master said she might amuse herself in the yard. This was kind of him, since the child was hateful to his sight. My task was to fit up the house for the reception of the bride. In the midst of sheets, tablecloths, towels, drapery, and carpeting, my head was as busy planning, as were my fingers with the needle. At noon I was allowed to go to Ellen. She had sobbed herself to sleep. I heard Mr. Flint say to a neighbor, "I've got her down here, and I'll soon take the town notions out of her head. My father is partly to blame for her nonsense. He ought to have broke her in long ago." The remark was made within my hearing, and it would have been quite as manly to have made it to my face. He had said things to my face which might, or might not, have surprised his neighbor if he had known of them. He was "a chip of the old block."

I resolved to give him no cause to accuse me of being too much of a lady, so far as work was concerned. I worked day and night, with wretchedness before me. When I lay down beside my child, I felt how much easier it would be to see her die than to see her master beat her about, as I daily saw him beat other little ones. The spirit of the mothers was so crushed by the lash, that they stood by, without courage to remonstrate.[1] How much more must I suffer, before I should be "broke in" to that degree?

I wished to appear as contented as possible. Sometimes I had an opportunity to send a few lines home; and this brought up recollections that made it difficult, for a time, to seem calm and indifferent to my lot. Notwithstanding my efforts, I saw that Mr. Flint regarded me with a suspicious eye. Ellen broke down under the trials of her new life. Separated from me, with no one to look after her, she wandered about, and in a few days cried herself sick. One day, she sat under the window where I was at work, crying that weary cry which makes a mother's heart bleed. I was obliged to steel myself to bear it.[2] After a while it ceased. I looked out, and she was gone. As it was near noon, I ventured to go down in search of her. The great house was raised two feet above the ground. I looked under it, and saw her about midway, fast asleep. I crept under and drew her out. As I held her in my arms, I thought how well it would be for her if she never waked up; and I uttered my thought aloud. I was startled to hear some one say, "Did you speak to me?" I looked up, and saw Mr. Flint standing beside me. He said nothing further, but turned, frowning away. That night he sent Ellen a biscuit and a cup of sweetened milk. This generosity surprised me. I learned afterwards, that in the afternoon he had killed a large snake, which crept from under the house; and I supposed that incident had prompted his unusual kindness.

The next morning the old cart was loaded with shingles for town. I put Ellen into it, and sent her to her grandmother. Mr. Flint said I ought to have asked his permission. I told him the child was sick, and required attention which I had no time to give. He let it pass; for he was aware that I had accomplished much work in a little time.

I had been three weeks on the plantation, when I planned a visit home. It must be at night, after every body was in bed. I was six miles from town, and the road was very dreary. I was to go with a young man, who, I knew often stole to town to see his mother. One night, when all was quiet, we started. Fear gave speed to our steps, and we were not long in performing the journey. I arrived at my grandmother's. Her bed room was on the first floor, and the window was open, the weather being warm. I spoke to her and she

---

1 To plead in protest; to offer reasons for complaint.
2 For powerful analysis that centers Black girlhood, see Curseen.

awoke. She let me in and closed the window, lest some late passer-by should see me. A light was brought, and the whole household gathered round me, some smiling and some crying. I went to look at my children, and thanked God for their happy sleep. The tears fell as I leaned over them. As I moved to leave, Benny stirred. I turned back, and whispered, "Mother is here." After digging at his eyes with his little first, they opened, and he sat up in bed, looking at me curiously. Having satisfied himself that it was I, he exclaimed, "O mother! you ain't dead, are you? They didn't cut off your head at the plantation, did they?"

My time was up too soon, and my guide was waiting for me. I laid Benny back in his bed, and dried his tears by a promise to come again soon. Rapidly we retraced our steps back to the plantation. About half way we were met by a company of four patrols.[1] Luckily we heard their horse's hoofs before they came in sight, and we had time to hide behind a large tree. They passed, hallooing and shouting in a manner that indicated a recent carousal. How thankful we were that they had not their dogs with them![2] We hastened our footsteps, and when we arrived on the plantation we heard the sound of the hand-mill. The slaves were grinding their corn. We were safely in the house before the horn summoned them to their labor. I divided my little parcel of food with my guide, knowing that he had lost the chance of grinding his corn, and must toil all day in the field.

Mr. Flint often took an inspection of the house, to see that no one was idle. The entire management of the work was trusted to me, because he knew nothing about it; and rather than hire a superintendent he contented himself with my arrangements. He had often urged upon his father the necessity of having me at the plantation to take charge of his affairs, and make clothes for the slaves; but the old man knew him too well to consent to that arrangement.

When I had been working a month at the plantation, the great aunt of Mr. Flint came to make him a visit. This was the good

---

1 White people on the lookout for enslaved people who might be moving about without permission. The cultural tendency to assume that white people should monitor Black people is so foundational to the culture of the United States that activists today remind Americans that the police evolved out of this precise dynamic of racial surveillance built on white license to punish Black mobility.

2 These patrols often included dogs that could see and smell what the patrollers could not and could intensify the brutality if an enslaved person were discovered.

old lady who paid fifty dollars for my grandmother, for the purpose of making her free, when she stood on the auction block. My grandmother loved this old lady, whom we all called Miss Fanny. She often came to take tea with us. On such occasions the table was spread with a snow-white cloth, and the china cups and silver spoons were taken from the old-fashioned buffet.[1] There were hot muffins, tea rusks, and delicious sweetmeats. My grandmother kept two cows, and the fresh cream was Miss Fanny's delight. She invariably declared that it was the best in town. The old ladies had cosey times together. They would work and chat, and sometimes, while talking over old times, their spectacles would get dim with tears, and would have to be taken off and wiped. When Miss Fanny bade us good by, her bag was filled with grandmother's best cakes, and she was urged to come again soon.

There had been a time when Dr. Flint's wife came to take tea with us, and when her children were also sent to have a feast of "Aunt Marthy's" nice cooking. But after I became an object of her jealousy and spite, she was angry with grandmother for giving a shelter to me and my children. She would not even speak to her in the street. This wounded my grandmother's feelings, for she could not retain ill will against the woman whom she had nourished with her milk when a babe. The doctor's wife would gladly have prevented our intercourse with Miss Fanny if she could have done it, but fortunately she was not dependent on the bounty of the Flints. She had enough to be independent; and that is more than can ever be gained from charity, however lavish it may be.

Miss Fanny was endeared to me by many recollections, and I was rejoiced to see her at the plantation. The warmth of her large, loyal heart made the house seem pleasanter while she was in it. She staid a week, and I had many talks with her. She said her principal object in coming was to see how I was treated, and whether any thing could be done for me. She inquired whether she could help me in any way. I told her I believed not. She condoled[2] with me in her own peculiar way; saying she wished that I and all my grandmother's family were at rest in our graves, for not until then should she feel any peace about us. The good old soul did not dream that I was planning to bestow peace upon her, with regard to myself and my children; not by death, but by securing our freedom.

---

1 Cabinet for holding table linen, china, etc.
2 Expressed sympathy.

Again and again I had traversed those dreary twelve miles, to and from the town; and all the way, I was meditating upon some means of escape for myself and my children. My friends had made every effort that ingenuity could devise to effect our purchase, but all their plans had proved abortive.[1] Dr. Flint was suspicious, and determined not to loosen his grasp upon us. I could have made my escape alone; but it was more for my helpless children than for myself that I longed for freedom. Though the boon would have been precious to me, above all price, I would not have taken it at the expense of leaving them in slavery. Every trial I endured, every sacrifice I made for their sakes, drew them closer to my heart, and gave me fresh courage to beat back the dark waves that rolled and rolled over me in a seemingly endless night of storms.

The six weeks were nearly completed, when Mr. Flint's bride was expected to take possession of her new home. The arrangements were all completed, and Mr. Flint said I had done well. He expected to leave home on Saturday, and return with his bride the following Wednesday. After receiving various orders from him, I ventured to ask permission to spend Sunday in town. It was granted; for which favor I was thankful. It was the first I had ever asked of him, and I intended it should be the last. It needed more than one night to accomplish the project I had in view; but the whole of Sunday would give me an opportunity. I spent the Sabbath with my grandmother. A calmer, more beautiful day never came down out of heaven. To me it was a day of conflicting emotions. Perhaps it was the last day I should ever spend under that dear, old sheltering roof! Perhaps these were the last talks I should ever have with the faithful old friend of my whole life! Perhaps it was the last time I and my children should be together! Well, better so, I thought, than that they should be slaves. I knew the doom that awaited my fair baby in slavery, and I determined to save her from it, or perish in the attempt. I went to make this vow at the graves of my poor parents, in the burying-ground of the slaves. "There the wicked cease from troubling, and there the weary be at rest. There the prisoners rest together; they hear not the voice of the oppressor; the servant is free from his master."[2] I knelt by the graves of my parents, and thanked God, as I had often done before, that they had not lived to witness my trials, or to mourn over my sins. I had received my mother's blessing when she died; and in many an hour of

1 Unsuccessful.
2 From biblical scripture, Job 3.17–19.

tribulation[1] I had seemed to hear her voice, sometimes chiding[2] me, sometimes whispering loving words into my wounded heart. I have shed many and bitter tears, to think that when I am gone from my children they cannot remember me with such entire satisfaction as I remembered my mother.

The graveyard was in the woods, and twilight was coming on. Nothing broke the death-like stillness except the occasional twitter of a bird. My spirit was overawed by the solemnity of the scene. For more than ten years I had frequented this spot, but never had it seemed to me so sacred as now. A black stump, at the head of my mother's grave, was all that remained of a tree my father had planted. His grave was marked by a small wooden board, bearing his name, the letters of which were nearly obliterated. I knelt down and kissed them, and poured forth a prayer to God for guidance and support in the perilous step I was about to take. As I passed the wreck of the old meeting house, where, before Nat Turner's time, the slaves had been allowed to meet for worship, I seemed to hear my father's voice come from it, bidding me not to tarry till I reached freedom or the grave. I rushed on with renovated hopes. My trust in God had been strengthened by that prayer among the graves.

My plan was to conceal myself at the house of a friend, and remain there a few weeks till the search was over. My hope was that the doctor would get discouraged, and, for fear of losing my value, and also of subsequently finding my children among the missing, he would consent to sell us; and I knew somebody would buy us. I had done all in my power to make my children comfortable during the time I expected to be separated from them. I was packing my things, when grandmother came into the room, and asked what I was doing. "I am putting my things in order," I replied. I tried to look and speak cheerfully; but her watchful eye detected something beneath the surface. She drew me towards her, and asked me to sit down. She looked earnestly at me, and said, "Linda, do you want to kill your old grandmother? Do you mean to leave your little, helpless children? I am old now, and cannot do for your babies as I once did for you."

I replied, that if I went away, perhaps their father would be able to secure their freedom.

"Ah, my child," said she, "don't trust too much to him. Stand by your own children, and suffer with them till death. Nobody

---

1 Severe trial or suffering.
2 Scolding.

respects a mother who forsakes her children; and if you leave them, you will never have a happy moment. If you go, you will make me miserable the short time I have to live. You would be taken and brought back, and your sufferings would be dreadful. Remember poor Benjamin. Do give it up, Linda. Try to bear a little longer. Things may turn out better than we expect."

My courage failed me, in view of the sorrow I should bring on that faithful, loving old heart. I promised that I would try longer, and that I would take nothing out of her house without her knowledge.

Whenever the children climbed on my knee, or laid their heads on my lap, she would say, "Poor little souls! what would you do without a mother? She don't love you as I do." And she would hug them to her own bosom, as if to reproach me for my want of affection; but she knew all the while that I loved them better than my life. I slept with her that night, and it was the last time. The memory of it haunted me for many a year.

On Monday I returned to the plantation, and busied myself with preparations for the important day. Wednesday came. It was a beautiful day, and the faces of the slaves were as bright as the sunshine. The poor creatures were merry. They were expecting little presents from the bride, and hoping for better times under her administration. I had no such hopes for them. I knew that the young wives of slaveholders often thought their authority and importance would be best established and maintained by cruelty; and what I had heard of young Mrs. Flint gave me no reason to expect that her rule over them would be less severe than that of the master and overseer. Truly, the colored race are the most cheerful and forgiving people on the face of the earth. That their masters sleep in safety is owing to their superabundance of heart; and yet they look upon their suffering with less pity than they would bestow on those of a horse or a dog.

I stood at the door with others to receive the bridegroom and bride. She was a handsome, delicate-looking girl, and her face flushed with emotion at sight of her new home. I thought it likely that visions of a happy future were rising before her. It made me sad; for I knew how soon clouds would come over her sunshine. She examined every part of the house, and told me she was delighted with the arrangements I had made. I was afraid old Mrs. Flint had tried to prejudice her against me, and I did my best to please her.

All passed off smoothly for me until dinner time arrived. I did not mind the embarrassment of waiting on a dinner party, for the first time in my life, half so much as I did the meeting with Dr. Flint and his wife, who would be among the guests. It was a mystery to me why Mrs. Flint had not made her appearance at the plantation during all the time I was putting the house in order. I had not met her, face to face, for five years, and I had no wish to see her now. She was a praying woman, and, doubtless, considered my present position a special answer to her prayers. Nothing could please her better than to see me humbled and trampled upon. I was just where she would have me—in the power of a hard, unprincipled master. She did not speak to me when she took her seat at table; but her satisfied, triumphant smile, when I handed her plate, was more eloquent than words. The old doctor was not so quiet in his demonstrations. He ordered me here and there, and spoke with peculiar emphasis when he said "your mistress." I was drilled like a disgraced soldier. When all was over, and the last key turned, I sought my pillow, thankful that God had appointed a season of rest for the weary.

The next day my new mistress began her housekeeping. I was not exactly appointed maid of all work; but I was to do whatever I was told. Monday evening came. It was always a busy time. On that night the slaves received their weekly allowance of food. Three pounds of meat, a peck of corn, and perhaps a dozen herring[1] were allowed to each man. Women received a pound and a half of meat, a peck of corn, and the same number of herring. Children over twelve years old had half the allowance of the women. The meat was cut and weighed by the foreman of the field hands, and piled on planks before the meat house. Then the second foreman went behind the building, and when the first foreman called out, "Who takes this piece of meat?" he answered by calling somebody's name. This method was resorted to as a means of preventing partiality in distributing the meat. The young mistress came out to see how things were done on her plantation, and she soon gave a specimen of her character. Among those in waiting for their allowance was a very old slave, who had faithfully served the Flint family through three generations. When he hobbled up to get his bit of meat, the mistress said he was too old to have any allowance; that when niggers were too old to work, they ought to be fed on grass. Poor old man! He suffered much before he found rest in the grave.

My mistress and I got along very well together. At the end of a week, old Mrs. Flint made us another visit, and was closeted

---

1 Fish.

a long time with her daughter-in-law. I had my suspicions what was the subject of the conference. The old doctor's wife had been informed that I could leave the plantation on one condition, and she was very desirous to keep me there. If she had trusted me, as I deserved to be trusted by her, she would have had no fears of my accepting that condition. When she entered her carriage to return home, she said to young Mrs. Flint, "Don't neglect to send for them as quick as possible." My heart was on the watch all the time, and I at once concluded that she spoke of my children. The doctor came the next day, and as I entered the room to spread the tea table, I heard him say, "Don't wait any longer. Send for them to-morrow." I saw through the plan. They thought my children's being there would fetter me to the spot, and that it was a good place to break us all in to abject submission to our lot as slaves. After the doctor left, a gentleman called, who had always manifested friendly feelings towards my grandmother and her family. Mr. Flint carried him over the plantation to show him the results of labor performed by men and women who were unpaid, miserably clothed, and half famished.[1] The cotton crop was all they thought of. It was duly admired, and the gentleman returned with specimens to show his friends. I was ordered to carry water to wash his hands. As I did so, he said, "Linda, how do you like your new home?" I told him I liked it as well as I expected. He replied, "They don't think you are contented, and to-morrow they are going to bring your children to be with you. I am sorry for you, Linda. I hope they will treat you kindly." I hurried from the room, unable to thank him. My suspicions were correct. My children were to be brought to the plantation to be "broke in."

To this day I feel grateful to the gentleman who gave me this timely information. It nerved me to immediate action.

---

1 Starved.

CHAPTER XVII.
THE FLIGHT.

Mr. Flint was hard pushed for house servants, and rather than lose me he had restrained his malice. I did my work faithfully, though not, of course, with a willing mind. They were evidently afraid I should leave them. Mr. Flint wished that I should sleep in the great house instead of the servants' quarters. His wife agreed to the proposition, but said I mustn't bring my bed into the house, because it would scatter feathers on her carpet. I knew when I went there that they would never think of such a thing as furnishing a bed of any kind for me and my little one. I therefore carried my own bed, and now I was forbidden to use it. I did as I was ordered. But now that I was certain my children were to be put in their power, in order to give them a stronger hold on me, I resolved to leave them that night. I remembered the grief this step would bring upon my dear old grandmother; and nothing less than the freedom of my children would have induced me to disregard her advice. I went about my evening work with trembling steps. Mr. Flint twice called from his chamber door to inquire why the house was not locked up. I replied that I had not done my work. "You have had time enough to do it," said he. "Take care how you answer me!"

I shut all the windows, locked all the doors, and went up to the third story, to wait till midnight. How long those hours seemed, and how fervently I prayed that God would not forsake me in this hour of utmost need! I was about to risk every thing on the throw of a die;[1] and if I failed, O what would become of me and my poor children? They would be made to suffer for my fault.

At half past twelve I stole softly down stairs. I stopped on the second floor, thinking I heard a noise. I felt my way down into the parlor, and looked out of the window. The night was so intensely dark that I could see nothing. I raised the window very softly and jumped out. Large drops of rain were falling, and the darkness bewildered me. I dropped on my knees, and breathed a short prayer to God for guidance and protection. I groped my way to the road, and rushed towards the town with almost lightning speed. I arrived at my grandmother's house, but dared not see her. She would say, "Linda, you are killing me;" and I knew that would unnerve me. I tapped softly at the window of a room, occupied by a woman, who had lived in the house several years. I knew she was

---

1 Singular of *dice*.

a faithful friend, and could be trusted with my secret. I tapped several times before she heard me. At last she raised the window, and I whispered, "Sally, I have run away. Let me in, quick." She opened the door softly, and said in low tones, "For God's sake, don't. Your grandmother is trying to buy you and de children. Mr. Sands was here last week. He tole her he was going away on business, but he wanted her to go ahead about buying you and de children, and he would help her all he could. Don't run away, Linda. Your grandmother is all bowed down wid trouble now."

I replied, "Sally, they are going to carry my children to the plantation to-morrow; and they will never sell them to any body so long as they have me in their power. Now, would you advise me to go back?"

"No, chile, no," answered she. "When dey finds you is gone, dey won't want de plague ob de children; but where is you going to hide? Dey knows ebery inch ob dis house."

I told her I had a hiding-place, and that was all it was best for her to know. I asked her to go into my room as soon as it was light, and take all my clothes out of my trunk, and pack them in hers; for I knew Mr. Flint and the constable would be there early to search my room. I feared the sight of my children would be too much for my full heart; but I could not go out into the uncertain future without one last look. I bent over the bed where lay my little Benny and baby Ellen. Poor little ones! fatherless and motherless! Memories of their father came over me. He wanted to be kind to them; but they were not all to him, as they were to my womanly heart. I knelt and prayed for the innocent little sleepers. I kissed them lightly, and turned away.

As I was about to open the street door, Sally laid her hand on my shoulder, and said, "Linda, is you gwine all alone? Let me call your uncle."

"No, Sally," I replied, "I want no one to be brought into trouble on my account."

I went forth into the darkness and rain. I ran on till I came to the house of the friend who was to conceal me.

Early the next morning Mr. Flint was at my grandmother's inquiring for me. She told him she had not seen me, and supposed I was at the plantation. He watched her face narrowly, and said, "Don't you know any thing about her running off?" She assured him that she did not. He went on to say, "Last night she ran off without the least provocation. We had treated her very kindly. My wife liked her. She will soon be found and brought back. Are her children with you?" When told that they were, he said, "I am very glad to hear that. If they are here, she cannot be far off. If I find out that any of my niggers have had any thing to do with this damned business, I'll give 'em five hundred lashes." As he started to go to his father's, he turned round and added, persuasively, "Let her be brought back, and she shall have her children to live with her."

The tidings made the old doctor rave and storm at a furious rate. It was a busy day for them. My grandmother's house was searched from top to bottom. As my trunk was empty, they concluded I had taken my clothes with me. Before ten o'clock every vessel northward bound was thoroughly examined, and the law against harboring fugitives was read to all on board. At night a watch was set over the town. Knowing how distressed my grandmother would be, I wanted to send her a message; but it could not be done. Every one who went in or out of her house was closely watched. The doctor said he would take my children, unless she became responsible for them; which of course she willingly did. The next day was spent in searching. Before night, the following advertisement was posted at every corner, and in every public place for miles round:—

"$300 Reward ! Ran away from the subscriber, an intelligent, bright, mulatto girl, named Linda, 21 years of age. Five feet four inches high. Dark eyes, and black hair inclined to curl; but it can be made straight. Has a decayed spot on a front tooth. She can read and write, and in all probability will try to get to the Free States. All persons are forbidden, under penalty of the law, to harbor or employ said slave. $150 will be given to whoever takes her in the state, and $300 if taken out of the state and delivered to me, or lodged in jail. Dr. Flint."

CHAPTER XVIII.
MONTHS OF PERIL.

The search for me was kept up with more perseverance than I had anticipated. I began to think that escape was impossible. I was in great anxiety lest I should implicate the friend who harbored me. I knew the consequences would be frightful; and much as I dreaded being caught, even that seemed better than causing an innocent person to suffer for kindness to me. A week had passed in terrible suspense, when my pursuers came into such close vicinity that I concluded they had tracked me to my hiding-place. I flew out of the house, and concealed myself in a thicket of bushes. There I remained in an agony of fear for two hours. Suddenly, a reptile of some kind seized my leg. In my fright, I struck a blow which loosened its hold, but I could not tell whether I had killed it; it was so dark, I could not see what it was; I only knew it was something cold and slimy. The pain I felt soon indicated that the bite was poisonous. I was compelled to leave my place of concealment, and I groped my way back into the house. The pain had become intense, and my friend was startled by my look of anguish. I asked her to prepare a poultice[1] of warm ashes and vinegar, and I applied it to my leg, which was already much swollen. The application gave me some relief, but the swelling did not abate. The dread of being disabled was greater than the physical pain I endured.

My friend asked an old woman, who doctored among the slaves, what was good for the bite of a snake or a lizard. She told her to steep a dozen coppers[2] in vinegar, over night, and apply the cankered vinegar to the inflamed part.[3]

I had succeeded in cautiously conveying some messages to my relatives. They were harshly threatened, and despairing of my having a chance to escape, they advised me to return to my master, ask his forgiveness, and let him make an example of me. But such counsel had no influence with me. When I started upon this hazardous undertaking, I had resolved that, come what would, there should be no turning back. "Give me liberty, or give me death,"[4] was my motto. When my friend contrived to make known to my relatives the painful situation I had been in for twenty-four hours, they said no more about my going back to my master. Something must be done, and that speedily; but

---

1 A soft, moist mass of cloth, bread, meal, herbs, etc., applied hot as a healing agent.

2 Copper coins.

3 [Lydia Maria Child's note:] The poison of a snake is a powerful acid, and is counteracted by powerful alkalies, such as potash, ammonia, &c. The Indians are accustomed to apply wet ashes, or plunge the limb into strong lie. White men, employed to lay out railroads in snaky places, often carry ammonia with them as an antidote.—Editor.

4 Famous words attributed to Patrick Henry (1736–99), a delegate attending the Second Virginia Convention in March 1775. While many advised caution and patience while awaiting diplomatic solutions to the colonists' complaints about imposition from the British Crown, Henry advocated organizing a militia to be prepared for armed defense.

where to turn for help, they knew not. God in his mercy raised up "a friend in need."

Among the ladies who were acquainted with my grandmother, was one who had known her from childhood, and always been very friendly to her. She had also known my mother and her children, and felt interested for them. At this crisis of affairs she called to see my grandmother, as she not unfrequently did. She observed the sad and troubled expression of her face, and asked if she knew where Linda was, and whether she was safe. My grandmother shook her head, without answering. "Come, Aunt Martha," said the kind lady, "tell me all about it. Perhaps I can do something to help you." The husband of this lady held many slaves, and bought and sold slaves. She also held a number in her own name; but she treated them kindly, and would never allow any of them to be sold. She was unlike the majority of slaveholders' wives. My grandmother looked earnestly at her. Something in the expression of her face said "Trust me!" and she did trust her. She listened attentively to the details of my story, and sat thinking for a while. At last she said, "Aunt Martha, I pity you both. If you think there is any chance of Linda's getting to the Free States, I will conceal her for a time. But first you must solemnly promise that my name shall never be mentioned. If such a thing should become known, it would ruin me and my family. No one in my house must know of it, except the cook. She is so faithful that I would trust my own life with her; and I know she likes Linda. It is a great risk; but I trust no harm will come of it. Get word to Linda to be ready as soon as it is dark, before the patrols are out. I will send the housemaids on errands, and Betty shall go to meet Linda." The place where we were to meet was designated and agreed upon. My grandmother was unable to thank the lady for this noble deed; overcome by her emotions, she sank on her knees and sobbed like a child.

I received a message to leave my friend's house at such an hour, and go to a certain place where a friend would be waiting for me. As a matter of prudence[1] no names were mentioned. I had no means of conjecturing who I was to meet, or where I was going. I did not like to move thus blindfolded, but I had no choice. It would not do for me to remain where I was. I disguised myself, summoned up courage to meet the worst, and went to the appointed place. My friend Betty was there; she was the last person I expected to see. We hurried along in silence. The pain in my leg was so intense that it seemed as if I should drop; but

---

1 Wisdom and caution regarding practical matters.

fear gave me strength. We reached the house and entered unobserved. Her first words were: "Honey, now you is safe. Dem devils ain't coming to search dis house. When I get you into missis' safe place, I will bring some nice hot supper. I specs you need it after all dis skeering." Betty's vocation led her to think eating the most important thing in life. She did not realize that my heart was too full for me to care much about supper.

The mistress came to meet us, and led me up stairs to a small room over her own sleeping apartment. "You will be safe here, Linda," said she; "I keep this room to store away things that are out of use. The girls are not accustomed to be sent to it, and they will not suspect any thing unless they hear some noise. I always keep it locked, and Betty shall take care of the key. But you must be very careful, for my sake as well as your own; and you must never tell my secret; for it would ruin me and my family. I will keep the girls busy in the morning, that Betty may have a chance to bring your breakfast; but it will not do for her to come to you again till night. I will come to see you sometimes. Keep up your courage. I hope this state of things will not last long." Betty came with the "nice hot supper," and the mistress hastened down stairs to keep things straight till she returned. How my heart overflowed with gratitude! Words choked in my throat; but I could have kissed the feet of my benefactress. For that deed of Christian womanhood, may God forever bless her!

I went to sleep that night with the feeling that I was for the present the most fortunate slave in town. Morning came and filled my little cell with light. I thanked the heavenly Father for this safe retreat. Opposite my window was a pile of feather beds. On the top of these I could lie perfectly concealed, and command a view of the street through which Dr. Flint passed to his office. Anxious as I was, I felt a gleam of satisfaction when I saw him. Thus far I had outwitted him, and I triumphed over it. Who can blame slaves for being cunning? They are constantly compelled to resort to it. It is the only weapon of the weak and oppressed against the strength of their tyrants.

I was daily hoping to hear that my master had sold my children; for I knew who was on the watch to buy them. But Dr. Flint cared even more for revenge than he did for money. My brother William, and the good aunt who had served in his family twenty years, and my little Benny, and Ellen, who was a little over two years old, were thrust into jail, as a means of compelling my relatives to give some information about me. He swore my grandmother should never see one of them again till I was brought back. They kept these facts from me for several days. When I heard that my little ones were in a loathsome jail, my first impulse was to go to them. I was encountering dangers for the sake of freeing them, and must I be the cause of their death? The thought was agonizing. My benefactress tried to soothe me by telling me that my aunt would take good care of the children while they remained in jail. But it added to my pain to think that the good old aunt, who had always been so kind to her sister's orphan children, should be shut up in prison for no other crime than loving them. I suppose my friends feared a reckless movement on my part, knowing, as they did, that my life was bound up in my children. I received a note from my brother William. It was scarcely legible, and ran thus: "Wherever you are, dear sister, I beg of you not to come here. We are all much better off than you are. If you come, you will ruin us all. They would force you to tell where you had been, or they would kill you. Take the advice of your friends; if not for the sake of me and your children, at least for the sake of those you would ruin."

Poor William! He also must suffer for being my brother. I took his advice and kept quiet. My aunt was taken out of jail at the end of a month, because Mrs. Flint could not spare her any longer. She was tired of being her own housekeeper. It was quite too fatiguing to order her dinner and eat it too. My children remained in jail, where brother William did all he could for their comfort. Betty went to see them sometimes, and brought me tidings. She was not permitted to enter the jail; but William would hold them up to the grated window while she chatted with them. When she repeated their prattle, and told me how they wanted to see their ma, my tears would flow. Old Betty would exclaim, "Lors, chile! what's you crying 'bout? Dem young uns vil kill you dead. Don't be so chick'n hearted! If you does, you vil nebber git thro' dis world."

Good old soul! She had gone through the world childless. She had never had little ones to clasp their arms round her neck; she had never seen their soft eyes looking into hers; no sweet little voices had called her mother; she had never pressed her own infants to her heart, with the feeling that even in fetters there was something to live for. How could she realize my feelings? Betty's husband loved children dearly, and wondered why God had denied them to him. He expressed great sorrow when he came to Betty with the tidings that Ellen had been taken out of jail and carried to Dr. Flint's. She had the measles a short time before they carried her to jail, and the disease had left her eyes affected. The doctor had taken her home to attend to them. My children had always been afraid of the doctor and his wife. They had never been inside of their house. Poor little Ellen cried all day to be carried back to prison. The instincts of childhood are true. She knew she was loved in the jail. Her screams and sobs annoyed Mrs. Flint. Before night she called one of the slaves, and said, "Here, Bill, carry this brat back to the jail. I can't stand her noise. If she would be quiet I should like to keep the little minx.[1] She would make a handy waiting-maid for my daughter by and by. But if she staid here, with her white face, I suppose I should either kill her or spoil her. I hope the doctor will sell them as far as wind and water can carry them. As for their mother, her ladyship will find out yet what she gets by running away. She hasn't so much feeling for her children as a cow has for its calf. If she had, she would have come back long ago, to get them out of jail, and save all this expense and trouble. The good-for-nothing hussy![2] When she is caught, she shall stay in jail, in irons, for one six months, and then be sold to a sugar plantation. I shall see her broke in yet. What do you stand there for, Bill? Why don't you go off with the brat? Mind, now, that you don't let any of the niggers speak to her in the street!"

When these remarks were reported to me, I smiled at Mrs. Flint's saying that she should either kill my child or spoil her. I thought to myself there was very little danger of the latter. I have always considered it as one of God's special providences that Ellen screamed till she was carried back to jail.

That same night Dr. Flint was called to a patient, and did not return till near morning. Passing my grandmother's, he saw a light in the house, and thought to himself, "Perhaps this has something to do with Linda." He knocked, and the door was opened. "What calls you up so early?" said he. "I saw your light, and I thought I would just stop and tell you that I have found out where Linda is. I know where to put my hands on her, and I shall have her before twelve o'clock." When he had turned away, my grandmother and my uncle looked anxiously at each other. They did not know whether or not it was merely one of the doctor's tricks to frighten them. In their uncertainty, they thought it was best to have a message conveyed to my friend Betty. Unwilling to alarm her mistress, Betty resolved to dispose of me herself. She

---

1 A bold or flirtatious girl. (Notice the characterization given to a child of two or three years old. It is worth considering this comment in the context of research and activism today that emphasizes the dangerous "adultification" of Black girls. See, for example, Morris; Epstein et al.)

2 An immoral woman.

came to me, and told me to rise and dress quickly. We hurried down stairs, and across the yard, into the kitchen. She locked the door, and lifted up a plank in the floor. A buffalo skin and a bit of carpet were spread for me to lie on, and a quilt thrown over me. "Stay dar," said she, "till I sees if dey know 'bout you. Dey say dey vil put thar hans on you afore twelve o'clock. If dey did know whar you are, dey won't know now. Dey'll be disapinted dis time. Dat's all I got to say. If dey comes rummaging 'mong my things, dey'll get one bressed sarssin from dis 'ere nigger." In my shallow bed I had but just room enough to bring my hands to my face to keep the dust out of my eyes; for Betty walked over me twenty times in an hour, passing from the dresser to the fire-place. When she was alone, I could hear her pronouncing anathemas[1] over Dr. Flint and all his tribe, every now and then saying, with a chuckling laugh, "Dis nigger's too cute for 'em dis time." When the housemaids were about, she had sly ways of drawing them out, that I might hear what they would say. She would repeat stories she had heard about my being in this, or that, or the other place. To which they would answer, that I was not fool enough to be staying round there; that I was in Philadelphia or New York before this time. When all were abed and asleep, Betty raised the plank, and said, "Come out, chile; come out. Dey don't know nottin 'bout you. 'Twas only white folks' lies, to skeer de niggers."

Some days after this adventure I had a much worse fright. As I sat very still in my retreat above stairs, cheerful visions floated through my mind. I thought Dr. Flint would soon get discouraged, and would be willing to sell my children, when he lost all hopes of making them the means of my discovery. I knew who was ready to buy them. Suddenly I heard a voice that chilled my blood. The sound was too familiar to me, it had been too dreadful, for me not to recognize at once my old master. He was in the house, and I at once concluded he had come to seize me. I looked round in terror. There was no way of escape. The voice receded. I supposed the constable was with him, and they were searching the house. In my alarm I did not forget the trouble I was bringing on my generous benefactress. It seemed as if I were born to bring sorrow on all who befriended me, and that was the bitterest drop in the bitter cup of my life. After a while I heard approaching footsteps; the key was turned in my door. I braced myself against the wall to keep from falling. I ventured to look up, and there stood

---

1 Curses.

my kind benefactress alone. I was too much overcome to speak, and sunk down upon the floor.

"I thought you would hear your master's voice," she said; "and knowing you would be terrified, I came to tell you there is nothing to fear. You may even indulge in a laugh at the old gentleman's expense. He is so sure you are in New York, that he came to borrow five hundred dollars to go in pursuit of you. My sister had some money to loan on interest. He has obtained it, and proposes to start for New York to-night. So, for the present, you see you are safe. The doctor will merely lighten his pocket hunting after the bird he has left behind."

CHAPTER XIX.
THE CHILDREN SOLD.

The doctor came back from New York, of course without accomplishing his purpose. He had expended considerable money, and was rather disheartened. My brother and the children had now been in jail two months, and that also was some expense. My friends thought it was a favorable time to work on his discouraged feelings. Mr. Sands sent a speculator to offer him nine hundred dollars for my brother William, and eight hundred for the two children. These were high prices, as slaves were then selling; but the offer was rejected. If it had been merely a question of money, the doctor would have sold any boy of Benny's age for two hundred dollars; but he could not bear to give up the power of revenge. But he was hard pressed for money, and he revolved the matter in his mind. He knew that if he could keep Ellen till she was fifteen, he could sell her for a high price; but I presume he reflected that she might die, or might be stolen away. At all events, he came to the conclusion that he had better accept the slave-trader's offer. Meeting him in the street, he inquired when he would leave town. "To-day, at ten o'clock," he replied. "Ah, do you go so soon?" said the doctor; "I have been reflecting upon your proposition, and I have concluded to let you have the three negroes if you will say nineteen hundred dollars." After some parley,[1] the trader agreed to his terms. He wanted the bill of sale drawn up and signed immediately, as he had a great deal to attend to during the short time he remained in town. The doctor went to the jail and told William he would take him back into his service if

---

1 Discussion.

he would promise to behave himself; but he replied that he would rather be sold. "And you shall be sold, you ungrateful rascal!" exclaimed the doctor. In less than an hour the money was paid, the papers were signed, sealed, and delivered, and my brother and children were in the hands of the trader.

It was a hurried transaction; and after it was over, the doctor's characteristic caution returned. He went back to the speculator, and said, "Sir, I have come to lay you under obligations of a thousand dollars not to sell any of those negroes in this state." "You come too late," replied the trader; "our bargain is closed." He had, in fact, already sold them to Mr. Sands, but he did not mention it. The doctor required him to put irons on "that rascal, Bill," and to pass through the back streets when he took his gang out of town. The trader was privately instructed to concede to his wishes. My good old aunt went to the jail to bid the children good by, supposing them to be the speculator's property, and that she should never see them again. As she held Benny in her lap, he said, "Aunt Nancy, I want to show you something." He led her to the door and showed her a long row of marks, saying, "Uncle Will taught me to count. I have made a mark for every day I have been here, and it is sixty days. It is a long time; and the speculator is going to take me and Ellen away. He's a bad man. It's wrong for him to take grandmother's children. I want to go to my mother."

My grandmother was told that the children would be restored to her, but she was requested to act as if they were really to be sent away. Accordingly, she made up a bundle of clothes and went to the jail. When she arrived, she found William handcuffed among the gang, and the children in the trader's cart. The scene seemed too much like reality. She was afraid there might have been some deception or mistake. She fainted, and was carried home.

When the wagon stopped at the hotel, several gentlemen came out and proposed to purchase William, but the trader refused their offers, without stating that he was already sold. And now came the trying hour for that drove[1] of human beings, driven away like cattle, to be sold they knew not where. Husbands were torn from wives, parents from children, never to look upon each other again this side the grave. There was wringing of hands and cries of despair.

Dr. Flint had the supreme satisfaction of seeing the wagon leave town, and Mrs. Flint had the gratification of supposing that my children were going "as far as wind and water would carry

---

1 A substantial number.

them." According to agreement, my uncle followed the wagon some miles, until they came to an old farm house. There the trader took the irons from William, and as he did so, he said, "You are a damned clever fellow. I should like to own you myself. Them gentlemen that wanted to buy you said you was a bright, honest chap, and I must git you a good home. I guess your old master will swear to-morrow, and call himself an old fool for selling the children. I reckon he'll never git their mammy back again. I expect she's made tracks for the north. Good by, old boy. Remember, I have done you a good turn. You must thank me by coaxing all the pretty gals to go with me next fall. That's going to be my last trip. This trading in niggers is a bad business for a fellow that's got any heart. Move on, you fellows!" And the gang went on, God alone knows where.

Much as I despise and detest the class of slave-traders, whom I regard as the vilest wretches on earth, I must do this man the justice to say that he seemed to have some feeling. He took a fancy to William in the jail, and wanted to buy him. When he heard the story of my children, he was willing to aid them in getting out of Dr. Flint's power, even without charging the customary fee.

My uncle procured a wagon and carried William and the children back to town. Great was the joy in my grandmother's house! The curtains were closed, and the candles lighted. The happy grandmother cuddled the little ones to her bosom. They hugged her, and kissed her, and clapped their hands, and shouted. She knelt down and poured forth one of her heartfelt prayers of thanksgiving to God. The father was present for a while; and though such a "parental relation" as existed between him and my children takes slight hold of the hearts or consciences of slaveholders, it must be that he experienced some moments of pure joy in witnessing the happiness he had imparted.

I had no share in the rejoicings of that evening.

The events of the day had not come to my knowledge. And now I will tell you something that happened to me; though you will, perhaps, think it illustrates the superstition of slaves. I sat in my usual place on the floor near the window, where I could hear much that was said in the street without being seen. The family had retired for the night, and all was still. I sat there thinking of my children, when I heard a low strain of music. A band of serenaders[1] were under the window, playing "Home, sweet home." I listened till the sounds did not seem like music, but like the

---

1 Singers.

moaning of children. It seemed as if my heart would burst. I rose from my sitting posture, and knelt. A streak of moonlight was on the floor before me, and in the midst of it appeared the forms of my two children. They vanished; but I had seen them distinctly. Some will call it a dream, others a vision. I know not how to account for it, but it made a strong impression on my mind, and I felt certain something had happened to my little ones.

I had not seen Betty since morning. Now I heard her softly turning the key. As soon as she entered, I clung to her, and begged her to let me know whether my children were dead, or whether they were sold; for I had seen their spirits in my room, and I was sure something had happened to them. "Lor, chile," said she, putting her arms round me, "you's got de highsterics. I'll sleep wid you to-night, 'cause you'll make a noise, and ruin missis. Something has stirred you up mightily. When you is done crying, I'll talk wid you. De chillern is well, and mighty happy. I seed 'em myself. Does dat satisfy you? Dar, chile, be still! Somebody vill hear you." I tried to obey her. She lay down, and was soon sound asleep; but no sleep would come to my eyelids.

At dawn, Betty was up and off to the kitchen. The hours passed on, and the vision of the night kept constantly recurring to my thoughts. After a while I heard the voices of two women in the entry. In one of them I recognized the housemaid. The other said to her, "Did you know Linda Brent's children was sold to the speculator yesterday. They say ole massa Flint was mighty glad to see 'em drove out of town; but they say they've come back again. I 'spect it's all their daddy's doings. They say he's bought William too. Lor! how it will take hold of ole massa Flint! I'm going roun' to aunt Marthy's to see 'bout it."

I bit my lips till the blood came to keep from crying out. Were my children with their grandmother, or had the speculator carried them off? The suspense was dreadful. Would Betty never come, and tell me the truth about it? At last she came, and I eagerly repeated what I had overheard. Her face was one broad, bright smile. "Lor, you foolish ting!" said she. "I'se gwine to tell you all 'bout it. De gals is eating thar breakfast, and missus tole me to let her tell you; but, poor creeter! t'aint right to keep you waitin', and I'se gwine to tell you. Brudder, children, all is bought by de daddy! I'se laugh more dan nuff, thinking 'bout ole massa Flint. Lor, how he vill swar! He's got ketched dis time, any how; but I must be getting out o' dis, or dem gals vill come and ketch me."

Betty went off laughing; and I said to myself, "Can it be true that my children are free? I have not suffered for them in vain. Thank God!"

Great surprise was expressed when it was known that my children had returned to their grandmother's. The news spread through the town, and many a kind word was bestowed on the little ones.

Dr. Flint went to my grandmother's to ascertain who was the owner of my children, and she informed him. "I expected as much," said he. "I am glad to hear it. I have had news from Linda lately, and I shall soon have her. You need never expect to see her free. She shall be my slave as long as I live, and when I am dead she shall be the slave of my children. If I ever find out that you or Phillip had any thing to do with her running off I'll kill him. And if I meet William in the street, and he presumes to look at me, I'll flog him within an inch of his life. Keep those brats out of my sight!"

As he turned to leave, my grandmother said something to remind him of his own doings. He looked back upon her, as if he would have been glad to strike her to the ground.

I had my season of joy and thanksgiving. It was the first time since my childhood that I had experienced any real happiness. I heard of the old doctor's threats, but they no longer had the same power to trouble me. The darkest cloud that hung over my life had rolled away. Whatever slavery might do to me, it could not shackle my children. If I fell a sacrifice, my little ones were saved. It was well for me that my simple heart believed all that had been promised for their welfare. It is always better to trust than to doubt.

CHAPTER XX.
NEW PERILS.

The doctor, more exasperated than ever, again tried to revenge himself on my relatives. He arrested uncle Phillip on the charge of having aided my flight. He was carried before a court, and swore truly that he knew nothing of my intention to escape, and that he had not seen me since I left my master's plantation. The doctor then demanded that he should give bail for five hundred dollars that he would have nothing to do with me. Several gentlemen offered to be security for him; but Mr. Sands told him he had better go back to jail, and he would see that he came out without giving bail.

The news of his arrest was carried to my grandmother, who conveyed it to Betty. In the kindness of her heart, she again stowed me away under the floor; and as she walked back and forth, in the performance of her culinary duties, she talked apparently to herself, but with the intention that I should hear what was going on. I hoped that my uncle's imprisonment would last but few days; still I was anxious. I thought it likely Dr. Flint would do his utmost to taunt and insult him, and I was afraid my uncle might lose control of himself, and retort in some way that would be construed into a punishable offence; and I was well aware that in court his word would not be taken against any white man's. The search for me was renewed. Something had excited suspicions that I was in the vicinity. They searched the house I was in. I heard their steps and their voices. At night, when all were asleep, Betty came to release me from my place of confinement. The fright I had undergone, the constrained posture, and the dampness of the ground, made me ill for several days. My uncle was soon after taken out of prison; but the movements of all my relatives, and of all our friends, were very closely watched.

We all saw that I could not remain where I was much longer. I had already staid longer than was intended, and I knew my presence must be a source of perpetual anxiety to my kind benefactress. During this time, my friends had laid many plans for my escape, but the extreme vigilance of my persecutors made it impossible to carry them into effect.

One morning I was much startled by hearing somebody trying to get into my room. Several keys were tried, but none fitted. I instantly conjectured it was one of the housemaids; and I concluded she must either have heard some noise in the room, or have noticed the entrance of Betty. When my friend came, at her usual time, I told her what had happened. "I knows who it was," said she. "'Pend upon it, 'twas dat Jenny. Dat nigger allers got de debble in her." I suggested that she might have seen or heard something that excited her curiosity.

"Tut! tut! chile!" exclaimed Betty, "she ain't seen notin', nor hearn notin'. She only 'spects something. Dat's all. She wants to fine out who hab cut and make my gownd. But she won't nebber know. Dat's sartin. I'll git missis to fix her."

I reflected a moment, and said, "Betty, I must leave here to-night."

"Do as you tink best, poor chile," she replied. "I'se mighty 'fraid dat 'ere nigger vill pop on you some time."

She reported the incident to her mistress, and received orders to keep Jenny busy in the kitchen till she could see my uncle Phillip. He told her he would send a friend for me that very evening. She told him she hoped I was going to the north, for it was very dangerous for me to remain any where in the vicinity. Alas, it was not an easy thing, for one in my situation, to go to the north. In order to leave the coast quite clear for me, she went into the country to spend the day with her brother, and took Jenny with her. She was afraid to come and bid me good by, but she left a kind message with Betty. I heard her carriage roll from the door, and I never again saw her who had so generously befriended the poor, trembling fugitive! Though she was a slaveholder, to this day my heart blesses her!

I had not the slightest idea where I was going. Betty brought me a suit of sailor's clothes,—jacket, trowsers, and tarpaulin[1] hat. She gave me a small bundle, saying I might need it where I was going. In cheery tones, she exclaimed, "I'se so glad you is gwine to free parts! Don't forget ole Betty. P'raps I'll come 'long by and by."

I tried to tell her how grateful I felt for all her kindness, but she interrupted me. "I don't want no tanks, honey. I'se glad I could help you, and I hope de good Lord vill open de path for you. I'se gwine wid you to de lower gate. Put your hands in your pockets, and walk ricketty, like de sailors."

I performed to her satisfaction. At the gate I found Peter, a young colored man, waiting for me. I had known him for years. He had been an apprentice to my father, and had always borne a good character. I was not afraid to trust to him. Betty bade me a hurried good by, and we walked off. "Take courage, Linda," said

---

1 Material made waterproof with, for example, wax or tar.

my friend Peter. "I've got a dagger, and no man shall take you from me, unless he passes over my dead body."

It was a long time since I had taken a walk out of doors, and the fresh air revived me. It was also pleasant to hear a human voice speaking to me above a whisper. I passed several people whom I knew, but they did not recognize me in my disguise. I prayed internally that, for Peter's sake, as well as my own, nothing might occur to bring out his dagger. We walked on till we came to the wharf. My aunt Nancy's husband was a seafaring man, and it had been deemed necessary to let him into our secret. He took me into his boat, rowed out to a vessel not far distant, and hoisted me on board. We three were the only occupants of the vessel. I now ventured to ask what they proposed to do with me. They said I was to remain on board till near dawn, and then they would hide me in Snaky Swamp, till my uncle Phillip had prepared a place of concealment for me. If the vessel had been bound north, it would have been of no avail to me, for it would certainly have been searched. About four o'clock, we were again seated in the boat, and rowed three miles to the swamp. My fear of snakes had been increased by the venomous bite I had received, and I dreaded to enter this hiding-place. But I was in no situation to choose, and I gratefully accepted the best that my poor, persecuted friends could do for me.

Peter landed first, and with a large knife cut a path through bamboos and briers[1] of all descriptions. He came back, took me in his arms, and carried me to a seat made among the bamboos. Before we reached it, we were covered with hundreds of mosquitos. In an hour's time they had so poisoned my flesh that I was a pitiful sight to behold. As the light increased, I saw snake after snake crawling round us. I had been accustomed to the sight of snakes all my life, but these were larger than any I had ever seen. To this day I shudder when I remember that morning. As evening approached, the number of snakes increased so much that we were continually obliged to thrash them with sticks to keep them from crawling over us. The bamboos were so high and so thick that it was impossible to see beyond a very short distance. Just before it became dark we procured a seat nearer to the entrance of the swamp, being fearful of losing our way back to the boat. It was not long before we heard the paddle of oars, and the low whistle, which had been agreed upon as a signal. We made haste to enter the boat, and were rowed back to the vessel. I passed a

---

1 Sharp, prickly plants.

wretched night; for the heat of the swamp, the mosquitos, and the constant terror of snakes, had brought on a burning fever. I had just dropped asleep, when they came and told me it was time to go back to that horrid swamp. I could scarcely summon courage to rise. But even those large, venomous snakes were less dreadful to my imagination than the white men in that community called civilized. This time Peter took a quantity of tobacco to burn, to keep off the mosquitos. It produced the desired effect on them, but gave me nausea and severe headache. At dark we returned to the vessel. I had been so sick during the day, that Peter declared I should go home that night, if the devil himself was on patrol. They told me a place of concealment had been provided for me at my grandmother's. I could not imagine how it was possible to hide me in her house, every nook and corner of which was known to the Flint family. They told me to wait and see. We were rowed ashore, and went boldly through the streets, to my grandmother's. I wore my sailor's clothes, and had blackened my face with charcoal. I passed several people whom I knew. The father of my children came so near that I brushed against his arm; but he had no idea who it was.[1]

"You must make the most of this walk," said my friend Peter, "for you may not have another very soon."

I thought his voice sounded sad. It was kind of him to conceal from me what a dismal hole was to be my home for a long, long time.

---

1 Besides highlighting the mobility of Black sailors (Appendix B5), this scenario underscores how gender and race can be manipulated. William and Ellen Craft also used this kind of cross-dressing performance to escape slavery. With an emphasis on "the racial history of trans identity," C. Riley Snorton theorizes "performances *for* rather than *of* freedom" (58) and highlights how gender and race can be "rearranged in [the] quest for freedom" (74). For more on the Crafts especially, see McCaskill; McMillan.

CHAPTER XXI.
THE LOOPHOLE OF RETREAT.

A small shed had been added to my grandmother's house years ago. Some boards were laid across the joists at the top, and between these boards and the roof was a very small garret,[1] never occupied by any thing but rats and mice. It was a pent roof, covered with nothing but shingles, according to the southern custom for such buildings. The garret was only nine feet long and seven wide. The highest part was three feet high, and sloped down abruptly to the loose board floor. There was no admission for either light or air. My uncle Philip, who was a carpenter, had very skillfully made a concealed trap-door, which communicated with the storeroom. He had been doing this while I was waiting in the swamp. The storeroom opened upon a piazza. To this hole I was conveyed as soon as I entered the house. The air was stifling; the darkness total. A bed had been spread on the floor. I could sleep quite comfortably on one side; but the slope was so sudden that I could not turn on the other without hitting the roof. The rats and mice ran over my bed; but I was weary, and I slept such sleep as the wretched may, when a tempest has passed over them. Morning came. I knew it only by the noises I heard; for in my small den day and night were all the same. I suffered for air even more than for light. But I was not comfortless. I heard the voices of my children.

There was joy and there was sadness in the sound. It made my tears flow. How I longed to speak to them! I was eager to look on their faces; but there was no hole, no crack, through which I could peep. This continued darkness was oppressive. It seemed horrible to sit or lie in a cramped position day after day, without one gleam of light. Yet I would have chosen this, rather than my lot as a slave, though white people considered it an easy one; and it was so compared with the fate of others. I was never cruelly over-worked; I was never lacerated with the whip from head to foot; I was never so beaten and bruised that I could not turn from one side to the other; I never had my heel-strings cut to prevent my running away; I was never chained to a log and forced to drag it about, while I toiled in the fields from morning till night; I was never branded with hot iron, or torn by bloodhounds. On the contrary, I had always been kindly treated, and tenderly cared for, until I came into the hands of Dr. Flint. I had never wished for freedom till then. But though my life in slavery was comparatively devoid

---

1 An attic, especially a small, miserable one.

of hardships, God pity the woman who is compelled to lead such a life!

My food was passed up to me through the trap-door my uncle had contrived; and my grandmother, my uncle Phillip, and aunt Nancy would seize such opportunities as they could, to mount up there and chat with me at the opening. But of course this was not safe in the daytime. It must all be done in darkness. It was impossible for me to move in an erect position, but I crawled about my den for exercise. One day I hit my head against something, and found it was a gimlet.[1]

My uncle had left it sticking there when he made the trap-door. I was as rejoiced as Robinson Crusoe[2] could have been at finding such a treasure. It put a lucky thought into my head. I said to myself, "Now I will have some light. Now I will see my children." I did not dare to begin my work during the daytime, for fear of attracting attention. But I groped round; and having found the side next the street, where I could frequently see my children, I stuck the gimlet in and waited for evening. I bored three rows of holes, one above another; then I bored out the interstices between. I thus succeeded in making one hole about an inch long and an inch broad. I sat by it till late into the night, to enjoy the little whiff of air that floated in. In the morning I watched for my children. The first person I saw in the street was Dr. Flint. I had a shuddering, superstitious feeling that it was a bad omen. Several familiar faces passed by. At last I heard the merry laugh of children, and presently two sweet little faces were looking up at me, as though they knew I was there, and were conscious of the joy they imparted. How I longed to tell them I was there!

My condition was now a little improved. But for weeks I was tormented by hundreds of little red insects, fine as a needle's point, that pierced through my skin, and produced an intolerable burning. The good grandmother gave me herb teas and cooling medicines, and finally I got rid of them. The heat of my den was intense, for nothing but thin shingles protected me from the scorching summer's sun. But I had my consolations. Through my peeping-hole I could watch the children, and when they were near enough, I could hear their talk.

Aunt Nancy brought me all the news she could hear at Dr.

---

1 A small tool for creating holes.

2 A reference to the main character in Daniel Defoe's *Robinson Crusoe* (1719), who, shipwrecked on a desert island, survived by finding tools and other useful items.

Flint's. From her I learned that the doctor had written to New York to a colored woman, who had been born and raised in our neighborhood, and had breathed his contaminating atmosphere. He offered her a reward if she could find out any thing about me. I know not what was the nature of her reply; but he soon after started for New York in haste, saying to his family that he had business of importance to transact. I peeped at him as he passed on his way to the steam-boat. It was a satisfaction to have miles of land and water between us, even for a little while; and it was a still greater satisfaction to know that he believed me to be in the Free States. My little den seemed less dreary than it had done. He returned, as he did from his former journey to New York, without obtaining any satisfactory information. When he passed our house next morning, Benny was standing at the gate. He had heard them say that he had gone to find me, and he called out, "Dr. Flint, did you bring my mother home? I want to see her." The doctor stamped his foot at him in a rage, and exclaimed, "Get out of the way, you little damned rascal! If you don't, I'll cut off your head."

Benny ran terrified into the house, saying, "You can't put me in jail again. I don't belong to you now." It was well that the wind carried the words away from the doctor's ear. I told my grandmother of it, when we had our next conference at the trap-door; and begged of her not to allow the children to be impertinent[1] to the irascible[2] old man.

Autumn came, with a pleasant abatement of heat.

My eyes had become accustomed to the dim light, and by holding my book or work in a certain position near the aperture[3] I contrived to read and sew. That was a great relief to the tedious monotony of my life. But when winter came, the cold penetrated through the thin shingle roof, and I was dreadfully chilled. The winters there are not so long, or so severe, as in northern latitudes; but the houses are not built to shelter from cold, and my little den was peculiarly comfortless. The kind grandmother brought me bed-clothes and warm drinks. Often I was obliged to lie in bed all day to keep comfortable; but with all my precautions, my shoulders and feet were frostbitten. O, those long, gloomy days, with no object for my eye to rest upon, and no thoughts to occupy my mind, except the dreary past and the uncertain future! I was thankful when there came a day sufficiently mild for me to

---

1 Brash.
2 Easily angered.
3 Slit, gap, or small opening.

wrap myself up and sit at the loophole to watch the passers by. Southerners have the habit of stopping and talking in the streets, and I heard many conversations not intended to meet my ears. I heard slave-hunters planning how to catch some poor fugitive. Several times I heard allusions[1] to Dr. Flint, myself, and the history of my children, who, perhaps, were playing near the gate. One would say, "I wouldn't move my little finger to catch her, as old Flint's property." Another would say, "I'll catch any nigger for the reward. A man ought to have what belongs to him, if he is a damned brute." The opinion was often expressed that I was in the Free States. Very rarely did any one suggest that I might be in the vicinity. Had the least suspicion rested on my grandmother's house, it would have been burned to the ground.

But it was the last place they thought of. Yet there was no place, where slavery existed, that could have afforded me so good a place of concealment.

Dr. Flint and his family repeatedly tried to coax[2] and bribe my children to tell something they had heard said about me. One day the doctor took them into a shop, and offered them some bright little silver pieces and gay handkerchiefs if they would tell where their mother was. Ellen shrank away from him, and would not speak; but Benny spoke up, and said, "Dr. Flint, I don't know where my mother is. I guess she's in New York; and when you go there again, I wish you'd ask her to come home, for I want to see her; but if you put her in jail, or tell her you'll cut her head off, I'll tell her to go right back."

CHAPTER XXII.
CHRISTMAS FESTIVITIES.

Christmas was approaching. Grandmother brought me materials, and I busied myself making some new garments and little playthings for my children. Were it not that hiring day is near at hand, and many families are fearfully looking forward to the probability of separation in a few days, Christmas might be a happy season for the poor slaves. Even slave mothers try to gladden the hearts of their little ones on that occasion. Benny and Ellen had their Christmas stockings filled. Their imprisoned mother could not have the privilege of witnessing their surprise and joy. But I had

---

1 Casual references.
2 To influence by flattery; to manipulate.

the pleasure of peeping at them as they went into the street with their new suits on. I heard Benny ask a little playmate whether Santa Claus brought him any thing. "Yes," replied the boy; "but Santa Claus ain't a real man. It's the children's mothers that put things into the stockings." "No, that can't be," replied Benny, "for Santa Claus brought Ellen and me these new clothes, and my mother has been gone this long time."

How I longed to tell him that his mother made those garments, and that many a tear fell on them while she worked!

Every child rises early on Christmas morning to see the Johnkannaus.[1] Without them, Christmas would be shorn of its greatest attraction. They consist of companies of slaves from the plantations, generally of the lower class. Two athletic men, in calico wrappers, have a net thrown over them, covered with all manner of bright-colored stripes. Cows' tails are fastened to their backs, and their heads are decorated with horns. A box, covered with sheepskin, is called the gumbo box. A dozen beat on this, while others strike triangles and jawbones, to which bands of dancers keep time. For a month previous they are composing songs, which are sung on this occasion. These companies, of a hundred each, turn out early in the morning, and are allowed to go round till twelve o'clock, begging for contributions. Not a door is left unvisited where there is the least chance of obtaining a penny or a glass of rum. They do not drink while they are out, but carry the rum home in jugs, to have a carousal.[2] These Christmas donations frequently amount to twenty or thirty dollars. It is seldom that any white man or child refuses to give them a trifle. If he does, they regale his ears with the following song:—

"Poor massa, so dey say;
Down in de heel, so dey say;
Got no money, so dey say;
Not one shillin,[3] so dey say;
God A'mighty bress you, so dey say."

---

1 Pronounced "John Canoe." Also known as *Jonkonnu*. Celebrations with roots on the African continent, suggesting that enslaved people retained some of their cultural knowledge and managed to keep practicing according to some of that knowledge even in a system that worked to strip them of their native languages, their names, their families, and everything else associated with being people, not property.
2 A drunken feast or gathering.
3 An old unit of currency from the United Kingdom, equal to 12 pence.

Christmas is a day of feasting, both with white and colored people. Slaves, who are lucky enough to have a few shillings, are sure to spend them for good eating; and many a turkey and pig is captured, without saying, "By your leave, sir." Those who cannot obtain these, cook a 'possum, or a raccoon, from which savory dishes can be made. My grandmother raised poultry and pigs for sale; and it was her established custom to have both a turkey and a pig roasted for Christmas dinner.

On this occasion, I was warned to keep extremely quiet, because two guests had been invited. One was the town constable, and the other was a free colored man, who tried to pass himself off for white, and who was always ready to do any mean work for the sake of currying favor with white people. My grandmother had a motive for inviting them. She managed to take them all over the house. All the rooms on the lower floor were thrown open for them to pass in and out; and after dinner, they were invited up stairs to look at a fine mocking bird my uncle had just brought home. There, too, the rooms were all thrown open, that they might look in. When I heard them talking on the piazza, my heart almost stood still. I knew this colored man had spent many nights hunting for me. Every body knew he had the blood of a slave father in his veins; but for the sake of passing himself off for white, he was ready to kiss the slaveholders' feet. How I despised him! As for the constable, he wore no false colors. The duties of his office were despicable, but he was superior to his companion, inasmuch as he did not pretend to be what he was not. Any white man, who could raise money enough to buy a slave, would have considered himself degraded by being a constable; but the office enabled its possessor to exercise authority. If he found any slave out after nine o'clock, he could whip him as much as he liked; and that was a privilege to be coveted. When the guests were ready to depart, my grandmother gave each of them some of her nice pudding, as a present for their wives. Through my peep-hole I saw them go out of the gate, and I was glad when it closed after them. So passed the first Christmas in my den.

CHAPTER XXIII.
STILL IN PRISON.

When spring returned, and I took in the little patch of green the aperture commanded, I asked myself how many more summers and winters I must be condemned to spend thus. I longed to draw in a plentiful draught of fresh air, to stretch my cramped limbs, to have room to stand erect, to feel the earth under my feet again. My relatives were constantly on the lookout for a chance of escape; but none offered that seemed practicable, and even tolerably safe. The hot summer came again, and made the turpentine[1] drop from the thin roof over my head.

During the long nights I was restless for want of air, and I had no room to toss and turn. There was but one compensation; the atmosphere was so stifled that even mosquitos would not condescend to buzz in it. With all my detestation of Dr. Flint, I could hardly wish him a worse punishment, either in this world or that which is to come, than to suffer what I suffered in one single summer. Yet the laws allowed him to be out in the free air, while I, guiltless of crime, was pent up here, as the only means of avoiding the cruelties the laws allowed him to inflict upon me! I don't know what kept life within me. Again and again, I thought I should die before long; but I saw the leaves of another autumn whirl through the air, and felt the touch of another winter. In summer the most terrible thunder storms were acceptable, for the rain came through the roof, and I rolled up my bed that it might cool the hot boards under it. Later in the season, storms sometimes wet my clothes through and through, and that was not comfortable when the air grew chilly. Moderate storms I could keep out by filling the chinks with oakum.[2]

But uncomfortable as my situation was, I had glimpses of things out of doors, which made me thankful for my wretched hiding-place. One day I saw a slave pass our gate, muttering, "It's his own, and he can kill it if he will." My grandmother told me that woman's history. Her mistress had that day seen her baby for the first time, and in the lineaments of its fair face she saw a likeness to her husband. She turned the bondwoman and her child out of doors, and forbade her ever to return. The slave went to her master, and told him what had happened. He promised to talk

---

1 The oil that seeps from the wood of pine or fir trees.
2 The loose fiber obtained by untwisting rope.

with her mistress, and make it all right. The next day she and her baby were sold to a Georgia trader.

Another time I saw a woman rush wildly by, pursued by two men. She was a slave, the wet nurse of her mistress's children. For some trifling offence her mistress ordered her to be stripped and whipped. To escape the degradation and the torture, she rushed to the river, jumped in, and ended her wrongs in death.

Senator Brown, of Mississippi,[1] could not be ignorant of many such facts as these, for they are of frequent occurrence in every Southern State. Yet he stood up in the Congress of the United States, and declared that slavery was "a great moral, social, and political blessing; a blessing to the master, and a blessing to the slave!"

I suffered much more during the second winter than I did during the first. My limbs were benumbed by inaction, and the cold filled them with cramp. I had a very painful sensation of coldness in my head; even my face and tongue stiffened, and I lost the power of speech. Of course it was impossible, under the circumstances, to summon any physician. My brother William came and did all he could for me. Uncle Phillip also watched tenderly over me; and poor grandmother crept up and down to inquire whether there were any signs of returning life. I was restored to consciousness by the dashing of cold water in my face, and found myself leaning against my brother's arm, while he bent over me with streaming eyes. He afterwards told me he thought I was dying, for I had been in an unconscious state sixteen hours. I next became delirious, and was in great danger of betraying myself and my friends. To prevent this, they stupefied me with drugs. I remained in bed six weeks, weary in body and sick at heart. How to get medical advice was the question. William finally went to a Thompsonian doctor,[2] and described himself as having all my pains and aches. He returned with herbs, roots, and ointment. He was especially charged to rub on the ointment by a fire; but how could a fire be made in my little den? Charcoal in a furnace was tried, but there was no outlet for the gas, and it nearly cost me my life. Afterwards coals, already kindled, were brought up in an iron pan, and placed on bricks. I was so weak, and it was so long since I had enjoyed the warmth of a fire, that those few coals actually made me weep. I think the medicines did me some good; but my

---

1 Albert G. Brown (1830–80).

2 Practitioner of alternative medicine; herbalist.

recovery was very slow. Dark thoughts passed through my mind as I lay there day after day. I tried to be thankful for my little cell, dismal as it was, and even to love it, as part of the price I had paid for the redemption of my children. Sometimes I thought God was a compassionate Father, who would forgive my sins for the sake of my sufferings. At other times, it seemed to me there was no justice or mercy in the divine government. I asked why the curse of slavery was permitted to exist, and why I had been so persecuted and wronged from youth upward. These things took the shape of mystery, which is to this day not so clear to my soul as I trust it will be hereafter.

In the midst of my illness, grandmother broke down under the weight of anxiety and toil. The idea of losing her, who had always been my best friend and a mother to my children, was the sorest trial I had yet had. O, how earnestly I prayed that she might recover! How hard it seemed, that I could not tend upon her, who had so long and so tenderly watched over me!

One day the screams of a child nerved me with strength to crawl to my peeping-hole, and I saw my son covered with blood. A fierce dog, usually kept chained, had seized and bitten him. A doctor was sent for, and I heard the groans and screams of my child while the wounds were being sewed up. O, what torture to a mother's heart, to listen to this and be unable to go to him!

But childhood is like a day in spring, alternately shower and sunshine. Before night Benny was bright and lively, threatening the destruction of the dog; and great was his delight when the doctor told him the next day that the dog had bitten another boy and been shot. Benny recovered from his wounds; but it was long before he could walk.

When my grandmother's illness became known, many ladies, who were her customers, called to bring her some little comforts, and to inquire whether she had every thing she wanted. Aunt Nancy one night asked permission to watch with her sick mother, and Mrs. Flint replied, "I don't see any need of your going. I can't spare you." But when she found other ladies in the neighborhood were so attentive, not wishing to be outdone in Christian charity, she also sallied forth,[1] in magnificent condescension, and stood by the bedside of her who had loved her in her infancy, and who

---

1 Moved forth suddenly. The term has roots in describing a band of soldiers moving forward suddenly for a surprise attack, so Jacobs remains consistent in characterizing all of these unjust interactions as part of a larger war.

had been repaid by such grievous wrongs. She seemed surprised to find her so ill, and scolded uncle Phillip for not sending for Dr. Flint. She herself sent for him immediately, and he came. Secure as I was in my retreat, I should have been terrified if I had known he was so near me. He pronounced my grandmother in a very critical situation, and said if her attending physician wished it, he would visit her. Nobody wished to have him coming to the house at all hours, and we were not disposed to give him a chance to make out a long bill.

As Mrs. Flint went out, Sally told her the reason Benny was lame was, that a dog had bitten him. "I'm glad of it," replied she. "I wish he had killed him. It would be good news to send to his mother. Her day will come. The dogs will grab her yet." With these Christian words she and her husband departed, and, to my great satisfaction, returned no more.

I heard from uncle Phillip, with feelings of unspeakable joy and gratitude, that the crisis was passed and grandmother would live. I could now say from my heart, "God is merciful. He has spared me the anguish of feeling that I caused her death."

CHAPTER XXIV.
THE CANDIDATE FOR CONGRESS.

The summer had nearly ended, when Dr. Flint made a third visit to New York, in search of me. Two candidates were running for Congress, and he returned in season to vote. The father of my children was the Whig candidate.[1] The doctor had hitherto been a stanch Whig; but now he exerted all his energies for the defeat of Mr. Sands. He invited large parties of men to dine in the shade of his trees, and supplied them with plenty of rum and brandy. If any poor fellow drowned his wits in the bowl, and, in the openness of his convivial heart, proclaimed that he did not mean to vote the Democratic ticket, he was shoved into the street without ceremony.

The doctor expended his liquor in vain. Mr. Sands was elected; an event which occasioned me some anxious thoughts. He had

---

1 The Whig party formed in 1834 in opposition to President Andrew Jackson (1776–1845), whom many saw as too much like a monarch. The name is inspired by the party's counterparts in England, who opposed absolute monarchy even while supporting the idea of a constitutional monarchy. The party had faded in the United States by the mid–1850s.

not emancipated my children, and if he should die they would be at the mercy of his heirs. Two little voices, that frequently met my ear, seemed to plead with me not to let their father depart without striving to make their freedom secure. Years had passed since I had spoken to him. I had not even seen him since the night I passed him, unrecognized, in my disguise of a sailor. I supposed he would call before he left, to say something to my grandmother concerning the children, and I resolved what course to take.

The day before his departure for Washington I made arrangements, towards evening, to get from my hiding-place into the storeroom below. I found myself so stiff and clumsy that it was with great difficulty I could hitch[1] from one resting place to another. When I reached the storeroom my ankles gave way under me, and I sank exhausted on the floor. It seemed as if I could never use my limbs again. But the purpose I had in view roused all the strength I had. I crawled on my hands and knees to the window, and, screened behind a barrel, I waited for his coming. The clock struck nine, and I knew the steamboat would leave between ten and eleven. My hopes were failing. But presently I heard his voice, saying to some one, "Wait for me a moment. I wish to see aunt Martha." When he came out, as he passed the window, I said, "Stop one moment, and let me speak for my children." He started, hesitated, and then passed on, and went out of the gate. I closed the shutter I had partially opened, and sank down behind the barrel. I had suffered much; but seldom had I experienced a keener pang than I then felt. Had my children, then, become of so little consequence to him? And had he so little feeling for their wretched mother that he would not listen a moment while she pleaded for them? Painful memories were so busy within me, that I forgot I had not hooked the shutter, till I heard some one opening it. I looked up. He had come back. "Who called me?" said he, in a low tone. "I did," I replied. "Oh, Linda," said he, "I knew your voice; but I was afraid to answer, lest my friend should hear me. Why do you come here? Is it possible you risk yourself in this house? They are mad to allow it. I shall expect to hear that you are all ruined." I did not wish to implicate him, by letting him know my place of concealment; so I merely said, "I thought you would come to bid grandmother good by, and so I came here to speak a few words to you about emancipating my children. Many changes may take place during the six months you are gone to Washington, and it does not seem right for you to expose them to the risk of

---

1 To move by jerks or with a tug.

such changes. I want nothing for myself; all I ask is, that you will free my children, or authorize some friend to do it, before you go."

He promised he would do it, and also expressed a readiness to make any arrangements whereby I could be purchased.

I heard footsteps approaching, and closed the shutter hastily. I wanted to crawl back to my den, without letting the family know what I had done; for I knew they would deem it very imprudent. But he stepped back into the house, to tell my grandmother that he had spoken with me at the storeroom window, and to beg of her not to allow me to remain in the house over night. He said it was the height of madness for me to be there; that we should certainly all be ruined. Luckily, he was in too much of a hurry to wait for a reply, or the dear old woman would surely have told him all.

I tried to go back to my den, but found it more difficult to go up than I had to come down. Now that my mission was fulfilled, the little strength that had supported me through it was gone, and I sank helpless on the floor. My grandmother, alarmed at the risk I had run, came into the storeroom in the dark, and locked the door behind her. "Linda," she whispered, "where are you?"

"I am here by the window," I replied. "I couldn't have him go away without emancipating the children. Who knows what may happen?"

"Come, come, child," said she, "it won't do for you to stay here another minute. You've done wrong; but I can't blame you, poor thing!"

I told her I could not return without assistance, and she must call my uncle. Uncle Phillip came, and pity prevented him from scolding me. He carried me back to my dungeon, laid me tenderly on the bed, gave me some medicine, and asked me if there was any thing more he could do. Then he went away, and I was left with my own thoughts—starless as the midnight darkness around me.

My friends feared I should become a cripple for life; and I was so weary of my long imprisonment that, had it not been for the hope of serving my children, I should have been thankful to die; but, for their sakes, I was willing to bear on.

CHAPTER XXV.
COMPETITION IN CUNNING.

Dr. Flint had not given me up. Every now and then he would say to my grandmother that I would yet come back, and voluntarily surrender myself; and that when I did, I could be purchased by my relatives, or any one who wished to buy me. I knew his cunning nature too well not to perceive that this was a trap laid for me; and so all my friends understood it. I resolved to match my cunning against his cunning. In order to make him believe that I was in New York, I resolved to write him a letter dated from that place. I sent for my friend Peter, and asked him if he knew any trustworthy seafaring person, who would carry such a letter to New York, and put it in the post office there. He said he knew one that he would trust with his own life to the ends of the world. I reminded him that it was a hazardous thing for him to undertake. He said he knew it, but he was willing to do any thing to help me. I expressed a wish for a New York paper, to ascertain the names of some of the streets. He ran his hand into his pocket, and said, "Here is half a one, that was round a cap I bought of a peddler yesterday." I told him the letter would be ready the next evening. He bade me good by, adding, "Keep up your spirits, Linda; brighter days will come by and by."

My uncle Phillip kept watch over the gate until our brief interview was over. Early the next morning, I seated myself near the little aperture to examine the newspaper. It was a piece of the New York Herald; and, for once, the paper that systematically abuses the colored people, was made to render them a service. Having obtained what information I wanted concerning streets and numbers, I wrote two letters, one to my grandmother, the other to Dr. Flint. I reminded him how he, a gray-headed man, had treated a helpless child, who had been placed in his power, and what years of misery he had brought upon her. To my grandmother, I expressed a wish to have my children sent to me at the north, where I could teach them to respect themselves, and set them a virtuous example; which a slave mother was not allowed to do at the south. I asked her to direct her answer to a certain street in Boston, as I did not live in New York, though I went there sometimes. I dated these letters ahead, to allow for the time it would take to carry them, and sent a memorandum of the date to the messenger. When my friend came for the letters, I said, "God bless and reward you, Peter, for this disinterested kindness. Pray be careful. If you are detected, both you and I will have to suffer

dreadfully. I have not a relative who would dare to do it for me."
He replied, "You may trust to me, Linda. I don't forget that your
father was my best friend, and I will be a friend to his children so
long as God lets me live."

It was necessary to tell my grandmother what I had done, in
order that she might be ready for the letter, and prepared to hear
what Dr. Flint might say about my being at the north. She was
sadly troubled.

She felt sure mischief would come of it. I also told my plan to
aunt Nancy, in order that she might report to us what was said
at Dr. Flint's house. I whispered it to her through a crack, and
she whispered back, "I hope it will succeed. I shan't mind being a
slave all my life, if I can only see you and the children free."

I had directed that my letters should be put into the New York
post office on the 20th of the month. On the evening of the 24th
my aunt came to say that Dr. Flint and his wife had been talking
in a low voice about a letter he had received, and that when he
went to his office he promised to bring it when he came to tea.
So I concluded I should hear my letter read the next morning. I
told my grandmother Dr. Flint would be sure to come, and asked
her to have him sit near a certain door, and leave it open, that
I might hear what he said. The next morning I took my station
within sound of that door, and remained motionless as a statue.
It was not long before I heard the gate slam, and the well-known
footsteps enter the house. He seated himself in the chair that was
placed for him, and said, "Well, Martha, I've brought you a letter
from Linda. She has sent me a letter, also. I know exactly where to
find her; but I don't choose to go to Boston for her. I had rather
she would come back of her own accord, in a respectable manner.
Her uncle Phillip is the best person to go for her. With him, she
would feel perfectly free to act. I am willing to pay his expenses
going and returning. She shall be sold to her friends. Her children
are free; at least I suppose they are; and when you obtain her freedom, you'll make a happy family. I suppose, Martha, you have no
objection to my reading to you the letter Linda has written to you."

He broke the seal, and I heard him read it. The old villain! He
had suppressed the letter I wrote to grandmother, and prepared a
substitute of his own, the purport of which was as follows:—

"Dear Grandmother:
I have long wanted to write to you; but the disgraceful manner
in which I left you and my children made me ashamed to do it. If

you knew how much I have suffered since I ran away, you would pity and forgive me. I have purchased freedom at a dear rate. If any arrangement could be made for me to return to the south without being a slave, I would gladly come. If not, I beg of you to send my children to the north. I cannot live any longer without them. Let me know in time, and I will meet them in New York or Philadelphia, whichever place best suits my uncle's convenience. Write as soon as possible to your unhappy daughter, Linda."

"It is very much as I expected it would be," said the old hypocrite, rising to go. "You see the foolish girl has repented of her rashness, and wants to return. We must help her to do it, Martha. Talk with Phillip about it. If he will go for her, she will trust to him, and come back. I should like an answer tomorrow. Good morning, Martha."

As he stepped out on the piazza, he stumbled over my little girl. "Ah, Ellen, is that you?" he said, in his most gracious manner. "I didn't see you. How do you do?"

"Pretty well, sir," she replied. "I heard you tell grandmother that my mother is coming home. I want to see her."

"Yes, Ellen, I am going to bring her home very soon," rejoined he; "and you shall see her as much as you like, you little curly-headed nigger."

This was as good as a comedy to me, who had heard it all; but grandmother was frightened and distressed, because the doctor wanted my uncle to go for me.

The next evening Dr. Flint called to talk the matter over. My uncle told him that from what he had heard of Massachusetts, he judged he should be mobbed if he went there after a runaway slave. "All stuff and nonsense, Phillip!" replied the doctor. "Do you suppose I want you to kick up a row in Boston? The business can all be done quietly. Linda writes that she wants to come back. You are her relative, and she would trust you. The case would be different if I went. She might object to coming with me; and the damned abolitionists, if they knew I was her master, would not believe me, if I told them she had begged to go back. They would get up a row; and I should not like to see Linda dragged through the streets like a common negro. She has been very ungrateful to me for all my kindness; but I forgive her, and want to act the part of a friend towards her. I have no wish to hold her as my slave. Her friends can buy her as soon as she arrives here."

Finding that his arguments failed to convince my uncle, the doctor "let the cat out of the bag," by saying that he had written to the mayor of Boston, to ascertain whether there was a person of my description at the street and number from which my letter was dated. He had omitted this date in the letter he had made up to read to my grandmother. If I had dated from New York, the old man would probably have made another journey to that city. But even in that dark region, where knowledge is so carefully excluded from the slave, I had heard enough about Massachusetts to come to the conclusion that slaveholders did not consider it a comfortable place to go to in search of a runaway. That was before the Fugitive Slave Law[1] was passed; before Massachusetts had consented to become a "nigger hunter" for the south.

My grandmother, who had become skittish[2] by seeing her family always in danger, came to me with a very distressed countenance, and said, "What will you do if the mayor of Boston sends him word that you haven't been there? Then he will suspect the letter was a trick; and maybe he'll find out something about it, and we shall all get into trouble. O Linda, I wish you had never sent the letters."

"Don't worry yourself, grandmother," said I. "The mayor of Boston won't trouble himself to hunt niggers for Dr. Flint. The letters will do good in the end. I shall get out of this dark hole some time or other."

"I hope you will, child," replied the good, patient old friend. "You have been here a long time; almost five years; but whenever you do go, it will break your old grandmother's heart. I should be expecting every day to hear that you were brought back in irons

---

1 The *Fugitive Slave Act* was part of the Compromise of 1850, a multifaceted measure to preserve the Union. Because California wanted to be admitted into the Union as a free state, the act helped satisfy those who would otherwise want to balance California by insisting that a slave state be admitted immediately. The act required all citizens to assist in the recovery of fugitives, and it obliterated a fugitive's right to a jury trial. In fact, cases would be handled by special commissioners who would be paid $5 if an alleged fugitive were released and $10 if handed over to the claimant (see Appendix A2).

2 Easily startled. (Notice the many ways that Jacobs's narrator acknowledges the emotional and psychological consequences for her grandmother of constantly encountering injustice. The text consistently disrupts the "strong Black woman" stereotype, the idea that Black women are strong and can withstand anything. This pervasive idea helped to justify the cruelty visited on Black women centuries ago, and it serves a similar purpose today.)

and put in jail. God help you, poor child! Let us be thankful that some time or other we shall go 'where the wicked cease from troubling, and the weary are at rest.'"[1] My heart responded, Amen.

The fact that Dr. Flint had written to the mayor of Boston convinced me that he believed my letter to be genuine, and of course that he had no suspicion of my being any where in the vicinity. It was a great object to keep up this delusion, for it made me and my friends feel less anxious, and it would be very convenient whenever there was a chance to escape. I resolved, therefore, to continue to write letters from the north from time to time.

Two or three weeks passed, and as no news came from the mayor of Boston, grandmother began to listen to my entreaty to be allowed to leave my cell, sometimes, and exercise my limbs to prevent my becoming a cripple. I was allowed to slip down into the small storeroom, early in the morning, and remain there a little while. The room was all filled up with barrels, except a small open space under my trap-door. This faced the door, the upper part of which was of glass, and purposely left uncurtained, that the curious might look in. The air of this place was close; but it was so much better than the atmosphere of my cell, that I dreaded to return. I came down as soon as it was light, and remained till eight o'clock, when people began to be about, and there was danger that some one might come on the piazza.[2] I had tried various applications to bring warmth and feeling into my limbs, but without avail. They were so numb and stiff that it was a painful effort to move; and had my enemies come upon me during the first mornings I tried to exercise them a little in the small unoccupied space of the storeroom, it would have been impossible for me to have escaped.

---

1 A reference to biblical scripture, Job 14.13.
2 Porch.

CHAPTER XXVI.
IMPORTANT ERA IN MY BROTHER'S LIFE.

I missed the company and kind attentions of my brother William, who had gone to Washington with his master, Mr. Sands. We received several letters from him, written without any allusion to me, but expressed in such a manner that I knew he did not forget me. I disguised my hand, and wrote to him in the same manner. It was a long session; and when it closed, William wrote to inform us that Mr. Sands was going to the north, to be gone some time, and that he was to accompany him. I knew that his master had promised to give him his freedom, but no time had been specified. Would William trust to a slave's chances? I remembered how we used to talk together, in our young days, about obtaining our freedom, and I thought it very doubtful whether he would come back to us.

Grandmother received a letter from Mr. Sands, saying that William had proved a most faithful servant, and he would also say a valued friend; that no mother had ever trained a better boy. He said he had traveled through the Northern States and Canada; and though the abolitionists had tried to decoy him away, they had never succeeded. He ended by saying they should be at home shortly.

We expected letters from William, describing the novelties of his journey, but none came. In time, it was reported that Mr. Sands would return late in the autumn, accompanied by a bride. Still no letters from William. I felt almost sure I should never see him again on southern soil; but had he no word of comfort to send to his friends at home? to the poor captive in her dungeon?[1] My thoughts wandered through the dark past, and over the uncertain future. Alone in my cell, where no eye but God's could see me, I wept bitter tears. How earnestly I prayed to him to restore

---

1 This scene exemplifies the self-determination enabled by being what cultural critic Xine Yao calls *disaffected*. Notice the changing tone Jacobs gives to Linda's narration. Linda matter-of-factly states that Sands has married and then expresses downright distress about not hearing from her brother. Young women are supposed to pine after men like Sands, but Linda yearns for her brother. As Yao might put it, "it is not that she does not care: rather she refuses to care in the ways demanded" by dominant American culture (117). Here and elsewhere, "strategic unfeeling toward whiteness makes possible the healing work of transformative Black love" (26).

me to my children, and enable me to be a useful woman and a good mother!

At last the day arrived for the return of the travellers. Grandmother had made loving preparations to welcome her absent boy back to the old hearthstone. When the dinner table was laid, William's plate occupied its old place. The stage coach went by empty. My grandmother waited dinner. She thought perhaps he was necessarily detained by his master. In my prison I listened anxiously, expecting every moment to hear my dear brother's voice and step. In the course of the afternoon a lad was sent by Mr. Sands to tell grandmother that William did not return with him; that the abolitionists had decoyed him away. But he begged her not to feel troubled about it, for he felt confident she would see William in a few days. As soon as he had time to reflect he would come back, for he could never expect to be so well off at the north as he had been with him.

If you had seen the tears, and heard the sobs, you would have thought the messenger had brought tidings of death instead of freedom. Poor old grandmother felt that she should never see her darling boy again. And I was selfish. I thought more of what I had lost, than of what my brother had gained. A new anxiety began to trouble me. Mr. Sands had expended a good deal of money, and would naturally feel irritated by the loss he had incurred. I greatly feared this might injure the prospects of my children, who were now becoming valuable property. I longed to have their emancipation made certain. The more so, because their master and father was now married. I was too familiar with slavery not to know that promises made to slaves, though with kind intentions, and sincere at the time, depend upon many contingencies for their fulfilment.

Much as I wished William to be free, the step he had taken made me sad and anxious. The following Sabbath was calm and clear; so beautiful that it seemed like a Sabbath in the eternal world. My grandmother brought the children out on the piazza, that I might hear their voices. She thought it would comfort me in my despondency;[1] and it did. They chatted merrily, as only children can. Benny said, "Grandmother, do you think uncle Will has gone for good? Won't he ever come back again? May be he'll find mother. If he does, won't she be glad to see him! Why don't you and uncle Phillip, and all of us, go and live where mother is? I should like it; wouldn't you, Ellen?"

"Yes, I should like it," replied Ellen; "but how could we find

---

1 Depression of spirits from loss of hope.

her? Do you know the place, grandmother? I don't remember how mother looked—do you, Benny?"

Benny was just beginning to describe me when they were interrupted by an old slave woman, a near neighbor, named Aggie. This poor creature had witnessed the sale of her children, and seen them carried off to parts unknown, without any hopes of ever hearing from them again. She saw that my grandmother had been weeping, and she said, in a sympathizing tone, "What's the matter, aunt Marthy?"

"O Aggie," she replied, "it seems as if I shouldn't have any of my children or grandchildren left to hand me a drink when I'm dying, and lay my old body in the ground. My boy didn't come back with Mr. Sands. He staid at the north."

Poor old Aggie clapped her hands for joy. "Is dat what you's crying fur?" she exclaimed. "Git down on your knees and bress de Lord! I don't know whar my poor children is, and I nebber 'spect to know. You don't know whar poor Linda's gone to; but you do know whar her brudder is. He's in free parts; and dat's de right place. Don't murmur at de Lord's doings, but git down on your knees and tank him for his goodness."

My selfishness was rebuked by what poor Aggie said. She rejoiced over the escape of one who was merely her fellow-bondman, while his own sister was only thinking what his good fortune might cost her children. I knelt and prayed God to forgive me; and I thanked him from my heart, that one of my family was saved from the grasp of slavery.

It was not long before we received a letter from William. He wrote that Mr. Sands had always treated him kindly, and that he had tried to do his duty to him faithfully. But ever since he was a boy, he had longed to be free; and he had already gone through enough to convince him he had better not lose the chance that offered. He concluded by saying, "Don't worry about me, dear grandmother. I shall think of you always; and it will spur me on to work hard and try to do right. When I have earned money enough to give you a home, perhaps you will come to the north, and we can all live happy together."

Mr. Sands told my uncle Phillip the particulars about William's leaving him. He said, "I trusted him as if he were my own brother, and treated him as kindly. The abolitionists talked to him in several places; but I had no idea they could tempt him. However, I don't blame William. He's young and inconsiderate, and those Northern rascals decoyed him. I must confess the scamp was very bold about it. I met him coming down the steps of the Astor

House with his trunk on his shoulder, and I asked him where he was going. He said he was going to change his old trunk. I told him it was rather shabby, and asked if he didn't need some money. He said, No, thanked me, and went off. He did not return so soon as I expected; but I waited patiently. At last I went to see if our trunks were packed, ready for our journey. I found them locked, and a sealed note on the table informed me where I could find the keys. The fellow even tried to be religious. He wrote that he hoped God would always bless me, and reward me for my kindness; that he was not unwilling to serve me; but he wanted to be a free man; and that if I thought he did wrong, he hoped I would forgive him. I intended to give him his freedom in five years. He might have trusted me. He has shown himself ungrateful; but I shall not go for him, or send for him. I feel confident that he will soon return to me."

I afterwards heard an account of the affair from William himself. He had not been urged away by abolitionists. He needed no information they could give him about slavery to stimulate his desire for freedom. He looked at his hands, and remembered that they were once in irons. What security had he that they would not be so again? Mr. Sands was kind to him; but he might indefinitely postpone the promise he had made to give him his freedom. He might come under pecuniary[1] embarrassments, and his property be seized by creditors; or he might die, without making any arrangements in his favor. He had too often known such accidents to happen to slaves who had kind masters, and he wisely resolved to make sure of the present opportunity to own himself. He was scrupulous about taking any money from his master on false pretences; so he sold his best clothes to pay for his passage to Boston. The slaveholders pronounced him a base, ungrateful wretch, for thus requiting his master's indulgence. What would they have done under similar circumstances?

When Dr. Flint's family heard that William had deserted Mr. Sands, they chuckled greatly over the news. Mrs. Flint made her usual manifestations of Christian feeling, by saying, "I'm glad of it. I hope he'll never get him again. I like to see people paid back in their own coin. I reckon Linda's children will have to pay for it. I should be glad to see them in the speculator's hands again, for I'm tired of seeing those little niggers march about the streets."

---

1 Relating to money.

CHAPTER XXVII.
NEW DESTINATION FOR THE CHILDREN.

Mrs. Flint proclaimed her intention of informing Mrs. Sands who was the father of my children. She likewise proposed to tell her what an artful devil I was; that I had made a great deal of trouble in her family; that when Mr. Sands was at the north, she didn't doubt I had followed him in disguise, and persuaded William to run away. She had some reason to entertain such an idea; for I had written from the north, from time to time, and I dated my letters from various places. Many of them fell into Dr. Flint's hands, as I expected they would; and he must have come to the conclusion that I travelled about a good deal. He kept a close watch over my children, thinking they would eventually lead to my detection.

A new and unexpected trial was in store for me. One day, when Mr. Sands and his wife were walking in the street, they met Benny. The lady took a fancy to him, and exclaimed, "What a pretty little negro! Whom does he belong to?"

Benny did not hear the answer; but he came home very indignant with the stranger lady, because she had called him a negro. A few days afterwards, Mr. Sands called on my grandmother, and told her he wanted her to take the children to his house. He said he had informed his wife of his relation to them, and told her they were motherless; and she wanted to see them.

When he had gone, my grandmother came and asked what I would do. The question seemed a mockery. What could I do? They were Mr. Sands's slaves, and their mother was a slave, whom he had represented to be dead. Perhaps he thought I was. I was too much pained and puzzled to come to any decision; and the children were carried without my knowledge.

Mrs. Sands had a sister from Illinois staying with her. This lady, who had no children of her own, was so much pleased with Ellen, that she offered to adopt her, and bring her up as she would a daughter. Mrs. Sands wanted to take Benjamin. When grandmother reported this to me, I was tried almost beyond endurance. Was this all I was to gain by what I had suffered for the sake of having my children free? True, the prospect seemed fair; but I knew too well how lightly slaveholders held such "parental relations." If pecuniary troubles should come, or if the new wife required more money than could conveniently be spared, my children might be thought of as a convenient means of raising funds. I had no trust in thee, O Slavery! Never should I know peace till my children were emancipated with all due formalities of law.

I was too proud to ask Mr. Sands to do any thing for my own benefit; but I could bring myself to become a supplicant for my children. I resolved to remind him of the promise he had made me, and to throw myself upon his honor for the performance of it. I persuaded my grandmother to go to him, and tell him I was not dead, and that I earnestly entreated him to keep the promise he had made me; that I had heard of the recent proposals concerning my children, and did not feel easy to accept them; that he had promised to emancipate them, and it was time for him to redeem his pledge. I knew there was some risk in thus betraying that I was in the vicinity; but what will not a mother do for her children? He received the message with surprise, and said, "The children are free. I have never intended to claim them as slaves. Linda may decide their fate. In my opinion, they had better be sent to the north. I don't think they are quite safe here. Dr. Flint boasts that they are still in his power. He says they were his daughter's property, and as she was not of age when they were sold, the contract is not legally binding."

So, then, after all I had endured for their sakes, my poor children were between two fires; between my old master and their new master! And I was powerless. There was no protecting arm of the law for me to invoke. Mr. Sands proposed that Ellen should go, for the present, to some of his relatives, who had removed to Brooklyn, Long Island. It was promised that she should be well taken care of, and sent to school. I consented to it, as the best arrangement I could make for her. My grandmother, of course, negotiated it all; and Mrs. Sands knew of no other person in the transaction. She proposed that they should take Ellen with them to Washington, and keep her till they had a good chance of sending her, with friends, to Brooklyn. She had an infant daughter. I had had a glimpse of it, as the nurse passed with it in her arms. It was not a pleasant thought to me, that the bondwoman's child should tend her free-born sister; but there was no alternative.

Ellen was made ready for the journey. O, how it tried my heart to send her away, so young, alone, among strangers! Without a mother's love to shelter her from the storms of life; almost without memory of a mother! I doubted whether she and Benny would have for me the natural affection that children feel for a parent. I thought to myself that I might perhaps never see my daughter again, and I had a great desire that she should look upon me, before she went, that she might take my image with her in her memory. It seemed to me cruel to have her brought to my dungeon. It was sorrow enough for her young heart to know that her mother was a victim of slavery, without seeing the wretched hiding-place to which it had driven her. I begged permission to pass the last night in one of the open chambers, with my little girl. They thought I was crazy to think of trusting such a young child with my perilous secret. I told them I had watched her character, and I felt sure she would not betray me; that I was determined to have an interview, and if they would not facilitate it, I would take my own way to obtain it. They remonstrated against the rashness of such a proceeding; but finding they could not change my purpose, they yielded. I slipped through the trap-door into the storeroom, and my uncle kept watch at the gate, while I passed into the piazza and went up stairs, to the room I used to occupy. It was more than five years since I had seen it; and how the memories crowded on me! There I had taken shelter when my mistress drove me from her house; there came my old tyrant, to mock, insult, and curse me; there my children were first laid in my arms; there I had watched over them, each day with a deeper and sadder love; there I had knelt to God, in anguish of heart, to forgive the wrong I had done. How vividly it all came back! And after this long, gloomy interval, I stood there such a wreck!

In the midst of these meditations, I heard footsteps on the stairs. The door opened, and my uncle Phillip came in, leading Ellen by the hand. I put my arms round her, and said, "Ellen, my dear child, I am your mother." She drew back a little, and looked at me; then, with sweet confidence, she laid her cheek against mine, and I folded her to the heart that had been so long desolated.[1] She was the first to speak. Raising her head, she said, inquiringly, "You really are my mother?" I told her I really was; that during all the long time she had not seen me, I had loved her most tenderly; and that now she was going away, I wanted to see her and talk with her, that she might remember me. With a sob in her voice, she said, "I'm glad you've come to see me; but why didn't you ever come before? Benny and I have wanted so much to see you! He remembers you, and sometimes he tells me about you. Why didn't you come home when Dr. Flint went to bring you?"

I answered, "I couldn't come before, dear. But now that I am with you, tell me whether you like to go away." "I don't know," said she, crying. "Grandmother says I ought not to cry; that I am going to a good place, where I can learn to read and write, and that by and by I can write her a letter. But I shan't have Benny, or

---

1 Devastated.

grandmother, or uncle Phillip, or any body to love me. Can't you go with me? O, do go, dear mother!"

I told her I couldn't go now; but sometime I would come to her, and then she and Benny and I would live together, and have happy times. She wanted to run and bring Benny to see me now. I told her he was going to the north, before long, with uncle Phillip, and then I would come to see him before he went away. I asked if she would like to have me stay all night and sleep with her. "O, yes," she replied. Then, turning to her uncle, she said, pleadingly, "May I stay? Please, uncle! She is my own mother." He laid his hand on her head, and said, solemnly, "Ellen, this is the secret you have promised grandmother never to tell. If you ever speak of it to any body, they will never let you see your grandmother again, and your mother can never come to Brooklyn." "Uncle," she replied, "I will never tell." He told her she might stay with me; and when he had gone, I took her in my arms and told her I was a slave, and that was the reason she must never say she had seen me. I exhorted her to be a good child, to try to please the people where she was going, and that God would raise her up friends. I told her to say her prayers, and remember always to pray for her poor mother, and that God would permit us to meet again. She wept, and I did not check her tears. Perhaps she would never again have a chance to pour her tears into a mother's bosom. All night she nestled in my arms, and I had no inclination to slumber. The moments were too precious to lose any of them. Once, when I thought she was asleep, I kissed her forehead softly, and she said, "I am not asleep, dear mother."

Before dawn they came to take me back to my den.

I drew aside the window curtain, to take a last look of my child. The moonlight shone on her face, and I bent over her, as I had done years before, that wretched night when I ran away. I hugged her close to my throbbing heart; and tears, too sad for such young eyes to shed, flowed down her cheeks, as she gave her last kiss, and whispered in my ear, "Mother, I will never tell." And she never did.

When I got back to my den, I threw myself on the bed and wept there alone in the darkness. It seemed as if my heart would burst. When the time for Ellen's departure drew nigh, I could hear neighbors and friends saying to her, "Good by, Ellen. I hope your poor mother will find you out. Won't you be glad to see her!" She replied, "Yes, ma'am;" and they little dreamed of the weighty secret that weighed down her young heart. She was an affectionate child, but naturally very reserved, except with those she loved, and I felt secure that my secret would be safe with her. I heard the gate close after her, with such feelings as only a slave mother can experience. During the day my meditations were very sad. Sometimes I feared I had been very selfish not to give up all claim to her, and let her go to Illinois, to be adopted by Mrs. Sands's sister. It was my experience of slavery that decided me against it. I feared that circumstances might arise that would cause her to be sent back. I felt confident that I should go to New York myself; and then I should be able to watch over her, and in some degree protect her.

Dr. Flint's family knew nothing of the proposed arrangement till after Ellen was gone, and the news displeased them greatly. Mrs. Flint called on Mrs. Sands's sister to inquire into the matter. She expressed her opinion very freely as to the respect Mr. Sands showed for his wife, and for his own character, in acknowledging those "young niggers." And as for sending Ellen away, she pronounced it to be just as much stealing as it would be for him to come and take a piece of furniture out of her parlor. She said her daughter was not of age to sign the bill of sale, and the children were her property; and when she became of age, or was married, she could take them, wherever she could lay hands on them.

Miss Emily Flint, the little girl to whom I had been bequeathed, was now in her sixteenth year. Her mother considered it all right and honorable for her, or her future husband, to steal my children; but she did not understand how any body could hold up their heads in respectable society, after they had purchased their own children, as Mr. Sands had done. Dr. Flint said very little. Perhaps he thought that Benny would be less likely to be sent away if he kept quiet. One of my letters, that fell into his hands, was dated from Canada; and he seldom spoke of me now. This state of things enabled me to slip down into the storeroom more frequently, where I could stand upright, and move my limbs more freely.

Days, weeks, and months passed, and there came no news of Ellen. I sent a letter to Brooklyn, written in my grandmother's name, to inquire whether she had arrived there. Answer was returned that she had not. I wrote to her in Washington; but no notice was taken of it. There was one person there, who ought to have had some sympathy with the anxiety of the child's friends at home; but the links of such relations as he had formed with me, are easily broken and cast away as rubbish. Yet how protectingly and persuasively he once talked to the poor, helpless slave girl!

And how entirely I trusted him! But now suspicions darkened my mind. Was my child dead, or had they deceived me, and sold her?

If the secret memoirs of many members of Congress should be published, curious details would be unfolded. I once saw a letter from a member of Congress to a slave, who was the mother of six of his children. He wrote to request that she would send her children away from the great house before his return, as he expected to be accompanied by friends. The woman could not read, and was obliged to employ another to read the letter. The existence of the colored children did not trouble this gentleman, it was only the fear that friends might recognize in their features a resemblance to him.

At the end of six months, a letter came to my grandmother, from Brooklyn. It was written by a young lady in the family, and announced that Ellen had just arrived. It contained the following message from her: "I do try to do just as you told me to, and I pray for you every night and morning." I understood that these words were meant for me; and they were a balsam to my heart. The writer closed her letter by saying, "Ellen is a nice little girl, and we shall like to have her with us. My cousin, Mr. Sands, has given her to me, to be my little waiting maid. I shall send her to school, and I hope some day she will write to you herself." This letter perplexed and troubled me. Had my child's father merely placed her there till she was old enough to support herself? Or had he given her to his cousin, as a piece of property? If the last idea was correct, his cousin might return to the south at any time, and hold Ellen as a slave. I tried to put away from me the painful thought that such a foul wrong could have been done to us. I said to myself, "Surely there must be some justice in man;" then I remembered, with a sigh, how slavery perverted all the natural feelings of the human heart. It gave me a pang to look on my light-hearted boy. He believed himself free; and to have him brought under the yoke of slavery, would be more than I could bear. How I longed to have him safely out of the reach of its power!

CHAPTER XXVIII.
AUNT NANCY.

I have mentioned my great-aunt,[1] who was a slave in Dr. Flint's family, and who had been my refuge during the shameful persecutions I suffered from him. This aunt had been married at twenty years of age; that is, as far as slaves can marry. She had the consent of her master and mistress, and a clergyman performed the ceremony. But it was a mere form, without any legal value. Her master or mistress could annul[2] it any day they pleased. She had always slept on the floor in the entry, near Mrs. Flint's chamber door, that she might be within call. When she was married, she was told she might have the use of a small room in an outhouse. Her mother and her husband furnished it. He was a seafaring man, and was allowed to sleep there when he was at home. But on the wedding evening, the bride was ordered to her old post on the entry floor.

Mrs. Flint, at that time, had no children; but she was expecting to be a mother, and if she should want a drink of water in the night, what could she do without her slave to bring it? So my aunt was compelled to lie at her door, until one midnight she was forced to leave, to give premature birth to a child. In a fortnight she was required to resume her place on the entry floor, because Mrs. Flint's babe needed her attentions. She kept her station there through summer and winter, until she had given premature birth to six children; and all the while she was employed as night-nurse to Mrs. Flint's children. Finally, toiling all day, and being deprived of rest at night, completely broke down her constitution, and Dr. Flint declared it was impossible she could ever become the mother of a living child. The fear of losing so valuable a servant by death, now induced them to allow her to sleep in her little room in the out-house, except when there was sickness in the family. She afterwards had two feeble babes, one of whom died in a few days, and the other in four weeks. I well remember her patient sorrow as she held the last dead baby in her arms. "I wish it could have lived," she said; "it is not the will of God that any of my children should live. But I will try to be fit to meet their little spirits in heaven."

---

1 Aunt Nancy seems to be Linda Brent's aunt, not great-aunt. As she says in this chapter, Nancy is her mother's twin sister. Perhaps she is just saying she is a great aunt, but the hyphenation is in the original text.

2 Cancel; invalidate; to make void.

Aunt Nancy was housekeeper and waiting-maid in Dr. Flint's family. Indeed, she was the factotum[1] of the household. Nothing went on well without her. She was my mother's twin sister, and, as far as was in her power, she supplied a mother's place to us orphans. I slept with her all the time I lived in my old master's house, and the bond between us was very strong. When my friends tried to discourage me from running away, she always encouraged me. When they thought I had better return and ask my master's pardon, because there was no possibility of escape, she sent me word never to yield. She said if I persevered I might, perhaps, gain the freedom of my children; and even if I perished in doing it, that was better than to leave them to groan under the same persecutions that had blighted my own life. After I was shut up in my dark cell, she stole away, whenever she could, to bring me the news and say something cheering. How often did I kneel down to listen to her words of consolation, whispered through a crack! "I am old, and have not long to live," she used to say; "and I could die happy if I could only see you and the children free. You must pray to God, Linda, as I do for you, that he will lead you out of this darkness." I would beg her not to worry herself on my account; that there was an end of all suffering sooner or later, and that whether I lived in chains or in freedom, I should always remember her as the good friend who had been the comfort of my life. A word from her always strengthened me; and not me only. The whole family relied upon her judgment, and were guided by her advice.

I had been in my cell six years when my grandmother was summoned to the bedside of this, her last remaining daughter. She was very ill, and they said she would die. Grandmother had not entered Dr. Flint's house for several years. They had treated her cruelly, but she thought nothing of that now. She was grateful for permission to watch by the death-bed of her child. They had always been devoted to each other; and now they sat looking into each other's eyes, longing to speak of the secret that had weighed so much on the hearts of both. My aunt had been stricken with paralysis. She lived but two days, and the last day she was speechless. Before she lost the power of utterance, she told her mother not to grieve if she could not speak to her; that she would try to hold up her hand, to let her know that all was well with her. Even the hard-hearted doctor was a little softened when he saw the dying woman try to smile on the aged mother, who was kneeling by her side. His eyes moistened for a moment,

---

1 Employee or official with many different responsibilities.

as he said she had always been a faithful servant, and they should never be able to supply her place. Mrs. Flint took to her bed, quite overcome by the shock. While my grandmother sat alone with the dead, the doctor came in, leading his youngest son, who had always been a great pet with aunt Nancy, and was much attached to her. "Martha," said he, "aunt Nancy loved this child, and when he comes where you are, I hope you will be kind to him, for her sake." She replied, "Your wife was my foster-child, Dr. Flint, the foster-sister of my poor Nancy, and you little know me if you think I can feel any thing but good will for her children."

"I wish the past could be forgotten, and that we might never think of it," said he; "and that Linda would come to supply her aunt's place. She would be worth more to us than all the money that could be paid for her. I wish it for your sake also, Martha. Now that Nancy is taken away from you, she would be a great comfort to your old age."

He knew he was touching a tender chord. Almost choking with grief, my grandmother replied, "It was not I that drove Linda away. My grandchildren are gone; and of my nine children only one is left. God help me!"

To me, the death of this kind relative was an inexpressible sorrow. I knew that she had been slowly murdered; and I felt that my troubles had helped to finish the work. After I heard of her illness, I listened constantly to hear what news was brought from the great house; and the thought that I could not go to her made me utterly miserable. At last, as uncle Phillip came into the house, I heard some one inquire, "How is she?" and he answered, "She is dead." My little cell seemed whirling round, and I knew nothing more till I opened my eyes and found uncle Phillip bending over me. I had no need to ask any questions. He whispered, "Linda, she died happy." I could not weep. My fixed gaze troubled him. "Don't look so," he said. "Don't add to my poor mother's trouble. Remember how much she has to bear, and that we ought to do all we can to comfort her." Ah, yes, that blessed old grandmother, who for seventy-three years had borne the pelting storms of a slave-mother's life. She did indeed need consolation!

Mrs. Flint had rendered her poor foster-sister childless, apparently without any compunction;[1] and with cruel selfishness had ruined her health by years of incessant, unrequited toil, and broken rest. But now she became very sentimental. I suppose she

---

1 A feeling of uneasiness of the conscience caused by regret for doing wrong or causing pain.

thought it would be a beautiful illustration of the attachment existing between slaveholder and slave, if the body of her old worn-out servant was buried at her feet. She sent for the clergyman and asked if he had any objection to burying aunt Nancy in the doctor's family burial-place. No colored person had ever been allowed interment in the white people's burying-ground, and the minister knew that all the deceased of our family reposed together in the old graveyard of the slaves. He therefore replied, "I have no objection to complying with your wish; but perhaps aunt Nancy's mother may have some choice as to where her remains shall be deposited."

It had never occurred to Mrs. Flint that slaves could have any feelings. When my grandmother was consulted, she at once said she wanted Nancy to lie with all the rest of her family, and where her own old body would be buried. Mrs. Flint graciously complied with her wish, though she said it was painful to her to have Nancy buried away from her. She might have added with touching pathos, "I was so long used to sleep with her lying near me, on the entry floor."

My uncle Phillip asked permission to bury his sister at his own expense; and slaveholders are always ready to grant such favors to slaves and their relatives. The arrangements were very plain, but perfectly respectable. She was buried on the Sabbath, and Mrs. Flint's minister read the funeral service. There was a large concourse of colored people, bond and free, and a few white persons who had always been friendly to our family. Dr. Flint's carriage was in the procession; and when the body was deposited in its humble resting place, the mistress dropped a tear, and returned to her carriage, probably thinking she had performed her duty nobly.

It was talked of by the slaves as a mighty grand funeral. Northern travellers, passing through the place, might have described this tribute of respect to the humble dead as a beautiful feature in the "patriarchal institution;" a touching proof of the attachment between slaveholders and their servants; and tender-hearted Mrs. Flint would have confirmed this impression, with handkerchief at her eyes. We could have told them a different story. We could have given them a chapter of wrongs and sufferings, that would have touched their hearts, if they had any hearts to feel for the colored people. We could have told them how the poor old slave-mother had toiled, year after year, to earn eight hundred dollars to buy her son Phillip's right to his own earnings; and how that same Phillip paid the expenses of the funeral, which they regarded as doing so much credit to the master. We could also have told them of a poor, blighted young creature, shut up in a living grave for years, to avoid the tortures that would be inflicted on her, if she ventured to come out and look on the face of her departed friend.

All this, and much more, I thought of, as I sat at my loophole, waiting for the family to return from the grave; sometimes weeping, sometimes falling asleep, dreaming strange dreams of the dead and the living.

It was sad to witness the grief of my bereaved grandmother. She had always been strong to bear, and now, as ever, religious faith supported her. But her dark life had become still darker, and age and trouble were leaving deep traces on her withered face. She had four places to knock for me to come to the trap-door, and each place had a different meaning. She now came oftener than she had done, and talked to me of her dead daughter, while tears trickled slowly down her furrowed[1] checks. I said all I could to comfort her; but it was a sad reflection, that instead of being able to help her, I was a constant source of anxiety and trouble. The poor old back was fitted to its burden. It bent under it, but did not break.

CHAPTER XXIX.
PREPARATIONS FOR ESCAPE.

I hardly expect that the reader will credit me, when I affirm that I lived in that little dismal hole, almost deprived of light and air, and with no space to move my limbs, for nearly seven years. But it is a fact; and to me a sad one, even now; for my body still suffers from the effects of that long imprisonment, to say nothing of my soul. Members of my family, now living in New York and Boston, can testify to the truth of what I say.

Countless were the nights that I sat late at the little loophole scarcely large enough to give me a glimpse of one twinkling star. There, I heard the patrols and slave-hunters conferring together about the capture of runaways, well knowing how rejoiced they would be to catch me.

Season after season, year after year, I peeped at my children's faces, and heard their sweet voices, with a heart yearning all the while to say, "Your mother is here." Sometimes it appeared to me as if ages had rolled away since I entered upon that gloomy,

---

1 Wrinkled.

monotonous existence. At times, I was stupefied and listless; at other times I became very impatient to know when these dark years would end, and I should again be allowed to feel the sunshine, and breathe the pure air.

After Ellen left us, this feeling increased. Mr. Sands had agreed that Benny might go to the north whenever his uncle Phillip could go with him; and I was anxious to be there also, to watch over my children, and protect them so far as I was able. Moreover, I was likely to be drowned out of my den, if I remained much longer; for the slight roof was getting badly out of repair, and uncle Phillip was afraid to remove the shingles, lest some one should get a glimpse of me. When storms occurred in the night, they spread mats and bits of carpet, which in the morning appeared to have been laid out to dry; but to cover the roof in the daytime might have attracted attention. Consequently, my clothes and bedding were often drenched; a process by which the pains and aches in my cramped and stiffened limbs were greatly increased. I revolved various plans of escape in my mind, which I sometimes imparted to my grandmother, when she came to whisper with me at the trap-door. The kind-hearted old woman had an intense sympathy for runaways. She had known too much of the cruelties inflicted on those who were captured. Her memory always flew back at once to the sufferings of her bright and handsome son, Benjamin, the youngest and dearest of her flock. So, whenever I alluded to the subject, she would groan out, "O, don't think of it, child. You'll break my heart." I had no good old aunt Nancy now to encourage me; but my brother William and my children were continually beckoning me to the north.

And now I must go back a few months in my story. I have stated that the first of January was the time for selling slaves, or leasing them out to new masters. If time were counted by heart-throbs, the poor slaves might reckon years of suffering during that festival so joyous to the free. On the New Year's day preceding my aunt's death, one of my friends, named Fanny, was to be sold at auction, to pay her master's debts. My thoughts were with her during all the day, and at night I anxiously inquired what had been her fate. I was told that she had been sold to one master, and her four little girls to another master, far distant; that she had escaped from her purchaser, and was not to be found. Her mother was the old Aggie I have spoken of. She lived in a small tenement[1] belonging to my grandmother, and built on the same lot with her own house. Her

---

1 Usually refers to a small, cramped habitation.

dwelling was searched and watched, and that brought the patrols so near me that I was obliged to keep very close in my den. The hunters were somehow eluded; and not long afterwards Benny accidentally caught sight of Fanny in her mother's hut. He told his grandmother, who charged him never to speak of it, explaining to him the frightful consequences; and he never betrayed the trust. Aggie little dreamed that my grandmother knew where her daughter was concealed, and that the stooping form of her old neighbor was bending under a similar burden of anxiety and fear; but these dangerous secrets deepened the sympathy between the two old persecuted mothers.

My friend Fanny and I remained many weeks hidden within call of each other; but she was unconscious of the fact. I longed to have her share my den, which seemed a more secure retreat than her own; but I had brought so much trouble on my grandmother, that it seemed wrong to ask her to incur greater risks. My restlessness increased. I had lived too long in bodily pain and anguish of spirit. Always I was in dread that by some accident, or some contrivance, slavery would succeed in snatching my children from me. This thought drove me nearly frantic, and I determined to steer for the North Star at all hazards. At this crisis, Providence opened an unexpected way for me to escape. My friend Peter came one evening, and asked to speak with me. "Your day has come, Linda," said he. "I have found a chance for you to go to the Free States. You have a fortnight to decide." The news seemed too good to be true; but Peter explained his arrangements, and told me all that was necessary was for me to say I would go. I was going to answer him with a joyful yes, when the thought of Benny came to my mind. I told him the temptation was exceedingly strong, but I was terribly afraid of Dr. Flint's alleged power over my child, and that I could not go and leave him behind. Peter remonstrated earnestly. He said such a good chance might never occur again; that Benny was free, and could be sent to me; and that for the sake of my children's welfare I ought not to hesitate a moment. I told him I would consult with uncle Phillip. My uncle rejoiced in the plan, and bade me go by all means. He promised, if his life was spared, that he would either bring or send my son to me as soon as I reached a place of safety. I resolved to go, but thought nothing had better be said to my grandmother till very near the time of departure. But my uncle thought she would feel it more keenly if I left her so suddenly. "I will reason with her," said he, "and convince her how necessary it is, not only for your sake, but for hers also. You cannot be blind to the fact that she is sinking under her burdens." I was not blind to it. I knew that my concealment was an ever-present source of anxiety, and that the older she grew the more nervously fearful she was of discovery. My uncle talked with her, and finally succeeded in persuading her that it was absolutely necessary for me to seize the chance so unexpectedly offered.

The anticipation of being a free woman proved almost too much for my weak frame. The excitement stimulated me, and at the same time bewildered me. I made busy preparations for my journey, and for my son to follow me. I resolved to have an interview with him before I went, that I might give him cautions and advice, and tell him how anxiously I should be waiting for him at the north. Grandmother stole up to me as often as possible to whisper words of counsel. She insisted upon my writing to Dr. Flint, as soon as I arrived in the Free States, and asking him to sell me to her. She said she would sacrifice her house, and all she had in the world, for the sake of having me safe with my children in any part of the world. If she could only live to know that she could die in peace. I promised the dear old faithful friend that I would write to her as soon as I arrived, and put the letter in a safe way to reach her; but in my own mind I resolved that not another cent of her hard earnings should be spent to pay rapacious[1] slaveholders for what they called their property. And even if I had not been unwilling to buy what I had already a right to possess, common humanity would have prevented me from accepting the generous offer, at the expense of turning my aged relative out of house and home, when she was trembling on the brink of the grave.

I was to escape in a vessel; but I forbear to mention any further particulars. I was in readiness, but the vessel was unexpectedly detained several days. Meantime, news came to town of a most horrible murder committed on a fugitive slave, named James. Charity, the mother of this unfortunate young man, had been an old acquaintance of ours. I have told the shocking particulars of his death, in my description of some of the neighboring slaveholders. My grandmother, always nervously sensitive about runaways, was terribly frightened. She felt sure that a similar fate awaited me, if I did not desist from my enterprise. She sobbed, and groaned, and entreated me not to go. Her excessive fear was somewhat contagious, and my heart was not proof against her extreme-agony. I was grievously disappointed, but I promised to relinquish my project.

---

1 Predatory; excessively greedy.

When my friend Peter was apprised[1] of this, he was both disappointed and vexed. He said, that judging from our past experience, it would be a long time before I had such another chance to throw away. I told him it need not be thrown away; that I had a friend concealed near by, who would be glad enough to take the place that had been provided for me. I told him about poor Fanny, and the kind-hearted, noble fellow, who never turned his back upon any body in distress, white or black, expressed his readiness to help her. Aggie was much surprised when she found that we knew her secret. She was rejoiced to hear of such a chance for Fanny, and arrangements were made for her to go on board the vessel the next night. They both supposed that I had long been at the north, therefore my name was not mentioned in the transaction. Fanny was carried on board at the appointed time, and stowed away in a very small cabin. This accommodation had been purchased at a price that would pay for a voyage to England. But when one proposes to go to fine old England, they stop to calculate whether they can afford the cost of the pleasure; while in making a bargain to escape from slavery, the trembling victim is ready to say, "Take all I have, only don't betray me!"

The next morning I peeped through my loophole, and saw that it was dark and cloudy. At night I received news that the wind was ahead, and the vessel had not sailed. I was exceedingly anxious about Fanny, and Peter too, who was running a tremendous risk at my instigation. Next day the wind and weather remained the same. Poor Fanny had been half dead with fright when they carried her on board, and I could readily imagine how she must be suffering now. Grandmother came often to my den, to say how thankful she was I did not go. On the third morning she rapped for me to come down to the storeroom. The poor old sufferer was breaking down under her weight of trouble. She was easily flurried now. I found her in a nervous, excited state, but I was not aware that she had forgotten to lock the door behind her, as usual. She was exceedingly worried about the detention of the vessel. She was afraid all would be discovered, and then Fanny, and Peter, and I, would all be tortured to death, and Phillip would be utterly ruined, and her house would be torn down. Poor Peter! If he should die such a horrible death as the poor slave James had lately done, and all for his kindness in trying to help me, how dreadful it would be for us all! Alas, the thought was familiar to me, and had sent many a sharp pang through my heart. I tried to suppress my

---

1 Informed.

own anxiety, and speak soothingly to her. She brought in some allusion to aunt Nancy, the dear daughter she had recently buried, and then she lost all control of herself. As she stood there, trembling and sobbing, a voice from the piazza called out, "Whar is you, aunt Marthy?" Grandmother was startled, and in her agitation opened the door, without thinking of me. In stepped Jenny, the mischievous housemaid, who had tried to enter my room, when I was concealed in the house of my white benefactors. "I's bin huntin ebery whar for you, aunt Marthy," said she. "My missis wants you to send her some crackers." I had slunk down behind a barrel, which entirely screened me, but I imagined that Jenny was looking directly at the spot, and my heart beat violently. My grandmother immediately thought what she had done, and went out quickly with Jenny to count the crackers, locking the door after her. She returned to me, in a few minutes, the perfect picture of despair. "Poor child!" she exclaimed, "my carelessness has ruined you. The boat ain't gone yet. Get ready immediately, and go with Fanny. I ain't got another word to say against it now; for there's no telling what may happen this day."

Uncle Phillip was sent for, and he agreed with his mother in thinking that Jenny would inform Dr. Flint in less than twenty-four hours. He advised getting me on board the boat, if possible; if not, I had better keep very still in my den, where they could not find me without tearing the house down. He said it would not do for him to move in the matter, because suspicion would be immediately excited; but he promised to communicate with Peter. I felt reluctant to apply to him again, having implicated him too much already; but there seemed to be no alternative. Vexed as Peter had been by my indecision, he was true to his generous nature, and said at once that he would do his best to help me, trusting I should show myself a stronger woman this time.

He immediately proceeded to the wharf, and found that the wind had shifted, and the vessel was slowly beating down stream. On some pretext of urgent necessity, he offered two boatmen a dollar apiece to catch up with her. He was of lighter complexion than the boatmen he hired, and when the captain saw them coming so rapidly, he thought officers were pursuing his vessel in search of the runaway slave he had on board. They hoisted sails, but the boat gained upon them, and the indefatigable Peter sprang on board.

The captain at once recognized him. Peter asked him to go below, to speak about a bad bill he had given him. When he told his errand, the captain replied, "Why, the woman's here already;

and I've put her where you or the devil would have a tough job to find her."

"But it is another woman I want to bring," said Peter. "She is in great distress, too, and you shall be paid any thing within reason, if you'll stop and take her."

"What's her name?" inquired the captain.

"Linda," he replied.

"That's the name of the woman already here," rejoined the captain. "By George! I believe you mean to betray me."

"O!" exclaimed Peter, "God knows I wouldn't harm a hair of your head. I am too grateful to you. But there really is another woman in great danger. Do have the humanity to stop and take her!"

After a while they came to an understanding. Fanny, not dreaming I was any where about in that region, had assumed my name, though she called herself Johnson. "Linda is a common name," said Peter, "and the woman I want to bring is Linda Brent."

The captain agreed to wait at a certain place till evening, being handsomely paid for his detention.

Of course, the day was an anxious one for us all. But we concluded that if Jenny had seen me, she would be too wise to let her mistress know of it; and that she probably would not get a chance to see Dr. Flint's family till evening, for I knew very well what were the rules in that household. I afterwards believed that she did not see me; for nothing ever came of it, and she was one of those base characters that would have jumped to betray a suffering fellow being for the sake of thirty pieces of silver.[1]

I made all my arrangements to go on board as soon as it was dusk. The intervening time I resolved to spend with my son. I had not spoken to him for seven years, though I had been under the same roof, and seen him every day, when I was well enough to sit at the loophole. I did not dare to venture beyond the storeroom; so they brought him there, and locked us up together, in a place concealed from the piazza door. It was an agitating interview for both of us. After we had talked and wept together for a little while, he said, "Mother, I'm glad you're going away. I wish I could go with you. I knew you was here; and I have been so afraid they would come and catch you!"

---

1 In describing the potential danger, Jacobs links her story to that of Jesus Christ, who, according Matthew 26.15, was betrayed by Judas for thirty pieces of silver.

I was greatly surprised, and asked him how he had found it out.

He replied, "I was standing under the eaves, one day, before Ellen went away, and I heard somebody cough up over the wood shed. I don't know what made me think it was you, but I did think so. I missed Ellen, the night before she went away; and grandmother brought her back into the room in the night; and I thought maybe she'd been to see you, before she went, for I heard grandmother whisper to her, 'Now go to sleep; and remember never to tell.'"

I asked him if he ever mentioned his suspicions to his sister. He said he never did; but after he heard the cough, if he saw her playing with other children on that side of the house, he always tried to coax her round to the other side, for fear they would hear me cough, too. He said he had kept a close lookout for Dr. Flint, and if he saw him speak to a constable, or a patrol, he always told grandmother. I now recollected that I had seen him manifest uneasiness, when people were on that side of the house, and I had at the time been puzzled to conjecture[1] a motive for his actions. Such prudence may seem extraordinary in a boy of twelve years, but slaves, being surrounded by mysteries, deceptions, and dangers, early learn to be suspicious and watchful, and prematurely cautious and cunning. He had never asked a question of grandmother, or uncle Phillip, and I had often heard him chime in with other children, when they spoke of my being at the north.

I told him I was now really going to the Free States, and if he was a good, honest boy, and a loving child to his dear old grandmother, the Lord would bless him, and bring him to me, and we and Ellen would live together. He began to tell me that grandmother had not eaten any thing all day. While he was speaking, the door was unlocked, and she came in with a small bag of money, which she wanted me to take. I begged her to keep a part of it, at least, to pay for Benny's being sent to the north; but she insisted, while her tears were falling fast, that I should take the whole. "You may be sick among strangers," she said, "and they would send you to the poorhouse to die." Ah, that good grandmother!

For the last time I went up to my nook. Its desolate appearance no longer chilled me, for the light of hope had risen in my soul. Yet, even with the blessed prospect of freedom before me, I felt very sad at leaving forever that old homestead, where I had been sheltered so long by the dear old grandmother; where I had dreamed my first young dream of love; and where, after that had

---

1 To form a conclusion without sufficient evidence to prove it.

faded away, my children came to twine themselves so closely round my desolate heart. As the hour approached for me to leave, I again descended to the storeroom. My grandmother and Benny were there. She took me by the hand, and said, "Linda, let us pray." We knelt down together, with my child pressed to my heart, and my other arm round the faithful, loving old friend I was about to leave forever. On no other occasion has it ever been my lot to listen to so fervent a supplication for mercy and protection. It thrilled through my heart, and inspired me with trust in God.

Peter was waiting for me in the street. I was soon by his side, faint in body, but strong of purpose. I did not look back upon the old place, though I felt that I should never see it again.

CHAPTER XXX.
NORTHWARD BOUND.

I never could tell how we reached the wharf. My brain was all of a whirl, and my limbs tottered under me. At an appointed place we met my uncle Phillip, who had started before us on a different route, that he might reach the wharf first, and give us timely warning if there was any danger. A row-boat was in readiness. As I was about to step in, I felt something pull me gently, and turning round I saw Benny, looking pale and anxious. He whispered in my ear, "I've been peeping into the doctor's window, and he's at home. Good by, mother. Don't cry; I'll come." He hastened away. I clasped the hand of my good uncle, to whom I owed so much, and of Peter, the brave, generous friend who had volunteered to run such terrible risks to secure my safety. To this day I remember how his bright face beamed with joy, when he told me he had discovered a safe method for me to escape. Yet that intelligent, enterprising, noble-hearted man was a chattel! liable, by the laws of a country that calls itself civilized, to be sold with horses and pigs! We parted in silence. Our hearts were all too full for words!

Swiftly the boat glided over the water. After a while, one of the sailors said, "Don't be down-hearted, madam. We will take you safely to your husband, in—." At first I could not imagine what he meant; but I had presence of mind to think that it probably referred to something the captain had told him; so I thanked him, and said I hoped we should have pleasant weather.

When I entered the vessel the captain came forward to meet me. He was an elderly man, with a pleasant countenance. He showed me to a little box of a cabin, where sat my friend Fanny.

She started as if she had seen a spectre. She gazed on me in utter astonishment, and exclaimed, "Linda, can this be you? or is it your ghost?" When we were locked in each other's arms, my over-wrought feelings could no longer be restrained. My sobs reached the ears of the captain, who came and very kindly reminded us, that for his safety, as well as our own, it would be prudent for us not to attract any attention. He said that when there was a sail in sight he wished us to keep below; but at other times, he had no objection to our being on deck. He assured us that he would keep a good lookout, and if we acted prudently, he thought we should be in no danger. He had represented us as women going to meet our husbands in—. We thanked him, and promised to observe carefully all the directions he gave us.

Fanny and I now talked by ourselves, low and quietly, in our little cabin. She told me of the sufferings she had gone through in making her escape, and of her terrors while she was concealed in her mother's house. Above all, she dwelt on the agony of separa-tion from all her children on that dreadful auction day. She could scarcely credit me, when I told her of the place where I had passed nearly seven years. "We have the same sorrows," said I. "No," replied she, "you are going to see your children soon, and there is no hope that I shall ever even hear from mine."

The vessel was soon under way, but we made slow progress. The wind was against us. I should not have cared for this, if we had been out of sight of the town; but until there were miles of water between us and our enemies, we were filled with constant apprehensions that the constables would come on board. Neither could I feel quite at ease with the captain and his men. I was an entire stranger to that class of people, and I had heard that sail-ors were rough, and sometimes cruel. We were so completely in their power, that if they were bad men, our situation would be dreadful. Now that the captain was paid for our passage, might he not be tempted to make more money by giving us up to those who claimed us as property? I was naturally of a confiding dispo-sition, but slavery had made me suspicious of every body. Fanny did not share my distrust of the captain or his men. She said she was afraid at first, but she had been on board three days while the vessel lay in the dock, and nobody had betrayed her, or treated her otherwise than kindly.

The captain soon came to advise us to go on deck for fresh air. His friendly and respectful manner, combined with Fanny's testimony, reassured me, and we went with him. He placed us in a comfortable seat, and occasionally entered into conversation. He told us he was a Southerner by birth, and had spent the greater part of his life in the Slave States, and that he had recently lost a brother who traded in slaves. "But," said he, "it is a pitiable and degrading business, and I always felt ashamed to acknowledge my brother in connection with it." As we passed Snaky Swamp, he pointed to it, and said, "There is a slave territory that defies all the laws." I thought of the terrible days I had spent there, and though it was not called Dismal Swamp, it made me feel very dismal as I looked at it.

I shall never forget that night. The balmy air of spring was so refreshing! And how shall I describe my sensations when we were fairly sailing on Chesapeake Bay? O, the beautiful sunshine! the exhilarating breeze! and I could enjoy them without fear or restraint. I had never realized what grand things air and sunlight are till I had been deprived of them.

Ten days after we left land we were approaching Philadelphia. The captain said we should arrive there in the night, but he thought we had better wait till morning, and go on shore in broad daylight, as the best way to avoid suspicion.

I replied, "You know best. But will you stay on board and protect us?"

He saw that I was suspicious, and he said he was sorry, now that he had brought us to the end of our voyage, to find I had so little confidence in him. Ah, if he had ever been a slave he would have known how difficult it was to trust a white man. He assured us that we might sleep through the night without fear; that he would take care we were not left unprotected. Be it said to the honor of this captain, Southerner as he was, that if Fanny and I had been white ladies, and our passage lawfully engaged, he could not have treated us more respectfully. My intelligent friend, Peter, had rightly estimated the character of the man to whose honor he had intrusted us.

The next morning I was on deck as soon as the day dawned. I called Fanny to see the sun rise, for the first time in our lives, on free soil; for such I then believed it to be. We watched the reddening sky, and saw the great orb come up slowly out of the water, as it seemed. Soon the waves began to sparkle, and every thing caught the beautiful glow. Before us lay the city of strangers. We looked at each other, and the eyes of both were moistened with tears. We had escaped from slavery, and we supposed ourselves to be safe from the hunters. But we were alone in the world, and we had left dear ties behind us; ties cruelly sundered by the demon Slavery.

CHAPTER XXXI.
INCIDENTS IN PHILADELPHIA.

I had heard that the poor slave had many friends at the north. I trusted we should find some of them. Meantime, we would take it for granted that all were friends, till they proved to the contrary. I sought out the kind captain, thanked him for his attentions, and told him I should never cease to be grateful for the service he had rendered us. I gave him a message to the friends I had left at home, and he promised to deliver it. We were placed in a row-boat, and in about fifteen minutes were landed on a wood wharf in Philadelphia. As I stood looking round, the friendly captain touched me on the shoulder, and said, "There is a respectable-looking colored man behind you. I will speak to him about the New York trains, and tell him you wish to go directly on." I thanked him, and asked him to direct me to some shops where I could buy gloves and veils. He did so, and said he would talk with the colored man till I returned. I made what haste I could. Constant exercise on board the vessel, and frequent rubbing with salt water, had nearly restored the use of my limbs. The noise of the great city confused me, but I found the shops, and bought some double veils and gloves for Fanny and myself. The shopman told me they were so many levies. I had never heard the word before, but I did not tell him so. I thought if he knew I was a stranger he might ask me where I came from. I gave him a gold piece, and when he returned the change, I counted it, and found out how much a levy was. I made my way back to the wharf, where the captain introduced me to the colored man, as the Rev. Jeremiah Durham, minister of Bethel church.[1] He took me by the hand, as if I had been an old friend. He told us we were too late for the morning cars to New York, and must wait until the evening, or the next morning. He invited me to go home with him, assuring me that his wife would give me a cordial welcome; and

---

1 An instance when a person is not given a pseudonym in Jacobs's narrative. As Yellin explains, "In 1842, Philadelphia housed 19,000 African Americans, the largest free black population in the country. The community supported fifteen churches, twenty-one day schools, sixty-four Mutual Relief or Benevolent Societies, and a Vigilant Committee.... Routinely placing themselves at risk by helping fugitives, the Vigilant Committee lived up to its name by aiding 'colored persons in distress' and regularly sent its members to the city docks looking for fugitives. Today was Durham's turn" (*Life* 65–66).

for my friend he would provide a home with one of his neighbors. I thanked him for so much kindness to strangers, and told him if I must be detained, I should like to hunt up some people who formerly went from our part of the country. Mr. Durham insisted that I should dine with him, and then he would assist me in finding my friends. The sailors came to bid us good by. I shook their hardy hands, with tears in my eyes. They had all been kind to us, and they had rendered us a greater service than they could possibly conceive of.

I had never seen so large a city, or been in contact with so many people in the streets. It seemed as if those who passed looked at us with an expression of curiosity. My face was so blistered and peeled, by sitting on deck, in wind and sunshine, that I thought they could not easily decide to what nation I belonged.

Mrs. Durham met me with a kindly welcome, without asking any questions. I was tired, and her friendly manner was a sweet refreshment. God bless her! I was sure that she had comforted other weary hearts, before I received her sympathy. She was surrounded by her husband and children, in a home made sacred by protecting laws. I thought of my own children, and sighed.

After dinner Mr. Durham went with me in quest of the friends I had spoken of. They went from my native town, and I anticipated much pleasure in looking on familiar faces. They were not at home, and we retraced our steps through streets delightfully clean. On the way, Mr. Durham observed that I had spoken to him of a daughter I expected to meet; that he was surprised, for I looked so young he had taken me for a single woman. He was approaching a subject on which I was extremely sensitive. He would ask about my husband next, I thought, and if I answered him truly, what would he think of me? I told him I had two children, one in New York, the other at the south. He asked some further questions, and I frankly told him some of the most important events of my life. It was painful for me to do it; but I would not deceive him. If he was desirous of being my friend, I thought he ought to know how far I was worthy of it. "Excuse me, if I have tried your feelings," said he. "I did not question you from idle curiosity. I wanted to understand your situation, in order to know whether I could be of any service to you, or your little girl. Your straight-forward answers do you credit; but don't answer every body so openly. It might give some heartless people a pretext for treating you with contempt."

That word contempt burned me like coals of fire. I replied, "God alone knows how I have suffered; and He, I trust, will forgive me. If I am permitted to have my children, I intend to be a good mother, and to live in such a manner that people cannot treat me with contempt."

"I respect your sentiments," said he. "Place your trust in God, and be governed by good principles, and you will not fail to find friends."

When we reached home, I went to my room, glad to shut out the world for a while. The words he had spoken made an indelible impression upon me. They brought up great shadows from the mournful past. In the midst of my meditations I was startled by a knock at the door. Mrs. Durham entered, her face all beaming with kindness, to say that there was an anti-slavery friend down stairs, who would like to see me. I overcame my dread of encountering strangers, and went with her. Many questions were asked concerning my experiences, and my escape from slavery; but I observed how careful they all were not to say any thing that might wound my feelings. How gratifying this was, can be fully understood only by those who have been accustomed to be treated as if they were not included within the pale of human beings. The antislavery friend had come to inquire into my plans, and to offer assistance, if needed. Fanny was comfortably established, for the present, with a friend of Mr. Durham. The Anti-Slavery Society agreed to pay her expenses to New York. The same was offered to me, but I declined to accept it; telling them that my grandmother had given me sufficient to pay my expenses to the end of my journey. We were urged to remain in Philadelphia a few days, until some suitable escort could be found for us. I gladly accepted the proposition, for I had a dread of meeting slaveholders, and some dread also of railroads. I had never entered a railroad car in my life, and it seemed to me quite an important event.

That night I sought my pillow with feelings I had never carried to it before. I verily believed myself to be a free woman. I was wakeful for a long time, and I had no sooner fallen asleep, than I was roused by fire-bells. I jumped up, and hurried on my clothes. Where I came from, every body hastened to dress themselves on such occasions. The white people thought a great fire might be used as a good opportunity for insurrection, and that it was best to be in readiness; and the colored people were ordered out to labor in extinguishing the flames. There was but one engine in our town, and colored women and children were often required to drag it to the river's edge and fill it. Mrs. Durham's daughter slept in the same room with me, and seeing that she slept through all the din,[1] I thought it was my duty to wake her. "What's the matter?" said she, rubbing her eyes.

"They're screaming fire in the streets, and the bells are ringing," I replied.

"What of that?" said she, drowsily. "We are used to it. We never get up, without the fire is very near. What good would it do?"

I was quite surprised that it was not necessary for us to go and help fill the engine. I was an ignorant child, just beginning to learn how things went on in great cities.

At daylight, I heard women crying fresh fish, berries, radishes, and various other things. All this was new to me. I dressed myself at an early hour, and sat at the window to watch that unknown tide of life. Philadelphia seemed to me a wonderfully great place. At the breakfast table, my idea of going out to drag the engine was laughed over, and I joined in the mirth.

I went to see Fanny, and found her so well contented among her new friends that she was in no haste to leave. I was also very happy with my kind hostess. She had had advantages for education, and was vastly my superior. Every day, almost every hour, I was adding to my little stock of knowledge. She took me out to see the city as much as she deemed prudent. One day she took me to an artist's room, and showed me the portraits of some of her children. I had never seen any paintings of colored people before, and they seemed to me beautiful.

At the end of five days, one of Mrs. Durham's friends offered to accompany us to New York the following morning. As I held the hand of my good hostess in a parting clasp, I longed to know whether her husband had repeated to her what I had told him. I supposed he had, but she never made any allusion to it. I presume it was the delicate silence of womanly sympathy.

When Mr. Durham handed us our tickets, he said, "I am afraid you will have a disagreeable ride; but I could not procure tickets for the first class cars."

Supposing I had not given him money enough, I offered more. "O, no," said he, "they could not be had for any money. They don't allow colored people to go in the first-class cars."

This was the first chill to my enthusiasm about the Free States. Colored people were allowed to ride in a filthy box, behind white people, at the south, but there they were not required to pay for the privilege. It made me sad to find how the north aped the customs of slavery.

---

1 Loud, confused noise.

We were stowed away in a large, rough car, with windows on each side, too high for us to look out without standing up. It was crowded with people, apparently of all nations. There were plenty of beds and cradles, containing screaming and kicking babies. Every other man had a cigar or pipe in his mouth, and jugs of whiskey were handed round freely. The fumes of the whiskey and the dense tobacco smoke were sickening to my senses, and my mind was equally nauseated by the coarse jokes and ribald songs around me. It was a very disagreeable ride. Since that time there has been some improvement in these matters.

CHAPTER XXXII.
THE MEETING OF MOTHER AND DAUGHTER.

When we arrived in New York, I was half crazed by the crowd of coachmen calling out, "Carriage, ma'am?" We bargained with one to take us to Sullivan Street for twelve shillings. A burly Irishman stepped up and said, "I'll tak' ye for sax shillings." The reduction of half the price was an object to us, and we asked if he could take us right away. "Troth an I will, ladies," he replied. I noticed that the hackmen smiled at each other, and I inquired whether his conveyance was decent. "Yes, it's dacent it is, marm. Devil a bit would I be after takin' ladies in a cab that was not dacent." We gave him our checks. He went for the baggage, and soon reappeared, saying, "This way, if you plase, ladies." We followed, and found our trunks on a truck, and we were invited to take our seats on them. We told him that was not what we bargained for, and he must take the trunks off. He swore they should not be touched till we had paid him six shillings. In our situation it was not prudent to attract attention, and I was about to pay him what he required, when a man near by shook his head for me not to do it. After a great ado we got rid of the Irishman, and had our trunks fastened on a hack. We had been recommended to a boarding-house in Sullivan Street, and thither we drove. There Fanny and I separated. The Anti-Slavery Society provided a home for her, and I afterwards heard of her in prosperous circumstances. I sent for an old friend from my part of the country, who had for some time been doing business in New York. He came immediately. I told him I wanted to go to my daughter, and asked him to aid me in procuring an interview.

I cautioned him not to let it be known to the family that I had just arrived from the south, because they supposed I had been at the north seven years. He told me there was a colored woman in Brooklyn who came from the same town I did, and I had better go to her house, and have my daughter meet me there. I accepted the proposition thankfully, and he agreed to escort me to Brooklyn. We crossed Fulton ferry, went up Myrtle Avenue, and stopped at the house he designated. I was just about to enter, when two girls passed. My friend called my attention to them. I turned, and recognized in the eldest, Sarah, the daughter of a woman who used to live with my grandmother, but who had left the south years ago. Surprised and rejoiced at this unexpected meeting, I threw my arms round her, and inquired concerning her mother.

"You take no notice of the other girl," said my friend. I turned, and there stood my Ellen! I pressed her to my heart, then held her away from me to take a look at her. She had changed a good deal in the two years since I parted from her. Signs of neglect could be discerned by eyes less observing than a mother's. My friend invited us all to go into the house; but Ellen said she had been sent on an errand, which she would do as quickly as possible, and go home and ask Mrs. Hobbs to let her come and see me. It was agreed that I should send for her the next day. Her companion, Sarah, hastened to tell her mother of my arrival. When I entered the house, I found the mistress of it absent, and I waited for her return. Before I saw her, I heard her saying, "Where is Linda Brent? I used to know her father and mother." Soon Sarah came with her mother. So there was quite a company of us, all from my grandmother's neighborhood. These friends gathered round me and questioned me eagerly. They laughed, they cried, and they shouted. They thanked God that I had got away from my persecutors and was safe on Long Island. It was a day of great excitement. How different from the silent days I had passed in my dreary den!

The next morning was Sunday. My first waking thoughts were occupied with the note I was to send to Mrs. Hobbs, the lady with whom Ellen lived. That I had recently come into that vicinity was evident; otherwise I should have sooner inquired for my daughter. It would not do to let them know I had just arrived from the south, for that would involve the suspicion of my having been harbored there, and might bring trouble, if not ruin, on several people.

I like a straightforward course, and am always reluctant to resort to subterfuges.[1] So far as my ways have been crooked, I

---

1 Artificial contrivances used to escape a rule or consequence. (In Jacobs's case, the rules and consequences are dehumanizing, brutal, and unjust.)

charge them all upon slavery. It was that system of violence and wrong which now left me no alternative but to enact a falsehood. I began my note by stating that I had recently arrived from Canada, and was very desirous to have my daughter come to see me. She came and brought a message from Mrs. Hobbs, inviting me to her house, and assuring me that I need not have any fears. The conversation I had with my child did not leave my mind at ease. When I asked if she was well treated, she answered yes; but there was no heartiness in the tone, and it seemed to me that she said it from an unwillingness to have me troubled on her account. Before she left me, she asked very earnestly, "Mother, when will you take me to live with you?" It made me sad to think that I could not give her a home till I went to work and earned the means; and that might take me a long time. When she was placed with Mrs. Hobbs, the agreement was that she should be sent to school. She had been there two years, and was now nine years old, and she scarcely knew her letters. There was no excuse for this, for there were good public schools in Brooklyn, to which she could have been sent without expense.

She staid with me till dark, and I went home with her. I was received in a friendly manner by the family, and all agreed in saying that Ellen was a useful, good girl. Mrs. Hobbs looked me coolly in the face, and said, "I suppose you know that my cousin, Mr. Sands, has given her to my eldest daughter. She will make a nice waiting-maid for her when she grows up." I did not answer a word. How could she, who knew by experience the strength of a mother's love, and who was perfectly aware of the relation Mr. Sands bore to my children,—how could she look me in the face, while she thrust such a dagger into my heart?

I was no longer surprised that they had kept her in such a state of ignorance. Mr. Hobbs had formerly been wealthy, but he had failed, and afterwards obtained a subordinate situation in the Custom House.[1] Perhaps they expected to return to the south some day; and Ellen's knowledge was quite sufficient for a slave's condition. I was impatient to go to work and earn money, that I might change the uncertain position of my children. Mr. Sands had not kept his promise to emancipate them. I had also

---

1 A government building for collecting fees. (Such jobs are not automatically bad or lowly but Jacobs suggests that the position Mr. Hobbs was able to attain was subordinate, especially in comparison to his previous status.)

been deceived about Ellen. What security had I with regard to Benjamin? I felt that I had none.

I returned to my friend's house in an uneasy state of mind. In order to protect my children, it was necessary that I should own myself. I called myself free, and sometimes felt so; but I knew I was insecure. I sat down that night and wrote a civil letter to Dr. Flint, asking him to state the lowest terms on which he would sell me; and as I belonged by law to his daughter, I wrote to her also, making a similar request.

Since my arrival at the north I had not been unmindful of my dear brother William. I had made diligent inquiries for him, and having heard of him in Boston, I went thither. When I arrived there, I found he had gone to New Bedford. I wrote to that place, and was informed he had gone on a whaling voyage, and would not return for some months. I went back to New York to get employment near Ellen. I received an answer from Dr. Flint, which gave me no encouragement. He advised me to return and submit myself to my rightful owners, and then any request I might make would be granted. I lent this letter to a friend, who lost it; otherwise I would present a copy to my readers.

CHAPTER XXXIII.
A HOME FOUND.

My greatest anxiety now was to obtain employment. My health was greatly improved, though my limbs continued to trouble me with swelling whenever I walked much. The greatest difficulty in my way was, that those who employed strangers required a recommendation; and in my peculiar position, I could, of course, obtain no certificates from the families I had so faithfully served.

One day an acquaintance told me of a lady who wanted a nurse for her babe, and I immediately applied for the situation. The lady told me she preferred to have one who had been a mother, and accustomed to the care of infants. I told her I had nursed two babes of my own. She asked me many questions, but, to my great relief, did not require a recommendation from my former employers. She told me she was an English woman, and that was a pleasant circumstance to me, because I had heard they had less prejudice against color than Americans entertained. It was agreed that we should try each other for a week. The trial proved satisfactory to both parties, and I was engaged for a month.

The heavenly Father had been most merciful to me in leading me to this place. Mrs. Bruce was a kind and gentle lady, and proved a true and sympathizing friend. Before the stipulated month expired, the necessity of passing up and down stairs frequently, caused my limbs to swell so painfully, that I became unable to perform my duties. Many ladies would have thoughtlessly discharged me; but Mrs. Bruce made arrangements to save me steps, and employed a physician to attend upon me. I had not yet told her that I was a fugitive slave. She noticed that I was often sad, and kindly inquired the cause. I spoke of being separated from my children, and from relatives who were dear to me; but I did not mention the constant feeling of insecurity which oppressed my spirits. I longed for some one to confide in; but I had been so deceived by white people, that I had lost all confidence in them. If they spoke kind words to me, I thought it was for some selfish purpose. I had entered this family with the distrustful feelings I had brought with me out of slavery; but ere six months had passed, I found that the gentle deportment of Mrs. Bruce and the smiles of her lovely babe were thawing my chilled heart. My narrow mind also began to expand under the influences of her intelligent conversation, and the opportunities for reading, which were gladly allowed me whenever I had leisure from my duties. I gradually became more energetic and more cheerful.

The old feeling of insecurity, especially with regard to my children, often threw its dark shadow across my sunshine. Mrs. Bruce offered me a home for Ellen; but pleasant as it would have been, I did not dare to accept it, for fear of offending the Hobbs family. Their knowledge of my precarious situation placed me in their power; and I felt that it was important for me to keep on the right side of them, till, by dint of labor and economy, I could make a home for my children. I was far from feeling satisfied with Ellen's situation. She was not well cared for. She sometimes came to New York to visit me; but she generally brought a request from Mrs. Hobbs that I would buy her a pair of shoes, or some article of clothing. This was accompanied by a promise of payment when Mr. Hobbs's salary at the Custom House became due; but some how or other the pay-day never came. Thus many dollars of my earnings were expended to keep my child comfortably clothed. That, however, was a slight trouble, compared with the fear that their pecuniary embarrassments might induce them to sell my precious young daughter. I knew they were in constant communication with Southerners, and had frequent opportunities to do it. I have stated that when Dr. Flint put Ellen in jail, at two years old, she had an inflammation of the eyes, occasioned by measles. This disease still troubled her; and kind Mrs. Bruce proposed that she should come to New York for a while, to be under the care of Dr. Elliott, a well known oculist. It did not occur to me that there was any thing improper in a mother's making such a request; but Mrs. Hobbs was very angry, and refused to let her go. Situated as I was, it was not politic to insist upon it. I made no complaint, but I longed to be entirely free to act a mother's part towards my children. The next time I went over to Brooklyn, Mrs. Hobbs, as if to apologize for her anger, told me she had employed her own physician to attend to Ellen's eyes, and that she had refused my request because she did not consider it safe to trust her in New York. I accepted the explanation in silence; but she had told me that my child belonged to her daughter, and I suspected that her real motive was a fear of my conveying her property away from her. Perhaps I did her injustice; but my knowledge of Southerners made it difficult for me to feel otherwise.

Sweet and bitter were mixed in the cup of my life, and I was thankful that it had ceased to be entirely bitter. I loved Mrs. Bruce's babe. When it laughed and crowed in my face, and twined its little tender arms confidingly about my neck, it made me think of the time when Benny and Ellen were babies, and my wounded heart was soothed. One bright morning, as I stood at the window, tossing baby in my arms, my attention was attracted by a young man in sailor's dress, who was closely observing every house as he passed. I looked at him earnestly. Could it be my brother William? It must be he—and yet, how changed! I placed the baby safely, flew down stairs, opened the front door, beckoned to the sailor, and in less than a minute I was clasped in my brother's arms. How much we had to tell each other! How we laughed, and how we cried, over each other's adventures! I took him to Brooklyn, and again saw him with Ellen, the dear child whom he had loved and tended so carefully, while I was shut up in my miserable den. He staid in New York a week. His old feelings of affection for me and Ellen were as lively as ever. There are no bonds so strong as those which are formed by suffering together.

CHAPTER XXXIV.
THE OLD ENEMY AGAIN.

My young mistress, Miss Emily Flint, did not return any answer to my letter requesting her to consent to my being sold. But after a while, I received a reply, which purported to be written by her younger brother. In order rightly to enjoy the contents of this letter, the reader must bear in mind that the Flint family supposed I had been at the north many years. They had no idea that I knew of the doctor's three excursions to New York in search of me; that I had heard his voice, when he came to borrow five hundred dollars for that purpose; and that I had seen him pass on his way to the steamboat. Neither were they aware that all the particulars of aunt Nancy's death and burial were conveyed to me at the time they occurred. I have kept the letter, of which I herewith subjoin a copy:—

"Your letter to sister was received a few days ago. I gather from it that you are desirous of returning to your native place, among your friends and relatives. We were all gratified with the contents of your letter; and let me assure you that if any members of the family have had any feeling of resentment towards you, they feel it no longer. We all sympathize with you in your unfortunate condition, and are ready to do all in our power to make you contented and happy. It is difficult for you to return home as a free person. If you were purchased by your grandmother, it is doubtful whether you would be permitted to remain, although it would be lawful for you to do so. If a servant should be allowed to purchase herself, after absenting herself so long from her owners, and return free, it would have an injurious effect. From your letter, I think your situation must be hard and uncomfortable. Come home. You have it in your power to be reinstated in our affections. We would receive you with open arms and tears of joy. You need not apprehend[1] any unkind treatment, as we have not put ourselves to any trouble or expense to get you. Had we done so, perhaps we should feel otherwise. You know my sister was always attached to you, and that you were never treated as a slave. You were never put to hard work, nor exposed to field labor. On the contrary, you were taken into the house, and treated as one of us, and almost as free; and we, at least, felt that you were above disgracing yourself by running away. Believing you may be induced to come home voluntarily has induced me to write for my sister. The family will

---

1 To be apprehensive, suspicious, or fearful.

be rejoiced to see you; and your poor old grandmother expressed a great desire to have you come, when she heard your letter read. In her old age she needs the consolation of having her children round her. Doubtless you have heard of the death of your aunt. She was a faithful servant, and a faithful member of the Episcopal church. In her Christian life she taught us how to live—and, O, too high the price of knowledge, she taught us how to die! Could you have seen us round her death bed, with her mother, all mingling our tears in one common stream, you would have thought the same heartfelt tie existed between a master and his servant, as between a mother and her child. But this subject is too painful to dwell upon. I must bring my letter to a close. If you are contented to stay away from your old grandmother, your child, and the friends who love you, stay where you are. We shall never trouble ourselves to apprehend you. But should you prefer to come home, we will do all that we can to make you happy. If you do not wish to remain in the family, I know that father, by our persuasion, will be induced to let you be purchased by any person you may choose in our community. You will please answer this as soon as possible, and let us know your decision. Sister sends much love to you. In the mean time believe me your sincere friend and well wisher."

This letter was signed by Emily's brother, who was as yet a mere lad. I knew, by the style, that it was not written by a person of his age, and though the writing was disguised, I had been made too unhappy by it, in former years, not to recognize at once the hand of Dr. Flint. O, the hypocrisy of slaveholders! Did the old fox suppose I was goose enough to go into such a trap? Verily, he relied too much on "the stupidity of the African race." I did not return the family of Flints any thanks for their cordial invitation—a remissness[1] for which I was, no doubt, charged with base ingratitude.

Not long afterwards I received a letter from one of my friends at the south, informing me that Dr. Flint was about to visit the north. The letter had been delayed, and I supposed he might be already on the way. Mrs. Bruce did not know I was a fugitive. I told her that important business called me to Boston, where my brother then was, and asked permission to bring a friend to supply my place as nurse, for a fortnight. I started on my journey immediately; and as soon as I arrived, I wrote to my grandmother that if Benny came, he must be sent to Boston. I knew she was only waiting for a good chance to send him north, and, fortunately, she had

---

1 Negligence or carelessness.

the legal power to do so, without asking leave of any body. She was a free woman; and when my children were purchased, Mr. Sands preferred to have the bill of sale drawn up in her name. It was conjectured that he advanced the money, but it was not known. At the south, a gentleman may have a shoal[1] of colored children without any disgrace; but if he is known to purchase them, with the view of setting them free, the example is thought to be dangerous to their "peculiar institution," and he becomes unpopular.

There was a good opportunity to send Benny in a vessel coming directly to New York. He was put on board with a letter to a friend, who was requested to see him off to Boston. Early one morning, there was a loud rap at my door, and in rushed Benjamin, all out of breath. "O mother!" he exclaimed, "here I am! I run all the way; and I come all alone. How d'you do?"

O reader, can you imagine my joy? No, you cannot, unless you have been a slave mother. Benjamin rattled away as fast as his tongue could go. "Mother, why don't you bring Ellen here? I went over to Brooklyn to see her, and she felt very bad when I bid her good by. She said, 'O Ben, I wish I was going too.' I thought she'd know ever so much; but she don't know so much as I do; for I can read, and she can't. And, mother, I lost all my clothes coming. What can I do to get some more? I 'spose free boys can get along here at the north as well as white boys."

I did not like to tell the sanguine,[2] happy little fellow how much he was mistaken. I took him to a tailor, and procured a change of clothes. The rest of the day was spent in mutual asking and answering of questions, with the wish constantly repeated that the good old grandmother was with us, and frequent injunctions from Benny to write to her immediately, and be sure to tell her every thing about his voyage, and his journey to Boston.

Dr. Flint made his visit to New York, and made every exertion to call upon me, and invite me to return with him; but not being able to ascertain where I was, his hospitable intentions were frustrated, and the affectionate family, who were waiting for me with "open arms," were doomed to disappointment.

As soon as I knew he was safely at home, I placed Benjamin in the care of my brother William, and returned to Mrs. Bruce. There I remained through the winter and spring, endeavoring to perform my duties faithfully, and finding a good degree of happiness in the attractions of baby Mary, the considerate kindness

---

1 Any large number of persons or things.
2 Cheerfully optimistic or confident.

of her excellent mother, and occasional interviews with my darling daughter.

But when summer came, the old feeling of insecurity haunted me. It was necessary for me to take little Mary out daily, for exercise and fresh air, and the city was swarming with Southerners, some of whom might recognize me. Hot weather brings out snakes and slaveholders, and I like one class of the venomous creatures as little as I do the other. What a comfort it is, to be free to say so!

CHAPTER XXXV.
PREJUDICE AGAINST COLOR.

It was a relief to my mind to see preparations for leaving the city. We went to Albany in the steamboat Knickerbocker. When the gong sounded for tea, Mrs. Bruce said, "Linda, it is late, and you and baby had better come to the table with me." I replied, "I know it is time baby had her supper, but I had rather not go with you, if you please. I am afraid of being insulted." "O no, not if you are with me," she said. I saw several white nurses go with their ladies, and I ventured to do the same. We were at the extreme end of the table. I was no sooner seated, than a gruff voice said, "Get up! You know you are not allowed to sit here." I looked up, and, to my astonishment and indignation, saw that the speaker was a colored man. If his office required him to enforce the by-laws of the boat, he might, at least, have done it politely. I replied, "I shall not get up, unless the captain comes and takes me up." No cup of tea was offered me, but Mrs. Bruce handed me hers and called for another. I looked to see whether the other nurses were treated in a similar manner. They were all properly waited on.

Next morning, when we stopped at Troy for breakfast, every body was making a rush for the table. Mrs. Bruce said, "Take my arm, Linda, and we'll go in together." The landlord heard her, and said, "Madam, will you allow your nurse and baby to take breakfast with my family?" I knew this was to be attributed to my complexion; but he spoke courteously, and therefore I did not mind it.

At Saratoga we found the United States Hotel[1] crowded, and Mr. Bruce took one of the cottages belonging to the hotel. I had

---

1 A hotel in Saratoga, New York. See Yellin, *Life*, for more about how differently Jacobs experienced this hotel than did her employers, especially Nathaniel Parker Willis, who wrote about it in his columns for periodicals (72–73).

thought, with gladness, of going to the quiet of the country, where I should meet few people, but here I found myself in the midst of a swarm of Southerners. I looked round me with fear and trembling, dreading to see some one who would recognize me. I was rejoiced to find that we were to stay but a short time.

We soon returned to New York, to make arrangements for spending the remainder of the summer at Rockaway. While the laundress was putting the clothes in order, I took an opportunity to go over to Brooklyn to see Ellen. I met her going to a grocery store, and the first words she said, were, "O, mother, don't go to Mrs. Hobbs's. Her brother, Mr. Thorne, has come from the south, and may be he'll tell where you are." I accepted the warning. I told her I was going away with Mrs. Bruce the next day, and would try to see her when I came back.

Being in servitude to the Anglo-Saxon race, I was not put into a "Jim Crow car,"[1] on our way to Rockaway, neither was I invited to ride through the streets on the top of trunks in a truck; but every where I found the same manifestations of that cruel prejudice, which so discourages the feelings, and represses the energies of the colored people. We reached Rockaway before dark, and put up at the Pavilion—a large hotel, beautifully situated by the sea-side—a great resort of the fashionable world. Thirty or forty nurses were there, of a great variety of nations. Some of the ladies had colored waiting-maids and coachmen, but I was the only nurse tinged with the blood of Africa. When the tea bell rang, I took little Mary and followed the other nurses. Supper was served in a long hall. A young man, who had the ordering of things, took the circuit of the table two or three times, and finally pointed me to a seat at the lower end of it. As there was but one chair, I sat down and took the child in my lap. Whereupon the young man came to me and said, in the blandest manner possible, "Will you please to seat the little girl in the chair, and stand behind it and feed her? After they have done, you will be shown to the kitchen, where you will have a good supper."

This was the climax! I found it hard to preserve my self-control, when I looked round, and saw women who were nurses, as I was, and only one shade lighter in complexion, eyeing me with

1 A reference to racially segregated public accommodations. Even before "separate but equal" was codified into US law via *Plessy v. Ferguson* (Appendix A12), African Americans were customarily relegated to separate spaces that were never equal, as historians such as Blair L.M. Kelley have shown.

a defiant look, as if my presence were a contamination. However, I said nothing. I quietly took the child in my arms, went to our room, and refused to go to the table again. Mr. Bruce ordered meals to be sent to the room for little Mary and I. This answered for a few days; but the waiters of the establishment were white, and they soon began to complain, saying they were not hired to wait on negroes. The landlord requested Mr. Bruce to send me down to my meals, because his servants rebelled against bringing them up, and the colored servants of other boarders were dissatisfied because all were not treated alike.

My answer was that the colored servants ought to be dissatisfied with themselves, for not having too much self-respect to submit to such treatment; that there was no difference in the price of board for colored and white servants, and there was no justification for difference of treatment. I staid a month after this, and finding I was resolved to stand up for my rights, they concluded to treat me well. Let every colored man and woman do this, and eventually we shall cease to be trampled under foot by our oppressors.

CHAPTER XXXVI.
THE HAIR-BREADTH ESCAPE.

After we returned to New York, I took the earliest opportunity to go and see Ellen. I asked to have her called down stairs; for I supposed Mrs. Hobbs's southern brother might still be there, and I was desirous to avoid seeing him, if possible. But Mrs. Hobbs came to the kitchen, and insisted on my going up stairs. "My brother wants to see you," said she, "and he is sorry you seem to shun him. He knows you are living in New York. He told me to say to you that he owes thanks to good old aunt Martha for too many little acts of kindness for him to be base enough to betray her grandchild."

This Mr. Thorne had become poor and reckless long before he left the south, and such persons had much rather go to one of the faithful old slaves to borrow a dollar, or get a good dinner, than to go to one whom they consider an equal. It was such acts of kindness as these for which he professed to feel grateful to my grandmother. I wished he had kept at a distance, but as he was here, and knew where I was, I concluded there was nothing to be gained by trying to avoid him; on the contrary, it might be the means of exciting his ill will. I followed his sister up stairs. He met me in a very friendly manner, congratulated me on my escape from slavery, and hoped I had a good place, where I felt happy.

I continued to visit Ellen as often as I could. She, good thoughtful child, never forgot my hazardous situation, but always kept a vigilant lookout for my safety. She never made any complaint about her own inconveniences and troubles; but a mother's observing eye easily perceived that she was not happy. On the occasion of one of my visits I found her unusually serious. When I asked her what was the matter, she said nothing was the matter. But I insisted upon knowing what made her look so very grave. Finally, I ascertained that she felt troubled about the dissipation[1] that was continually going on in the house. She was sent to the store very often for rum and brandy, and she felt ashamed to ask for it so often; and Mr. Hobbs and Mr. Thorne drank a great deal, and their hands trembled so that they had to call her to pour out the liquor for them. "But for all that," said she, "Mr. Hobbs is good to me, and I can't help liking him. I feel sorry for him." I tried to comfort her, by telling her that I had laid up a hundred dollars, and that before long I hoped to be able to give her and Benjamin a home, and send them to school. She was always desirous not to add to my troubles more than she could help, and I did not discover till years afterwards that Mr. Thorne's intemperance was not the only annoyance she suffered from him. Though he professed too much gratitude to my grandmother to injure any of her descendants, he had poured vile language into the ears of her innocent great-grandchild.

I usually went to Brooklyn to spend Sunday afternoon. One Sunday, I found Ellen anxiously waiting for me near the house. "O, mother," said she, "I've been waiting for you this long time. I'm afraid Mr. Thorne has written to tell Dr. Flint where you are. Make haste and come in. Mrs. Hobbs will tell you all about it!"

The story was soon told. While the children were playing in the grape-vine arbor, the day before, Mr. Thorne came out with a letter in his hand, which he tore up and scattered about. Ellen was sweeping the yard at the time, and having her mind full of suspicions of him, she picked up the pieces and carried them to the children, saying, "I wonder who Mr. Thorne has been writing to."

"I'm sure I don't know, and don't care," replied the oldest of the children; "and I don't see how it concerns you."

"But it does concern me," replied Ellen; "for I'm afraid he's been writing to the south about my mother."

---

1 Indulgence in extravagant, wasteful pleasure.

They laughed at her, and called her a silly thing, but good-naturedly put the fragments of writing together, in order to read them to her. They were no sooner arranged, than the little girl exclaimed, "I declare, Ellen, I believe you are right."

The contents of Mr. Thorne's letter, as nearly as I can remember, were as follows: "I have seen your slave, Linda, and conversed with her. She can be taken very easily, if you manage prudently. There are enough of us here to swear to her identity as your property. I am a patriot, a lover of my country, and I do this as an act of justice to the laws." He concluded by informing the doctor of the street and number where I lived. The children carried the pieces to Mrs. Hobbs, who immediately went to her brother's room for an explanation. He was not to be found. The servants said they saw him go out with a letter in his hand, and they supposed he had gone to the post office. The natural inference was, that he had sent to Dr. Flint a copy of those fragments. When he returned, his sister accused him of it, and he did not deny the charge. He went immediately to his room, and the next morning he was missing. He had gone over to New York, before any of the family were astir.

It was evident that I had no time to lose; and I hastened back to the city with a heavy heart. Again I was to be torn from a comfortable home, and all my plans for the welfare of my children were to be frustrated by that demon Slavery! I now regretted that I never told Mrs. Bruce my story. I had not concealed it merely on account of being a fugitive; that would have made her anxious, but it would have excited sympathy in her kind heart. I valued her good opinion, and I was afraid of losing it, if I told her all the particulars of my sad story. But now I felt that it was necessary for her to know how I was situated. I had once left her abruptly, without explaining the reason, and it would not be proper to do it again. I went home resolved to tell her in the morning. But the sadness of my face attracted her attention, and, in answer to her kind inquiries, I poured out my full heart to her, before bed time. She listened with true womanly sympathy, and told me she would do all she could to protect me. How my heart blessed her!

Early the next morning, Judge Vanderpool and Lawyer Hopper[1] were consulted. They said I had better leave the city at once, as the risk would be great if the case came to trial. Mrs. Bruce took me in a carriage to the house of one of her friends,

---

1 Another instance of Jacobs not creating pseudonyms. Her employer Mary Willis (Mrs. Bruce) had contacted anti-slavery judge Arent Van der Poel and attorney John Hopper. See Yellin, *Life* 74.

where she assured me I should be safe until my brother could arrive, which would be in a few days. In the interval my thoughts were much occupied with Ellen. She was mine by birth, and she was also mine by Southern law, since my grandmother held the bill of sale that made her so. I did not feel that she was safe unless I had her with me. Mrs. Hobbs, who felt badly about her brother's treachery, yielded to my entreaties, on condition that she should return in ten days. I avoided making any promise. She came to me clad in very thin garments, all outgrown, and with a school satchel on her arm, containing a few articles. It was late in October, and I knew the child must suffer; and not daring to go out in the streets to purchase any thing, I took off my own flannel skirt and converted it into one for her. Kind Mrs. Bruce came to bid me good by, and when she saw that I had taken off my clothing for my child, the tears came to her eyes. She said, "Wait for me, Linda," and went out. She soon returned with a nice warm shawl and hood for Ellen. Truly, of such souls as hers are the kingdom of heaven.

My brother reached New York on Wednesday. Lawyer Hopper advised us to go to Boston by the Stonington route, as there was less Southern travel in that direction. Mrs. Bruce directed her servants to tell all inquirers that I formerly lived there, but had gone from the city.

We reached the steamboat Rhode Island in safety. That boat employed colored hands, but I knew that colored passengers were not admitted to the cabin. I was very desirous for the seclusion of the cabin, not only on account of exposure to the night air, but also to avoid observation. Lawyer Hopper was waiting on board for us. He spoke to the stewardess, and asked, as a particular favor, that she would treat us well. He said to me, "Go and speak to the captain yourself by and by. Take your little girl with you, and I am sure that he will not let her sleep on deck." With these kind words and a shake of the hand he departed.

The boat was soon on her way, bearing me rapidly from the friendly home where I had hoped to find security and rest. My brother had left me to purchase the tickets, thinking that I might have better success than he would. When the stewardess came to me, I paid what she asked, and she gave me three tickets with clipped corners. In the most unsophisticated manner I said, "You have made a mistake; I asked you for cabin tickets. I cannot possibly consent to sleep on deck with my little daughter." She assured me there was no mistake. She said on some of the routes colored people were allowed to sleep in the cabin, but not on this route, which was much travelled by the wealthy. I asked her to show me to the captain's office, and she said she would after tea. When the time came, I took Ellen by the hand and went to the captain, politely requesting him to change our tickets, as we should be very uncomfortable on deck. He said it was contrary to their custom, but he would see that we had berths[1] below; he would also try to obtain comfortable seats for us in the cars; of that he was not certain, but he would speak to the conductor about it, when the boat arrived. I thanked him, and returned to the ladies' cabin. He came afterwards and told me that the conductor of the cars was on board, that he had spoken to him, and he had promised to take care of us. I was very much surprised at receiving so much kindness. I don't know whether the pleasing face of my little girl had won his heart, or whether the stewardess inferred from Lawyer Hopper's manner that I was a fugitive, and had pleaded with him in my behalf.

When the boat arrived at Stonington, the conductor kept his promise, and showed us to seats in the first car, nearest the engine. He asked us to take seats next the door, but as he passed through, we ventured to move on toward the other end of the car. No incivility was offered us, and we reached Boston in safety.

The day after my arrival was one of the happiest of my life. I felt as if I was beyond the reach of the bloodhounds; and, for the first time during many years, I had both my children together with me. They greatly enjoyed their reunion, and laughed and chatted merrily. I watched them with a swelling heart. Their every motion delighted me.

I could not feel safe in New York, and I accepted the offer of a friend, that we should share expenses and keep house together. I represented to Mrs. Hobbs that Ellen must have some schooling, and must remain with me for that purpose. She felt ashamed of being unable to read or spell at her age, so instead of sending her to school with Benny, I instructed her myself till she was fitted to enter an intermediate school. The winter passed pleasantly, while I was busy with my needle, and my children with their books.

---

1 Allotted spaces, often for sleeping.

CHAPTER XXXVII.
A VISIT TO ENGLAND.

In the spring, sad news came to me. Mrs. Bruce was dead. Never again, in this world, should I see her gentle face, or hear her sympathizing voice. I had lost an excellent friend, and little Mary had lost a tender mother. Mr. Bruce wished the child to visit some of her mother's relatives in England, and he was desirous that I should take charge of her. The little motherless one was accustomed to me, and attached to me, and I thought she would be happier in my care than in that of a stranger. I could also earn more in this way than I could by my needle. So I put Benny to a trade, and left Ellen to remain in the house with my friend and go to school.

We sailed from New York, and arrived in Liverpool after a pleasant voyage of twelve days. We proceeded directly to London, and took lodgings at the Adelaide Hotel.[1] The supper seemed to me less luxurious than those I had seen in American hotels; but my situation was indescribably more pleasant. For the first time in my life I was in a place where I was treated according to my deportment, without reference to my complexion. I felt as if a great millstone[2] had been lifted from my breast. Ensconced in a pleasant room, with my dear little charge, I laid my head on my pillow, for the first time, with the delightful consciousness of pure, unadulterated freedom.

As I had constant care of the child, I had little opportunity to see the wonders of that great city; but I watched the tide of life that flowed through the streets, and found it a strange contrast to the stagnation in our Southern towns. Mr. Bruce took his little daughter to spend some days with friends in Oxford Crescent, and of course it was necessary for me to accompany her. I had heard much of the systematic method of English education, and I was very desirous that my dear Mary should steer straight in the midst of so much propriety. I closely observed her little playmates and their nurses, being ready to take any lessons in the science of good management. The children were more rosy than American children, but I did not see that they differed materially in other respects. They were like all children—sometimes docile[3] and sometimes wayward.[4]

---

1 Jacobs has not changed the name of the hotel in her narrative. See Yellin, *Life* 85.

2 Anything that grinds or crushes.

3 Easily managed.

4 Disobedient.

We next went to Steventon, in Berkshire. It was a small town, said to be the poorest in the county. I saw men working in the fields for six shillings, and seven shillings, a week, and women for sixpence, and sevenpence, a day, out of which they boarded themselves. Of course they lived in the most primitive manner; it could not be otherwise, where a woman's wages for an entire day were not sufficient to buy a pound of meat. They paid very low rents, and their clothes were made of the cheapest fabrics, though much better than could have been procured in the United States for the same money. I had heard much about the oppression of the poor in Europe. The people I saw around me were, many of them, among the poorest poor. But when I visited them in their little thatched cottages, I felt that the condition of even the meanest and most ignorant among them was vastly superior to the condition of the most favored slaves in America. They labored hard; but they were not ordered out to toil while the stars were in the sky, and driven and slashed by an overseer, through heat and cold, till the stars shone out again. Their homes were very humble; but they were protected by law. No insolent patrols could come, in the dead of night, and flog them at their pleasure. The father, when he closed his cottage door, felt safe with his family around him. No master or overseer could come and take from him his wife, or his daughter. They must separate to earn their living; but the parents knew where their children were going, and could communicate with them by letters. The relations of husband and wife, parent and child, were too sacred for the richest noble in the land to violate with impunity. Much was being done to enlighten these poor people. Schools were established among them, and benevolent societies were active in efforts to ameliorate their condition. There was no law forbidding them to learn to read and write; and if they helped each other in spelling out the Bible, they were in no danger of thirty-nine lashes, as was the case with myself and poor, pious, old uncle Fred. I repeat that the most ignorant and the most destitute of these peasants was a thousand fold better off than the most pampered American slave.

I do not deny that the poor are oppressed in Europe. I am not disposed to paint their condition so rose-colored as the Hon. Miss Murray paints the condition of the slaves in the United States.[1] A small portion of my experience would enable her to read her own

---

1 A reference to the 1856 volume *Letters from the United States, Cuba and Canada* by English visitor to the United States Amelia Matilda Murray (1795–1884).

pages with anointed eyes. If she were to lay aside her title, and, instead of visiting among the fashionable, become domesticated, as a poor governess, on some plantation in Louisiana or Alabama, she would see and hear things that would make her tell quite a different story.

My visit to England is a memorable event in my life, from the fact of my having there received strong religious impressions. The contemptuous manner in which the communion had been administered to colored people, in my native place; the church membership of Dr. Flint, and others like him; and the buying and selling of slaves, by professed ministers of the gospel, had given me a prejudice against the Episcopal church. The whole service seemed to me a mockery and a sham. But my home in Steventon was in the family of a clergyman, who was a true disciple of Jesus. The beauty of his daily life inspired me with faith in the genuineness of Christian professions. Grace entered my heart, and I knelt at the communion table, I trust, in true humility of soul.

I remained abroad ten months, which was much longer than I had anticipated. During all that time, I never saw the slightest symptom of prejudice against color.[1] Indeed, I entirely forgot it, till the time came for us to return to America.

---

1 Throughout African American literature, there are testimonies like this about not being treated according to color in Europe. In the nineteenth century, this is often a way of highlighting how horribly Americans treat African Americans. However, the rhetorical power of these representations of better treatment should not keep readers from remembering that European countries have populations of color that they treat as horribly as white Americans treat African Americans and other people of color. Just because racism can be culturally specific doesn't make it any less racist. To put it plainly, I'm a dark-skinned Black woman. When I travel to London, I am treated much better than I am in the US, but I notice that Black Britons are treated as I am in the US. Likewise, when I travel to Paris, I get to feel like my color doesn't matter, but I notice that white Parisians treat French-speaking people from Senegal, for example, or even light-skinned people from Martinique—basically, places the French colonized—the way white Americans treat me when I'm trying to live my life in peace in the US.

CHAPTER XXXVIII.
RENEWED INVITATIONS TO GO SOUTH.

We had a tedious winter passage, and from the distance spectres seemed to rise up on the shores of the United States. It is a sad feeling to be afraid of one's native country. We arrived in New York safely, and I hastened to Boston to look after my children. I found Ellen well, and improving at her school; but Benny was not there to welcome me. He had been left at a good place to learn a trade, and for several months every thing worked well. He was liked by the master, and was a favorite with his fellow-apprentices; but one day they accidentally discovered a fact they had never before suspected—that he was colored! This at once transformed him into a different being. Some of the apprentices were Americans, others American-born Irish; and it was offensive to their dignity to have a "nigger" among them, after they had been told that he was a "nigger." They began by treating him with silent scorn, and finding that he returned the same, they resorted to insults and abuse. He was too spirited a boy to stand that, and he went off. Being desirous to do something to support himself, and having no one to advise him, he shipped for a whaling voyage. When I received these tidings I shed many tears, and bitterly reproached myself for having left him so long. But I had done it for the best, and now all I could do was to pray to the heavenly Father to guide and protect him.

Not long after my return, I received the following letter from Miss Emily Flint, now Mrs. Dodge:—

"In this you will recognize the hand of your friend and mistress. Having heard that you had gone with a family to Europe, I have waited to hear of your return to write to you. I should have answered the letter you wrote to me long since, but as I could not then act independently of my father, I knew there could be nothing done satisfactory to you. There were persons here who were willing to buy you and run the risk of getting you. To this I would not consent. I have always been attached to you, and would not like to see you the slave of another, or have unkind treatment. I am married now, and can protect you. My husband expects to move to Virginia this spring, where we think of settling. I am very anxious that you should come and live with me. If you are not willing to come, you may purchase yourself; but I should prefer having you live with me. If you come, you may, if you like, spend a month with your grandmother and friends, then come to me in Norfolk, Virginia. Think this over, and write as soon as possible, and let me know the conclusion. Hoping that your children are well, I remain your friend and mistress."

Of course I did not write to return thanks for this cordial invitation. I felt insulted to be thought stupid enough to be caught by such professions.

"'Come up into my parlor,' said the spider to the fly; "Tis the prettiest little parlor that ever you did spy.'"[1]

It was plain that Dr. Flint's family were apprised of my movements, since they knew of my voyage to Europe. I expected to have further trouble from them; but having eluded them thus far, I hoped to be as successful in future. The money I had earned, I was desirous to devote to the education of my children, and to secure a home for them. It seemed not only hard, but unjust, to pay for myself. I could not possibly regard myself as a piece of property. Moreover, I had worked many years without wages, and during that time had been obliged to depend on my grandmother for many comforts in food and clothing. My children certainly belonged to me; but though Dr. Flint had incurred no expense for their support, he had received a large sum of money for them. I knew the law would decide that I was his property, and would probably still give his daughter a claim to my children; but I regarded such laws as the regulations of robbers, who had no rights that I was bound to respect.[2]

The Fugitive Slave Law had not then passed. The judges of Massachusetts had not then stooped under chains to enter her courts of justice, so called. I knew my old master was rather skittish of Massachusetts. I relied on her love of freedom, and felt safe on her soil. I am now aware that I honored the old Commonwealth beyond her deserts.[3]

---

1 Lines from "The Spider and the Fly," an 1829 poem by British author and translator Mary Howitt (1799–1888).

2 Jacobs powerfully recasts the language of the 1857 *Dred Scott* decision, which declared that African Americans had no rights that white people were bound to respect. See Appendix A4.

3 The state or condition of being worthy.

CHAPTER XXXIX.
THE CONFESSION.

For two years my daughter and I supported ourselves comfortably in Boston. At the end of that time, my brother William offered to send Ellen to a boarding school. It required a great effort for me to consent to part with her, for I had few near ties, and it was her presence that made my two little rooms seem home-like. But my judgment prevailed over my selfish feelings. I made preparations for her departure. During the two years we had lived together I had often resolved to tell her something about her father; but I had never been able to muster sufficient courage. I had a shrinking dread of diminishing my child's love. I knew she must have curiosity on the subject, but she had never asked a question. She was always very careful not to say any thing to remind me of my troubles. Now that she was going from me, I thought if I should die before she returned, she might hear my story from some one who did not understand the palliating circumstances;[1] and that if she were entirely ignorant on the subject, her sensitive nature might receive a rude shock.

When we retired for the night, she said, "Mother, it is very hard to leave you alone. I am almost sorry I am going, though I do want to improve myself. But you will write to me often; won't you, mother?"

I did not throw my arms round her. I did not answer her. But in a calm, solemn way, for it cost me great effort, I said, "Listen to me, Ellen; I have something to tell you!" I recounted my early sufferings in slavery, and told her how nearly they had crushed me. I began to tell her how they had driven me into a great sin, when she clasped me in her arms, and exclaimed, "O, don't, mother! Please don't tell me any more."

I said, "But, my child, I want you to know about your father."

"I know all about it, mother," she replied; "I am nothing to my father, and he is nothing to me. All my love is for you. I was with him five months in Washington, and he never cared for me. He never spoke to me as he did to his little Fanny. I knew all the time he was my father, for Fanny's nurse told me so; but she said I must never tell any body, and I never did. I used to wish he would take me in his arms and kiss me, as he did Fanny; or that he would sometimes smile at me, as he did at her. I thought

---

1 Circumstances that lessen the wrong and/or should lessen the harshness of judgment.

if he was my own father, he ought to love me. I was a little girl then, and didn't know any better. But now I never think any thing about my father. All my love is for you." She hugged me closer as she spoke, and I thanked God that the knowledge I had so much dreaded to impart had not diminished the affection of my child. I had not the slightest idea she knew that portion of my history. If I had, I should have spoken to her long before; for my pent-up feelings had often longed to pour themselves out to some one I could trust. But I loved the dear girl better for the delicacy she had manifested towards her unfortunate mother.

The next morning, she and her uncle started on their journey to the village in New York, where she was to be placed at school. It seemed as if all the sunshine had gone away. My little room was dreadfully lonely. I was thankful when a message came from a lady, accustomed to employ me, requesting me to come and sew in her family for several weeks. On my return, I found a letter from brother William. He thought of opening an anti-slavery reading room in Rochester, and combining with it the sale of some books and stationery; and he wanted me to unite with him. We tried it, but it was not successful. We found warm anti-slavery friends there, but the feeling was not general enough to support such an establishment. I passed nearly a year in the family of Isaac and Amy Post,[1] practical believers in the Christian doctrine of human brotherhood. They measured a man's worth by his character, not by his complexion. The memory of those beloved and honored friends will remain with me to my latest hour.

---

1 Another instance of Jacobs not creating pseudonyms. Also note that Amy Post (1802–89) wrote one of the two letters in the original appendix to the narrative.

CHAPTER XL.
THE FUGITIVE SLAVE LAW.

My brother, being disappointed in his project, concluded to go to California; and it was agreed that Benjamin should go with him. Ellen liked her school, and was a great favorite there. They did not know her history, and she did not tell it, because she had no desire to make capital out of their sympathy. But when it was accidentally discovered that her mother was a fugitive slave, every method was used to increase her advantages and diminish her expenses.

I was alone again. It was necessary for me to be earning money, and I preferred that it should be among those who knew me. On my return from Rochester, I called at the house of Mr. Bruce, to see Mary, the darling little babe that had thawed my heart, when it was freezing into a cheerless distrust of all my fellow-beings. She was growing a tall girl now, but I loved her always. Mr. Bruce had married again, and it was proposed that I should become nurse to a new infant. I had but one hesitation, and that was my feeling of insecurity in New York, now greatly increased by the passage of the Fugitive Slave Law. However, I resolved to try the experiment. I was again fortunate in my employer. The new Mrs. Bruce was an American, brought up under aristocratic influences, and still living in the midst of them; but if she had any prejudice against color, I was never made aware of it; and as for the system of slavery, she had a most hearty dislike of it. No sophistry of Southerners could blind her to its enormity. She was a person of excellent principles and a noble heart. To me, from that hour to the present, she has been a true and sympathizing friend. Blessings be with her and hers!

About the time that I reëntered the Bruce family, an event occurred of disastrous import to the colored people. The slave Hamlin,[1] the first fugitive that came under the new law, was given up by the bloodhounds of the north to the bloodhounds of the south. It was the beginning of a reign of terror to the colored population. The great city rushed on in its whirl of excitement, taking no note of the "short and simple annals of the poor."[2] But while fashionables were listening to the thrilling voice of Jenny Lind in

---

1 Apparently a misspelled or misremembered reference to James Hamlet, generally thought to be the first person recaptured in New York under the provisions of the *Fugitive Slave Act* of 1850 (Appendix A2).

2 A reference to "Elegy Written in a Country Churchyard" (1751) by British poet Thomas Gray (1716–71).

Metropolitan Hall,[1] the thrilling voices of poor hunted colored people went up, in an agony of supplication, to the Lord, from Zion's church. Many families, who had lived in the city for twenty years, fled from it now. Many a poor washerwoman, who, by hard labor, had made herself a comfortable home, was obliged to sacrifice her furniture, bid a hurried farewell to friends, and seek her fortune among strangers in Canada. Many a wife discovered a secret she had never known before—that her husband was a fugitive, and must leave her to insure his own safety. Worse still, many a husband discovered that his wife had fled from slavery years ago, and as "the child follows the condition of its mother," the children of his love were liable to be seized and carried into slavery. Every where, in those humble homes, there was consternation and anguish. But what cared the legislators of the "dominant race" for the blood they were crushing out of trampled hearts?

When my brother William spent his last evening with me, before he went to California, we talked nearly all the time of the distress brought on our oppressed people by the passage of this iniquitous[2] law; and never had I seen him manifest such bitterness of spirit, such stern hostility to our oppressors. He was himself free from the operation of the law; for he did not run from any Slave holding State, being brought into the Free States by his master. But I was subject to it; and so were hundreds of intelligent and industrious people all around us. I seldom ventured into the streets; and when it was necessary to do an errand for Mrs. Bruce, or any of the family, I went as much as possible through back streets and by-ways. What a disgrace to a city calling itself free, that inhabitants, guiltless of offense, and seeking to perform their duties conscientiously, should be condemned to live in such incessant[3] fear, and have nowhere to turn for protection! This state of things, of course, gave rise to many impromptu vigilance committees.[4] Every colored

---

1 The popular name for Tripler Hall, which was built in 1850 specifically for performances by opera singer Jenny Lind (1820–87), known as the "Swedish Nightingale." Yellin reports that it was not ready for Lind's earliest New York appearances, but it was the site of many of her performances (*Incidents* 289).

2 Wicked; sinful.

3 Constant; unending.

4 Groups of people who made it their business to watch for those who would kidnap and enslave African Americans and then discreetly share information that would empower people to avoid capture. By calling them "impromptu," Jacobs suggests that this worked well even

person, and every friend of their persecuted race, kept their eyes wide open. Every evening I examined the newspapers carefully, to see what Southerners had put up at the hotels. I did this for my own sake, thinking my young mistress and her husband might be among the list; I wished also to give information to others, if necessary; for if many were "running to and fro," I resolved that "knowledge should be increased."[1]

This brings up one of my southern reminiscences, which I will here briefly relate. I was somewhat acquainted with a slave named Luke, who belonged to a wealthy man in our vicinity. His master died, leaving a son and daughter heirs to his large fortune. In the division of the slaves, Luke was included in the son's portion. This young man became a prey to the vices growing out of the "patriarchal institution," and when he went to the north, to complete his education, he carried his vices with him. He was brought home, deprived of the use of his limbs, by excessive dissipation. Luke was appointed to wait upon his bed-ridden master, whose despotic[2] habits were greatly increased by exasperation at his own helplessness. He kept a cowhide beside him, and, for the most trivial occurrence, he would order his attendant to bare his back, and kneel beside the couch, while he whipped him till his strength was exhausted. Some days he was not allowed to wear anything but his shirt, in order to be in readiness to be flogged. A day seldom passed without his receiving more or less blows. If the slightest resistance was offered, the town constable was sent for to execute the punishment, and Luke learned from experience how much more the constable's strong arm was to be dreaded than the comparatively feeble one of his master. The arm of his tyrant grew weaker, and was finally palsied;[3] and then the constable's services were in constant requisition. The fact that he was entirely dependent on Luke's care, and was obliged to be tended like an infant, instead of inspiring any gratitude or compassion towards his poor slave, seemed only to increase his irritability and cruelty. As he

---

when it was spontaneous. That is, being officially organized into actual committees was not necessary for people acting based on a sense of community and care. They did not need to be directed in advance to operate according to common goals. Also see Appendix A3.

1 Jacobs links the Black community's ethos of care to biblical scripture, Daniel 12.4.

2 Characterized by the assertion of absolute power and control; tyrannical.

3 Unable to move or control certain muscles; paralyzed.

lay there on his bed, a mere degraded wreck of manhood, he took into his head the strangest freaks of despotism; and if Luke hesitated to submit to his orders, the constable was immediately sent for. Some of these freaks were of a nature too filthy to be repeated. When I fled from the house of bondage, I left poor Luke still chained to the bedside of this cruel and disgusting wretch.

One day, when I had been requested to do an errand for Mrs. Bruce, I was hurrying through back streets, as usual, when I saw a young man approaching, whose face was familiar to me. As he came nearer, I recognized Luke. I always rejoiced to see or hear of any one who had escaped from the black pit; but, remembering this poor fellow's extreme hardships, I was peculiarly glad to see him on Northern soil, though I no longer called it free soil. I well remembered what a desolate feeling it was to be alone among strangers, and I went up to him and greeted him cordially. At first, he did not know me; but when I mentioned my name, he remembered all about me. I told him of the Fugitive Slave Law, and asked him if he did not know that New York was a city of kidnappers.

He replied, "De risk ain't so bad for me, as 'tis fur you. 'Cause I runned away from de speculator, and you runned away from de massa. Dem speculators vont spen dar money to come here fur a runaway, if dey ain't sartin sure to put dar hans right on him. An I tell you I's tuk good car 'bout dat. I had too hard times down dar, to let 'em ketch dis nigger."

He then told me of the advice he had received, and the plans he had laid. I asked if he had money enough to take him to Canada. "'Pend upon it, I hab," he replied. "I tuk car fur dat. I'd bin workin all my days fur dem cussed whites, an got no pay but kicks and cuffs. So I tought dis nigger had a right to money nuff to bring him to de Free States. Massa Henry he lib till ebery body vish him dead; an ven he did die, I knowed de debbil would hab him, an vouldn't vant him to bring his money 'long too. So I tuk some of his bills, and put 'em in de pocket of his ole trousers. An ven he was buried, dis nigger ask fur dem ole trousers, an dey gub 'em to me." With a low, chuckling laugh, he added, "You see I didn't steal it; dey gub it to me. I tell you, I had mighty hard time to keep de speculator from findin it; but he didn't git it."

This is a fair specimen of how the moral sense is educated by slavery. When a man has his wages stolen from him, year after year, and the laws sanction and enforce the theft, how can he be expected to have more regard to honesty than has the man who robs him? I have become somewhat enlightened, but I confess that I agree with poor, ignorant, much-abused Luke, in thinking he had a right to that money, as a portion of his unpaid wages. He went to Canada forth-with, and I have not since heard from him.

All that winter I lived in a state of anxiety. When I took the children out to breathe the air, I closely observed the countenances of all I met. I dreaded the approach of summer, when snakes and slaveholders make their appearance. I was, in fact, a slave in New York, as subject to slave laws as I had been in a Slave State. Strange incongruity in a State called free!

Spring returned, and I received warning from the south that Dr. Flint knew of my return to my old place, and was making preparations to have me caught. I learned afterwards that my dress, and that of Mrs. Bruce's children, had been described to him by some of the Northern tools, which slaveholders employ for their base purposes, and then indulge in sneers at their cupidity[1] and mean servility.[2]

I immediately informed Mrs. Bruce of my danger, and she took prompt measures for my safety. My place as nurse could not be supplied immediately, and this generous, sympathizing lady proposed that I should carry her baby away. It was a comfort to me to have the child with me; for the heart is reluctant to be torn away from every object it loves. But how few mothers would have consented to have one of their own babes become a fugitive, for the sake of a poor, hunted nurse, on whom the legislators of the country had let loose the bloodhounds! When I spoke of the sacrifice she was making, in depriving herself of her dear baby, she replied, "It is better for you to have baby with you, Linda; for if they get on your track, they will be obliged to bring the child to me; and then, if there is a possibility of saving you, you shall be saved."

This lady had a very wealthy relative, a benevolent gentleman in many respects, but aristocratic and proslavery. He remonstrated with her for harboring a fugitive slave; told her she was violating the laws of her country; and asked her if she was aware of the penalty. She replied, "I am very well aware of it. It is imprisonment and one thousand dollars fine. Shame on my country that it is so! I am ready to incur the penalty. I will go to the state's prison, rather than have any poor victim torn from my house, to be carried back to slavery."

The noble heart! The brave heart! The tears are in my eyes while I write of her. May the God of the helpless reward her for her sympathy with my persecuted people!

---

1 Excessive desire, especially to possess something; greed.
2 Slavish submissiveness.

I was sent into New England, where I was sheltered by the wife of a senator, whom I shall always hold in grateful remembrance.[1] This honorable gentleman would not have voted for the Fugitive Slave Law, as did the senator in "Uncle Tom's Cabin;"[2] on the contrary, he was strongly opposed to it; but he was enough under its influence to be afraid of having me remain in his house many hours. So I was sent into the country, where I remained a month with the baby. When it was supposed that Dr. Flint's emissaries had lost track of me, and given up the pursuit for the present, I returned to New York.

CHAPTER XLI.
FREE AT LAST.

Mrs. Bruce, and every member of her family, were exceedingly kind to me. I was thankful for the blessings of my lot, yet I could not always wear a cheerful countenance. I was doing harm to no one; on the contrary, I was doing all the good I could in my small way; yet I could never go out to breathe God's free air without trepidation at my heart. This seemed hard; and I could not think it was a right state of things in any civilized country.

From time to time I received news from my good old grandmother. She could not write; but she employed others to write for her. The following is an extract from one of her last letters:—

"Dear Daughter: I cannot hope to see you again on earth; but I pray to God to unite us above, where pain will no more rack this feeble body of mine; where sorrow and parting from my children will be no more. God has promised these things if we are faithful unto the end. My age and feeble health deprive me of going to church now; but God is with me here at home. Thank your brother for his kindness. Give much love to him, and tell him to remember the Creator in the days of his youth, and strive to meet me in the Father's kingdom. Love to Ellen and Benjamin. Don't neglect him. Tell him for me, to be a good boy. Strive, my child,

---

1 This is a reference to the baby's grandparents in New Bedford, Massachusetts. Joseph Grinnell was not a senator, though; he served in the House of Representatives as a Whig from 1843 to 1851. Like many Northerners, he avoided voting on the slave bill (Yellin, *Incidents* 290n10).

2 A reference to Chapter IX of Harriet Beecher Stowe's famous 1852 novel.

to train them for God's children. May he protect and provide for you, is the prayer of your loving old mother."

These letters both cheered and saddened me. I was always glad to have tidings from the kind, faithful old friend of my unhappy youth; but her messages of love made my heart yearn to see her before she died, and I mourned over the fact that it was impossible. Some months after I returned from my flight to New England, I received a letter from her, in which she wrote, "Dr. Flint is dead. He has left a distressed family. Poor old man! I hope he made his peace with God."

I remembered how he had defrauded my grandmother of the hard earnings she had loaned; how he had tried to cheat her out of the freedom her mistress had promised her, and now he had persecuted her children; and I thought to myself that she was a better Christian than I was, if she could entirely forgive him. I cannot say, with truth, that the news of my old master's death softened my feelings towards him. There are wrongs which even the grave does not bury. The man was odious to me while he lived, and his memory is odious now.

His departure from this world did not diminish my danger. He had threatened my grandmother that his heirs should hold me in slavery after he was gone; that I never should be free so long as a child of his survived. As for Mrs. Flint, I had seen her in deeper afflictions than I supposed the loss of her husband would be, for she had buried several children; yet I never saw any signs of softening in her heart. The doctor had died in embarrassed circumstances, and had little to will to his heirs, except such property as he was unable to grasp. I was well aware what I had to expect from the family of Flints; and my fears were confirmed by a letter from the south, warning me to be on my guard, because Mrs. Flint openly declared that her daughter could not afford to lose so valuable a slave as I was.

I kept close watch of the newspapers for arrivals; but one Saturday night, being much occupied, I forgot to examine the Evening Express as usual. I went down into the parlor for it, early in the morning, and found the boy about to kindle a fire with it. I took it from him and examined the list of arrivals. Reader, if you have never been a slave, you cannot imagine the acute sensation of suffering at my heart, when I read the names of Mr. and Mrs. Dodge, at a hotel in Courtland Street.[1] It was a third-rate hotel,

---

1 Yellin located the notice in "Arrivals at City Hotels" in the Saturday 28 February 1852 issue of the New York *Evening Express* (*Incidents* 290n5).

and that circumstance convinced me of the truth of what I had heard, that they were short of funds and had need of my value, as they valued me; and that was by dollars and cents. I hastened with the paper to Mrs. Bruce. Her heart and hand were always open to every one in distress, and she always warmly sympathized with mine. It was impossible to tell how near the enemy was. He might have passed and repassed the house while we were sleeping. He might at that moment be waiting to pounce upon me if I ventured out of doors. I had never seen the husband of my young mistress, and therefore I could not distinguish him from any other stranger. A carriage was hastily ordered; and, closely veiled, I followed Mrs. Bruce, taking the baby again with me into exile. After various turnings and crossings, and returnings, the carriage stopped at the house of one of Mrs. Bruce's friends, where I was kindly received. Mrs. Bruce returned immediately, to instruct the domestics what to say if any one came to inquire for me.

It was lucky for me that the evening paper was not burned up before I had a chance to examine the list of arrivals. It was not long after Mrs. Bruce's return to her house, before several people came to inquire for me. One inquired for me, another asked for my daughter Ellen, and another said he had a letter from my grandmother, which he was requested to deliver in person.

They were told, "She has lived here, but she has left."

"How long ago?"

"I don't know, sir."

"Do you know where she went?"

"I do not, sir." And the door was closed.

This Mr. Dodge, who claimed me as his property, was originally a Yankee peddler in the south; then he became a merchant, and finally a slaveholder. He managed to get introduced into what was called the first society, and married Miss Emily Flint. A quarrel arose between him and her brother, and the brother cowhided him. This led to a family feud, and he proposed to remove to Virginia. Dr. Flint left him no property, and his own means had become circumscribed, while a wife and children depended upon him for support. Under these circumstances, it was very natural that he should make an effort to put me into his pocket.

I had a colored friend, a man from my native place, in whom I had the most implicit confidence. I sent for him, and told him that Mr. and Mrs. Dodge had arrived in New York. I proposed that he should call upon them to make inquiries about his friends at the south, with whom Dr. Flint's family were well acquainted.

He thought there was no impropriety in his doing so, and he consented. He went to the hotel, and knocked at the door of Mr. Dodge's room, which was opened by the gentleman himself, who gruffly inquired, "What brought you here? How came you to know I was in the city?"

"Your arrival was published in the evening papers, sir; and I called to ask Mrs. Dodge about my friends at home. I didn't suppose it would give any offence."

"Where's that negro girl, that belongs to my wife?"

"What girl, sir?"

"You know well enough. I mean Linda, that ran away from Dr. Flint's plantation, some years ago. I dare say you've seen her, and know where she is."

"Yes, sir, I've seen her, and know where she is. She is out of your reach, sir."

"Tell me where she is, or bring her to me, and I will give her a chance to buy her freedom."

"I don't think it would be of any use, sir. I have heard her say she would go to the ends of the earth, rather than pay any man or woman for her freedom, because she thinks she has a right to it. Besides, she couldn't do it, if she would, for she has spent her earnings to educate her children."

This made Mr. Dodge very angry, and some high words passed between them. My friend was afraid to come where I was; but in the course of the day I received a note from him. I supposed they had not come from the south, in the winter, for a pleasure excursion; and now the nature of their business was very plain.

Mrs. Bruce came to me and entreated me to leave the city the next morning. She said her house was watched, and it was possible that some clew to me might be obtained. I refused to take her advice. She pleaded with an earnest tenderness, that ought to have moved me; but I was in a bitter, disheartened mood. I was weary of flying from pillar to post. I had been chased during half my life, and it seemed as if the chase was never to end. There I sat, in that great city, guiltless of crime, yet not daring to worship God in any of the churches. I heard the bells ringing for afternoon service, and, with contemptuous sarcasm, I said, "Will the preachers take for their text, 'Proclaim liberty to the captive, and the opening of prison doors to them that are bound'?[1] or will they preach

---

1 Reference to biblical scripture, Isaiah 61.1: The spirit of the Lord God is upon me; because the Lord hath anointed one to preach [*continued*]

from the text, 'Do unto others as ye would they should do unto you'?"[1] Oppressed Poles and Hungarians could find a safe refuge in that city; John Mitchell[2] was free to proclaim in the City Hall his desire for "a plantation well stocked with slaves;" but there I sat, an oppressed American, not daring to show my face. God forgive the black and bitter thoughts I indulged on that Sabbath day! The Scripture says, "Oppression makes even a wise man mad;"[3] and I was not wise.

I had been told that Mr. Dodge said his wife had never signed away her right to my children, and if he could not get me, he would take them. This it was, more than any thing else, that roused such a tempest in my soul. Benjamin was with his uncle William in California, but my innocent young daughter had come to spend a vacation with me. I thought of what I had suffered in slavery at her age, and my heart was like a tiger's when a hunter tries to seize her young.

Dear Mrs. Bruce! I seem to see the expression of her face, as she turned away discouraged by my obstinate[4] mood. Finding her expostulations[5] unavailing, she sent Ellen to entreat me. When ten o'clock in the evening arrived and Ellen had not returned, this watchful and unwearied friend became anxious. She came to us in a carriage, bringing a well-filled trunk for my journey—trusting that by this time I would listen to reason. I yielded to her, as I ought to have done before.

The next day, baby and I set out in a heavy snow storm, bound for New England again. I received letters from the City of Iniquity, addressed to me under an assumed name. In a few days

---

good tidings unto the meek; he hath sent me to bind up the broken-hearted, to proclaim liberty to the captives, and the opening of the prison to them that are bound.

1 From biblical scripture, Matthew 7.12: Therefore all things whatso-ever ye would that men should do to you, do ye even so to them: for this is the law and the prophets.

2 Irish nationalist John Mitchel (1815–75) founded the pro-slavery New York newspaper *The Citizen*. In 1854, he wrote, "We, for our part, wish we had a good plantation, well-stocked with healthy negroes, in Alabama," and this statement provoked considerable discussion in William Lloyd Garrison's anti-slavery newspaper *Liberator*.

3 From biblical scripture, Ecclesiastes 7.17: Surely oppression maketh a wise man mad; and a bribe destroyeth the heart.

4 Not yielding to persuasion.

5 Kind, earnest protests, arguments, or reasonings.

one came from Mrs. Bruce, informing me that my new master was still searching for me, and that she intended to put an end to this persecution by buying my freedom. I felt grateful for the kindness that prompted this offer, but the idea was not so pleasant to me as might have been expected. The more my mind had become enlightened, the more difficult it was for me to consider myself an article of property; and to pay money to those who had so grievously oppressed me seemed like taking from my sufferings the glory of triumph. I wrote to Mrs. Bruce, thanking her, but saying that being sold from one owner to another seemed too much like slavery; that such a great obligation could not be easily cancelled; and that I preferred to go to my brother in California.

Without my knowledge, Mrs. Bruce employed a gentleman in New York to enter into negotiations with Mr. Dodge. He proposed to pay three hundred dollars down, if Mr. Dodge would sell me, and enter into obligations to relinquish all claim to me or my children forever after.[1] He who called himself my master said he scorned so small an offer for such a valuable servant. The gentleman replied, "You can do as you choose, sir. If you reject this offer you will never get any thing; for the woman has friends who will convey her and her children out of the country."

Mr. Dodge concluded that "half a loaf was better than no bread," and he agreed to the proffered terms. By the next mail I received this brief letter from Mrs. Bruce: "I am rejoiced to tell you that the money for your freedom has been paid to Mr. Dodge. Come home to-morrow. I long to see you and my sweet babe."

My brain reeled as I read these lines. A gentleman near me said, "It's true; I have seen the bill of sale." "The bill of sale!" Those words struck me like a blow. So I was sold at last! A human being sold in the free city of New York! The bill of sale is on record, and future generations will learn from it that women were articles of traffic in New York, late in the nineteenth century of the Christian religion. It may hereafter prove a useful document to antiquaries, who are seeking to measure the progress of civilization in the United States. I well know the value of that bit of paper; but much as I love freedom, I do not like to look upon it. I am deeply grateful to the generous friend who procured it, but I despise the miscreant who demanded payment for what never rightfully belonged to him or his.

---

1 Daniel Messmore correctly assumed that Jacobs did not know that Dr. Norcom had actually relinquished claim to Jacobs's children in the sale that freed them years earlier. See Yellin, *Incidents* 291n10.

I had objected to having my freedom bought, yet I must confess that when it was done I felt as if a heavy load had been lifted from my weary shoulders. When I rode home in the cars I was no longer afraid to unveil my face and look at people as they passed. I should have been glad to have met Daniel Dodge himself; to have had him seen me and known me, that he might have mourned over the untoward[1] circumstances which compelled him to sell me for three hundred dollars.

When I reached home, the arms of my benefactress were thrown round me, and our tears mingled. As soon as she could speak, she said, "O Linda, I'm so glad it's all over! You wrote to me as if you thought you were going to be transferred from one owner to another. But I did not buy you for your services. I should have done just the same, if you had been going to sail for California to-morrow. I should, at least, have the satisfaction of knowing that you left me a free woman."

My heart was exceedingly full. I remembered how my poor father had tried to buy me, when I was a small child, and how he had been disappointed. I hoped his spirit was rejoicing over me now. I remembered how my good old grandmother had laid up her earnings to purchase me in later years, and how often her plans had been frustrated. How that faithful, loving old heart would leap for joy, if she could look on me and my children now that we were free! My relatives had been foiled in all their efforts, but God had raised me up a friend among strangers, who had bestowed on me the precious, long-desired boon. Friend! It is a common word, often lightly used. Like other good and beautiful things, it may be tarnished by careless handling; but when I speak of Mrs. Bruce as my friend, the word is sacred.

My grandmother lived to rejoice in my freedom; but not long after, a letter came with a black seal. She had gone "where the wicked cease from troubling, and the weary are at rest."

Time passed on, and a paper came to me from the south, containing an obituary notice of my uncle Phillip. It was the only case I ever knew of such an honor conferred upon a colored person. It was written by one of his friends, and contained these words: "Now that death has laid him low, they call him a good man and a useful citizen; but what are eulogies to the black man, when the world has faded from his vision? It does not require man's praise to obtain rest in God's kingdom." So they called a colored man a citizen! Strange words to be uttered in that region!

---

1 Unfavorable; unfortunate.

Reader, my story ends with freedom; not in the usual way, with marriage. I and my children are now free! We are as free from the power of slaveholders as are the white people of the north; and though that, according to my ideas, is not saying a great deal, it is a vast improvement in my condition. The dream of my life is not yet realized. I do not sit with my children in a home of my own. I still long for a hearthstone of my own, however humble. I wish it for my children's sake far more than for my own. But God so orders circumstances as to keep me with my friend Mrs. Bruce. Love, duty, gratitude, also bind me to her side. It is a privilege to serve her who pities my oppressed people, and who has bestowed the inestimable boon of freedom on me and my children.

It has been painful to me, in many ways, to recall the dreary years I passed in bondage. I would gladly forget them if I could. Yet the retrospection is not altogether without solace; for with those gloomy recollections come tender memories of my good old grandmother, like light, fleecy clouds floating over a dark and troubled sea.

APPENDIX.

The following statement is from Amy Post, a member of the Society of Friends in the State of New York, well known and highly respected by friends of the poor and the oppressed. As has been already stated, in the preceding pages, the author of this volume spent some time under her hospitable roof. L.M.C.[1]

"The author of this book is my highly-esteemed friend. If its readers knew her as I know her, they could not fail to be deeply interested in her story. She was a beloved inmate of our family nearly the whole of the year 1849. She was introduced to us by her affectionate and conscientious brother, who had previously related to us some of the almost incredible events in his sister's life. I immediately became much interested in Linda; for her appearance was prepossessing, and her deportment indicated remarkable delicacy of feeling and purity of thought.

"As we became acquainted, she related to me, from time to time some of the incidents in her bitter experiences as a slave-woman. Though impelled by a natural craving for human sympathy, she passed through a baptism of suffering, even in recounting her trials to me, in private confidential conversations. The burden of these memories lay heavily upon her spirit—naturally virtuous and refined. I repeatedly urged her to consent to the publication of her narrative; for I felt that it would arouse people to a more earnest work for the disinthralment of millions still remaining in that soul-crushing condition, which was so unendurable to her. But her sensitive spirit shrank from publicity. She said, 'You know a woman can whisper her cruel wrongs in the ear of a dear friend much easier than she can record them for the world to read.' Even in talking with me, she wept so much, and seemed to suffer such mental agony, that I felt her story was too sacred to be drawn from her by inquisitive questions, and I left her free to tell as much, or as little, as she chose. Still, I urged upon her the duty of publishing her experience, for the sake of the good it might do; and, at last, she undertook the task.

"Having been a slave so large a portion of her life, she is unlearned; she is obliged to earn her living by her own labor, and she has worked untiringly to procure education for her children; several times she has been obliged to leave her employments, in order to fly from the man-hunters and woman-hunters of our

---

1   Editor Lydia Maria Child.

land; but she pressed through all these obstacles and overcame them. After the labors of the day were over, she traced secretly and wearily, by the midnight lamp, a truthful record of her eventful life.

"This Empire State is a shabby place of refuge for the oppressed; but here, through anxiety, turmoil, and despair, the freedom of Linda and her children was finally secured, by the exertions of a generous friend. She was grateful for the boon; but the idea of having been bought was always galling to a spirit that could never acknowledge itself to be a chattel. She wrote to us thus, soon after the event: 'I thank you for your kind expressions in regard to my freedom; but the freedom I had before the money was paid was dearer to me. God gave me that freedom; but man put God's image in the scales with the paltry sum of three hundred dollars. I served for my liberty as faithfully as Jacob served for Rachel.[1] At the end, he had large possessions; but I was robbed of my victory; I was obliged to resign my crown, to rid myself of a tyrant.'

"Her story, as written by herself, cannot fail to interest the reader. It is a sad illustration of the condition of this country, which boasts of its civilization, while it sanctions laws and customs which make the experiences of the present more strange than any fictions of the past. Amy Post.
"Rochester, N.Y., Oct. 30th, 1859."

The following testimonial is from a man who is now a highly respectable colored citizen of Boston. L.M.C.

"This narrative contains some incidents so extraordinary, that, doubtless, many persons, under whose eyes it may chance to fall, will be ready to believe that it is colored highly, to serve a special purpose. But, however it may be regarded by the incredulous, I know that it is full of living truths. I have been well acquainted with the author from my boyhood. The circumstances recounted in her history are perfectly familiar to me. I knew of her treatment from her master; of the imprisonment of her children; of their sale and redemption; of her seven years' concealment; and of her

---

1 In biblical scripture, Jacob wants to marry Rachel, so he serves her father for seven years, "and they seemed *only* a few days to him because of the love he had for her." However, the father substitutes Rachel's older sister Leah, and Jacob serves him another seven years to win Rachel. See Genesis 29.15–30.

subsequent escape to the North. I am now a resident of Boston, and am a living witness to the truth of this interesting narrative. George W. Lowther."[1]

---

1   George W. Lowther (1822–98) was the son of a free Black neighbor of
    Jacobs's grandmother. Lowther was privately educated in their home-
    town of Edenton, North Carolina, and he moved to Boston in 1838.
    During the 1850s, he was part of William C. Nell's circle and renewed
    his friendship with Jacobs. After the Civil War, he became active in
    the Republican Party and was elected to the Massachusetts House of
    Representatives in 1878 and 1879 (Yellin, Incidents 292).

Appendix A: Historical Contexts

[This appendix places at readers' fingertips historical documents that articulate the values of powerful Americans as well as the suffering those values created for the less powerful. A 1788 petition from a Northern state provides just one early example of how enslaved people pressed for humane treatment. The *Fugitive Slave Act* reminds readers that slavery could not have survived without cooperation from the North—cooperation that created terror. The 1857 *Dred Scott* decision demonstrates that disregarding Black people's rights and basic humanity took many forms, not just enslavement. In fact, once the Civil War was underway, the Union's willingness to see African Americans as property helped it to win battles, as illustrated by the *Confiscation Acts*. Because the Union ultimately defeated the Confederacy while he was president, most learn to regard Abraham Lincoln as "the great emancipator," but few consider what his Emancipation Proclamation actually said; the full text appears here.

After the Civil War, legislators created what is commonly known as the Freedmen's Bureau. While most think of the Bureau as an entity that helped newly free African Americans, the text of the legislation shows concern for "refugees," the white people who were loyal to the Union while living in the Confederacy. Constant concern for white Americans' comfort and status never dissipated, even as the 13th, 14th, and 15th amendments emerged in 1865, 1868, and 1870. Indeed, it helps explain why the investment in inequality articulated by the 1857 *Dred Scott* decision was intensified by the 1897 *Plessy v. Ferguson* decision.]

1. "Handed by the Blacks of New Haven City," Petition (1788)

[Petition submitted by unidentified enslaved people who "beg for murcy" and liberation. It describes harsh treatment received in the northern state of Connecticut. All irregularities of spelling, spacing, capitalization, etc. have been retained. Full text at http://www.hartford-hwp.com/archives/45a/023.html.]

1ly
gentlemen wee are Dragd from our native Country for Life lyis Cruil Slavirre Leving our mothers our farthers our Sisters and our Brothers is this humen pea[p]le

4th
Now gentlemen wee wold wish to act a wisely part and with a mile Temper and good Dispersisan but can we help but Beg for murcy in this accation Don[t] gentlemen think us impirtinent for asking this favor for the Lord bath saide ask and it Shal [be] given we that can live prary let you us Liv[e]

5th
Now gentlemen we would wish to say nom₁ore apon thi[s] Subject all our wishes ar that your Honours wou[ld] grant us a Liberration wee are all Deturmand we Can to[il] As Long as thir is Labor we woul wish no more to be in Sl[avery] to Sin Seene Christ is maid us free and nald our tanants to the Cross and Bought our Liberty

2. From the *Fugitive Slave Act* (1850)

[Passed to appease slave states, this act required all citizens to assist in the recovery of "fugitives from slavery," or self-emancipators, and it obliterated a fugitive's right to a jury trial. Cases would be handled by special commissioners who would be paid $5 if an alleged fugitive was released and $10 if handed over to the claimant. The law literally offered incentives for being hostile to African Americans' desire for freedom.]

SEC. 6. And be it further enacted, That when a person held to service or labor in any State or Territory of the United States, has heretofore or shall hereafter escape into another State or Territory of the United States, the person or persons to whom such service or labor may be due, or his, her, or their agent or attorney, duly authorized, by power of attorney, in writing ... may Pursue and reclaim such fugitive person, either by procuring a warrant from some one of the courts, judges, or commissioners aforesaid ... or by seizing and arresting such fugitive, where the same can be done without process, and by taking, or causing such person to be taken, forthwith before such court, judge, or commissioner, whose duty it shall be to hear and determine the case of such claimant in a summary manner.... In no trial or hearing under this act shall the testimony of such alleged fugitive be admitted in evidence; and the certificates in this ... section mentioned, shall be conclusive of the right of the person or persons in whose favor granted, to remove such fugitive to the State or Territory from which he escaped, and shall prevent all molestation of such person or persons by any process issued by any court, judge, magistrate, or other person whomsoever.

SEC. 7. *And be it further enacted,* That any person who shall knowingly and willingly obstruct, hinder, or prevent such claimant, his agent or attorney, or any person or persons lawfully assisting him, her, or them, from arresting such a fugitive from service or labor, either with or without process as aforesaid, or shall rescue, or attempt to rescue, such fugitive from service or labor, from the custody of such claimant, his or her agent or attorney, or other person or persons lawfully assisting as aforesaid, when so arrested, pursuant to the authority herein given and declared; or shall aid, abet, or assist such person so owing service or labor as aforesaid, directly or indirectly, to escape from such claimant, his agent or attorney, or other person or persons legally authorized as aforesaid; or shall harbor or conceal such fugitive, so as to prevent the discovery and arrest of such person, after notice or knowledge of the fact that such person was a fugitive from service or labor as aforesaid, shall, for either of said offences, be subject to a fine not exceeding one thousand dollars, and imprisonment not exceeding six months...; and shall moreover forfeit and pay, by way of civil damages to the party injured by such illegal conduct, the sum of one thousand dollars for each fugitive so lost....

SEC. 8. *And be it further enacted,* That the marshals, their deputies, and the clerks of the said District and Territorial Courts, shall be paid, for their services, the like fees as may be allowed for similar services in other cases; ... and in all cases where the proceedings are before a commissioner, he shall be entitled to a fee of ten dollars in full for his services in each case, upon the delivery of the said certificate to the claimant, his agent or attorney; or a fee of five dollars in cases where the proof shall not, in the opinion of such commissioner, warrant such certificate and delivery....

Approved, September 18, 1850.

3. Notice warning Black people in Boston to be on guard
   after the passage of the *Fugitive Slave Act* (24 April 1851),
   Library of Congress, Rare Book and Special Collections
   Division, Printed Ephemera Collection

[In *Incidents*, Jacobs highlights the *Fugitive Slave Act* as a key example of the nation's hypocrisy. She also describes how it intensified the terror that characterized Black life in the North. Her habit of regularly reading newspapers for announcements about enslavers' hotel arrivals predated the *Act*, but this image, which circulated after the *Act* went into effect, reflects the same kind of community-oriented watchfulness. Jacobs sought information for her own benefit and to share with others, and she was not alone in how she thought about what community members do for each other.]

CAUTION!!
COLORED PEOPLE
OF BOSTON, ONE & ALL,

You are hereby respectfully CAUTIONED and
advised, to avoid conversing with the

Watchmen and Police Officers
of Boston,

For since the recent ORDER OF THE MAYOR &
ALDERMEN, they are empowered to act as

KIDNAPPERS
AND
Slave Catchers,

And they have already been actually employed in
KIDNAPPING, CATCHING, AND KEEPING
SLAVES. Therefore, if you value your LIBERTY,
and the *Welfare of the Fugitives* among you, *Shun*
them in every possible manner, as so many *HOUNDS*
on the track of the most unfortunate of your race.

Keep a Sharp Look Out for
KIDNAPPERS, and have
TOP EYE open.
APRIL 24, 1851.

4. United States Supreme Court Justice Roger Taney, The *Dred Scott* Decision (6 March 1857)

[Commonly known as The *Dred Scott* Decision, the case before the Supreme Court of the United States was *Dred Scott v. Sandford*, and the ruling was issued on 6 March 1857. Dred Scott, an enslaved man, had been taken to the free territories of Illinois and Minnesota, where he and his enslaver remained during the late 1830s and early 1840s. Upon returning to the slave state of Missouri in 1847, Scott (with the help of white allies) sued for his freedom. The St. Louis County Circuit Court acknowledged his freedom, the Missouri State Supreme Court reversed that decision, and the US Supreme Court upheld the latter ruling. Chief Justice Roger B. Taney wrote the Court's majority opinion. Transcription from Trotter A–27.]

The question is simply this: Can a negro, whose ancestors were imported into this country, and sold as slaves, become a member of the political community formed and brought into existence by the Constitution of the United States, and as such become entitled to all the rights, and privileges, and immunities, guaranteed by that instrument to the citizen? One of which rights is the privilege of suing in a court of the United States in the cases specified in the Constitution....

It is difficult at this day to realize the state of public opinion in relation to that unfortunate race, which prevailed in the civilized and enlightened portions of the world at the time of the Declaration of Independence, and when the Constitution of the United States was framed and adopted. But the public history of every European nation displays it in a manner too plain to be mistaken.

They had for more than a century before been regarded as beings of an inferior order, and altogether unfit to associate with the white race, either in social or political relations; and so far inferior, that they had no rights which the white man was bound to respect; and that the negro might justly and lawfully be reduced to slavery for his benefit....

And upon a full and careful consideration of the subject, the court is of opinion, that, upon the facts stated in the plea in abatement, Dred Scot was not a citizen of Missouri within the meaning of the Constitution of the United States, and not entitled as such to sue in its courts; and consequently, that the Circuit Court had no jurisdiction of the case, and that the judgment on the plea in abatement is erroneous....

Its judgment for the defendant must, consequently, be reversed, and a mandate issued, directing the suit to be dismissed for want of jurisdiction.

5. From the *First Confiscation Act* (1861)

[This act was based on the idea that warring factions will use whatever resources they can to defeat each other. Because it was crafted by federal authorities, the act declared that "all property" used to rebel against the government would become Union property even if "found" in the Confederacy. It therefore labeled enslaved men and women who were willing to help the Union "contraband" of war; it treated them as confiscated property that the Union could use to advance its cause. The act helped the Union while keeping slavery intact. Contrabands were repurposed property; they were not necessarily viewed as people and certainly not as citizens.]

An Act to confiscate Property used for Insurrectionary Purposes.

Be it enacted by the Senate and House of Representatives of the United States of America in Congress assembled, That if, during the present or any future insurrection against the Government of the United States, after the President of the United States shall have declared, by proclamation, that the laws of the United States are opposed, and the execution thereof obstructed, by combinations too powerful to be suppressed by the ordinary course of judicial proceedings, or by the power vested in the marshals by law, any person or persons, his, her, or their agent, attorney, or employé, shall purchase or acquire, sell or give, any property of whatsoever kind or description, with intent to use or employ the same, or suffer the same to be used or employed, in aiding, abetting, or promoting such insurrection or resistance to the laws, or any person or persons engaged therein; or if any person or persons, being the owner or owners of any such property, shall knowingly use or employ, or consent to the use or employment of the same as aforesaid, all such property is hereby declared to be lawful subject of prize and capture wherever found; and it shall be the duty of the President of the United States to cause the same to be seized, confiscated, and condemned.

SEC. 4. And be it further enacted, That whenever hereafter, during the present insurrection against the Government of the

United States, any person claimed to be held to labor or service under the law of any State, shall be required or permitted by the person to whom such labor or service is claimed to be due, or by the lawful agent of such person, to take up arms against the United States, or shall be required or permitted by the person to whom such labor or service is claimed to be due, or his lawful agent, to work or to be employed in or upon any fort, navy yard, dock, armory, ship, entrenchment, or in any military or naval service whatsoever, against the Government and lawful authority of the United States, then, and in every such case, the person to whom such labor or service is claimed to be due shall forfeit his claim to such labor, any law of the State or of the United States to the contrary notwithstanding. And whenever thereafter the person claiming such labor or service shall seek to enforce his claim, it shall be a full and sufficient answer to such claim that the person whose service or labor is claimed had been employed in hostile service against the Government of the United States, contrary to the provisions of this act.

APPROVED, August 6, 1861.

6. From the *Second Confiscation Act* (1862)

[Only with the passage of this act were "contrabands" declared to be "free."]

An Act to suppress Insurrection, to punish Treason and Rebellion, to seize and confiscate the Property of Rebels, and for other Purposes.

Be it enacted by the Senate and House of Representatives of the United States of America in Congress assembled, That every person who shall hereafter commit the crime of treason against the United States, and shall be adjudged guilty thereof, shall suffer death, and all his slaves, if any, shall be declared and made free; or, at the discretion of the court, he shall be imprisoned for not less than five years and fined not less than ten thousand dollars, and all his slaves, if any, shall be declared and made free; said fine shall be levied and collected on any or all of the property, real and personal, excluding slaves, of which the said person so convicted was the owner at the time of committing the said crime, any sale or conveyance to the contrary notwithstanding.

SEC. 3. And be it further enacted, That every person guilty of either of the offences described in this act shall be forever incapable and disqualified to hold any office under the United States.

SEC. 10. And be it further enacted, That no slave escaping into any State, Territory, or the District of Columbia, from any other State, shall be delivered up, or in any way impeded or hindered of his liberty, except for crime, or some offence against the laws, unless the person claiming said fugitive shall first make oath that the person to whom the labor or service of such fugitive is alleged to be due is his lawful owner, and has not borne arms against the United States in the present rebellion, nor in any way given aid and comfort thereto; and no person engaged in the military or naval service of the United States shall, under any pretence whatever, assume to decide on the validity of the claim of any person to the service or labor of any other person, or surrender up any such person to the claimant, on pain of being dismissed from the service.

SEC. 11. And be it further enacted, That the President of the United States is authorized to employ as many persons of African descent as he may deem necessary and proper for the suppression of this rebellion, and for this purpose he may organize and use them in such manner as he may judge best for the public welfare.

SEC. 13. And be it further enacted, That the President is hereby authorized, at any time hereafter, by proclamation, to extend to persons who may have participated in the existing rebellion in any State or part thereof, pardon and amnesty, with such exceptions and at such time and on such conditions as he may deem expedient for the public welfare.

... APPROVED, July 17, 1862.

7. The Emancipation Proclamation (1863)

[This is the complete text of the famous proclamation. Please note that it did not immediately release enslaved people from bondage. Also note that it placed a priority on reassuring enslavers who had been loyal to the Union of their "rights" over enslaved men, women, and children. As attorney Lurie Daniel Favors[1] points out, the proclamation offered freedom only in territories where it had no authority; where its authority was acknowledged, it honored slavery.]

---

1 I owe this insight to *The Lurie Daniel Favors Show,* which airs Monday through Friday from 10 a.m. to noon Eastern time on SiriusXM Urbanview, Channel 126.

By the President of the United States of America:
A Proclamation.

Whereas, on the twenty-second day of September, in the year of our Lord one thousand eight hundred and sixty-two, a proclamation was issued by the President of the United States, containing, among other things, the following, to wit:

"That on the first day of January, in the year of our Lord one thousand eight hundred and sixty-three, all persons held as slaves within any State or designated part of a State, the people whereof shall then be in rebellion against the United States, shall be then, thenceforward, and forever free; and the Executive Government of the United States, including the military and naval authority thereof, will recognize and maintain the freedom of such persons, and will do no act or acts to repress such persons, or any of them, in any efforts they may make for their actual freedom.

"That the Executive will, on the first day of January aforesaid, by proclamation, designate the States and parts of States, if any, in which the people thereof, respectively, shall then be in rebellion against the United States; and the fact that any State, or the people thereof, shall on that day be, in good faith, represented in the Congress of the United States by members chosen thereto at elections wherein a majority of the qualified voters of such State shall have participated, shall, in the absence of strong countervailing testimony, be deemed conclusive evidence that such State, and the people thereof, are not then in rebellion against the United States."

Now, therefore I, Abraham Lincoln, President of the United States, by virtue of the power in me vested as Commander-in-Chief, of the Army and Navy of the United States in time of actual armed rebellion against the authority and government of the United States, and as a fit and necessary war measure for suppressing said rebellion, do, on this first day of January, in the year of our Lord one thousand eight hundred and sixty-three, and in accordance with my purpose so to do publicly proclaimed for the full period of one hundred days, from the day first above mentioned, order and designate as the States and parts of States wherein the people thereof respectively, are this day in rebellion against the United States, the following, to wit:

Arkansas, Texas, Louisiana, (except the Parishes of St. Bernard, Plaquemines, Jefferson, St. John, St. Charles, St. James Ascension, Assumption, Terrebonne, Lafourche, St. Mary, St. Martin, and Orleans, including the City of New Orleans)

Mississippi, Alabama, Florida, Georgia, South Carolina, North Carolina, and Virginia, (except the forty-eight counties designated as West Virginia, and also the counties of Berkley, Accomac, Northampton, Elizabeth City, York, Princess Ann, and Norfolk, including the cities of Norfolk and Portsmouth), and which excepted parts, are for the present, left precisely as if this proclamation were not issued.

And by virtue of the power, and for the purpose aforesaid, I do order and declare that all persons held as slaves within said designated States, and parts of States, are, and henceforward shall be free; and that the Executive government of the United States, including the military and naval authorities thereof, will recognize and maintain the freedom of said persons.

And I hereby enjoin upon the people so declared to be free to abstain from all violence, unless in necessary self-defense; and I recommend to them that, in all cases when allowed, they labor faithfully for reasonable wages.

And I further declare and make known, that such persons of suitable condition, will be received into the armed service of the United States to garrison forts, positions, stations, and other places, and to man vessels of all sorts in said service.

And upon this act, sincerely believed to be an act of justice, warranted by the Constitution, upon military necessity, I invoke the considerate judgment of mankind, and the gracious favor of Almighty God.

In witness whereof, I have hereunto set my hand and caused the seal of the United States to be affixed.

Done at the City of Washington, this first day of January, in the year of our Lord one thousand eight hundred and sixty-three, and of the Independence of the United States of America the eighty-seventh.

By the President: ABRAHAM LINCOLN
WILLIAM H. SEWARD, Secretary of State.

8. From the *Freedmen's Bureau Act* (1865)

[The act that established what is commonly known as the Freedmen's Bureau.]

An Act to Establish a Bureau for the Relief of Freedmen and Refugees.[1]

Be it enacted by the Senate and House of Representatives of the United States of America in Congress assembled, That there is hereby established in the War Department, to continue during the present war of rebellion, and for one year thereafter, a bureau of refugees, freedmen, and abandoned lands, to which shall be committed, as hereinafter provided, the supervision and management of all abandoned lands, and the control of all subjects relating to refugees and freedmen from rebel states, or from any district of [the] country within the territory embraced in the operations of the army, under such rules and regulations as may be prescribed by the head of the bureau and approved by the President....

SEC. 2. And be it further enacted, That the Secretary of War may direct such issues of provisions, clothing, and fuel, as he may deem needful for the immediate and temporary shelter and supply of destitute and suffering refugees and freedmen and their wives and children, under such rules and regulations as he may direct....

SEC. 3. And be it further enacted, That the President may, by and with the advice and consent of the Senate, appoint an assistant commissioner for each of the states declared to be in insurrection, not exceeding ten in number, who shall, under the direction of the commissioner, aid in the execution of the provisions of this act.... The commissioner shall, before the commencement of each regular session of congress, make full report of his proceedings with exhibits of the state of his accounts to the President, who shall communicate the same to congress, and shall also make special reports whenever required to do so by the President or either house of congress; and the assistant commissioners shall make quarterly reports of their proceedings to the commissioner, and also such other special reports as from time to time may be required.

SEC. 4. And be it further enacted, That the commissioner, under the direction of the President, shall have authority to set apart, for

---

1 White Southerners who were loyal to the United States during the Confederacy's rebellion.

the use of loyal refugees and freedmen, such tracts of land within the insurrectionary states as shall have been abandoned, or to which the United States shall have acquired title by confiscation or sale, or otherwise, and to every male citizen, whether refugee or freedman, as aforesaid, there shall be assigned not more than forty acres[1] of such land, and the person to whom it was so assigned shall be protected in the use and enjoyment of the land for the term of three years at an annual rent not exceeding six per centum upon the value of such land, as it was appraised by the state authorities in the year eighteen hundred and sixty, for the purpose of taxation, and in case no such appraisal can be found, then the rental shall be based upon the estimated value of the land in said year, to be ascertained in such manner as the commissioner may by regulation prescribe. At the end of said term, or at any time during said term, the occupants of any parcels so assigned may purchase the land and receive such title thereto as the United States can convey, upon paying therefor the value of the land, as ascertained and fixed for the purpose of determining the annual rent aforesaid.

SEC. 5. *And be it further enacted,* That all acts and parts of acts inconsistent with the provisions of this act, are hereby repealed.

APPROVED, March 3, 1865.

---

1 The federal government gained control of 850,000 acres of land after defeating the Confederacy, and Freedmen's Bureau leadership believed that Southern economic recovery required helping not only white "refugees" but also the formerly enslaved. With the approval of Freedman's Bureau leadership, General Rufus Saxton (1824–1908) began settling Black people on forty-acre farms in the summer of 1865. By September, President Johnson ordered that all allocations to formerly enslaved people cease, and he insisted that land already distributed to African Americans be restored to previous owners, who were generally ex-Confederates who had betrayed the United States. Only a small fraction of the formerly enslaved who had gained land this way were allowed to keep it.

9. The Thirteenth Amendment (1865)

Amendment XIII

SEC. 1. Neither slavery nor involuntary servitude, except as a punishment for crime whereof the party shall have been duly convicted, shall exist within the United States, or any place subject to their jurisdiction.

SEC. 2. Congress shall have power to enforce this article by appropriate legislation.

10. From the Fourteenth Amendment (1868)

Amendment XIV

SEC. 1. All persons born or naturalized in the United States, and subject to the jurisdiction thereof, are citizens of the United States and of the state wherein they reside. No state shall make or enforce any law which shall abridge the privileges or immunities of citizens of the United States; nor shall any state deprive any person of life, liberty, or property, without due process of law; nor deny to any person within its jurisdiction the equal protection of the laws.

SEC. 2. Representatives shall be apportioned among the several states according to their respective numbers, counting the whole number[1] of persons in each state, excluding Indians not taxed....

SEC. 3. No person shall be a Senator or Representative in Congress, or elector of President and Vice President, or hold any office, civil or military, under the United States, or under any state, who, having previously taken an oath, as a member of Congress, or as an officer of the United States, or as a member of any state legislature, or as an executive or judicial officer of any state, to support the Constitution of the United States, shall have engaged in insurrection or rebellion against the same, or given aid or comfort to the enemies thereof. But Congress may by a vote of two-thirds of each House, remove such disability.

SEC. 5. The Congress shall have power to enforce, by appropriate legislation, the provisions of this article.

---

1 At the 1787 United States Constitutional Convention, leaders decided to count the enslaved as three-fifths of a person. It was one of many compromises with enslavers because it allowed them to demand higher representation in government based on people they brutalized.

11. From the Fifteenth Amendment (1870)

Amendment XV

SEC. 1. The right of citizens of the United States to vote shall not be denied or abridged by the United States or by any state on account of race, color, or previous condition of servitude.

SEC. 2. The Congress shall have power to enforce this article by appropriate legislation.

12. From United States Supreme Court Justice Billings Brown, *Plessy v. Ferguson* (1896)

[By the 1880s, many states had laws insisting upon the separation of Black and white people in public spaces. Hoping to demonstrate that state laws were impinging on rights guaranteed by the federal government, Homer Plessy (1862–1925) brought a case against the judge that convicted him of having violated Louisiana law by purchasing a first-class train ticket and sitting in a whites-only car while being seven-eighths white and one-eighth Black. The Supreme Court declared that states had a right to create these laws and insisted that if African Americans viewed segregation as inherently degrading, it was because they chose to give it that meaning. But, in any case, the majority opinion argued, the court cannot make African Americans socially equal nor prevent all infringements upon their rights.]

This case turns upon the constitutionality of an act of the General Assembly of the State of Louisiana, passed in 1890, providing for separate railway carriages for the white and colored races....

The constitutionality of this act is attacked upon the ground that it conflicts both with the Thirteenth Amendment of the Constitution, abolishing slavery, and the Fourteenth Amendment, which prohibits certain restrictive legislation on the part of the States.

1. That it does not conflict with the Thirteenth Amendment, which abolished slavery and involuntary servitude, except as a punishment for crime, is too clear for argument. Slavery implies involuntary servitude—a state of bondage; the ownership of mankind as a chattel, or at least the control of the labor and services of one man for the benefit of another, and the absence of a legal right to the disposal of his own person, property and services.... It was intimated, however, ... that this amendment was regarded

by the statesmen of that day as insufficient to protect the colored race from certain laws which had been enacted in the Southern States, imposing upon the colored race onerous disabilities and burdens, and curtailing their rights in the pursuit of life, liberty and property to such an extent that their freedom was of little value; and that the Fourteenth Amendment was devised to meet this exigency....

The object of the [14th] amendment was undoubtedly to enforce the absolute equality of the two races before the law, but, in the nature of things, it could not have been intended to abolish distinctions based upon color, or to enforce social, as distinguished from political, equality, or a commingling of the two races upon terms unsatisfactory to either. Laws permitting, and even requiring, their separation in places where they are liable to be brought into contact do not necessarily imply the inferiority of either race to the other, and have been generally, if not universally, recognized as within the competency of the state legislatures in the exercise of their police power. The most common instance of this is connected with the establishment of separate schools for white and colored children, which has been held to be a valid exercise of the legislative power even by courts of States where the political rights of the colored race have been longest and most earnestly enforced.

The distinction between laws interfering with the political equality of the negro and those requiring the separation of the two races in schools, theatres and railway carriages has been frequently drawn by this court....

[Even if the court conceded that the reputation of belonging to the dominant race is *property*], we are unable to see how this statute deprives [the plaintiff] of, or in any way affects his right to, such property. If he be a white man and assigned to a colored coach, he may have his action for damages against the company for being deprived of his so called property. Upon the other hand, if he be a colored man and be so assigned, he has been deprived of no property, since he is not lawfully entitled to the reputation of being a white man.

... [W]e cannot say that a law which authorizes or even requires the separation of the two races in public conveyances is unreasonable, or more obnoxious to the Fourteenth Amendment than the acts of Congress requiring separate schools for colored children in the District of Columbia, the constitutionality of which does not seem to have been questioned, or the corresponding acts of state legislatures.

We consider the underlying fallacy of the plaintiff's argument to consist in the assumption that the enforced separation of the two races stamps the colored race with a badge of inferiority. If this be so, it is not by reason of anything found in the act, but solely because the colored race chooses to put that construction upon it. The argument necessarily assumes that if, as has been more than once the case, and is not unlikely to be so again, the colored race should become the dominant power in the state legislature, and should enact a law in precisely similar terms, it would thereby relegate the white race to an inferior position. We imagine that the white race, at least, would not acquiesce in this assumption. The argument also assumes that social prejudices may be overcome by legislation, and that equal rights cannot be secured to the negro except by an enforced commingling of the two races. We cannot accept this proposition. If the two races are to meet upon terms of social equality, it must be the result of nat-ural affinities, a mutual appreciation of each other's merits and a voluntary consent of individuals....

Legislation is powerless to eradicate racial instincts or to abol-ish distinctions based upon physical differences, and the attempt to do so can only result in accentuating the difficulties of the pres-ent situation. If the civil and political rights of both races be equal one cannot be inferior to the other civilly or politically. If one race be inferior to the other socially, the Constitution of the United States cannot put them upon the same plane.

Appendix B: Additional Historical Connections

1. Laws of Virginia, Act XII (1662)

[An example of the laws enacted to ensure that Black women's bodies would produce profit for enslavers. According to British common law, children inherited their father's status, so when colonists based a child's fate on the mother's status, they reversed the practices that had shaped their own lives. The shift demonstrates how deliberate such laws were in creating a population that would be treated differently from how one treats people whose humanity and rights are recognized. This reversal was clearly motivated by the determination to prioritize exploitation, which required dehumanization. The Latin in this except was added by William Henig, *The Statutes at Large* (1819).]

Whereas some doubts have arisen whether children got by any Englishman upon a negro woman shall be slave or free, Be it therefore enacted and declared by this present grand assembly, that all children borne in this country shall be held bond or free only according to the condition of the mother—*Partus Sequitur Ventrem*. And that if any Christian shall commit fornication with a negro man or woman, hee or shee soe offending shall pay double the fines imposed by the former act.

2. From Olive Gilbert, *The Narrative of Sojourner Truth* (1850)

[This excerpt provides a sense of what "slave marriage" did and did not mean, given the nation's hostility toward Black humanity. *Incidents* honors enslaved people's view of their unions when speaking of Linda's mother (p. 143) and her aunt Nancy (p. 203), but it also notes the nation's disregard. Truth's as-told-to biography offers further context. Written by Olive Gilbert (1801–84), a white woman who lived with Truth (and others) in an interracial utopian community, this narrative was originally published in

1850.[1] It was re-released in 1884 to include "a memorial chapter" "giving the particulars of [Truth's] last sickness and death" in 1883. Transcribed from docsouth.unc.edu.]

As she advanced in years, an attachment sprung up between herself and a slave named Robert. But his master, an Englishman by the name of Catlin, anxious that no one's property but his own should be enhanced by the increase of his slaves, forbade Robert's visits to Isabella,[2] and commanded him to take a wife among his fellow-servants. Notwithstanding this interdiction, Robert, following the bent of his inclinations, continued his visits to Isabel, though very stealthily, and, as he believed, without exciting the suspicion of his master; but one Saturday afternoon, hearing that Bell was ill, he took the liberty to go and see her. The first intimation she had of his visit was the appearance of her master, inquiring "If she had seen Bob." On her answering in the negative, he said to her, "If you see him, tell him to take care of himself, for the Catlins are after him." Almost at that instant, Bob made his appearance; and the first people he met were his old and his young masters. They were terribly enraged at finding him there, and the eldest began cursing, and calling upon his son to "Knock down the d——d black rascal"; at the same time, they both fell upon him like tigers, beating him with the heavy ends of their canes, bruising and mangling his head and face in the most awful manner, and causing the blood, which streamed from his wounds, to cover him like a slaughtered beast, constituting him a most shocking spectacle. Mr. Dumont[3] interposed at this point, telling the ruffians they could no longer thus spill human blood on his premises—he would have "no niggers killed there." The Catlins then took

1 Gilbert's text was published with Truth's blessing while she was alive, and it was not the only indication of interest in formerly enslaved people's biographies. Decades before Truth's 1883 death, Harriet Beecher Stowe (1811–96) published "Sojourner Truth, The Libyan Sibyl" in the April 1863 issue of *The Atlantic*. It represents Truth in striking ways that underscore Jacobs's achievement in having written and published her own story. Though Truth was born in New York among Dutch settlers, Stowe gives her a Middle Passage experience (claiming she was on a boat from the African continent to the United States) and gives her a manner of speaking that aligns more with that of enslaved people in the South. The piece is still easily accessible on *The Atlantic* website.
2 Truth's birth name.
3 Truth's enslaver.

a rope they had taken with them for the purpose, and tied Bob's hands behind him in such a manner, that Mr. Dumont insisted on loosening the cord, declaring that no brute should be tied in that manner, where he was. And as they led him away, like the greatest of criminals, the more humane Dumont followed them to their homes, as Robert's protector; and when he returned, he kindly went to Bell, as he called her, telling her he did not think they would strike him any more, as their wrath had greatly cooled before he left them. Isabella had witnessed this scene from her window, and was greatly shocked at the murderous treatment of poor Robert, whom she truly loved, and whose only crime, in the eye of his persecutors, was his affection for her. This beating, and we know not what after treatment, completely subdued the spirit of its victim, for Robert ventured no more to visit Isabella, but like an obedient and faithful chattel, took himself a wife from the house of his master. Robert did not live many years after his last visit to Isabel, but took his departure to that country, where "they neither marry nor are given in marriage," and where the oppressor cannot molest.

ISABELLA'S MARRIAGE.

Subsequently, Isabella was married to a fellow-slave, named Thomas, who had previously had two wives, one of whom, if not both, had been torn from him and sold far away.[1] And it is more than probable, that he was not only allowed but encouraged to take another at each successive sale. I say it is probable, because the writer of this knows from personal observation, that such is the custom among slaveholders at the present day; and that in a twenty months' residence among them,[2] we never knew any one to open the lip against the practice; and when we severely censured it, the slaveholder had nothing to say; and the slave pleaded that, under existing circumstances, he could do no better.

---

1 Gilbert here emphasizes that violent disregard is what often determined not only enslaved people's separations but also their unions. This aspect of Truth's story resonates with that of a Mrs. Everett, preserved by historian Deirdre Cooper Owens in *Medical Bondage* (57–58).

2 The community in which Gilbert and Truth met disbanded in 1846, and Gilbert spent almost two years in Kentucky, directly observing life among the enslaved.

Such an abominable state of things is silently tolerated, to say the least, by slaveholders—deny it who may. And what is that religion that sanctions, even by its silence, all that is embraced in the "Peculiar Institution"? If there can be any thing more diametrically opposed to the religion of Jesus, than the working of this soul-killing system—which is as truly sanctioned by the religion of America as are her ministers and churches—we wish to be shown where it can be found.

We have said, Isabella was married to Thomas—she was, after the fashion of slavery, one of the slaves performing the ceremony for them; as no true minister of Christ can perform, as in the presence of God, what he knows to be a mere farce, a mock marriage, unrecognized by any civil law, and liable to be annulled any moment, when the interest or caprice of the master should dictate....

Slaveholders appear to me to take the same notice of the vices of the slave, as one does of the vicious disposition of his horse. They are often an inconvenience; further than that, they care not to trouble themselves about the matter.

ISABELLA AS A MOTHER.

In process of time, Isabella found herself the mother of five children, and she rejoiced in being permitted to be the instrument of increasing the property of her oppressors! Think, dear reader, without a blush, if you can, for one moment, of a mother thus willingly, and with pride, laying her own children, the "flesh of her flesh," on the altar of slavery.... But we must remember that beings capable of such sacrifices are not mothers; they are only "things," "chattels," "property."

3. Documents regarding Nat Turner's Insurrection

[Anonymous letter expressing anxiety and insisting upon the need for a bounty on Turner's head, followed by a decree by the governor that fulfills that request. Transcribed from https://www.lva.virginia.gov.]

a. "Anonymus" to Governor John Floyd (28 August 1831)

To the Governor of Virginia
Sir
It has been humbly & respectfully suggested that as Nat. Turner
the leader & mover of the insurrection in Southampton has not
been caught or killed that it would be adviseable to offer a large
reward for him if caught by a white or free man, or manumission
to any slave who will bring him dead or alive so that he may be
punished. It is perhaps idle to think that this insurrection is ended
until the Leader is killed

Aug 28th
Anonymus.

b. Proclamation by Governor John Floyd (17 September 1831)

A Proclamation

Whereas the slave Nat, otherwise called Nat Turner, the contriver
and leader of the late Insurrection in Southampton, is still going
at large: Therefore I, John Floyd, Governor of the Commonwealth
of Virginia have thought proper, and do hereby offer a reward of
five hundred dollars[1] to any person or persons who will apprehend and convey to the Jail of Southampton County, the said
slave Nat: and I do moreover require all officers civil and military,
and exhort the good people of the Commonwealth to use their
best endeavors to cause the said fugitive to be apprehended, that
he may be dealt with as the law directs.

Given under my hand as Governor, and under the lesser Seal of
the Commonwealth at Richmond, this 17th. day of Septemr: 1831.

John Floyd

Nat is between 30 & 35 years old, 5 feet 6 or 8 inches high, weighs
between 150 and 160 lbs. rather bright complexion but not a
mulatto—broad shouldered—large flat nose—large eyes—broad
flat feet—rather knock-kneed—walks brisk and active—hair on the
top of the head very thin—no beard except on the upper lip, and the
tip of the chin—a scar on one of his temples produced by the kick of
a mule also one on the back of his neck by a bite a large knot on one
of the bones of his right arm, near the wrist, produced by a blow

---

1 According to officialdata.org, $500 in 1831 would be about $17,000
in 2023.

4. Advertisement, *American Beacon* (30 June 1835)

[A visual of the newspaper advertisement that Dr. James Norcom placed after Jacobs escaped from his son's plantation. Notice that when Jacobs/Brent included the ad in her narrative at the end of Chapter XVII (p. 160), she raised the reward from the $100 Norcom offered in real life to $300. Furthermore, "the first adjective she use[d] to describe the self-liberated Linda Brent is 'intelligent'" (Blackwood 61). Jacobs therefore "simultaneously increase[d] her value and disembodie[d] herself by emphasizing the mental acuity of the escaped Linda Brent rather than her physical features" (Blackwood 62). However, she also differently animated the physical traits emphasized in such advertisements by adding a detail that Norcom left out: her decayed tooth. In this way, she called attention to the abuse and neglect imposed by slavery's cruelty, a cruelty she wanted her readers to address.]

$100 REWARD

WILL be given for the apprehension and delivery of my Servant Girl HARRIET. She is a light mulatto, 21 years of age, about 5 feet 4 inches high, of a thick and corpulent habit, having on her head a thick covering of black hair that curls naturally, but which can be easily combed straight. She speaks easily and fluently, and has an agreeable carriage and address. Being a good seamstress, she has been accustomed to dress well, has a variety of very fine clothes, made in the prevailing fashion, and will probably appear, if abroad, tricked out in gay and fashionable finery. As this girl absconded from the plantation of my son without any known cause or provocation, it is probable she designs to transport herself to the North.

The above reward, with all reasonable charges, will be given for apprehending her, or securing her in any prison or jail within the U. States.

All persons are hereby forewarned against harboring or entertaining her, or being in any way instrumental in her escape, under the most rigorous penalties of the law.

JAMES NORCOM.

Edenton, N. C. June 30

5. South Carolina *Negro Seamen Act*, Proceedings of the United States Senate, on the Fugitive slave bill,—the abolition of the slave-trade in the District of Columbia,—and the imprisonment of free colored seamen in the southern ports (1 December 1822), p. 58

[Because Black men enjoyed relative freedom when they became sailors,[1] there was a huge investment in curbing that freedom. Seafaring black men in *Incidents* include Aunt Nancy's husband (p. 203) and the family friend Peter and his acquaintances, who mail Linda's letters to Dr. Flint from points north (pp. 188–89). Also, Linda's brother (p. 225) and son (p. 241) go on whaling voyages. Recall, too, that Linda walks in public in disguise as a sailor (pp. 173–75).]

Section 3. And be it further enacted by the authority aforesaid, that if any vessel shall come into any port or harbor in this State, from any other State or foreign port, having on board any free negroes or persons of color, as cooks, stewards, mariners, or in any other employment on board of said vessel, such free negroes or persons of color shall be liable to be seized and confined in jail, until said vessel shall clear out and depart from this State; and that, when said vessel is ready to sail, the captain of said vessel shall be bound to carry away the said free negro or free person of color, and to pay the expenses of his detention; and in case of his neglect or refusal so to do, he shall be liable to be indicted, and, on conviction thereof, shall be fined in a sum not less than one thousand dollars,[2] and imprisoned not less than two months; and such free negroes or persons of color shall be deemed and taken as absolute slaves, and sold in conformity to the provisions of the act passed on the twentieth day of December, one thousand eight hundred and twenty, aforesaid.

---

1 Scholars attribute this relative freedom to many factors, including the fact that life at sea was so deadly that sailors were motivated to focus more on an individual's skill than on enforcing subordination based on race. See Bolster. Racism often found ways to shape sea experiences, too, though.

2 According to officialdata.org, $1,000 in 1822 would be about $25,300 in 2023.

Appendix C: The Composition, Publication, and Reception of Incidents

1. Harriet Jacobs's First Forays into Writing for Publication

a. From *New York Daily Tribune* (21 June 1853), p. 6

[Jacobs targeted a public readership for the first time because she was upset about how inaccurately slavery had been represented in newspapers, which often reprinted material from each other's pages. After reading "The Women of England vs. the Women of America" by Julia Tyler,[1] Jacobs waited until the Willis family (which employed her as nanny and housekeeper) went to sleep; she then wrote all night in response. Tyler's piece had itself been a response to the "Stafford House Address" by the Duchess of Sutherland,[2] who urged American women to support abolition. Tyler offered common justifications for slavery and insisted that selling enslaved people and splitting up their families was rare, despite what British people believed based on Harriet Beecher Stowe's novel *Uncle Tom's Cabin*. Jacobs directly addressed Tyler's claims because she saw how they strengthened slavery by encouraging Americans to underestimate its violence and remain complacent about it. Transcribed from Yellin, *Harriet Jacobs Family Papers* 1.197–201.]

[We publish the subjoined communication exactly as written by the author, with the exception of corrections in punctuation and spelling, and the omission of one or two passages.—Ed.]

SIR: ... Would that I could write an article worthy of notice in your columns. As I never enjoyed the advantages of an education,

---

1 Julia Tyler (1820–89) had been First Lady of the United States for the last eight months of President John Tyler's term. She was an outspoken advocate for slavery and secession.
2 Harriet Elizabeth Georgiana Levenson-Gower (1806–68) was known for hosting anti-slavery gatherings at her home, Stafford House.

therefore I could not study the arts of reading and writing, yet poor as it may be, I had rather give it from my own hand, than have it said that I employed others to do it for me. The truth can never be told so well through the second and third person as from yourself....

I was born a slave, reared in the Southern hot-bed until I was the mother of two children, sold at the early age of two and four years old. I have been hunted through all of the Northern States, but no, I will not tell you of my own suffering—no, it would harrow up my soul, and defeat the object that I wish to pursue. Enough—the dregs of that bitter cup have been my bounty for many years.

And as this is the first time that I ever took my pen in hand to make such an attempt, you will not say that it is fiction, for had I the inclination I have neither the brain or talent to write it. But to this very peculiar circumstance[1] under which slaves are sold.

My mother was held as property by a maiden lady; when she marries, my younger sister was in her fourteenth year, whom they took into the family. She was as gentle as she was beautiful. Innocent and guileless child, the light of our desolate hearth! But oh, my heart bleeds to tell you of the misery and degradation she was forced to suffer in slavery. The monster who owned her had no humanity in his soul. The most sincere affection that his heart was capable of, could not make him faithful to his beautiful and wealthy bride the short time of three months, but every stratagem was used to seduce my sister.[2] Mortified and tormented beyond endurance, this child came and threw herself on her mother's bosom, the only place where she could seek refuge from her persecutor; and yet she could not protect her child that she bore into the world. On that bosom with bitter tears she told her troubles, and entreated her mother to save her. And oh, Christian mothers! you that have daughters of your own, can you think of your sable sisters without offering a prayer to that God who created all in their behalf! My poor mother, naturally high-spirited, smarting under what she considered as the wrongs and outrages which her child had to bear, sought her master, entreating him to spare her child. Nothing could exceed his rage at this what he called

---

1 Tyler had claimed that enslaved people were very rarely sold away from their kin and that it happened only under "peculiar circumstances."

2 When Jacobs answered Amy Post's questions about her newspaper writing, she noted that the events were true but that they were the experience of a friend rather than a biological sister (Yellin, *Life* 306).

impertinence.[1] My mother was dragged to jail, there remained twenty-five days, with Negro traders to come in as they liked to examine her, as she was offered for sale. My sister was told that she must yield, or never expect to see her mother again.[2] There were three younger children; on no other condition could she be restored to them, without the sacrifice of one. That child gave herself up to her master's bidding, to save one that was dearer to her than life itself. And can you, Christian, find it in your heart to despise her? Ah, no! not even Mrs. Tyler; for though we believe that the vanity of a name would lead her to bestow her hand where her heart could never go with it, yet, with all her faults and follies, she is nothing more than a woman. For if her domestic hearth is surrounded with slaves, ere long before this she has opened her eyes to the evils of slavery, and that the mistress as well as the slave must submit to the indignities and vices imposed on them by their lords of body and soul. But to one of those peculiar circumstances.

At fifteen, my sister held to her bosom an innocent offspring of her guilt and misery. In this way she dragged a miserable existence of two years, between the fires of her mistress's jealousy and her master's brutal passion. At seventeen, she gave birth to another helpless infant, heir to all the evils of slavery. Thus life and its sufferings was meted out to her until her twenty-first year. Sorrow and suffering has made its ravages upon her—she was less the object to be desired by the fiend who had crushed her to the earth; and as her children grew, they bore too strong a resemblance to him who desired to give them no other inheritance save Chains and Handcuffs, and in the dead hour of the night, when this young, deserted mother lay with her little ones clinging around her, little dreaming of the dark and inhuman plot that would be carried out into execution before another dawn, and when the sun

---

1 Inappropriate intrusion or presumption.

2 With not only individual physical violence but also incarceration hanging over their heads, this is a perfect example of what historian Emily Owens has found: namely, when enslavers asked for sex or made promises in exchange for it, requests and negotiations must be understood as sites of violence because they always occurred under the threat of not only interpersonal attacks but also the authority of the state. Furthermore, these women were being asked to "willingly participate in [their] own annihilation" (94). Then and now, because United States law defines rape based on "consent," it insists that "where there is transaction, there can be no violence" (32).

rose on God's beautiful earth, that broken-hearted mother was far on her way to the capitol of Virginia. That day should have refused her light to so disgraceful and inhuman an act in your boasted country of Liberty. Yet, reader, it is true, those two helpless children were the sons of one of your sainted Members in Congress; that agonized mother, his victim and slave. And where she now is God only knows, who has kept a record on high of all that she has suffered on earth.

And, you would exclaim, Could not the master have been more merciful to his children? God is merciful to all of his children, but it is seldom that a slaveholder has any mercy for his slave child. And you will believe it when I tell you that mother and her children were sold to make room for another sister, who was now the age of that mother when she entered the family. And this selling appeased the mistress's wrath, and satisfied her desire for revenge, and made the path more smooth for her young rival at first. For there is a strong rivalry between a handsome mulatto girl and a jealous and faded mistress, and her liege lord sadly neglects his wife or doubles his attentions, to save him being suspected by his wife. Would you not think that Southern Women had cause to despise that Slavery which forces them to bear so much deception practiced by their husbands? Yet all this is true, for a slaveholder seldom takes a white mistress,[1] for she is an expensive commodity, not as submissive as he would like to have her, but more apt to be tyrannical; and when his passion seeks another object, he must leave her in quiet possession of all the gewgaws[2] that she

---

1 Even if enslavers seldom had white mistresses, there was remarkable interest in having concubines that appeared and behaved as white as possible. All enslaved women were sexually vulnerable, but some were forced directly into prostitution via the "Fancy Trade." As historian Dorothy Sterling explains, "Slaves selected for their beauty, grace and light skins were shipped to the 'fancy-girl markets' of New Orleans and other cities. At a time when prime field hands sold for $1600, a fancy girl brought $5,000. Some ended up in bordellos, but the majority became the mistresses of wealthy planters, gamblers, or businessmen" (27). Historian Brenda Stevenson clarifies the stakes: "What, after all, could be more valuable than a woman of 'white' complexion who could be bought as one's private 'sex slave'?" (*Life* 180). Furthermore, Stevenson has found that white men of stature preferred a concubine that did "not only look like white women, but also dress, speak, clean, sew, cook, and worship like them as well" ("What's Love" 168).

2 Something that is gaudy or worthless; trinket.

has sold herself for. But not so with his poor slave victim, that he has robbed of everything that can make life desirable; she must be torn from the little that is left to bind her to life, and sold by her seducer and master, caring not where, so that it puts him in possession of enough to purchase another victim. And such are the peculiar circumstances of American Slavery—of all the evils in God's sight most to be abhorred.

... And oh ye Christians, while your arms are extended to receive the oppressed of all nations, while you exert every power of your soul to assist them to raise funds, put weapons in their hands, tell them to return to their own country to slay every foe until they break the accursed yoke from off their necks....

And because one friend of a slave has dared to tell of their wrongs you would annihilate her. But in Uncle Tom's Cabin she has not told the half. Would that I had one spark from her store house of genius and talent I would tell you of my own sufferings—I would tell you of wrongs that Hungary has never inflicted, nor England ever dreamed of in this free country where all nations fly for liberty, equal rights and protection under your stripes and stars. It should be stripes and scars, for they go along with Mrs. Tyler's peculiar circumstances, of which I have told you only one.

A FUGITIVE SLAVE.

b. *New York Tribune* (25 July 1853)

[Jacobs was again inspired to set the record straight in print when she saw doubts expressed in newspapers about the cruelty visited upon Black "outlaws." Besides testifying to what she had witnessed, Jacobs makes a point of disrupting assumptions about the differences between Southerners and Northerners.]

To the Editor of The N.Y. Tribune,

SIR: Having seen an article, a few days ago, that was going the rounds in some of the daily papers, denying the truth of an advertisement wherein Slaves were outlawed in North Carolina. I wish to reply to it through your columns. I was born in that good old State, and less than 20 years since I left it, and it is not that length of time since I witnessed there a sight which I can never forget. It was a slave that been a runaway from his master twelvemonths. After that time a white man is justified in shooting a slave, as he is considered an outlaw. This slave man was brought to the wharf, placed in a small boat, by two white men, early in the morning, with his *head* severed from his body, and remained there in an August sun until noon, before an inquest was held. Then he was buried, and not a word of murder or of arrest was heard. He was a negro and a runaway slave, and it was all right. It mattered not who murdered him—if he was a white man[1] he was sure of the reward, and the name of being a brave fellow, truly[.] The writer of that article has said, the people of North Carolina have hearts and souls like our own. Surely, many of them have. The poor slave, however, who had his head severed from his body was owned by a merchant in New-York.

A FUGITIVE.

2. Correspondence from Harriet Jacobs to Amy Post[2]

a. From Harriet Jacobs to Amy Post (after 28 December 1852), transcribed from Yellin, *Harriet Jacobs Family Papers* 1.190–91

[In what is clearly an ongoing conversation, Jacobs expresses why she hesitates to accept entreaties to share her life story. Even what she had shared previously with Post had been based on how kind and sympathetic she knows her friend to be. Jacobs never assumes others will be as compassionate, so having a larger audience is not appealing. Nevertheless, Jacobs is increasingly feeling compelled to overcome her misgivings because her story might help those still in bondage. And yet, there are many other writing obstacles.]

[some time after December 28, 1852]
Cornwall Orrange Co [N.Y.]

My Dear Friend

Yours of the 24 was received on the 27th and my pin will fail to describe my greatful feelings on reading it   although you could never be forgotten yet you do not know how much itt cheers my sad heart and how much I appreciate a word of Sympathy and friendship from those I love for you little know how much I have had to pass through since we last meet but it is a blessing that we can say a word in this way to each other   many far more deserving than myself has been debared from this privilege[3] ...

---

1 An example of Jacobs's awareness of the unearned advantages attending whiteness.

2 The ↑↓ indicate words that appear above, below, or between the lines.

3 Here, Jacobs acknowledges that the United States has made being able to read and write a privilege. That is, merit has nothing to do with who can and cannot read and write.

your proposal to me has been thought over and over again but not with out some painful remembrances   dear Amy if it was the life of a Heroine with no degradation associated with it   far better to have been one of the starving poor of Ireland whose bones had to bleach on the highways than to have been a slave with the curse of slavery stamped upon yourself and Children.   Your purity of heart and kindly sympathies won me at one time to speak of my children   it is the only words that has passed my lips since I left my Mothers door   I had determined to let others think as p they pleased but my lips should be sealed and no one had a right to question me   for this reason when I first came North I avoided the Anti-slavery people as much as possible because I felt that I could not be honest and tell the whole truth   often have I gone to my poor Brother with my grieved and mortified spirits   he would mingle his tears with mine while he would advise me to do what was right   my conscience approved ↑it↓ but my stubborn pride would not yeild   I have tried for the last two years to con-quer it and I feel that God has helped me or I never would con-sent to give my past life to any one for I would not do it with out giving whole truth   if it could help save another from my fate it would be selfish and unchristian in me to keep it back   situated as I am I do not see any way that I could put it forward   Mrs Willis thinks it would do much good in Mrs Stowe hand but I could not ask her to take any step   Mr W is too proslavery   he would tell me that it was very wrong and that I was trying to do harm or perhaps he was sorry for me to undertake ↑it↓ while I was in his family   Mrs Willis thinks if is not done in my day it will a good legacy for my children to do it after my death but now is the time when their is so much excitement everywhere ...

If the Antislavery society could prapare this I would be willing to exert myself in any way that they thought best for the welfare of the cause   they do not know me   they have heard of me as John Jacobs sister

my dear friend would you be willing to make this proposal   I would rather have you do it than any one else   you could do it better   I should be ... [obliterated] happier in remembering it was you   if Mrs Stowe would under take it I should like to be with her a Month   I should want the first History of my childhood and the first five years in one volume [...] and my home in the northern states in the secont   besids I could give her some fine sketches for her pen on slavery   give my love to your dear Husband and sons kiss Willie for me   love to all   God bless   Yours

Harriet

b. From Harriet Jacobs to Amy Post (14 February 1853),
transcribed from Yellin, *Harriet Jacobs Family Papers* 1.193–94

[Post had written to Harriet Beecher Stowe on Jacobs's behalf
with a sketch of her life that might interest the famous author in
writing Jacobs's biography. Before an answer could be received,
Jacobs saw newspaper announcements about Stowe's upcoming
trip to visit abolitionist activists in England. Now, no longer optimistic about being able to spend time with Stowe to make the
biography possible, Jacobs has devised another plan altogether
that her employer, Mrs. Cornelia Willis, has proposed to Stowe
on her behalf. Jacobs will keep Post updated about the response.]

Feby 14th [1853]

My Dear Friend

I received your kind letter yesterday   if silence is expressive
of ones deep feeling then in this way I must ask you to receive the
emotions of what my heart ↑and pen↓ cannot express   hoping the time is not far distant when we may see each other but
I must tell you what I am trying to accomplish   having seen
the notice in the paper of Mrs Stowe intention to visit England I
felt there would not be much hope of coming before her for some
time and I thought if I could get her to take Louisa with her she
might get interested enough   if she could do nothing herself she
might help Louisa to do something   besides I thought Louisa
would be a very good representative of a Southern Slave   she
has improved much in her studies and I think that she has energy
enough to do something for the cause   she only needs to be
put in the field   I told my Ideas to Mrs Willis   she thought
they were good and offered to write Mrs Stowe   she wrote last
Tuesday asking her protection and if she would place her in some
Antislavery family unless her services could be useful to her which
I would perfer myself intending to pay her expenses there   the
letter was directed as yours[1]   when it is answered you shall know
dear Amy since I haveno fear of my name coming before those
whom I have lived in dread of I can nott be happy without trying
to be useful in some way ...

---

1 Willis had reached out to Stowe in the same manner that Post had
used before.

c. Harriet Jacobs to Amy Post (4 April 1853), transcribed from
   Yellin, *Harriet Jacobs Family Papers* 1.194–95

[The update on the request made to Stowe. Upon receiving Mrs.
Willis's letter about possibly allowing Louisa Jacobs to join her
delegation to England, Stowe responded with her reasons for
objecting. However, Stowe also sent Mrs. Willis the letter from
Post that included a sketch of Jacobs's life. Stowe wanted veri-
fication from Jacobs's employer that the details were true, and
if so, she wanted Willis's permission to use them in her *Key to
Uncle Tom's Cabin*, a book she was preparing in response to critics
who said her novel contained events that bore no relationship to
the realities of Southern slavery. There were many details about
her life that Jacobs had not shared with her employer, so Stowe
exposed Jacobs, embarrassing her and forcing her to have an
unwanted conversation. Furthermore, Stowe's permission request
showed respect for Willis, not for Jacobs.]

~~March~~ April 4th [1853]

My Dear friend

   I steal this moment to scratch you a ~~few~~ lines   I should have
written you before but I have been waiting with the hope of having some thing to tell you from our friend Mrs Stowe but as it is
I hardly know where to begin   for my thoughts come rushing
down with such a ... [*obliterated*] ↑spirit↓ of rivalry   each wishing to be told you first   so that they fill my heart and ... [*obliterated*] make my eyes dim   therefore my silence must express to
you what my poor pen is not capable of doing   but you know
dear Amy that ... [*obliterated*] I have a heart towards you filled with
love and gratitude for all the interest you have so kindly shown in
my behalf   I wish that I could sit by you and talk instead of writing   but that pleasure is denied   and I am thankful ~~and I am
than~~ for this   Mrs Stowe received your letter   and Mrs Willis
she said it would be much care to her to take Louisa   as she went
by   invitation   it would not be right   and she was afraid that if
her situation as a Slave should be known   it would subject her
to much petting and patronizing   which would be more pleasing
to a young Girl than useful   and the English was very apt to do
it and sh was very much opposed to it with this class of people   I
will leave the rest for you to solve   but remem that I mene to pay
Louisa expenses   your letter she sent to Mrs Willis asking might
she trouble her so far as to ask if this most extraordinary event was

true in all its bearings   and if she might use it in her key   I had
never opend my lips to Mrs Willis concerning my Children   in
the Charitableness of her own heart   she sympathised with me
and never asked their origin   my suffering she knew   it embarrassed me at first   but I told her the truth   but we both thought
it was wrong in Mrs Stowe to have sent you letter   she might
have written to enquire if she liked   Mrs Willis wrote her a very
kind letter begang that she would not use any of the facts in he key
saying that I wished it to be a history of my life entirely by itsslf
which would do more good   and it needed no romance but if
she wanted some facts for her book that I would be most happy to
give her some   she never answered the letter   she wrote again
and I wrote twice with no better success   it was not Lady↑like↓
to treat Mrs Willis so   she would not have done it to ... [obliter-
ated] any one   I think she did not like my objectian   I cant help
it [letter breaks off]

d. From Harriet Jacobs to Amy Post (c. May 1853), transcribed
   from Yellin, *Harriet Jacobs Family Papers* 1.195–96

[Jacobs is as stretched as ever by her nanny and housekeeper
responsibilities in the Willis family, but she pauses to drop a note
to Post, who had written to Stowe about disrespecting her friend.
Jacobs also hints at her new plans for contributing to the anti-
slavery cause, given that collaboration of any sort with Stowe
seems increasingly unlikely.]

[ca. May 1853]
... I leave home to morrow to go to New Bedford on a visit with
Mrs Willis and the Children   I shall be gone two week   you
must write me there ... I have a project in my head   and when I
think more upon it I will tell you   I hope   dear Amy   you will
be able to read this miserable scrawl but I am so hurried   the
Children are calling to get up   and I don't want to leave without
sending you a line   pray burn it   Mrs W thought your letter
very Cleverly written   think dear Amy that a visit to Stafford
House[1] would spoil me as Mrs Stowe thinks peting is more than
my race car bear   weell what a pity   we poor blacks cant have

---

1 Now called Lancaster House, this was home in 1853 to Harriet
  Elizabeth Georgiana Levenson-Gower (1806–68), the Duchess of
  Sutherland. She was also a London abolitionist known for hosting
  anti-slavery gatherings.

the firmness and stability of character that you white people have
...
... heart full of love to all yours

e. From Harriet Jacobs to Amy Post (9 October 1853),
    transcribed from Yellin, *Harriet Jacobs Family Papers* 1.205–06

[In this letter, Jacobs shares that her grandmother has died. She also confirms that Stowe has remained silent since not gaining permission to extract from Jacobs's life to add credibility to her *Key to Uncle Tom's Cabin*. In addition, Jacobs reveals that she is the author of the "fugitive" responses recently published in newspapers, but she admits to having kept it a secret. Jacobs always had reasons for writing without her employer's knowledge, but without having received Post's reassurance about the pieces, she was not comfortable revealing her new author status even to her friend William C. Nell and her daughter (Yellin, *Life* 123). Here, she wants Post's honest assessment because she hopes to contribute to the anti-slavery cause through writing.]

Oct 9th [1853]

My Dear Friend
    I was more than glad to receive your welcome letter for I must acknowledge that your long silence had troubled me much ... and dear Amy I have lost that Dear old Grandmother ~~you~~ that I so dearly loved   oh her life has been one of sorrow and trial but he in whom she trusted has never forsaken her   her Death was beautiful   may my last end be like hers ...
    Mrs Stowe never answered any of my letters after I refused to have my history in her key   perhaps its for the best   at least I will try and think so   ~~did~~ ↑have↓ you seen any more of my scribling   they were marked fugitive[1]   William Nell told Louisa about the piece and sent her a Copy   I was careful to keep it from her and no one here never suspected me   I would not have Mrs W. to know it before I had undertaken my history for I must write just what I have lived and witnessed myself   dont expect much of me dear Amy   you shall have truth but not talent God did not give me that gift but he gave me a soul that burned for freedom and a heart nerved with determination to suffer even unto death in pursuit of that liberty which without makes life an intolerable burden   ... and now my my dear friend dont flatter

---

1 A reference to her newspaper letters signed *Fugitive*. See Appendix C1.

me   I am aware of my many mistakes and willing to be told of them   only let me come before the world as I have been an uneducated oppressed Slave   but I must stop   love to all   God bless you   excuse the Hasty scrawl   10 Clock   Your

Harriet

f. From Harriet Jacobs to Amy Post (March 1854), transcribed from Yellin, *Harriet Jacobs Family Papers* 1.212–13

[Jacobs gives voice to the many obstacles she is facing as she works to complete a draft of her autobiography.]

Cornwall [N.Y.] March [1854]

My Dear Friend

... as yet I have not written a single page by daylight   Mrs W dont know from my lips that I am writing for a Book and has never seen a line of what I have written   I told her in the Autumn that I would give her Louisa services through the winter if she would allow me my winter evenings to myself but with the care of the little baby and the big Babies and at the household calls I have but a little time to think or write but I have tried in my poor way to do my best and that is not much

And you my dear friend must not expect much where there has been so little given   Yes dear Amy there has been more than a bountiful share of suffering given enough to crush the finer feelings of stouter hearts than this poor timid one of mine but I will try and not send you a portraiture of feelings   just now the poor Book is in its Chrysalis state[1] and though I can never make it a butterfly I am satisfied to have it creep meekly among some of the humbler bugs   I sometimes wish that I could fall into a Rip Van Winkle sleep[2] and awake with the blest belief of that little Witch Topsy[3] that I never was born ...

---

1 The feeding stage of an insect's development when it is unformed, wingless, and immobile.

2 A reference to the title character who sleeps for 20 years in Washington Irving's 1819 collection *The Sketch Book of Geoffrey Crayon, Gent.*

3 Topsy is the Black girl character in Harriet Beecher Stowe's *Uncle Tom's Cabin* known for being wild and saying that she had not been born but "jes grew." Jacobs uses this reference as a way to comment critically on how American culture represents her people. Also see Robin Bernstein's *Racial Innocence* for powerful analysis of Topsy and other representations of Black children.

3. Correspondence from Lydia Maria Child to Harriet Jacobs

a. Lydia Maria Child to Harriet Jacobs (13 August 1860), transcribed from Yellin, *Harriet Jacobs Family Papers* 1.278–79

[Having received Jacobs's autobiography when they last met in person, Child writes to Jacobs with a progress report. The editing is going well, but she also requests more material.]

Wayland [Mass.] Aug. 13th 1860

Dear Mrs. Jacobs,

I have been busy with your M.S.[1] ever since I saw you; and have only done one third of it. I have very little occasion to alter the language, which is wonderfully good, for one whose opportunities for education have been so limited. The events are interesting, and well told; the remarks are also good, and to the purpose. But I am copying a great deal of it, for the purpose of transposing sentences and pages, so as to bring the story into continuous order, and the remarks into appropriate places. I think you will see that this renders the story much more clear and entertaining.

I should not take so much pains, if I did not consider the book unusually interesting, and likely to do much service to the Anti-Slavery cause. So you need not feel under great personal obligations. You know I would go through fire and water to help give a blow to Slavery. I suppose you will want to see the M.S. after I have exercised my bump of mental order upon it; and I will send it wherever you direct, a fortnight hence.

My object in writing at this time is to ask you to write what you can recollect of the outrages committed on the colored people, in Nat Turner's time. You say the reader would not believe what you saw "inflicted on men, women, and children, without the slightest ground of suspicion against them." What were those inflictions? Were any tortured to make them confess? and how? Where any killed? Please write down some of the most striking particulars, and let me have them to insert.

I think the last Chapter, about John Brown,[2] had better be omitted. It does not naturally come into your story, and the M.S.

---

1 Manuscript.

2 John Brown (1800–59) was a white anti-slavery activist who hoped to inspire a slave rebellion in 1859 by raiding the government's armory in Harpers Ferry, Virginia. He was joined in this raid by twenty-one

is already too long. Nothing can be so appropriate to end with, as the death of your grand mother.

Mr. Child desires to be respectfully remembered to you. Very cordially your friend,

L. Maria Child.

b. Lydia Maria Child to Harriet Jacobs (27 September 1860), transcribed from Yellin, *Harriet Jacobs Family Papers* 1.280–81

[Letter demonstrating that Child not only edited Jacobs's manuscript but also operated as her literary agent.]

Wayland [Mass.], Sep 27th, 1860

Dear Mrs. Jacobs,

I have signed and sealed the contract with Thayer & Eldridge, in my name, and told them to take out the copyright in my name. Under the circumstances your name could not be used, you know. I inquired of other booksellers, and could find none that were willing to undertake it, except Thayer & Eldridge. I have never heard a word to the disparagement of either of them, and I do not think you could do better than to let them have it. They ought to have the monopoly of it for some time, if they stereotype it, because that process involves considerable expense, and if you changed publishers, their plates would be worth nothing to them. When I spoke of limiting them to an edition of 2000, I did not suppose they intended to stereotype it. They have agreed to pay you ten per cent on the retail price of all sold, and to let you have as many as you want, at the lowest wholesale price. On your part, I have agreed that they may publish it for five years on those terms, and that you will not print any abridgement, or altered copy, meanwhile.

I have no reason whatever to think that Thayer & Eldridge are likely to fail. I merely made the suggestion because they were beginners. However, several of the oldest bookselling firms have failed within the last three years; mine among the rest.[1] We must run for luck in these matters.

I have promised to correct the proof-sheets, and I don't think

---

men who also believed that slavery should end immediately and that such a violent system could not be challenged effectively with words alone; armed resistance was required.

1 The firm that had published Child's 1857 prose and poetry collection had recently failed.

it would be of any use to the book to have you here at this time. They say they shall get it out by the 1'st Nov.

You had better let me know beforehand if you want to come to Wayland; because when I leave home, I generally stay over night, and in that case you would lose your time and your money. I saw your daughter a few minutes, and found her very prepossessing.

Write to me whenever you want to; and when I have time, I will answer.

I want you to sign the following paper, and send it back to me. It will make Thayer & Eldridge safe about the contract in <u>my</u> name, and in case of my death, will prove that the book is <u>your</u> property, not <u>mine</u>. Cordially your friend,

L. Maria Child.

4. Original Title Page of Jacobs's Narrative

[Once Boston publishers Thayer and Eldridge went bankrupt, Jacobs bought the plates from which her book would have been produced and had two thousand copies printed and bound. As Christy Pottroff emphasizes, given that Jacobs oversaw this process, it is clear that she made decisions that encouraged readers to "recognize her status as both publisher and author" (229). Notice, Pottroff encourages, that both "written by herself" and "published for the author" appear in "a font larger than Child's editorial attribution" (229).]

INCIDENTS

IN THE

LIFE OF A SLAVE GIRL.

WRITTEN BY HERSELF.

"Northerners know nothing at all about Slavery. They think it is perpetual bondage only. They have no conception of the depth of *degradation* involved in that word, SLAVERY; if they had, they would never cease their efforts until so horrible a system was overthrown."

A WOMAN OF NORTH CAROLINA.

"Rise up, ye women that are at ease! Hear my voice, ye careless daughters! Give ear unto my speech."

ISAIAH xxxii. 9.

EDITED BY L. MARIA CHILD.

BOSTON:
PUBLISHED FOR THE AUTHOR.
1861.

5. Correspondence from John Greenleaf Whittier to Lydia Maria Child (1 April 1861), transcribed from Yellin, *Harriet Jacobs Family Papers* 1.341

[Letter confirming that Jacobs's autobiography was circulating upon publication. Because it was not issued by a publishing firm with a network for publicity and distribution, Jacobs's personal activist connections mattered. Here, it is clear that Child helped promote the book by sending copies directly to associates. This letter was written less than two weeks before the 12 April Confederate attack on Fort Sumter that launched the Civil War.]

April 1, 1861

A thousand thanks for giving us that wonderful book 'Linda.' We have read it with the deepest interest. It ought to be circulated broadcast over the land. I laid it down with a deeper abhorrence than ever of the Fugitive Slave Law. Has thee seen Dr. Adams's new book?[1] It is the foulest blasphemy ever put in type—but weak as it is wicked. Get it; it is a curiosity of devilish theology worth studying.—What is to be the end of this disunion turmoil? I cannot but hope that, in spite of the efforts of the politicians and compromises, the Great Nuisance[2] is to fall off from us; and we are to be a free people.

6. William C. Nell, "Linda, the Slave Girl," *Liberator* (24 January 1861)

[William C. Nell (1816–74) was a friend to Jacobs and her daughter Louisa, and he was active in abolitionist circles. A Black man whose first job was with William Lloyd Garrison's abolitionist newspaper *The Liberator*, he was also active in the 1840s and 1850s in the Colored Conventions movement, the gatherings at which African Americans came together to develop and enact strategies for political empowerment (coloredconventions.org). Having regularly encouraged Jacobs to write her autobiography, he supported it in every way, including by connecting Jacobs to

---

1 A reference to *The Sable Cloud* (1861) by Nehemiah Adams (1806–78). Jacobs mentions him in "The Church and Slavery" chapter of *Incidents* (p. 139).

2 A reference to slavery. He is riffing critically on the words of a politician who had in an 1829 debate deemed African Americans to be the nation's "great nuisance."

Lydia Maria Child. He had promised to promote the book once it existed, and this review upon its release is one example of his doing so. Transcribed from Yellin, *Harriet Jacobs Family Papers* 1.292–94.]

BOSTON, January 21, 1861.
LINDA, THE SLAVE GIRL.

DEAR MR. GARRISON:

Crowded though I know the *Liberator* columns to be just now, I am constrained to solicit space for a word in announcement of a book just issued from the press, entitled "LINDA: *Incidents in the Life of a Slave Girl, seven years concealed in Slavery.*" It is a handsome volume of 306 pages, and is on sale at the Anti-Slavery Office, price $1.00. I feel confident that its circulation at this crisis in our country's history will render a signal and most acceptable service.

The lamented Mrs. Follen,[1] in her admirable tract addressed to Mothers in the Free States, and with which that indefatigable colporteur,[2] Miss Putnam,[3] is doing so much good in her visits to families, seems to have anticipated just such a contribution to anti-slavery literature as this book, "Linda." It presents features more attractive than many of its predecessors purporting to be histories of slave life in America, because, in contrast with their mingling of fiction with fact, this record of complicated experience in the life of a young woman, a doomed victim to America's peculiar institution—her seven years' concealment in slavery—continued persecutions—hopes, often deferred, but which at length culminated in her freedom—surely need not the charms that any pen of fiction, however gifted and graceful, could lend. They shine by the lustre of their own truthfulness—a rhetoric which always commends itself to the wise head and honest heart. In furtherance of the object of its author, LYDIA MARIA CHILD has furnished a graceful introduction and AMY POST a well-written letter; and wherever the names of these two devoted friends of humanity are known, no higher credentials can be required or given. My own acquaintance, too, with the author and

---

1 Eliza Follen (1787–1860), whose anti-slavery tract, *A Letter to Mothers in the Free States*, was published in 1855. In focusing on enslaved women, it aimed to prompt sympathy in white women by helping them consider the injustice of routine sexual exploitation.

2 A distributor of pamphlets.

3 Caroline F. Putnam (c. 1826–1917), who was known for circulating anti-slavery literature.

her relatives, of whom special mention is made in the book, warrants an expression of the hope that it will find its way into every family, where all, especially mothers and daughters, may learn yet more of the barbarism of American slavery and the character of its victims. Yours, for breaking every yoke,

WM. C. NELL.

7. From Unsigned Book Review, *Weekly Anglo-African* (13 April 1861)

[Transcribed from Yellin, *Harriet Jacobs Family Papers* 1.349.]

LINDA.

INCIDENTS IN THE LIFE OF A SLAVE GIRL, written by Herself. Edited by L. Maria Child. Boston: published for the author. 1861.

In such volumes as this, the true romance of American life and history is to be found. Patient suffering, heroic daring, untiring zeal, perseverance seemingly unparalleled, and growth from surroundings of degradation and ignorance to education, refinement, and power: all find in these modest pages their simple, yet affecting narrative. It is the "oft told tale" of American slavery, in another and more revolting phase than that which is generally seen. More revolting because it is of the spirit and not the flesh. In this volume, a woman tells in words of fire, yet never overstepping the bounds of the truest purity, not, how *she* was scourged and maimed, but that far more terrible sufferings endured by and inflicted upon woman, by a system which legalizes concubinage, and offers a premium to licentiousness. No one can read these pages without a feeling of horror, and a stronger determination arising in them to tear down the cursed system which makes such records possible. Wrath, the fiery messenger which goes flaming from the roused soul and overthrows in its divine fury the accursed tyrannies of the earth; will find in these pages new fuel for the fire, and new force for the storm which shall overthrow and sweep from existence American slavery.

The name of the editor of the volume, Mrs. Child, is a sufficient endorsement of its literary merit....

The volume is ... handsome, well printed.... It may be obtained at the Anti-Slavery Offices in Boston, New York, Philadelphia, and of Thos. Hamilton, 48 Beekman St., New York.

8. From Unsigned Book Review, *Anti-Slavery Advocate* (1 May 1861)

[According to Yellin, "abolitionists, determined to make Lincoln's war to preserve the Union into a war to oppose slavery, intensified their propaganda," and they embraced *Incidents* as a powerful tool. Therefore, this is only one of several British reviews, but it makes clear that Jacobs's authorship was known, so scholars who later labeled it fiction had to ignore evidence like this. Also worth noting: unlike its coverage in the United States, *Incidents* was reviewed in the mainstream press in England "as a major work of literature" (*Harriet Jacobs Family Papers* 1.292). Transcribed from *Harriet Jacobs Family Papers* 1.350–52.]

Incidents In The Life of a Slave Girl. Written by Herself. Edited by Lydia Maria Child. Boston: published for the Author. 1861. pp. 306, 12mo.

We have read this book with no ordinary interest, for we are acquainted with the writer; we have heard many of the incidents from her own lips, and have great confidence in her truthfulness and integrity. Between two and three years ago, a coloured woman, about as dark as a southern Spaniard or a Portuguese, aged about five-and-forty, and with a kind and pleasing expression of countenance, called on us, bearing an introductory letter from one of the most honoured friends[1] of the anti-slavery cause in the United States. This letter requested our friendly offices on behalf of Linda, who was desirous of publishing her narrative in England. It happened that the friends at whose house we were then staying were so much interested by this dusky stranger's conversation and demeanour, that they induced her to become their guest for some weeks.[2] Thus we had an excellent opportunity of becoming acquainted with one of the truest heroines we have ever met with. Her manners were marked by refinement and sensibility, and by an utter absence of pretence or affectation; and we

---

1 Maria Weston Chapman (1806–85).

2 Jacobs was welcomed to stay at the home of Harriet Elizabeth Georgiana Levenson-Gower, the Duchess of Sutherland (1806–68) when she traveled to England with her book manuscript in 1858. This was the famous Stafford House that was mentioned when Stowe suggested that being among British abolitionists would spoil African Americans (Appendix C2d).

were deeply touched by the circumstances of her early life which she then communicated, and which exactly coincide with those of the volume now before us. A lady who was also enjoying the hospitality thus extended to Linda kindly undertook to peruse her manuscript, from the publication of which she hoped to raise a small fund for the benefit of her two children. We have this friend's testimony that the manuscript and the printed volume are substantially the same; whilst the narrative has been condensed and rendered more fluent and compact by the friendly assistance of Mrs. Child, than whom no one is better qualified to perform such a task with delicacy and determination....

During Linda's stay on this side of the Atlantic, she was recommended to publish her book in America; and we think this has proved to be good advice, for she has thus secured the invaluable assistance of Mrs. Child in pruning some redundancies of matter and style. At the same time she will be sure to affect more good for her brethren and sisters still in bonds, by the diffusion of her story amongst the people of the Free States, whom it is above all others important to inform, since they alone are able, by withholding their support from it, to shake down the whole system of chattel slavery.

Appendix D: Life after Incidents

1. From Linda [Harriet Jacobs], "Life among the Contrabands," *Liberator* (5 September 1862), p. 3

[On 12 April 1862, Abraham Lincoln signed a bill that released from bondage the approximately 3,000 people enslaved in the nation's capital. This shift also made the city attractive to self-emancipators from other locations. Aware of the influx of people and the humanitarian crisis it created, Jacobs went to help those struggling to make a new life. Her activist comrades remained ready to support, so she kept them updated through the abolitionist press. She signed this report *Linda*, underscoring the value of her reputation as the person whose life is recounted in *Incidents*. Transcribed from Yellin, *Harriet Jacobs Family Papers* 2.399–415.]

DEAR MR. GARRISON:

I thank you for the request of a line on the condition of the contrabands, and what I have seen while among them.... I found men, women and children all huddled together, without any distinction or regard to age or sex. Some of them were in the most pitiable condition. Many were sick with measles, diptheria [sic], scarlet and typhoid fever. Some had a few filthy rags to lie on; others had nothing but the bare floor for a couch. There seemed to be no established rules among them; they were coming in at all hours, often through the night, in large numbers, and the Superintendent had enough to occupy his time in taking the names of those who came in, and of those who were sent out. His office was thronged through the day by persons who came to hire these poor creatures, who they say will not work and take care of themselves. Single women hire at four dollars a month; a woman with one child, two and a half or three dollars a month. Men's wages are ten dollars per month. Many of them, accustomed as they have been to field labor, and to living almost entirely out of doors, suffer much from the confinement in this crowded building. The little children pine like prison birds for their native element. It is almost impossible to keep the building in a healthy condition. Each day brings its fresh additions of the hungry, naked and sick. In the early part of June, there were, some days, as many as ten deaths reported at this place in twenty-four hours. At this time, there was no matron in the house, and nothing at hand to administer to the comfort of the sick and dying. I felt that their sufferings must be unknown to the people. I did not meet kindly, sympathizing people, trying to soothe the last agonies of death. Those tearful eyes often looked up to me with the language, "Is this freedom?"

[A new supervisor took charge, bringing greater compassion to the position, and white women known for their humane activism arrived, too.] They were the first white females whom I had seen among these poor creatures, except those who had come in to hire them. These noble ladies had come to work, and their names will be lisped in prayer by many a dying slave. Hoping to help a little in the good work they had begun, I wrote to a lady in New York, a true and tried friend of the slave, who from the first moment had responded to every call of humanity. This letter was to ask for such articles as would make comfortable the sick and dying in the hospital. On the Saturday following, the cots were put up. A few hours after, an immense box was received from New York. Before the sun went down, those ladies who have labored so hard for the comfort of these people had the satisfaction of seeing every man, woman and child with clean garments, lying in a clean bed. What a contrast! They seemed different beings. Every countenance beamed with gratitude and satisfied rest....

Still, there were other places in which I felt, if possible, more interest, where the poor creatures seemed so far removed from the immediate sympathy of those who would help them. These were the contrabands in Alexandria. This place is strongly secesh;[1] the inhabitants are kept quiet only at the point of Northern bayonets. In this place, the contrabands are distributed more over the city. In visiting those places, I had the assistance of two kind friends, women. True at heart, they felt the wrongs and degradation of their race. These ladies were always ready to aid me, as far as lay in their power.... All [of the people we assist] expressed a willingness to work, and were anxious to know what was to be done with them after the work was done. All of them said they had not received pay for their work, and some wanted to know if I thought it would be paid to their masters. One old man said, "I don't kere if dey don't pay, so dey give me freedom. I bin working for ole maas all de time; he nebber gib me five cent. I like de Unions fuss

---

1 Strongly secessionist: believing secession—removal from the United States to create the Confederacy—is justified and right.

rate. If de Yankee Unions didn't come long, I'd be working tu de old place now." All said they had plenty to eat, but no clothing, and no money to buy any.

Another place, the old school-house in Alexandria, is the Government head-quarters for the women. This I thought the most wretched of all the places. Any one who can find an apology for slavery should visit this place, and learn its curse. Here you see them from infancy up to a hundred years old. What but the love of freedom could bring these old people hither? ...

When in Washington for the day, ... [m]y first business would be to look into a small room on the ground floor. This room was covered with lime. Here I would learn how many deaths had occurred in the last twenty-four hours. Men, women and children lie here together, without a shadow of those rites which we give to our poorest dead. There they lie, in the filthy rags they wore from the plantation. Nobody seems to give it a thought. It is an every-day occurrence, and the scenes have become familiar. One morning, as I looked in, I saw lying there five children. By the side of them lay a young man. He escaped, was taken back to Virginia, whipped nearly to death, escaped again the next night, dragged his body to Washington, and died, literally cut to pieces. Around his feet I saw a rope; I could not see that put into the grave with him. Other cases similar to this came to my knowledge, but this I saw.

Amid all this sadness, we sometimes would hear a shout of joy. Some mother had come in, and found her long-lost child; some husband his wife. Brothers and sisters meet. Some, without knowing it, had lived years within twenty miles of each other.

A word about the schools. It is pleasant to see that eager group of old and young, striving to learn their A, B, C, and Scripture sentences. Their great desire is to learn to read. While in the school-room, I could not but feel how much these young women and children needed female teachers who could do something more than teach them their A, B, C. They need to be taught the right habits of living and the true principles of life.

My last visit intended for Alexandria was on Saturday. I spent the day with them, and received showers of thanks for myself and the good ladies who had sent me; for I had been careful to impress upon them that these kind friends sent me, and that all that was given by me was from them....

I left the contrabands feeling that the people were becoming more interested in their behalf, and much had been done to make their condition more comfortable. On my way home, I stopped a few days in Philadelphia. I called on a lady who had sent a large supply to the hospital, and told her of the many little orphans who needed a home. This lady advised me to call and see the Lady Managers of an institution for orphan children supported by those ladies. I did so, and they agreed to take the little orphans. They employed a gentleman to investigate the matter, and it was found impossible to bring them through Baltimore. This gentleman went to the captains of the propellers in Philadelphia, and asked if those orphan children could have a passage on their boats. Oh no, it could not be; it would make an unpleasant feeling among the people! Some of those orphans have died since I left, but the number is constantly increasing. Many mothers, on leaving the plantations, pick up the little orphans, and bring them with their own children; but they cannot provide for them; they come very destitute themselves.

To the ladies who have so nobly interested themselves in behalf of my much oppressed race, I feel the deepest debt of gratitude. Let me beg the reader's attention to these orphans.[1] They are the innocent and helpless of God's poor. If you cannot take one, you can do much by contributing your mite to the institution that will open its doors to receive them.

LINDA.

2. From "Jacobs (Linda) School, Alexandria, Va.,"
Freedmen's Record (February 1865)

[An account of Jacobs's success supporting the community of newly free people in the South. This is yet another example of her reputation as an author and her connections to activist circles. Transcribed from Yellin, *Harriet Jacobs Family Papers* 2.613–14.]

MANY of our readers are familiar with a book called "Linda; or, the Autobiography of a Slave Girl." Perhaps few of them know that this slave girl is now one of the most zealous and efficient workers in the Freedmen's cause. Mrs. Harriet Jacobs was sent to Alexandria more than two years ago, by a society of Friends in

---

1 As Yellin details, Jacobs's efforts on behalf of orphans was longstanding. She traveled more than once with several children in order to place them in homes (*Life* 168–69). Especially given that the injustice of slavery created this orphan crisis, readers interested in this issue and its implications today should consider the findings of Jessie Daniels in Chapter 5 of *Nice White Ladies* and of Laura Briggs in *Taking Children*.

New York, to look after the Freedmen who were gathered there. Her first winter's service was a very hard one. Small-pox and other diseases made fearful havoc among the people; and all her energies were exhausted in caring for their physical needs.

She has been unwearied in her labors, in providing orphan children with homes, in nursing the sick, in assisting the able-bodied to find work, and in encouraging all in habits of industry and self-reliance. They have established a school, and sent to the New-England Society[1] for assistance in maintaining it. We offered them a teacher, and sent them Miss Virginia Lawton, a young colored woman of good education and great worth of character....

... The most remarkable feature of Linda's slave life was this: to escape the persecution of a master not cruel, but cruelly kind, she hid in a small loft, under the roof of her grandmother's house, where light and air came only through the chinks in the boards, and where she lay concealed for seven years, within sound both of her children's voices and of her master's threats, before she succeeded in escaping altogether from the town.

No doubt, when she sank to sleep over-wearied with the monotony of suffering, visions of hope and joy came through the golden gate of slumber, which snatched her away from her vile den, and gave her strength and courage to endure still longer. But was any dream of the night dearer and sweeter to her than the present reality?—her people freed, and the school-house, built mainly by her own exertions, named in her honor, and presided over by black and white teachers, working harmoniously together.

And yet, this woman, this lady,—who for years has been treated as a friend in the family of one of our celebrated literary men, and who has won the respect and love of all who have associated with her,—cannot ride in the street-cars at Washington, and is insulted even in a concert-room in Boston, on account of the slight tinge of color in her skin.

We have made great progress; but much yet remains to be done.

---

1 The New England Freedmen's Aid Society, the organization that was also the publisher of the outlet in which this account appears.

3. "From Harriet Jacobs," *Freedman* (February 1866)

[An account written by Jacobs to keep activist circles updated. Transcribed from Yellin, *Harriet Jacobs Family Papers* 2.657–58.]

Savannah, Jan. 19th, 1866.

We have a great deal to do here. In every direction the colored people are being turned from the plantations when unwilling to comply with the hard proposals of the planters. The contracts proposed are sometimes very severe and unjust. The freedmen are not allowed to hire land or work it on shares, but must work under their former overseers. They cannot own a horse, cow, pigs, or poultry, nor keep a boat; and they cannot leave the plantation without permission. If a friend calls to see them a fine is imposed of one dollar, and a second offence breaks the contract. They work for ten dollars and rations. They are very unwilling to be placed under the overseers who formerly treated them with cruelty. I have this week visited several plantations on both the Georgia and Carolina sides of the river. In these places the people are expecting the return of their old masters. Poor things! some are excited; others so dispirited that they cannot work. They say, "I can't eat, I can't sleep, for tinking of de hard time coming on me again; my heart 'pears to be all de time quiverin'; I knows 'tis trouble." I wrote in another letter of the poor people who are daily landing at the wharf to be scattered as they can find homes. The Bureau only assists them in making contracts.[1]

A few days since I found a company on Ham Island[2] in a starving condition. The children were crying for bread. I had thirteen dollars belonging to the Society, six dollars of which I spent at the Commissary[3] to relieve their pressing needs. There were fifty women, fifty-six children, and twelve men. Among these I divided

---

1 Jacobs notes that the Freedmen's Bureau concerns itself with negotiating work contracts but does not address the fact that newly free people need places to live. She also calls attention to how the employment contracts honor the "right" of white people to subordinate Black people.

2 An island above Savannah where Yellin reports that twenty-five newly free African Americans had settled by April 1865. In January 1867, it was restored to the white family that had enslaved people there before (*Harriet Jacobs Family Papers* 2.658).

3 A store that sells food and supplies to the employees of a military post or work camp.

forty-six lbs. of salt pork and beef, twenty-five loaves of bread, and some salt. One old woman, too decrepid [*sic*] to walk, crawled to me to beg for food. The larger portion of the men were in the city, seeking work. The case must be presented to [the] Colonel.

4. "From Louisa Jacobs," *Freedmen's Record* (March 1866)

[Like Jacobs, Louisa offered reports on her work in the South and what she observed about the determination to subordinate African Americans and make their new freedom as meaningless as possible. Transcribed from Yellin, *Harriet Jacobs Family Papers* 2.660–62.]

I wish you could look up on my school of one hundred and thirty scholars. There are bright faces among them bent over puzzling books: a, b, and p are all one now. But these small perplexities will soon be conquered, and the conqueror, perhaps, feel as grand as a promising scholar of mine, who had no sooner mastered his A B C's when he conceived that he was persecuted on account of his knowledge. He preferred charges against the children for ill-treatment, concluding with the emphatic assurance that he knew a "little something now."[1]

I have called mine the Lincoln School.

... Employer and employed can never agree: the consequence is a new servant each week. The last comer had the look and air of one not easily crushed by circumstances. In the course of a few days, the neighbors were attracted to their doors by the loud voice of the would-be slaveholders. Out in the yard stood the mistress and her woman. The former had struck the latter. I am no pugilist, but, as I looked at the black woman's fiery eye, her quivering form, and heard her dare her assailant to strike again, I was proud of her metal. In a short time the husband of the white woman made his appearance, and was about to deal a second blow, when she drew back telling him that she was no man's slave; that she was as free as he, and would take the law upon his wife for striking her. He blustered, but there he stood deprived of his old power to kill her if it had so pleased him. He ordered her to leave his premises immediately, telling her he should not pay her a cent for the time she had been with them....

---

1 Louisa seems to suggest that when an adult student learned the alphabet, the children teased him. He considered teasing to be a small price to pay for learning what was withheld during slavery.

5. Linda [Harriet] Jacobs, "Savannah Freedmen's Orphan Asylum," *Anti-Slavery Reporter* (2 March 1868), pp. 57–58

[Early in 1868, Jacobs and Louisa were in England, fundraising. This written appeal supplemented their in-person efforts. Slavery had ended on paper, but they had witnessed the investment in keeping African Americans not only impoverished but also subordinate. British citizens who had worked for abolition should not consider their mission complete; now was the time to work for "human rights." Transcribed from Yellin, *Harriet Jacobs Family Papers* 2.722–24.]

We have much pleasure in publishing the following Appeal. It is made by a well-known victim of Slavery, Linda Brent, now Harriet Jacob[s], whose narrative, entitled "Linda," every one should read. We hope her appeal will be met with a generous response.

AN APPEAL.

"My object in visiting England is to solicit aid in the erection of an Orphan Asylum in connection with a home for the destitute among the aged freedmen of Savannah, Georgia. There are many thousand orphans in the Southern States. In a few of the States homes have been established through the benevolence of Northern friends; in others, no provision has been made except through the Freedmen's Bureau, which provides that the orphan be apprenticed till of age.[1] It not unfrequently happens that the apprenticeship is to the former owner. As the spirit of Slavery is not exorcised yet, the child, in many instances, is cruelly treated. It is our earnest desire to do something for this class of children; to give them a shelter surrounded by some home influences, and instruction that shall fit them for usefulness, and, when apprenticed, the right of an oversight. I know of the degradation of Slavery—the blight it leaves; and, thus knowing, feel how strong

---

1 Though the Freedmen's Bureau was supposed to help a population robbed of its labor for generations, it made a priority of avoiding alterations to the power dynamic that kept Black people subordinate to white people. Apprenticeships were part of this dynamic, locking Black children into work contracts that superseded anything their parents might want for them until age twenty-one (male) or age eighteen (female).

the necessity is of throwing around the young, who, through God's mercy, have come out of it, the most salutary influences.

"The aged freedmen have likewise a claim upon us. Many of them are worn out with field-labour. Some served faithfully as domestic slaves, nursing their masters and masters' children. Infirm, penniless, homeless, they wander about dependent on charity for bread and shelter. Many of them suffer and die from want. Freedom is a priceless boon, but its value is enhanced when accompanied with some of life's comforts. The old freed man and the old freed woman have obtained their's after a long weary march through a desolate way. If some peace and light can be shed on the steps so near the grave, it were but human kindness and Christian love.

"I was sent as an agent to Savannah in 1865 by the Friends of New-York city. I there found that a number of coloured persons had organized a Society for the relief of freed orphans and aged freedmen. Their object was to found an asylum,[1] and take the destitute of that class under their care. They asked my co-operation. I promised my assistance, with the understanding that they should raise among themselves the money to purchase the land. They are now working for that purpose. Their plan is to make the institution wholly, or in part, self-sustaining. It is proposed to cultivate the land (about fifteen acres) in vegetables and fruit. The institution will thereby be supplied, while a large surplus will remain for market sale. Poultry will also be raised for the market. This arrangement will afford a pleasant occupation to many of the old people, and a useful one to the older children out of school hours. I am deeply sensible of the interest taken and the aid rendered by the friends of Great Britain since the emancipation of Slavery. It is a noble evidence of their joy at the downfall of American Slavery and the advancement of human rights. I shall be grateful to any who shall respond to my efforts for the object in view. Every mite will tell in the balance.

"LINDA JACOBS."

[A list of names and addresses to which contributions can be sent.]

---

1 An institution for the care of persons needing specialized assistance.

6. Letters by an Adult Louisa Jacobs (1880–84)

a. "Ah me!" (25 March 1880)

[Though Jacobs was an entrepreneur when she was running boarding houses, the work was grueling, and the harsh realities are apparent as her adult daughter confides in a friend, Eugenie "Genie" Webb (1856–1919), niece of Frank J. Webb (1828–94), author of the 1857 novel *The Garies and Their Friends*. Letter transcribed from Maillard 64–65.]

Thursday [March] 25th [1880]

... We shall break up our home in June. Ah me! The thought is not pleasant. What a tramp life! I shall go north and as I pass through hope to see you. The time will soon be here.... My mother has not been at all well this winter, I am hoping she will feel stronger with the coming of the spring. Do you keep well Genie & Take care of yourself dear child. May the cares and responsibilities of your life press not too heavily on your young shoulders is the pray of

Your loving friend.

Lulu

b. "Rest and quiet is what she needs" (7 September 1884)

[Transcribed from Maillard 120.]

Washington, Sept. 7, 1884

My dear Genie

... I trust your doctor by this time understands your case and is going to make a new woman of you.... I want to see you happy, Genie....

You have not gone through life on flowery beds of ease. My love for you would have the way smoothed and sunned with many joys in the future.... Mother has been very miserable all Summer. You can fancy my life has been busy. On the 10 I must go back to Howard[1] with much of my work unfinished, which will have to be done between times. We must move the middle or last of October. The little house has yet to be found. When we are settled, dear, a load will be lifted from my shoulders and heart. Mother will be

---

1 Howard University in Washington, DC. At this point, Louisa had been appointed to teach needlework and sewing in the Industrial Department (Yellin, *Harriet Jacobs Family Papers* 2.775).

better I am sure. Rest and quiet is what she needs and cannot get as we are now situated. The doorbell is ringing so, for a time, good bye.

c. "I was sure Mother would not refuse him" (21 December 1884)

[Transcribed from Maillard 122–24.]

2125 L Street
Washington Dec. 21, 1884

My dear Genie

I know you think yourself an ill used childie. If you could look within my heart you would reverse your judgment. Scarcely a day has passed that has not brought some thought of you and self-re-proach at what may have appeared like neglect to you. Genie dear if you could but know just how I have been situated you would not wonder at my not writing. To begin at the beginning of this chapter (and I will endeavor not to make the story too long).

You know how busy I was in the Summer, and how I had to go back to my Howard work long before the other work was completed. When I left one occupation it was to go to another, and many times continue it late into the evening. Mother did all, and more than she ought to help me. She was feeble, and the responsibility of the work was upon me. To add to our care the son of a family of whom you have heard me speak—I mean the Willis's came here in the Summer for orders, having secured an appointment from the government in the Geological Survey.[1] We are bound by many ties—I may say obligations to his mother. When he heard we were going into a small home he said we must take him and his wife to board. To me this was not a welcome suggestion. I was tired of the boarding house life and wanted a quiet home of our own. I was sure Mother would not refuse him. He left us with the understanding of returning in November with his wife and we were to be in the home. The second week of October they wrote they were ready to come, were we ready for them. At this time we had not been able to find a small house such as we could afford to rent in a nice locality. Moreover I had not sent out one of my orders and knew it would be a great undertaking to move the things into another house. I advised Mother to write them we had not found a house, that if they must come then it would be best

---

1 Jacobs had been a constant presence in the lives of Nathaniel Parker Willis's children. As an adult, his son Bailey became a geologist.

for them to board until we could find a house to settle them in. She thought it best to let them come to the Conn Avenue house, that we might soon be able to find a house. Of course I felt this to be a bad arrangement, Mother not well and with so much to do, added to the additional care of two boarders. They were with us nearly three weeks before a house was found, and that not what we wanted. At all events we are here and must make the best of it. I did not move my Preserves and Pickles but went each day back and forth to the two houses, and slept at the former house nights. At last dear old girl I got so desperate over the conditions of things (after keeping up that kind of life for nearly four weeks) I had every thing moved here and gave up the keys. I could not have remained as long as I did had the house been taken. It has since been taken.

See how selfishly I have talked only of myself. I am truly glad to know you are improving and pray that the good work begun will go on until a complete cure is made. I regret you must go back to your school so soon. Oh! Genie what slaves necessity makes of us. I wish your old friend had means....

We have been having a few very cold and stormy days. After next Tuesday I shall have a short vacation for which blessing I shall be most grateful. I so much feel the need of a little rest. I wish dear I could spend a part of it with you. Genie you must not have that picture framed. I will frame it. I know you are under much expense and do not darling spend any thing for me. It is not right to. When you are rich you may bestow all you want to on me.

Get all the pleasure you can get out of the holidays....

Good night, with blessings and kisses.

Always lovingly,
Lulu

This is a poor scrawl, but I could not wait to do better.

Lou

7. Remembrances upon Jacobs's Death

a. From the Eulogy[1] by Reverend Francis Grimké

[Typed document in Grimké's (1850–1937) papers at the Moorland-Spingarn Research Center at Howard University in Washington, DC. He was the husband of a woman dear to Jacobs and Louisa and important to their life in the capital: Charlotte Forten Grimké (1837–1914) (Yellin, *Life* 234–37). Eulogy transcribed from Yellin, *Harriet Jacobs Family Papers* 2.827–30.[2]]

It has been some years since I first made the acquaintance of Mrs Jacobs. She was then living in Cambridge Mass. I took to her a letter of introduction from an intimate ↑<friend>↓, who a few years afterwards passed into the silent land, into which she has now also entered. I remember as distinctly, as though it were yesterday, our first meeting. The cordiality with which she received me and made me welcome to her pleasant and hospitable home, I shall never forget. I soon felt, in her presence, as much at home as though I had known her all my life. And from that day to the present, as I came to know her more intimately, to get a clearer and fuller insight into the inner workings of her soul, the more strongly was I drawn towards her, and the more highly did I esteem her. Since her residence in this city I have seen much of her. I called frequently at her home; and it was always a pleasure to meet her, to get a glimpse of her kind, benevolent face; to feel the pressure of the warm grasp of her friendly hand; and to hear her speak of the stirring times before the war when the great struggle for freedom was going on, and of the events immediately after the war. She was thoroughly alive to all that was ↑<transpiring>↓ and had a most vivid recollection of the events and of the actors, the prominent men and women, who figured on the stage of action at that time....

She was a woman of strong character. She possessed all the elements that go to make up such a character. She had great will

---

1 A speech or writing in praise of a person, especially on the occasion of their death.

2 This is a typed document with handwritten editorial markings, presumably by the author, Rev. Grimke. When transcribing, Yellin used < > to indicate a handwritten word meant to be inserted. Similarly, ↑ ↓ indicates handwritten words that appear above, below, or between typed lines.

power. She knew how to say, No, when it was necessary, and how to adhere to it. She was no reed shaken by the wind, va—cillating, easily moved from a position. She did her own thinking; had opinions of her own, and held to them with great tenacity. Only when her judgment *was* convinced could she be moved. <xx>

With great strength of character, there was also <combined> ↑<in her>↓ a heart as tender as that of little child. How wonderfully sympathetic she was; how readily did she enter into the sorrows, the heartaches of others; how natural it seemed for her to take up in the arms of her great love, all who needed to be soothed and comforted. The very Spirit of the Lord was upon her, that Spirit to which the prophet referred to when he said: "The spirit of the Lord God is upon me, because he hath sent me to bind up the broken hearted; to comfo<rt> all that mourn; to give unto them beauty for ashes, the oil of joy for mourning, the garment of praise for the spirit of heaviness." How divinely beautiful was her sympathy, her tenderness.

She was ↑<also>↓ the very <soul> of generosity; she possessed in a remarkable degree, what we sometimes call the milk of human kindness. Especially did her sympathies go out towards the poor, the suffering, the destitute. She never hesitated to share what she had, ↑<with others>↓ to deny herself for the sake of helping a suffering fellow creature. There are hundreds, who if they had the opportunity, ↑<to day>↓ would rise up and call her blessed.

b. From the Obituary for Harriet Jacobs, *Woman's Journal* (May 1897)

[Ednah Dow Cheney (1824–1904) was an activist and philanthropist who first became acquainted with Jacobs and Louisa when they were teaching in Alexandria and Cheney was serving as secretary of the teachers' committee of the New England Freedmen's Aid Society, which sent teachers from Boston to the South during Reconstruction. They remained in similar activist circles until Jacobs's death. Obituary transcribed from Yellin, *Harriet Jacobs Family Papers* 2.842–84.]

Mrs. Harriet Jacobs
Born in North Carolina, over eighty years ago, died in Washington,
March, 1897.

It is not fitting that a life so noble, so remarkable and so instruc-
tive, should pass away without some record of this admirable
character and this interesting story.

Inadequate as my sketch of her later life must be, her many
friends in all parts of our country will be glad to know something
of it.

From her autobiography, written more than forty-five years
ago and edited by Lydia Maria Child, I take the leading facts of
her early life. The book itself is of permanent interest....

The account of her sufferings in the household of her mistress
is too long to repeat here. As she grew to womanhood, she began
to experience the most degrading and insufferable evils of a slave
girl's lot, in the pitiless persecution of a vile master, and the jealousy of an angry mistress. Although she escaped the immediate
consequences of her master's evil wishes, yet her life was poisoned. She was separated from a young man of her own degree
who truly loved her, and when a white man gave her sympathy
and kindness, while she was yet but fifteen years old, shall we
blame her severely, that she yielded to his love, and became the
mother of two children without the form of marriage, which to the
slave girl could only be a mockery? She tells the story with perfect
simplicity, how even the good grandmother condemned her, but
at last, after hearing the whole sad story, laid her hand upon the
girl's head, murmuring "Poor child! Poor child!"

After long years of trial and suffering Harriet resolved on flight
from her tormentor....

Since her emancipation from the fear of renewed slavery, Mrs.
Jacobs' life has been one of earnest effort to support herself and
children and to benefit humanity in all ways in her power. She has
held honorable positions. She was for a time the matron of the
New England Women's Club, and has kept an excellent boarding house both in Cambridge and in Washington. She also taught
in Freedmen's schools under the New England Freedman's Aid
Society. During all these years, she has been well known to many
of the best people in our land, who will with one accord bear witness to the high intelligence, earnest truth, unselfish devotion, and
active benevolence of her life.

The unswerving kindness of the family who had guarded her
through so many dangers, and who were bound to her by such

strong ties of affection and mutual service, and the constant affectionate care of her daughter, soothed long months of suffering, and she was followed to her grave by affectionate mourners. A few friends gathered in the little rooms. The old Episcopal minister[1] read the service, and Mr. Grimke made a few remarks which, while being a tribute to her worth and useful life, were in good taste, and there was no jar to any one's feelings. "Nearer, my God, to Thee" and "Lead, Kindly Light" were sung without any instrumental accompaniment. The voices were sweet and mellow, and it was tender and fitting. Harriet looked not more than sixty years old. The sweet brow was free from all traces of suffering. Some violets were about her in the coffin, and ascension lilies and palm leaves on it. They were typical of her old-fashioned piety and her faith in the good Lord. The body was brought hither and laid in Mt. Auburn.

"So mayst thou rest in peace, dear sister, and thy life become fruitful in good to those who have known thee!"

Harriet's book called "Linda," which gives the record of her early life, written about the year 1858, and published in 1861, is now out of the market. It should be carefully preserved in our libraries, for it is a wonderful record of the suffering and heroism of those never to be forgotten days.

E.D.C.

---

1 Alexander Crummell (1819–97) was Jacobs and Louisa's pastor when they moved to Washington, DC (Yellin, *Harriet Jacobs Family Papers* 2.845). This is yet another indication of how well connected the figures who made significant contributions to history were.

Appendix E: Enduring Legacy

1. From Ellen Driscoll, "The Loophole of Retreat," displayed 4 December 1991–8 February 1992 at the Whitney Museum of American Art at Philip Morris. Photographer: George Hirose

[An artistic rendering of the attic in which Jacobs hid for nearly seven years. Museum visitors entered the tight space one at a time. The interior was dark, and the structure moved because of its cone shape, creating a destabilizing experience as the technology above the cone projected image fragments that drew the visitor's attention, intensifying the effect.][1]

---

1 Ellen Driscoll describes the artwork in her own words: "An artistic interpretation of the eaves in which Jacob hid for nearly seven years. Museum visitors entered the space one at a time. The interior was dark, and the structure moved slightly because of its cone shape, creating a slight destabilization as the viewer's eyes adjusted to the darkness. They would then see a series of moving images projected on a screen in the interior, created by light hitting the objects moving on a wheel suspended from the ceiling above the cone, and passing through a lens on the cone itself. The entire moving image sequence took about 7 minutes."

2. From Lydia Diamond, *Harriet Jacobs: A Play* (2011)

[An early exchange in the *Incidents*-inspired play developed as part of Steppenwolf Theatre Company's 2008 Steppenwolf for Young Adults programming. Diamond (b. 1969) is an acclaimed Black woman playwright. This and several other of her plays have been produced throughout the United States.]

CHARACTERS

Note: It is imperative that all cast members be Black. All "White" characters are represented by Black ensemble members, donning skeletal white hoopskirts, bonnets, top hats, and the like. It is important that some theatrical gesture (for example, putting on gloves or white skirts onstage) accompany the transforming of ensemble members into "White" characters.

Harriet Jacobs

Age fourteen to nineteen. The author of one of the first published slave narratives, Harriet possesses an intelligence and centeredness beyond her years. These traits are equally attributable to the strength that surely any slave must have had to possess and a personal wisdom and acuity passed down from insightful parents and grandparents. Harriet has a social savvy—a dexterity that serves her well both with her family or peers and with slave owners. She's very educated and slips easily between the more casual slave vernacular of the time and the formal language used in her writing and when addressing the audience. She is not "putting this on" or "talking proper"; she is an adept and unconscious "code-switcher." Historically, Harriet is described as having light-brown skin and dark eyes. She is the daughter of two Biracial parents. She is pretty but does not embrace or consciously exploit her looks; in her setting they are more often a liability than a blessing, and she is aware of this.

Grandma

Harriet's strong-willed, well-liked, free grandmother

[The action begins with Harriet addressing the audience directly. Then, *Light rises on an old lady kneading bread on a small table by a hearth: Harriet's* Grandma]

Grandma: Who are you talking to?
Harriet: To *whom* am I talking Grandma ...

Grandma: I am sure my granddaughter is not tellin' *me* how to
   speak ...
Harriet: I'm jes' teasing with you.
Grandma [*laughing*]: Better be ... 'cause seems to me, I'm the
   one taught you, in your diapers, to say your first words ...
   so, who were you talkin' to ...?
Harriet: Oh, I was just ... just thinking.
Grandma: Well stop that. Life *is*. We pray to the Lord for deliver-
   ance, love the people before us whom we must love,
   wipe our butts, roll up our sleeves, and work. No time for
   thinking.
Harriet [*laughing*]: Wipe our butts? What's gotten into you?
Grandma: Little bit of the devil today I s'pose. Did I add the
   leavening?[1]
Harriet: Probably.
Grandma: Take that batch out, they smell ready.
[Harriet *moves to look out of the window*.]
Harriet: It's getting late ...
Grandma: They burning ...
Harriet [*removing the crackers from the oven*]: She'll have my hide.
Grandma: So take the mistress a package of warm crackers. Tell
   her Grandmother wouldn't let you leave 'fore they come
   out. How many babies she drop, one a year fo de lass
   six years? Tell her maybe if she cross her legs and eat a
   cracker, wouldn't be in that condition all the time.

[Harriet's *removing crackers from a cookie sheet as they speak*.]

Harriet: If it's just the same to you, I think I won't tell her the
   latter.
Grandma: The latter? You need to watch it with the fancy talk.
Harriet: I speak from my heart, and so, if my heart is smarter
   than my master's I cannot help it, and I will not apologize
   for it.
Grandma: Just tell me this. How he have time to run after skirt
   like he do ...? Got her always in the family way, seem he
   gettin' enough where he lay.
Harriet: Grandmother stop ...
Grandma: That's why she so mean, can't lay down for rest 'fore
   he tryin' to climb on top of her ...

---

1 The ingredient that causes fermentation in dough, making it expand
   and allowing bread to rise.

Harriet: Grandmother ...
Grandma: And if she do lay down, cain't rest proper tryin' to
figure out who else he climbin' on top of. Should jes'
be grateful for a moment of peace on her back ... [*Both laugh.*]

3. Quotations from Lorna Ann Johnson, *Freedom Road* (2004)

[There is no way to represent a film effectively here, but I gesture toward this work in order to encourage readers to consider how consistently Jacobs brought attention to the ever-present threat of incarceration. Enslaving people was not violent enough; enslavement had to be underwritten by the violence of patrollers, constables, sheriffs, jails, and prisons. The 2004 independent film *Freedom Road* shines a light on women in prison who participated in a course called *Woman is the Word*. Developed by Dr. Michele Tarter, the course led incarcerated students in the reading of women's autobiographies, including *Incidents*, as a way of encouraging them to write their own life stories. As a reminder, *Incidents* references patrollers, constables, and jails frequently, including p. 82, p. 88, p. 90, p. 105, p. 111, p. 114, p. 129, p. 132, p. 135, p. 151, p. 159, p. 162, p. 164, p. 166, p. 181, p.207, p. 209, p. 214, p. 216, p. 239, p. 247, p. 248.]

"In our society, it's like people feel like you make your own bed and you lay in it. Whereas I don't see it being a balance there where they have a lot of opportunities to make the bed different."—Elaine Easterling, speaking as the mother of an imprisoned woman after the film has just featured an attorney who explains that, in the United States, a person's zip code is the largest determining factor for the kind of life they will have. The mother continues: prison is "a business. A booming business."

The film is titled *Freedom Road* because that is what the women in these classes call the road leading into and out of the prison.

"The question 'what is freedom?' comes up all the time. And freedom becomes for them a state of mind, a state of being. And they can create their safe space wherever they are, if they have the tools to do so."—Dr. Michele Tarter, professor and creator of the *Woman is the Word* course.

"I re-live these visits [with my daughter] in my dream, my sleeping state. This is my freedom. It is mine. All mine."—an imprisoned student's biographical creative writing.

"I would like to share ... my tools and my remedies I used to survive and make it through this without turning it into a nightmare."—Robin Easterling, imprisoned student who participated in *Woman is the Word*.

"I can't move but so far and then they want to pull my body back, but my mind is like the sky. It's open. I can reach the sky with my mind."—Melvina McClain, imprisoned woman and *Woman is the Word* student, age 62.

Appendix F: People and Places Relevant to Incidents

1. Who Is Who in *Incidents*

Linda Brent	Harriet Jacobs
Mother	Delilah Horniblow
Father	Elijah Knox
Brother/William	John S. Jacobs
Grandmother/Aunt Martha	Molly Horniblow
Aunt Martha's son/Uncle Phillip	Mark Ramsey
Aunt Martha's son/Uncle Benjamin	Joseph
Aunt Martha's daughter/Aunt Nancy	Betty
Dr. Flint	James Norcom
Mrs. Flint	Mary Matilda Horniblow Norcom
Mr. Sands	Samuel Tredwell Sawyer
Daughter/Ellen	Louisa Matilda Jacobs
Son/Benjamin	Joseph Jacobs
Miss Emily Flint/Mrs. Dodge	Mary Matilda Norcom/ Mrs. Daniel Messmore
Mr. and Mrs. Hobbs/Sands's cousins	James Iredell Tredwell and Mary Blount Tredwell
Mrs. Bruce/first northern employer	Mary Stace Willis
Mr. Bruce/employer's spouse	Nathaniel Parker Willis
Mrs. Bruce/second northern employer	Cornelia Grinnell Willis

2. Image of Dr. Norcom

[Jacobs encountered Norcom when he was fifty years old, and this portrait was likely created when he was much younger. Still, he reminds me of men of our own time who are said to have used their elevated social positions to sexually harass and exploit women, including actor James Franco and television journalist Matt Lauer.]

3. Image of Mrs. Norcom

4. Image of Louisa Jacobs

5. Visual Rendering of Floor Plan of Grandmother's House and Hiding Place

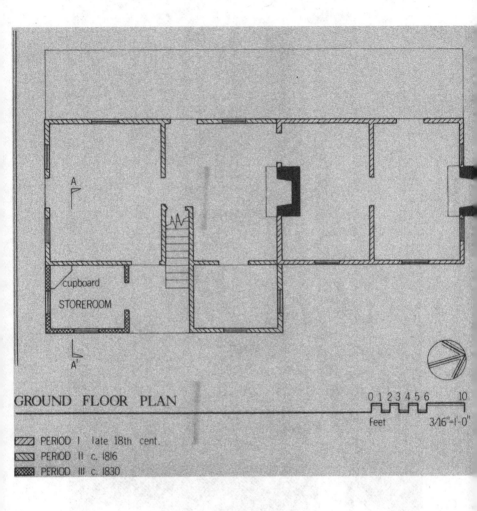

GROUND FLOOR PLAN

PERIOD I   late 18th cent.
PERIOD II c. 1816
PERIOD III c. 1830

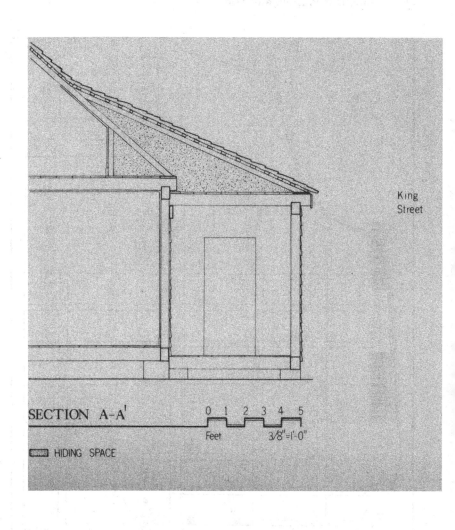

SECTION A-A'

0 1 2 3 4 5
Feet   3/8"=1'-0"

King
Street

▨ HIDING SPACE

6. Visual Rendering of the Edenton Neighborhood in Which Jacobs Was Born and Hid

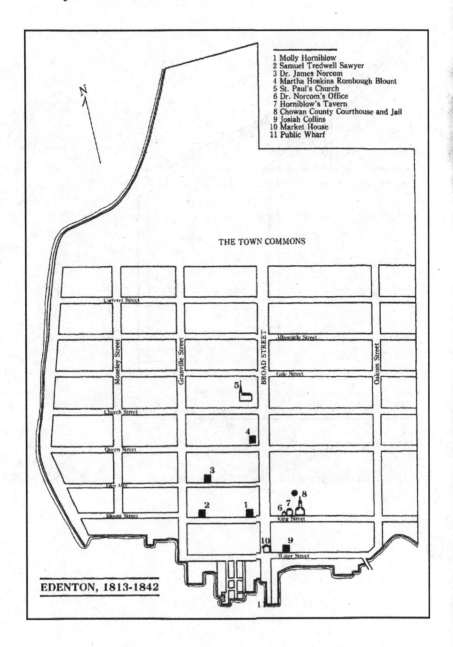

1 Molly Horniblow
2 Samuel Tredwell Sawyer
3 Dr. James Norcom
4 Martha Hoskins Rombough Blount
5 St. Paul's Church
6 Dr. Norcom's Office
7 Horniblow's Tavern
8 Chowan County Courthouse and Jail
9 Josiah Collins
10 Market House
11 Public Wharf

THE TOWN COMMONS

EDENTON, 1813-1842

7. Image of Amy Post

8. Image of Harriet Beecher Stowe

9. Image of Lydia Maria Child

Works Cited and Select Bibliography

Databases

Accessible Archives. www.accessible-archives.com.

African American Biographical Database. https://aabd.chad-wyck.com.

African American Periodicals 1825–1995. http://www.readex.com/content/african-american-periodicals–1825–1995.

America's Historical Newspapers. http://www.readex.com/content/americas-historical-newspapers.

Black Abolitionist Archive. University of Detroit Mercy, http://libraries.udmercy.edu/archives/special-collections/index.php.

Documenting the American South. University of North Carolina, docsouth.unc.edu.

Freedom on/the Move. Cornell University, https://freedomonthemove.org/.

Primary Sources

Berlin, Ira, et al., editors. *Free at Last: A Documentary History of Slavery, Freedom, and the Civil War*. New Press, 1992.

Foner, Eric. *Voices of Freedom: A Documentary History*. W.W. Norton, 2013.

Maillard, Mary. *Whispers of Cruel Wrongs: The Correspondence of Louisa Jacobs and Her Circle, 1879–1911*. U of Wisconsin P, 2017.

Yellin, Jean Fagan, editor. *The Harriet Jacobs Family Papers*. U of North Carolina P, 2008. 2 vols.

Secondary Sources (Books and Articles)

Abdur-Rahman, Aliyyah. *Against the Closet: Black Political Longing and the Erotics of Race*. Duke UP, 2012.

Ammons, Elizabeth. *Conflicting Stories: American Women Writers at the Turn into the Twentieth Century*. Oxford UP, 1991.

Anderson, Carol. "Self-Defense." *The 1619 Project: A New Origin Story*, created by Nikole Hannah-Jones and *The New York Times Magazine*, One World, 2021, pp. 249–66.

Andrews, William. "Class and Class Awareness in *Incidents in the Life of a Slave Girl*." *Auto/Biography across the Americas*, edited by Ricia Anne Chansky, Routledge, 2017, pp. 183–97.

——. "Slave Narratives, 1865–1900." *The Oxford Handbook of the African American Slave Narrative*, edited by John Ernest, Oxford UP, 2014.

——. *To Tell a Free Story: The First Century of Afro-American Autobiography, 1760–1865*. U of Illinois P, 1988.

Bay, Mia, et al., editors. *Toward an Intellectual History of Black Women*. U of North Carolina P, 2015.

Berlant, Lauren. "The Queen of America Goes to Washington City: Harriet Jacobs, Frances Harper, Anita Hill." *American Literary Studies: A Methodological Reader*, edited by Michael A. Elliott and Claudia Stokes, New York UP, 2003, pp. 98–123.

Bernstein, Robin. *Racial Innocence: Performing American Childhood and Race from Slavery to Civil Rights*. New York UP, 2011.

Berry, Daina. *The Price for Their Pound of Flesh: The Value of the Enslaved from Womb to Grave in the Building of a Nation*. Beacon P, 2017.

Berry, Daina, and Kali Nicole Gross. *A Black Women's History of the United States*. Beacon P, 2020.

Berry, Daina, and Leslie Harris, editors. *Sexuality and Slavery: Reclaiming Intimate Histories in the Americas*. U of Georgia P, 2018.

Blackwood, Sarah. *The Portrait's Subject: Inventing Inner Life in the Nineteenth-Century United States*. U of North Carolina P, 2019.

Bolster, W. Jeffrey. *Black Jacks: African American Seamen in the Age of Sail*. Harvard UP, 1997.

Bradford, Sarah Hopkins. *Scenes in the Life of Harriet Tubman*. Auburn, NY, W.J. Moses, 1869.

Braxton, Joanne. *Black Women Writing Autobiography: A Tradition within a Tradition*. Temple UP, 1989.

Briggs, Laura. *Taking Children: A History of American Terror*. U of California P, 2020.

Butler, Anthea. "Church." *The 1619 Project: A New Origin Story*, created by Nikole Hannah-Jones and *The New York Times Magazine*, One World, 2021, pp. 335–53.

Carby, Hazel. *Reconstructing Womanhood: The Emergence of the Afro-American Woman Novelist*. Oxford UP, 1987.

Chandler, Zala. "Voices Beyond the Veil: An Interview with

Toni Cade Bambara and Sonia Sanchez." *Wild Women in the Whirlwind: Afra-American Culture and the Contemporary Literary Renaissance,* edited by Joanne M. Braxton and Andrée Nicola McLaughlin, Rutgers UP, 1990, pp. 342–62.

Collins, Patricia Hill. *Black Feminist Thought: Knowledge, Consciousness, and the Politics of Empowerment.* Routledge, 2000.

Cottom, Tressie McMillan. *Thick and Other Essays.* New Press, 2019.

Crenshaw, Kimberlé. "Demarginalizing the Intersection of Race and Sex: A Black Feminist Critique of Antidiscrimination Doctrine, Feminist Theory and Antiracist Politics." *The University of Chicago Legal Forum,* vol. 140, 1989, pp. 139–67.

———. "Mapping the Margins: Intersectionality, Identity Politics, and Violence against Women of Color." *Stanford Law Review,* vol. 43, no. 6, July 1991, pp. 1241–99.

Curseen, Allison. "Black Girlish Departure and the 'Semiotics of Theater' in Harriet Jacobs's Narrative; Or, Lulu & Ellen: Four Opening Acts." *Theatre Survey,* vol. 60, no. 1, 2019, pp. 91–121.

Daniels, Jessie. *Nice White Ladies: The Truth about White Supremacy, Our Role in It, and How We Can Help Dismantle It.* Seal Press, 2021.

Daniels-Rauterkus, Melissa. "Civil Resistance and Procreative Agency in Harriet Jacobs's *Incidents in the Life of a Slave Girl.*" *Women's Studies,* vol. 48, no. 5, 2019, pp. 498–509.

Delchamps, Vivian. "Restoration and Reconstruction: Charlotte L. Forten and Black Feminist Self-Care." C19: The Society of Nineteenth-Century Americanists Conference, Miami, Florida, 2 April 2022.

DeLombard, Jeannine. "'Eye-Witness to the Cruelty': Southern Violence and Northern Testimony in Frederick Douglass's 1845 Narrative." *American Literature,* vol. 73, no. 2, 2001, pp. 245–75.

Deloria, Philip. *Playing Indian.* Yale UP, 1999.

Desmond, Matthew. "Capitalism." *The 1619 Project: A New Origin Story,* created by Nikole Hannah-Jones and *The New York Times Magazine,* One World, 2021, pp. 165–85.

DuCille, Ann. "Where in the World Is William Wells Brown? Thomas Jefferson, Sally Hemings, and the DNA of African-American Literary History." *American Literary History,* vol. 12, no. 3, 2000, pp. 443–62.

Dunbar, Erica Armstrong. *Never Caught: The Washingtons' Relentless Pursuit of Their Runaway Slave, Ona Judge*. Atria, 2017.

———. *She Came to Slay: The Life and Times of Harriet Tubman*. 37 Ink, 2019.

Dunbar-Ortiz, Roxanne. *An Indigenous Peoples' History of the United States*. Beacon P, 2014.

Epstein, Rebecca, et al. *Girlhood Interrupted: The Erasure of Black Girls' Girlhood*. Georgetown Law, Center on Poverty and Inequality, 2017.

Ernest, John. *Resistance and Reformation in Nineteenth-Century African-America Literature: Brown, Wilson, Jacobs, Delany, Douglass, and Harper*. UP of Mississippi, 1995.

Esty, Kaisha. "'I Told Him to Let Me Alone, That He Hurt Me': Black Women and Girls and the Battle over Labor and Sexual Consent in Union-Occupied Territory." *Labor*, vol. 19, no. 1, 2021, pp. 32–51.

Fagan, Benjamin. "Harriet Jacobs and the Lessons of Rogue Reading." *Legacy*, vol. 33, no. 1, 2016, pp. 19–21.

Fielder, Brigitte. *Relative Races: Genealogies of Interracial Kinship in Nineteenth-Century America*. Duke UP, 2020.

Foner, Eric. *Reconstruction: America's Unfinished Revolution, 1863–1877*. History Book Club, 2005.

Foreman, P. Gabrielle. *Activist Sentiments: Reading Black Women in the Nineteenth Century*. U of Illinois P, 2009.

———, founder. *The Colored Conventions Project*. https://colored conventions.org/.

Foreman, P. Gabrielle, et al. Community-sourced guide: *Writing about Slavery? This Might Help*. https://naacpculpeper.org/resources/writing-about-slavery-this-might-help/.

Foster, Frances Smith. "Resisting *Incidents*." Garfield and Zafar, pp. 57–75.

Foster, Frances Smith, and Richard Yarborough, editors. "Introduction." *Incidents in the Life of Slave Girl*, by Harriet Jacobs, W.W. Norton, 2019, pp. vii–xix.

Freeman, Tyrone McKinley. *Madam C.J. Walker's Gospel of Giving: Black Women's Philanthropy during Jim Crow*. U of Illinois P, 2020.

Fulton, DoVeanna. *Speaking Power: Black Feminist Orality in Women's Narratives of Slavery*. SUNY P, 2006.

Furui, Yoshiaki. *Modernizing Solitude: The Networked Individual in Nineteenth-Century American Literature*. U of Alabama P, 2019.

Gardner, Eric. *Unexpected Places: Relocating Nineteenth-Century African American Literature.* U of Mississippi P, 2009.

Garfield, Deborah M., and Rafia Zafar, editors. *Harriet Jacobs and* Incidents in the Life of a Slave Girl: *New Critical Essays.* Cambridge UP, 1996.

Gilbert, Olive. *Narrative of the Life of Sojourner Truth.* Boston, 1850.

Glymph, Thavolia. *Out of the House of Bondage: The Transformation of the Plantation Household.* Cambridge UP, 2012.

Goldberg, Shari. "Harriet Jacobs's Taxonomy of an Enslaved Heart." Paper delivered at *Pain, Disability, and Nineteenth-Century American Literature* symposium, Oxford University, 8 June 2022.

Goldsby, Jacqueline. "'I Disguised My Hand': Writing Version of the Truth in Harriet Jacob's *Incidents in the Life of a Slave Girl* and John Jacob's 'A True Tale of Slavery.'" Garfield and Zafar, pp. 11–43.

Gordon-Reed, Annette. *On Juneteenth.* W.W. Norton, 2021.

——. *Thomas Jefferson and Sally Hemings: An American Controversy.* UP of Virginia, 1997.

Gunning, Sandra. "Reading and Redemption in Incidents in the Life of a Slave Girl." Garfield and Zafar, pp. 131–55.

Hannah-Jones, Nikole. "Democracy." *The 1619 Project: A New Origin Story,* created by Nikole Hannah-Jones and *The New York Times Magazine,* One World, 2021, pp. 7–36.

Harris, Trudier. *Saints, Sinners, Saviors: Strong Black Women in African American Literature.* Palgrave, 2001.

Harris-Perry, Melissa. *Sister Citizen: Shame, Stereotypes, and Black Women in America.* Yale UP, 2011.

Hartman, Saidiya. *Scenes of Subjection: Terror, Slavery, and Self-Making in Nineteenth-Century America.* Oxford UP, 1997.

——. *Wayward Lives, Beautiful Experiments: Intimate Histories of Social Upheaval.* W.W. Norton, 2019.

Hoang, Kimberly. *Dealing in Desire: Asian Ascendancy, Western Decline, and the Hidden Currencies of Global Sex Work.* U of California P, 2015.

Holden, Vanessa. *Surviving Southampton: African American Women and Resistance in Nat Turner's Community.* U of Illinois P, 2021.

Hunter, Tera. *Bound in Wedlock: Slave and Free Black Marriage in the Nineteenth Century.* Harvard UP, 2017.

Hyde, Carrie. *Civic Longing: The Speculative Origins of U.S. Citizenship*. Harvard UP, 2018.

Jeffers, Honorée Fanonne. *The Age of Phillis*. Wesleyan UP, 2020.

Johnson, Jessica Marie. *Wicked Flesh: Black Women, Intimacy, and Freedom in the Atlantic World*. U of Pennsylvania P, 2020.

Jones, Martha S. *Birthright Citizens: A History of Race and Rights in Antebellum America*. Cambridge UP, 2018.

Jones-Rogers, Stephanie. *They Were Her Property: White Women as Slave Owners in the American South*. Yale UP, 2019.

Kaba, Mariame. *We Do This 'Til We Free Us: Abolitionist Organizing and Transforming Justice*. Edited by Tamara K. Nopper, Haymarket Books, 2021.

Kelley, Blair L.M. *Right to Ride: Streetcar Boycotts and African American Citizenship in the Era of* Plessy v. Ferguson. U of North Carolina P, 2010.

Kelley, Robin D.G. *Freedom Dreams*. Beacon, 2002.

Leonard, David. "The Unbearable Invisibility of White Masculinity: Innocence in the Age of White Male Mass Shootings." *Gawker*, 12 Jan. 2013, www.gawker.com/5973485/the-unbearable-invisibility-of-white-masculinity-innocence-in-the-age-of-white-male-mass-shootings.

Lindsey, Treva. *America Goddam: Violence, Black Women, and the Struggle for Justice*. U of California P, 2022.

——. "The 'Strong Black Woman' Trope Is a Trap." *Huffington Post*, 24 June 2022.

Lindsey, Treva, and Jessica Marie Johnson. "Searching for Climax: Black Erotic Lives in Slavery and Freedom." *Meridians*, vol. 12, no. 2, 2014, pp. 169–95.

Louis, Diana Martha. "Pro-Slavery Psychiatry and Psychological Costs of Black Women's Enslavement in Harriet Jacobs's *Incidents in the Life of a Slave Girl*." *Literature and Medicine*, vol. 39, no. 2, 2021, pp. 273–95.

Lowry, Beverly. "1851 Uncle Tom's Cabin." *A New Literary History of America*, edited by Werner Sollors and Greil Marcus, Harvard UP, 2021, pp. 287–91.

Manne, Kate. *Entitled: How Male Privilege Hurts Women*. Crown, 2020.

Masur, Kate. "The African American Delegation to Abraham Lincoln: A Reappraisal." *Civil War History*, vol. 56, 2010, pp. 117–44.

——. "'A Rare Phenomenon of Philological Vegetation': The Word 'Contraband' and the Meanings of Emancipation in the United States." *Journal of American History*, vol. 93, 2007, pp. 1050–84.

McBride, Dwight. *Impossible Witnesses: Truth, Abolitionism, and Slave Testimony*. New York UP, 2001.

McCaskill, Barbara. *Love, Liberation, and Escaping Slavery: William and Ellen Craft in Cultural Memory*. U of Georgia P, 2015.

McKittrick, Katherine. *Demonic Grounds: Black Women and the Cartographies of Struggle*. U of Minnesota P, 2006.

McMillan, Uri. *Embodied Avatars: Genealogies of Black Feminist Art and Performance*. New York UP, 2015.

Miles, Tiya. *All That She Carried: The Journey of Ashley's Sack, a Black Family Keepsake*. Random House, 2021.

———. "Introduction." *Incidents in the Life of a Slave Girl*, by Harriet Jacobs, Modern Library, 2021, pp. vii–xii.

Mitchell, Koritha. *From Slave Cabins to the White House: Homemade Citizenship in African American Culture*. U of Illinois P, 2020.

Moody, Joycelyn. "Crafting a Credible Black Self in African American Life Writing." *A History of African American Autobiography*, edited by Joycelyn Moody, Cambridge UP, 2021, pp. 1–20.

———, editor. *A History of African American Autobiography*. Cambridge UP, 2021.

———. "Obscene Questions and Righteous Hysteria." *Legacy*, vol. 33, no. 1, 2016, pp. 1–7.

———. *Sentimental Confessions: Spiritual Narratives of Nineteenth-Century African American Women*. U of Georgia P, 2001.

———. "Silenced Women and Silent Language in Early Abolitionist Serials." *Cultural Narratives: Textuality and Performance in American Culture before 1900*, edited by Sandra M. Gustafson and Caroline F. Sloat, U of Notre Dame P, 2010, pp. 220–29.

Morris, Monique W. *Pushout: The Criminalization of Black Girls in Schools*. New Press, 2018.

Nazer, Mende. *Slave: My True Story*. PublicAffairs, 2003.

Neary, Janet. *Fugitive Testimony: On the Visual Logic of Slave Narratives*. Fordham UP, 2017.

Noble, Marianne. "The Ecstacies of Sentimental Wounding in *Uncle Tom's Cabin*." *Yale Journal of Criticism*, vol. 10, no. 2, 1997, pp. 295–320.

Nunley, Tamika. *At the Threshold of Liberty: Women, Slavery, and Shifting Identities in Washington, D.C.* U of North Carolina P,

2021.

Olou, Ijeoma. *Mediocre: The Dangerous Legacy of White Male America.* Seal Press, 2020.

Owens, Deirdre Cooper. *Medical Bondage: Race, Gender, and the Origins of American Gynecology.* U of Georgia P, 2018.

Owens, Emily A. *Consent in the Presence of Force: Sexual Violence and Black Women's Survival in Antebellum New Orleans.* U of North Carolina P, 2023.

Painter, Nell. *Sojourner Truth: A Life, a Symbol.* W.W. Norton, 1997.

Penningroth, Dylan. *Claims of Kinfolk: African American Property and Community in the Nineteenth-Century South.* U of North Carolina P, 2003.

Perry, Imani. *South to America: A Journey Below the Mason-Dixon to Understand the Soul of a Nation.* Ecco, 2022.

Peterson, Carla. *"Doers of the Word": African-American Women Speakers and Writers in the North, 1830–1880.* Oxford UP, 1995.

Pottroff, Christy. "Incommensurate Labors: The Work Behind the Works of Harriet Jacobs and Walt Whitman." *American Literature*, vol. 94, no. 2, 2022, pp. 219–44.

Reed, Peter. "'There Was No Resisting John Canoe': Circum-Atlantic Transracial Performance." *Theatre History Studies*, vol. 27, 2007, pp. 65–85.

Reid-Pharr, Robert. *Conjugal Union: The Body, the House, and the Black American.* Oxford UP, 1999.

Rifkin, Mark. "'A Home Made Sacred by Protecting Laws': Black Activist Homemaking and Geographies of Citizenship in *Incidents in the Life of a Slave Girl*." *Differences*, vol. 18, no. 2, 2007, pp. 72–102.

Roberts, Dorothy. *Killing the Black Body: Race, Reproduction, and the Meaning of Liberty.* Vintage, 1997.

Ross, Kelly. "Watching from Below: Racialized Surveillance and Vulnerable Sousveillance." *PMLA*, vol. 135, no. 2, 2020, pp. 299–314.

Rusert, Britt. "From Black Lit to Black Print: The Return to the Archive in African American Literary Studies." *American Quarterly*, vol. 68, no. 4, 2016, pp. 993–1005.

Samuels, Shirley, editor. *The Culture of Sentiment: Race, Gender and Sentimentality in 19th Century America.* Oxford UP, 1992.

Schuller, Kyla. *The Trouble with White Women: A Counterhistory of Feminism.* Bold Type Books, 2021.

Sharpe, Christina. *In the Wake: On Blackness and Being.* Duke

UP, 2016.

Smith, Valerie. *Self-Discovery and Authority in Afro-American Narrative*. Harvard UP, 1987.

Snorton, C. Riley. *Black on Both Sides: A Racial History of Trans Identity*. U of Minnesota P, 2017.

Spillers, Hortense. *Black, White, and in Color: Essays on American Literature and Culture*. U of Chicago P, 2003.

Spires, Derrick R. *The Practice of Citizenship: Black Politics and Print Culture in the Early United States*. U of Pennsylvania P, 2019.

Sterling, Dorothy. *We Are Your Sisters: Black Women in the Nineteenth Century*. W.W. Norton, 1984.

Stevenson, Brenda. *Life in Black and White: Family and Community in the Slave South*. Oxford UP, 1996.

———. "What's Love Got to Do With It?: Concubinage and Enslaved Women and Girls in the Antebellum South." *Sexuality and Slavery: Reclaiming Intimate Histories in the Americas*, edited by Daina Berry and Leslie Harris, U of Georgia P, 2018, pp. 159–88.

Tompkins, Kyla Wazana. *Racial Indigestion: Eating Bodies in the Nineteenth Century*. New York UP, 2012.

Trotter, Joe William, Jr. *The African American Experience*. Houghton Mifflin, 2001.

Walker, Alice. "In Search of Our Mothers' Gardens." *Within the Circle: An Anthology of African American Literary Criticism from the Harlem Renaissance to the Present*, edited by Angelyn Mitchell, Duke UP, 1994, pp. 401–09.

Webster, Crystal. *Beyond the Boundaries of Childhood: African American Children in the Antebellum North*. U of North Carolina P, 2021.

Welter, Barbara. "The Cult of True Womanhood: 1820–1860." *American Quarterly*, no. 18, vol. 2, 1966, pp. 151–74.

Williams, Andreá. "Frances Watkins (Harper), Harriet Tubman and the Rhetoric of Single Blessedness." *Meridians*, vol. 12, no. 2, 2014, pp. 99–122.

Williams, Heather Andrea. *Self-Taught: African American Education in Slavery and Freedom*. U of North Carolina P, 2006.

Williamson, Jennifer. *Twentieth-Century Sentimentalism: Narrative Appropriation in American Literature*. Rutgers UP, 2013.

Winters, Lisa Ze. *The Mulatta Concubine: Terror, Intimacy, Freedom, and Desire in the Black Transatlantic*. U of Georgia

P, 2016.

Wong, Edlie. *Neither Fugitive nor Free: Atlantic Slavery, Freedom Suits, and the Legal Culture of Travel.* New York UP, 2009.

Wright, Nazera. *Black Girlhood in the Nineteenth Century.* U of Illinois P, 2015.

Yao, Xine. *Disaffected: The Cultural Politics of Unfeeling in Nineteenth-Century America.* Duke UP, 2021.

Yates-Richard, Meina. "'What Is Your Mother's Name?': Maternal Disavowal and the Reverberating Aesthetic of Black Women's Pain in Black Nationalist Literature." *American Literature*, vol. 88, no. 3, 2016, pp. 477–507.

Yellin, Jean Fagan. *Harriet Jacobs: A Life.* Basic Books, 2004.

———, editor. *Incidents in the Life of a Slave Girl.* Harvard UP, 1987.

Zafar, Rafia. "Introduction: Over-exposed, Under-exposed: Harriet Jacobs and *Incidents in the Life of a Slave Girl.*" Garfield and Zafar, pp. 1–10.

Permissions Acknowledgements

Page 299: Image of the 1861 Title Page. Courtesy of Wilson Special Collections Library, UNC-Chapel Hill.

Page 321: Driscoll, Ellen. *The Loophole of Retreat*, 1991, photograph by George Hirose, commissioned by The Whitney Museum of American Art at Phillip Morris. Copyright © 1991 Ellen Driscoll. Reprinted by permission of the artist.

Pages 327–28: Image of Dr. James Norcom and image of Mary Matilda Horniblow Norcom. Courtesy of the North Carolina Museum of History.

Pages 330–31: Visual Rendering of Floor Plan of Grandmother's House and Hiding Place. Courtesy of *The Colonial Williamsburg Foundation*.

Page 332: Visual Rendering of the Edenton Neighborhood in Which Jacobs Was Born and Hid. Courtesy of George Stevenson and Kathleen B. Wyche.

Page 333: Image of Amy Post. Courtesy of Rare Books, Special Collections and Preservation, River Campus Libraries, University of Rochester.

This book is made of paper from well-managed FSC® - certified
forests, recycled materials, and other controlled sources.

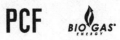